Canyoneering 3

Canyoneering 3

Loop Hikes in Utah's Escalante

Steve Allen
Foreword by Bert Fingerhut

The University of Utah Press
Salt Lake City

Library of Congress Cataloging-in-Publication Data

Allen, Steve, 1951–
    Canyoneering 3 : loop hikes in Utah's Escalante / Steve Allen ;
foreword by Bert Fingerhut.
        p.   cm.
    Includes bibliographical references (p.   ).
    ISBN 978-0-87480-545-1 (alk. paper)
    1. Hiking—Utah—Grand Staircase-Escalante National
Monument—Guidebooks. 2. Grand Staircase-Escalante
National Monument (Utah)—Guidebooks.   I. Title.
GV199.42.U82G733   1997
917.92'52—dc21   97-24495

For Barry, Celeste, Harvey, and Ginger

In memory:
Harold Graham
Tony Merten

Contents

Foreword

Steve Allen's accomplishments in the backcountry of southern Utah have become legendary among canyoneers. Well-deserved praise of Steve has centered on his epic searches for new routes and new slot canyons, his solo explorations of remote places for months at a time (often with his famous dog, Diz), his climbing skills, his knowledge of local history, geology, archaeology, and the natural world, and his ability to write clear and definitive guide books — guide books hikers can trust.

I have never met anyone as committed to exploring every nook, cranny, side canyon, mesa top, slot canyon, and crack as Steve. For most of us, it is hard not to compare canyons; but for Steve each and every canyon is exceptional and well worth visiting. Although he loves revisiting favorite places, his face absolutely glows at the thought of heading off into an unknown area with a group of friends. His love of the land, indomitable spirit, enthusiasm, and up-beat personality are contagious, making him a wonderful hiking companion.

Steve is a strong advocate for wild places in southern Utah. He is completely committed in his support of the Southern Utah Wilderness Alliance's (SUWA) campaign to designate 5.7 million acres — or more — in Utah as wilderness. Steve has worked to convince others to become involved in protecting the areas so meaningful to him. When he meets people in the backcountry or at trailheads he takes time to tell them about the dangers to the area and of new roads, mines, gas and oil wells, and off-road vehicles. He encourages them to write to those agencies that are supposed to be caring for our wildlands.

Whether it is reporting on cows in remote canyons or participating in lengthy discussions with local groups and federal agencies about where and what should be the appropriate use of off-road vehicles, Steve has done it. His slide show on the canyons of Utah and his educational trips into threatened canyons for the Sierra Club and SUWA have helped spread the word about the threats to southern Utah and the Colorado Plateau.

Thanks to the concerted efforts of conservation groups over the years, the Escalante region of Utah remains one of the more remote and pristine places in the lower forty-eight states. Wildlife and plant life are abundant and rock art and archaeological sites abound. Above all, the Escalante is a land of endless eloquence and splendor where every corner offers a new mystery or surprise.

There are combinations of colors, rocks, walls, emerald pools, and hanging gardens that have beauty beyond comprehension. There are slot canyons hundreds of feet deep that narrow down to inches. There are amphitheaters comparable to those found in the Grand Canyon. There are cottonwood groves and beaver ponds nestled in the canyon bottoms that provide shade and sustenance. There are traces of people who came long before us—people whose spirits pervade the landscape.

All of this—the many wonders and beauties of the Escalante— are bordered by some of America's most recognized treasures: Capitol Reef and Bryce Canyon national parks and Glen Canyon National Recreation Area. With the formation of the new Grand Staircase-Escalante National Monument, lands formerly unprotected in the Escalante have gained the recognition they deserve.

Steve's book is also important because of what is still at stake in the Escalante. The Utah Wilderness Coalition, an alliance of over one hundred pro-wilderness groups, has recommended that more than 350,000 acres of the Escalante region be designated wilderness. This is in sharp contrast to the 183,000 acres of designated wilderness included in the 1995 Utah congressional delegation's Utah Public Lands Management Act that was introduced in the 104th Congress. If that essentially anti-wilderness bill had passed, much of the land described in this guide would have been opened for development. Without the herculean efforts of many like Steve who love the Escalante, that bill would have become law in 1996.

The establishment of Grand Staircase-Escalante National Monument has changed the wilderness dynamic somewhat in the Escalante area. While the monument has stopped mining in the area, other threats—such as the proposed paving of the Hole-in-the-Rock road—remain. Wilderness designation of a large percentage of Escalante land within Grand Staircase-Escalante National Monument is still the goal of the ardent lovers of the land and represents yet another battle for the environmental community to undertake.

There are those who question the ethic of having guide books to wilderness areas. My own answer is simple: Where did the generals and soldiers for the neverending war to protect wild places come from and how did they get there? If it were not for guide books, photography books, slide shows, articles about exploration and backcountry adventure, and organizations like the Southern Utah Wilderness Alliance, many of us might never have taken the leap from the city or the farm to the wilderness.

The leap to wilderness, in the case of many of my friends, often led to their advocacy of protecting unprotected or threatened wild places. My own personal experience mirrors this. I can remember meeting a gentleman at a party in Colorado who seemed to want to fight because he recognized me as the guy from New York (at the time) who was leading all those people to places he considered secret and sacred. Well, many of those people who hiked with me then are now in the forefront of the battle to save those same places.

Brant Calkin, a great wilderness advocate who has fought conservation battles on the Colorado Plateau for more than thirty years, said it succinctly, "I wish, when we were fighting the [Glen Canyon] dam in 1960, that there had been a good guide book for Glen Canyon." People who hike in wild places and learn about the land from first-hand experience are the most likely to become wilderness advocates. Once you are in the backcountry, the land changes from a pretty image on a magazine cover to something much more tangible and very much worth fighting to save.

Canyoneering 3: Loop Hikes in Utah's Escalante provides more than the nuts-and-bolts route descriptions that help the dayhiker and backpacker find their way through a tortuous landscape. Chapters on geology, the pre-Columbian Native Americans who first inhabited the area, and the Mormon settlers who made the Escalante home help weave a tapestry that provides the foundation needed for a more full understanding of this complex canyon area. Interesting vignettes add color to the guide, and chapters on canyon travel and equipment will help you along the way. With the recent rash of accidents in canyon country, the essay "Technical Canyoneering" is important and in the future may be viewed as seminal.

Steve has done a wonderful job of making this guide book easy to use. It is designed for all canyon visitors, from the neophyte to the hardcore. For many years I have explored the canyons of the Escalante, and on many trips Steve was with our group. After tramping the landscape, then reading *Canyoneering 3*, I can safely say that you will do well to take this guide along. You will surely have a better trip. And Steve and I would hope that you will become more dedicated to the cause of Utah wilderness protection.

Bert Fingerhut

Introduction

The view to the south and southeast is dismal and suggestive of the terrible. It is almost unique even in the category of plateau scenery. The streams which head at the foot of the lava-cap on the southern wall of the Aquarius flow southward down its long slopes. The amphitheaters soon grow into canyons of profound depth and inaccessible walls. These passages open into a single trunk canyon, and their united waters form the Escalante River....At no point can its walls be scaled.

Clarence Dutton, 1880

A recent acquaintance, hearing that I hiked in the desert, mentioned that he too liked hiking there. "It's level," he said. "To the contrary," I thought, thinking of a letter I'd received about a certain canyon: "Never have I hiked so much uphill as I did trying to get down the damn canyon," my correspondent had written.

And therein lies the rub: the vast province called Escalante is not the seemingly flat plain familiar to so many as desert. It is a twisted, complex web of sandstone; a jigsaw puzzle of canyons, draws, defiles, gorges, slots, and washes that outline upland expanses of slickrock and soil, demarcate benches, mesas, and ridges, and delineate the towers, pinnacles, and peaks that stand above the rest.

The Escalante is a land of diversity, from the vivacious sub-alpine highlands of the Aquarius Plateau to the death-knell dryness of the lower desert. It has been called a lonely land, devoid of life, with little to recommend it. But that is a perception of those who have never hiked the desert skin or explored its underpinnings from the bottom of the abyss.

It is motion, the sine qua non of the desert, that precludes loneliness. Who cannot help but find joy in the changing shadows on a wall at first light, delight in the intensifying colors of slickrock and cloud as day turns to night, and relish in the swirl of water during a summer downpour or the quiet waters of a pothole under a scorching sun?

The purpose of *Canyoneering 3: Loop Hikes in Utah's Escalante* is to provide accurate information for those intent on discovering what this desert region has to offer. It is designed to be used by sightseers, photographers, dayhikers, backpackers, and rock-climbers. Desert enthusiasts from youngsters to seniors will find hikes to fulfill their objectives.

In comparison with other hiking guides, the material presented in this guide may seem complex. The text does not simply lead you from signpost to signpost along oft-trodden paths. There are few established trails in the Escalante. Most of the routes described in this book entail finding ways in and out of canyons, and often they include long stretches of cross-country hiking on benches or along rimrock.

Rugged terrain is the norm, not the exception, in the Escalante. This puts an added obligation on those hiking there. In a land with few trails, route-finding and map-reading skills are very important. On many routes, rock-climbing and rope-handling skills become paramount. For the more audacious, swimming skills may be needed while descending some of the canyons.

Several of the routes entail hiking long stretches between water sources. This may require carrying two or more gallons of water in packs that are already heavy. Those attempting the harder hikes or technical routes must be prepared both physically and mentally. Hikers must be willing to turn back if things do not go as planned.

As with any outdoor activity done far from medical help, basic CPR and first-aid skills, though rarely needed, become essential. A knowledge of both the prevention and the treatment of hyperthermia is crucial.

Thirty-seven major hikes are featured in the guide. Many short and side hikes also are described. There are hikes that will satisfy any canyoneer, from the novice to the expert. Dayhikers can choose routes from an hour to a very long day. Backpackers will find many multiday hikes. Those not satisfied with the standard hikes can use the information presented in the guide to chart their own course.

All of the hikes in the guide are designed as loops. This negates the need for tedious, time-consuming, and gas-wasting car shuttles.

One of the aggravating aspects of hiking in the Escalante is finding the trailhead. The miles of old mining roads and stock access tracks in the area can confuse even the veteran canyoneer. Fourteen main roads and several side roads are described in the Road sections. They will help ensure that time is not squandered trying to find a trailhead.

Each hike is prefaced with a brief description of the route. This includes details regarding the recommended hiking seasons, trip length, water availability, elevation range, maps, skill level needed, and special equipment required.

The route descriptions contain information on hiking time between known landmarks, side trips, and interesting route variations. Maps are included that show important water sources and routes in and out of canyon systems.

About half of the land in the Escalante is within Glen Canyon National Recreation Area and therefore has some environmental protection. With the exception of a small amount of Forest Service land permanently protected in Box-Death Hollow Wilderness Area, the rest of the Escalante is in the Grand Staircase-Escalante National Monument. Although this designation has stopped some adverse development within the region, problems remain. The influx of backcountry users has also led to detrimental impacts in the popular canyons. The chapters on "Wilderness" and "Protecting the Environment" discuss these problems.

Landscapes are defined by their history—the physical forces that molded the land, the ancient ones who first inhabited it, and the people who explored, exploited, or were enchanted by it. Each new generation, building on the knowledge of the land gleaned from the past, adds its own insights about the land and so redefines the present and future. A rewarding part of hiking the Escalante is melding your perception of the land with the history of the area.

Chapters on "The Geology of the Escalante" and "The Strata" describe the forming of the Escalante. Other chapters tell the story of pre-Columbian habitation and historic settlement. Notable historic tidbits are scattered throughout the guide.

Wilderness

Best of all, the Escalante country belongs to us. It lies entirely within the public domain, and is therefore the property not of land and cattle companies, not of oil and mining corporations, not of the Utah State Highway Department or any Utah Chamber of Commerce, but of all Americans. It's our country. Or should be. It's supposed to be.

Edward Abbey, 1971

The Grand Staircase-Escalante National Monument's vast and austere landscape embraces a spectacular array of scientific and historic resources. This high, rugged, and remote region, where bold plateaus and multi-hued cliffs run for distances that defy human perspective, was the last place in the continental United States to be mapped. Even today, this unspoiled natural area remains a frontier.

Bill Clinton, September 18, 1996

I started with a simple map of Escalante country, white paper crossed with a squiggle of black lines. Small print followed the contour of those lines and provided each with a name: Harris Wash, Stevens Canyon, Choprock Bench, Death Hollow, Llewellyn Gulch, and a hundred others. Every label was familiar to me, intimately so. I had spent nearly thirty years learning what all of them—each representing a canyon, ridge top, bench, peak, stream, or slot—had to offer. Mile after mile, season after season I had trudged through that country, learning, discovering, exploring, and loving. So many adventures, so much beauty, so many friends.

But now my task was serious as I took out a black pen and started to draw on the map. With a hardened hand I began blacking out the areas on the map that over the years had been proposed for alteration or development—that is, destruction. Canyons, benches, and ridges disappeared under the ink. Soon my simple map of a complex landscape showed only small areas of white. The rest of the map was black.

The black represented not only a piece of wilderness we could have lost forever, but potentially a piece of myself. Without those areas what would I, or you, have missed? I thought of the struggle my friend Rob and I had in the Long Branch of Sleepy Hollow—sixteen hours of danger and delight: the green room, the natural bridges, the swims, the rappels, our bloody hands and knees, and how we had hugged each other when it was over. Or the winter night on Pollywog Bench when incredible winds tried to sweep Harvey, Bud, and me into oblivion. Or the week Ginger and I nickled-and-dimed our way down The Gulch on an archaeological survey, all the while catching up on the months we had been apart—talking, laughing, and giggling. Or the warm spring evening on top of King Bench where a group of friends and I sat marveling at the views and reveling in each other's company.

How many others, I wonder, have shared similar adventures and intimate contact with and within the lands called Escalante? Thousands certainly, perhaps even hundreds of thousands over the years. If the lands represented by my penned black boxes and rectangles and circles had been lost, where would we have gone to find what we were seeking?

Since its initial exploration in the late 1800s, the Escalante has been a special place not only for outdoor enthusiasts but also for a few greedy souls who were intent on plundering the land for personal profit. The schemes the promoters have suggested over the years, when added together, would have spelled the destruction of the Escalante. It has only been through the tireless efforts of conservationists and environmentalists that the Escalante has remained the wonderful area we now enjoy. Detailed below are several of the serious development proposals that surfaced over the years.

Coal mining, dams, and power plants

In the early 1970s two coal-fired, steam-electric power plants were proposed near the town of Escalante. Coal was to come from mines located in the Straight Cliffs Formation at the base of the Kaiparowits Plateau near the head of Alvey Wash (the headwaters of Harris Wash). Water to run the steam generators was to come from reservoirs built along the Escalante River. Four dam sites were suggested.

The first, an earthen dam, was to be built just below the town of Escalante on the river. The second, an alternative to the first dam, would have entailed erecting a 133-foot concrete dam below the mouth of Pine Creek on the Escalante River. Water from either of these dams was to be used for both irrigation and to supply a 430-megawatt power plant.

The third dam would have been built on the Escalante River below the mouth of Horse Canyon. This dam, forming what was to be called the King Bench Reservoir, would have backed water up the main canyon for twelve miles and up Horse Canyon for several miles.

A system of canals and aqueducts ten miles long was to be used to pump water to the fourth proposed dam in the headwaters of Twentyfive Mile Wash. Water from this reservoir and the King Bench Reservoir was to be used exclusively for a coal-fired 1,500-megawatt power plant.

. . .

Oil Development

The Circle Cliffs Basin area of the Escalante drainage system contains the Circle Cliffs Special Tar Sands Area. Covering a total of 49,000 acres, the Tar Sands Area encloses the top and middle portions of Horse Canyon, Wolverine Creek, Little Death Hollow, and the North Fork of Silver Falls Creek. Some of the Tar Sands Area reaches the Escalante River.

In the 1980s developers proposed a massive oil drilling and recovery program in the bowl formed by the Circle Cliffs. Industry plans included drilling ninety-seven production wells and 27,000 injection and recovery wells, building 197 miles of power lines and pipelines, and assembling eleven four-story compressor-dehydrator plants. Access to the area would have been eased by widening and realigning the Burr Trail and constructing many miles of new roads, some cutting up through the Circle Cliffs to the benches above the canyons. Huge eighteen-wheel tank trucks would have run day and night—as many as 140 every twenty-four hours.

The work force would have been housed in a 640-acre industrial park at the head of Wolverine Creek that included power and sewage plants, an air strip, and housing for 500 employees. The payoff in terms of actual oil production would have been minuscule compared to the irreversible damage inflicted on a nearly pristine landscape: only 14 million barrels of oil—enough to supply the nation for only a single day—would have been recovered if the project was economically feasible, which it was not.

In 1993 Australian-owned, Houston-based BHP Petroleum proposed drilling in the Studhorse Peaks area just off the Burr Trail near the Capitol Reef National Park boundary. The project would have entailed building two miles of new road. The drilling plan was stopped by environmental groups.

In 1995 Viking Exploration, Inc. of Colorado proposed drilling an oil well near upper Middle Moody Canyon within the boundaries of Glen Canyon National Recreation Area. To make this possible, Viking will have to rebuild eight miles of old uranium mining roads that are now closed and construct five new miles of road. This oil well is still a possibility.

The 1996 hiking season started with the rhythmic thump-thump-thump of a diesel engine at an oil drilling rig on a state land parcel at the junction of the Hole-in-the-Rock road and the Fortymile Ridge road. We could hear the racket at our camp just below King Mesa several miles away. After more than eighty days of drilling, the hole was found to be dry.

Gas Development

In 1988 Box-Death Hollow Wilderness Area was threatened by carbon dioxide mining. Under a development plan approved by the U.S. Forest Service, sixty-five carbon dioxide wells, thirty-two oil wells, fifty-three miles of new roads, and 127 miles of pipelines and power lines were to be built on the high, thin ridges that divide Pine Creek, Death Hollow, and Sand Creek. The Forest Service admitted that "visual and auditory impacts" to the area would be "largely unavoidable and significant" and that sedimentation of the creeks and displacement of wildlife would be inevitable.

Roads

Perhaps the most senseless proposal for the Escalante region was the Trans-Escalante Federal Parkway. This 117-mile-long high-speed highway was to start at Bullfrog Basin on Lake Powell, traverse the top of the Waterpocket Fold, cross a bridge built over the Escalante River just below Stevens Arch, climb up and over the Kaiparowits Plateau, or under its eastern end, and terminate near Big Water, Arizona. The plan called for paving the Hole-in-the-Rock road to provide access from Escalante to contemplated marinas either at Hole-in-the-Rock or the mouth of Llewellyn Gulch.

The proposal was serious and, as part of a larger bill that established Glen Canyon National Recreation Area in 1971, funds were requested to finance the Trans-Escalante Federal Parkway. During hearings before Congress on the proposal, two opposing views of the parkway were presented.

The late Calvin Black, a commissioner from San Juan County and a well-known development advocate, stated in his testimony: "Without a road there will be less than 10 percent of that area that will ever be seen, even by the most vivid or avid outdoorsman there is. So I think this will give us some sort of perspective. Now, I think one other statement that really could be said of this, if we build these roads, compared to the vastness—the areas, the bench areas that will protect it from being seen—if we do this, if we build these roads, I think you can literally say that it will make about as much scar, when considering the whole area, as if you were to plow the ocean, and I think that is almost literal."

June Viavant, representing the Sierra Club and the Wasatch Mountain Club, testified against the parkway. She said: "The road planned across the Escalante wilderness would be, for all but a few miles, built for a design speed of 60 miles per hour. Driving through at 60 miles an hour would reduce the subtleties of that beautiful country, its own peculiar twists and turns, to a blur of slick-rock with an arch or two. This road would only enable more and more people to see less and less. People deserve to have a chance to be drawn into the Escalante naturally—to follow a canyon stream or a canyon rim on foot, wondering what is around the next bend."

Happily, the part of the bill establishing Glen Canyon National Recreation Area did pass Congress but the Trans-Escalante Federal Parkway part of the proposal did not.

The Burr Trail, a road that runs from Boulder to Capitol Reef National Park and on to Bullfrog Basin on Lake Powell, has been a source of contention between Garfield County officials and environmentalists. The county fought long and hard to pave the road, citing increased tourist business from Bullfrog Basin as its main reason for wanting to improve the road.

Environmentalists argued that a paved road would bring an influx of visitors to the area and damage the equanimity which exists on the Escalante's north side. The Bureau of Land Management's environmental assessment of the proposed paving agreed; it stated that traffic would increase 1,273 percent and that much of the area would lose its value of solitude and remoteness. Garfield County, nevertheless, paved the road from Boulder to the Capitol Reef National Park border in 1993. To date, the National Park Service has been unwilling to pave the portion of the Burr Trail that passes through the national park, thus making the paved portion a "highway to nowhere."

It just does not end

In 1989 the Bureau of Land Management transferred approximately 4,000 acres of land in Harris Wash to the State of Utah. The state planned to either open the area to development or sell it to private owners. The land transfer was not legal, however; and, after three years in the courts, the state agreed to return the land to the Bureau of Land Management. Part of the settlement called for the state to withdraw its claim to a right-of-way down Harris Wash. If implemented, the plan would have meant a road down magnificent Harris Wash, one of the most heavily hiked canyons in the Escalante area.

In 1992 Utah Congressman Jim Hansen proposed a bill to designate the Escalante region as a National Conservation Area. Despite its environmentally friendly name, the bill actually would have given the land less protection than it now enjoys. Part of the bill would have provided funding to pave the Hole-in-the-Rock road.

In 1994 Utah Governor Mike Leavitt advanced the Escalante Eco-Region Plan, which was a blueprint for developing the area. His proposal included a jetport, golf course, and hotel complex just outside Escalante and a visitor's center at the Hole-in-the-Rock road/Harris Wash road junction. Lands above many of the Escalante River tributaries would have been opened for development. The proposal died when locals, though mainly anti-wilderness, decided they were anti-development as well.

Cattle grazing

One of the most important issues facing the Escalante area is overgrazing by cattle. One only has to hike in The Gulch, upper Twentyfive Mile Wash, Dry Fork Coyote, Steep Creek, Llewellyn Gulch, Davis Gulch, and many other canyons that flow to the Escalante River to see the damage done by these four-footed bulldozers.

It is most revealing to compare these areas to those where cattle grazing has been eliminated. In 1992, a private foundation bought the 55,000-acre Glen Canyon grazing permit. This permit, though not covering all of the Escalante canyons that are in Glen Canyon National Recreation Area, did permanently stop grazing in such popular canyons as lower Harris Wash, lower Twentyfive Mile Wash, Scorpion Gulch, and Coyote Gulch.

The Bureau of Land Management oversees cattle grazing not only in Grand Staircase-Escalante National Monument but also on the lands administered by the National Park Service in Glen Canyon National Recreation Area. If you have comments about cattle grazing after you visit the Escalante, write the BLM office in Escalante. (See the "Access" chapter for the address.) Those interested in learning more about cattle grazing or in becoming actively involved in the cattle grazing issue in the Escalante should write or call:

Great Old Broads for Wilderness
1942 Broadway #206
Boulder, Colorado 80302
303-443-7024

The Great Old Broads for Wilderness is actively working on the grazing problems in the Escalante.

The wilderness issue

The first proposal to save the wildlands of southern Utah and the canyons of the Escalante was suggested in 1936. Secretary of the Interior Harold Ickes recommended the establishment of Escalante National Monument. It would have contained almost 7,000 square miles, or 4.5 million acres, and encompassed almost all of what we now term canyon country. In a preliminary report at the time to Governor Henry H. Blood, the Utah State Planning Board stated: "The principal advantages that will accrue from the designation of this area as a national monument will be the preservation for all time and under proper control of the many scenic wonders and areas of archaeological importance." The report went on to say: "It is reasonable to expect that the proceeds due directly or indirectly to tourist business will mean more to Southern Utah than those from any other use to which this barren and almost unproductive area may be put."

Pressure from extractive industries stopped the establishment of Escalante National Monument, however, and set the tone for future battles over the canyons: Was the drive for private profits more important than protecting the land for all Americans to enjoy?

Little happened on the conservation front until the passing of the Wilderness Act in 1964. That act defined wilderness as "an area where the earth and its community of life are untrammeled by man, where man himself is a visitor who does not remain." The Wilderness Act further stated that wilderness is an area where one can find solitude and where there is the opportunity for primitive and unconfined recreation.

Unfortunately, the Wilderness Act only applied to certain U.S. Forest Service, National Park Service, and Fish and Wildlife Service lands. These agencies were required to inventory their holdings and recommend areas that met the criteria for wilderness. This led to the establishment of the 26,000-acre Box-Death Hollow Wilderness Area in Dixie National Forest in the northwest part of the Escalante region in 1984. It protects just a tiny corner of the Aquarius Plateau: The Box of Pine Creek and small areas at the heads of Death Hollow and Sand Creek.

The Colorado River Storage Project Act of 1956 called for the construction of Glen Canyon Dam. Interim administration of the land around the soon-to-be-formed Lake Powell was given to the National Park Service in cooperation with the Bureau of Reclamation. Although the dam was finished and the lake started filling in 1963, a proposed Glen Canyon National Recreation Area (GCNRA) bill was not introduced in Congress until 1965. Battles between developers and environmentalists erupted over which land should be included in GCNRA.

In the Escalante, the initial bill would have protected the canyon only as far upriver as Twentyfive Mile Wash and Middle Moody Canyon. Conservationists countered with a proposal to extend GCNRA to Utah Highway 12 and to make all of the land in the Escalante a designated wilderness area. The GCNRA bill went through several revisions and was reintroduced in Congress in 1965, 1968, and 1970 before finally passing in 1971. A compromise was reached between the opposing groups—the Escalante was divided a couple of miles above Harris Wash and Silver Falls Creek and was not designated as wilderness.

Glen Canyon National Recreation Area, which is run by the National Park Service, provides superficial protection to most of the canyons of the lower Escalante. Unfortunately, development, mining, and grazing are allowed in GCNRA. This will be of concern in the future.

The Federal Lands Policy Management Act (FLPMA—pronounced "flipma") of 1976 was similar to the Wilderness Act, but it applied to areas under the control of the Bureau of Land Management (BLM). The Federal Lands Policy Management Act required the BLM to inventory its holdings to see which lands were suitable for wilderness designation. The BLM was to use the definition of wilderness provided in the Wilderness Act. Once the BLM had determined which lands met the criterion for wilderness, Congress then would decide their final disposition.

The BLM lands in the Escalante region include most of the main Escalante Canyon and its side drainages from the town of Escalante to Harris Wash and from the Circle Cliffs to the Kaiparowits Plateau. After inventorying its land, the BLM determined that 167,358 acres had wilderness qualities. These acres became Wilderness Study Areas (WSAs).

The BLM wilderness inventory process came under attack from environmental groups who felt that the BLM did not use the congressional definition of wilderness. They believed that the BLM had declared areas worthy or not worthy of wilderness designation based on the agency's various whims and fancies. The environmentalists noted that most of the lands excluded from wilderness consideration by the BLM had the potential for economic development—whether it be for mines, dam sites, or stock improvements.

For example, in the Escalante region the BLM left out much of the Circle Cliffs Basin and the Studhorse Peak area based on possible oil, gas, and uranium exploitation. Much of the Aquarius Plateau was left out due to its potential for carbon dioxide mining and timber harvesting.

Environmental groups decided that Congress needed an accurate description of the wildlands in southern Utah to counter the inaccurate information presented by the BLM. In 1985 they formed the Utah Wilderness Coalition (UWC), an association that now includes over a hundred conservation groups such as the Sierra Club, the Wilderness Society, the National Parks and Conservation Association, and the Southern Utah Wilderness Alliance.

Members of the UWC did an intensive survey of the Escalante area and found that close to another 100,000 acres met the congressional definition of wilderness. These acres have been included in the UWC-sponsored America's Red Rocks Wilderness Act. This bill has been introduced into Congress as H.R. 1500.

In the winter of 1995 the wilderness battle heated to hellish temperatures. The Utah congressional delegation, emboldened by the 1994 elections, introduced Senate Bill 884 and House of Representative Bill 1745, both of which sought to set aside only 1.8 million acres of land as wilderness in all of Utah. The bills also contained "hard release" language which meant that any land not designated as wilderness could never be considered for wilderness in the future. In addition, the House and Senate bills would have left wilderness areas open to off-road vehicles and the construction of roads, dams, pipelines, and communication antennas. It was only through the efforts of the Utah Wilderness Coalition and a filibuster led by New Jersey Senator Bill Bradley that the bills were defeated.

In the fall of 1996 Interior Secretary Bruce Babbitt and Utah Representative Jim Hansen, recognizing the inadequacies of the first wilderness inventory, initiated a reinventory of BLM lands in Utah. This reinventory raised the number of acres that met the congressional definition of wilderness from 5.7 million acres to more than 6.0 million acres.

Grand Staircase-Escalante National Monument

An important and unexpected development in protecting the Escalante took place in September 1996 when President Bill Clinton, using provisions of the Antiquities Act of 1906, established Grand Staircase-Escalante National Monument. Encompassing 1.7 million acres, including the Grand Staircase, Kaiparowits Plateau, and upper Paria Canyon and its tributaries, the new national monument will help protect some of the wildest land in America. In the Escalante area, several hundred thousand acres that were formerly managed by the Bureau of Land Management under its multiple-use mandate are now in Grand Staircase-Escalante National Monument.

The immediate effect of the national monument designation was to stop the issuance of all new mineral leases. This effectively put an end to the proposed Andalex coal mine on the Kaiparowits Plateau. This huge mine, fought intensely by the environmental community, would have changed the character of southern Utah and adversely impacted the Kaiparowits Plateau, a pristine 650,000-acre upland and canyon area that is south and west of the Escalante canyons. President Clinton, when announcing the formation of the monument, stated: "I am concerned about a large coal mine proposed for the area. Mining jobs are good jobs, and mining is important to our national economy and to our national security. But we can't have mines everywhere, and we shouldn't have mines that threaten our national treasures."

While Grand Staircase-Escalante National Monument does protect the area from some intrusions, it does not give the land the same protection as would wilderness designation. Wilderness designation stops all but the most rudimentary incursions. Environmentalists worry that if development is allowed in the national monument—in the form of constructed and signed trails, upgraded roads, visitor centers, and campgrounds—it will become a tourist draw like the popular national parks in southern Utah.

Designated wilderness is allowed within the national monument. For that reason, the wilderness battle in the Escalante is not over. Land that meets the definition of wilderness in the Escalante will still be included in America's Red Rocks Wilderness Act.

President Clinton, in his proclamation establishing Grand Staircase-Escalante National Monument, gave the Bureau of Land Management, which will manage the national monument, three years from September 1996 to prepare a management plan for the area. The public has been invited to participate in discussions about how the monument will be managed in the future. Those interested in participating should contact the Bureau of Land Management office in Escalante (see the "Access" chapter for the address) or the Southern Utah Wilderness Alliance (address below).

The new national monument gives added protection to some of the land in southern Utah. But much more is at stake. Areas such as the Dirty Devil River, Dark Canyon, White Canyon, Comb Ridge, Cedar Mesa, San Rafael Swell, Nokai Dome, and many others still have no permanent protection.

It is up to each of us to decide which side of the wilderness issue to support. The Southern Utah Wilderness Alliance (SUWA) has been leading the pro-wilderness battle since 1984. It is in great part due to its leadership that we have not lost the Escalante—and other wilderness-worthy canyon areas throughout southern Utah—to the developers and despoilers. The wilderness battle rages on in Utah and in the halls of Congress. Please make it a habit to donate to SUWA or other environmental organizations that are helping protect the Escalante and other wilderness lands in Utah. Consider it an essential part of every canyon hike you do—a tithing for wilderness.

Southern Utah Wilderness Alliance
1471 South 1100 East
Salt Lake City, Utah 84105
801-486-3161

Protecting the Environment

*Today's desert traveler must pick his way between the immensity and the
fragility. For many of us the refreshment of the waterless has become a ne-
cessity, whatever the warring concepts about our impact. Accepting the
fact of our flesh bringing down our boots with care, we can still, if briefly,
give predictability the slip. For to walk into the desert is to deal one's life a
wild card.*

Bruce Berger, 1990

The increase in backcountry use in the Escalante has led to un-
intentional degradation of the land. Our continued and unrestricted
use of this land is contingent on each person's commitment to protect the environment. There are a number of things we as individuals
can do. None are difficult; none take much effort. The goal is to
leave the desert as you found it—or better.

The meticulous practice of "leave-no-trace" camping techniques
can help spare the land; but this is no longer enough. We must now
become our brother's keeper. It is our responsibility to clean up the
mess left by others. Leave room in your pack for extra garbage.
Spend ten minutes breaking up an old fire ring, blocking off a redun-
dant trail, or restoring an ill-used campsite. Insensitive hikers can no
longer be tolerated. It is our obligation to help educate those who do
not know and to chastise those who do know but do not care.

Some of the techniques used to minimize impacts on desert
lands have changed over the years. Readers of *Canyoneering 1* and
Canyoneering 2 should read the following section and abide by the
changes it makes in earlier practices. All users of such lands should
adhere to these concepts and practices.

Please read the following section carefully.

Group size: One of the biggest problems land managers have in
the Escalante is overly large hiking groups. Although group size is
limited to twelve, a voluntary limit is eight people. If your group is
larger than twelve, it must break into two or more smaller groups.
The groups must hike and camp at least one-half mile apart.

Bill Wolverton, a backcountry ranger for many years in the Escalante, notes that: "Compliance with the [group size] rule is a joke.
Most groups seem to think that camping across the creek, around
the bend, or maybe 100 yards apart, is compliance. Very often, the
group has one stove or one set of pots, or their meals are packaged
together, so they end up together for meals anyway. Sometimes
groups even think that filling out two permits is good enough."

Most often, the group-size rule is broken by youth groups. In the past, it has been common to see groups as large as fifty camping in popular canyons such as Coyote Gulch, Harris Wash, and Willow Creek. The aggregate damage by large groups is usually extensive compared to that of smaller groups. Sanitation problems, multiple trails between groups, and excessive noise detract from the wilderness experience of others in the canyons. Leaders of large groups should contact the Interagency Office in Escalante and discuss their plans with the rangers there before heading into the backcountry.

Trash: The most obvious eyesore. Take out more than you bring in. Apple cores, orange peels, banana peels, and nut shells are garbage. Carry them out.

Bodily waste: Solid waste should be disposed of at least 300 feet from any water source or camp area. Avoid water courses. Dig a hole four to six inches deep near vegetation and with maximum exposure to sunlight. The microorganisms associated with the vegetation will speed the breakdown of the waste, as will the heat available from the sun. Do not dispose of waste or urinate in caves or under overhangs.

In the popular canyons it is no longer adequate to burn your toilet paper; you must carry it out. In areas of dense or dry vegetation do not burn your toilet paper; carry it out. Wildfires start quickly and are difficult to extinguish. Plastic bags make carrying out your toilet paper easy and odor free. Grand Canyon backpackers have been carrying out their toilet paper for years. The Interagency Office in Escalante dispenses plastic bags with sanitation instructions to all backcountry users.

The conventional wisdom was that you should not urinate on vegetation. It has been found, however, that there are no impacts from this and that urine is a good fertilizer. The only rule now is to urinate away from water sources.

Washing dishes: Have you ever wondered why some campsites are overrun with mice and others are not? Have you ever had to set up your tent to keep mice from running over your face in the night? Mice—and other animals—are attracted to the food scraps campers did not carry out. We used to use gray water holes for dishwater and leftovers; this is no longer acceptable. Instead, pour wastewater through a strainer into a second container. The wastewater can then be broadcast over a wide area away from camp. The dregs from the strainer, and any other leftovers, **must** be carried out.

Bathing: Water in backcountry Escalante is scarce and should be treated as a treasured commodity. Pothole water should be used only for cooking and drinking. Other backpackers may be depending on the water. Save your swimming and bathing for the creeks and rivers. Swim in potholes only if there is a substantial flow of water. If you need to lather up, use pots and canteens to carry water well away from the water source. Use only biodegradable soaps; they do not have the perfumes and additives that are damaging to the environment. Never swim until you have washed off your sun-tan lotion.

Indian artifacts and ruins: The relics left behind by Anasazi and Fremont Indians belong to all of us and are protected by law. Archaeological sites are being destroyed at an alarming rate by vandals, pot and artifact hunters, and the uninformed public. The Archeological Resources Protection Act of 1979 provides stiff penalties for those harming archaeological sites. If you witness vandalism to an archaeological site, notify the personnel at the Escalante Interagency Office in Escalante. (See the "Access" chapter for the address.) Information you provide that leads to a conviction may entitle you to a reward.

There are protocols you must follow when visiting Indian sites:

1. When visiting ruins, view them from a distance. Although a couple of people may not severely impact a site, the aggregate impact of many visitors over a period of years can destroy it. Stay on established paths, never enter a ruin, do not climb on the walls or roofs of a ruin, and do not touch the walls of a ruin.

2. Do not camp or build fires in or near ruins or Indian sites. This includes the caves that Indians used as temporary camps that do not contain obvious ruins. Sometimes it is difficult to determine if a cave has been used by Indians. Look first for large artifacts such as manos or metates or grinding surfaces on larger rocks or boulders. Rock art in or near a cave is ample evidence of Indian occupation. The presence of lithics—flakes of stone that are not native to the area—signify that ancient peoples once used the site. In the Escalante area these flakes are usually chert, jasper, or chalcedony.

3. It is illegal to remove any Indian artifact. These include pottery shards, lithics, arrowheads, pots, baskets, etc. Leave them where you find them.

4. Rock art should be viewed from a distance. Do not touch, brush, or use chalk to outline the figures.

In recent years federal agencies have come down hard on those who desecrate or loot Indian sites. A $3,000 fine was levied against a man caught vandalizing an Indian ruin near Escalante in 1990. In 1992 an individual caught destroying a petroglyph panel with a

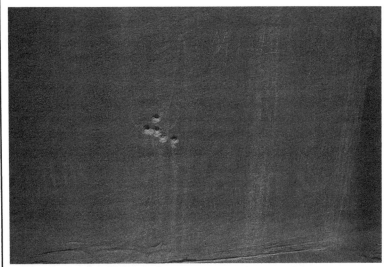

Vandalized petroglyph panel.

penknife near the Escalante River in Glen Canyon National Recreation Area was convicted as a felon and had to pay an $8,500 fine. Earl Shumway, a notorious artifact hunter from Moab, was given a six-and-a-half-year prison term for his criminal deeds.

Campsite selection: The area that takes the most abuse from backpackers is the campsite. For that reason, campsite selection is of primary importance. There are several things to consider when choosing a campsite: (1) Camp at least 200 feet from water sources. When camping near isolated potholes, springs, or ponds do not use the water source after dark, because you may scare away wild animals. (2) Use a well-established or totally trashed site. There the damage has already been done. If a site has been lightly used, it is best to find a heavily used site or move to a new site and let the lightly used site recover. (3) Camp on slickrock, sandy benches, or in a dry wash, weather permitting. These are the optimal sites since there are no lasting impacts from camping. (4) Do not camp in areas where cryptobiotic soil is present. (5) Do not remove vegetation in order to level or smooth out sleeping platforms. (6) If debris—branches, rocks, leaves—have been cleared to make a campsite, return them to their original location before moving on. Unless the campsite has been heavily used in the past, you should be able to erase all signs of use.

Fires: Campfires can no longer be tolerated in the wilderness setting. They do an immense amount of damage to the land. Not only are the blackened rocks of a fire ring ugly, the charcoal and ash residues seem to last forever. Fire rings demarcate campsites and tend to draw people to them. This promotes overuse. Use a light-weight stove for cooking and a candle lantern as a gathering beacon for nighttime socializing. It is illegal to build fires when camping in the Glen Canyon National Recreation Area portion of the Escalante.

Cryptobiotic soil: Also called cryptogamic or microbiotic soil, this is a conglomeration of algae, fungi, moss, and lichen that forms the black castlelike crust that is spread throughout the desert. It is invaluable in holding the soil together and reducing erosion. When walking through areas of cryptobiotic soil, stay on established trails. If there are no trails, walk footstep to footstep. Do not leave a trail where erosion can start.

Dogs: Dogs are allowed in all of the areas covered in the guide. In Glen Canyon National Recreation Area dogs must be leashed at all times. Be realistic about your animal. If it is loud, aggressive toward other hikers or wildlife, chases cattle, defecates on the trails, does not respond to your commands, or is in other ways obnoxious, leave it behind. In some areas, water sources are infrequent and become very valuable; do not let your dog muddy an isolated water source. Dog owners should make it a practice to leash their pet when other hikers are nearby.

Cairns: Both a bane and a boon, these short stacks of rocks are erected to mark the trail. Unfortunately, there are too many "cairns to nowhere," and these should be toppled. Some cairns can be an environmental plus—they keep hikers on established paths and reduce the incidence of multiple trails.

The Geology of the Escalante Region
by Tom Messenger and Steve Allen

The shifting sands! Slowly they move, wave upon wave, drift upon drift;
but by day and by night they gather, gather, gather. They overwhelm, they
bury, they destroy, and then a spirit of restlessness seizes them and they
move off elsewhere, swirl upon swirl, line upon line, in serpentine wind-
ings that enfold some new growth or fill in some new valley in waste.
John C. Van Dyke, 1901

The geology of the Escalante region is complicated. A basic understanding of how the canyons were created and a knowledge of
the characteristics of the common formations will prove valuable as
you follow the route descriptions. It will add insight and increase
your sensitivity while hiking in the area.

Most of the rocks in the Escalante area are sedimentary. Sedimentary rocks are most commonly composed of fragments (mainly
silica) that weathered from surrounding highlands. Geologists call
these fragments clastic particles. Volcanic ash is another source of
clastic particles. Some sediments, such as limestone and gypsum, are
biological or chemical precipitates in seas or lakes.

As the clastic particles were swept down from the highlands by
wind and water, the environments into which the material was deposited varied. The source of the particles, the length of deposition,
and the depositional environment—a lake, sea, tidal flat, or dry
ground—determined the final sedimentary structures of the formation. The rocks under discussion here are of two basic types, wind
deposited and water deposited.

The wind deposits are cross-bedded sandstone. Examples include Wingate Sandstone, Navajo Sandstone, Page Sandstone, and
Entrada Sandstone. They strikingly preserve evidence of massive
sand seas in which a large amount of material was deposited over a
geologically short span of time. The climate and environment during the period of deposition was similar to that of the present-day
Sahara Desert, hot and dry. Although from a distance cross-bedded
sandstone appears homogeneous, it does contain layers. These layers, which are up to seventy feet thick, are inclined about twenty-five
degrees to the horizontal. The layers formed on the downwind slip
faces of the dunes as steady seasonal winds moved them across the
landscape. The layers record the passage of successive waves of
dunes.

Water deposits are represented by horizontal-bedded layers that
range from paper-thin to many feet thick and include several rock
types. Some layers record the deposition of fine particles of silt and
clay in the quiet water of floodplains, lakes, lagoons, tidal flats, and

shallow seas. Other layers are coarser deposits of sand and gravel brought in by rivers. Current ripples (ripple rock), mud cracks, and raindrop impressions can often be seen. Flowing water also deposits cross-bedded layers, but these are generally much thinner than the wind deposits described above. (Other differences are too technical for this discussion.)

Horizontal-bedded layers are also formed by fossil-bearing limestone from shallow seas and by gypsum evaporated in basins with restricted connection to the open ocean (which concentrates the salts because the water does not mix very rapidly with the ocean). Alternating layers of marine and stream deposits record the migration of the shoreline in response to changes in sea level brought about by local and global climate changes and tectonic motions.

Few formations enjoyed exactly the same environment the whole time they were being laid down. Occasional wind-blown dune deposits occur in river sediments, and massive dune deposits often contain limestone layers that were deposited in interdune lakes. Once deposited, clastic particles are liable to be swept away eventually unless they are retained in a basin or held by rising groundwater. As the sediments become more deeply buried, heat, pressure, and fluids harden them into rock by chemical and physical processes of solution, replacement, recrystallization, compaction, and cementation.

By 250 million years ago the highlands to the east—the Ancestral Rocky Mountains and the Ancestral Uncompahgre Uplift—had greatly eroded and were becoming less important as sources for the sediment. To the west an oceanic plate was forcing its way under the western edge of the North American Plate. These forces were induced by plate tectonics, the shifting of the huge geologic plates driven by the churning of the earth's hot, fluid mantle. This subduction, or one plate diving under another, caused the formation of a volcanic arc to the south and west of the Colorado Plateau. The arc gradually spread north. The new highlands formed in the arc contributed more and more sediment, both as stream sediments and as volcanic ash. (The Ancestral Rockies resulted from earlier plate collisions that produced the supercontinent of Pangaea.)

Sixty-five million years ago the subduction process under the western edge of North America speeded up. Instead of plunging steeply into the mantle, it is thought that the subducted oceanic crust slid shallowly under the continent all the way to the Great Plains. This Laramide Orogeny both compressed and uplifted the West. The compression, acting at old zones of weakness, buckled the sediments laid down over a 500-million-year period.

In the Escalante region, the upheaval produced an upwarp running north and south through the Circle Cliffs. The upwarp is bordered on the east by the Henry Mountains Basin and on the west by the Kaiparowits Basin. The steep eastern side of the upwarp is the Waterpocket Fold. The upwarp recedes from its greatest height in the north under the Aquarius Plateau to its lowest point at Lake Powell to the south. Evidence of this structural relief can be seen by noting that Navajo Sandstone is present near the 9,000' level on the Aquarius Plateau and below the 4,000' level at Lake Powell.

Twenty-five million years ago volcanic activity in the form of lava flows on the Aquarius Plateau added another element to the geology we see today. Lava boulders, brought into the Escalante River Basin by the action of glaciers and running water in the last two million years, are strewn throughout the upper Escalante canyons and can readily be seen in Death Hollow, Sand Creek, Steep Creek, The Gulch, and Boulder Creek.

Uplifting of the Colorado Plateau has continued intermittently since the Laramide Orogeny, and erosion has altered the Laramide topography so that the land surface no longer follows the structural relief. As the land rose, the highest points were most exposed to erosion. Younger rocks on the crest of the upwarp eroded away to the point that the region's oldest exposed rocks are found in the Circle Cliffs. On the Aquarius Plateau younger rocks were preserved by a resistant volcanic cap.

In the structurally low Kaiparowits Basin, the younger rocks were less exposed to erosion. These rocks are preserved in the Straight Cliffs, where they stand as high as the older rocks now at the surface on the crest of the deeply eroded upwarp. This inversion is shown on the topographic map. Why does "Kaiparowits Basin" not appear? Because topographically the basin is really the lofty Kaiparowits Plateau. It still is a basin structurally: rocks of the same age are 8,000 feet lower in altitude on (or actually, under) the Kaiparowits Plateau than in the Circle Cliffs.

While the Colorado Plateau has risen, the land to the west has dropped. Once drainage was established, erosion rapidly cut into the western edge of the plateau and captured the upper course of the Colorado River. Following the path of least resistance as it flowed downward, water in the form of trickles, streams, and rivers remorselessly cut through hard and soft layers of rock to form the canyons we visit today.

The Strata
by Tom Messenger and Steve Allen

> *...the surface was diversified by columns, spires, castles, and battlemented towers of colossal but often beautiful proportions, closely resembling elaborate structures of art, but in effect far surpassing the most imposing monuments of human skill.*
>
> John S. Newberry, 1860

The formations detailed below are listed in order of age, from the oldest or lowest stratum to the youngest or highest stratum. Only the dominant formations found in the Escalante area are described. Other rock types and even other formations may be present elsewhere on the Colorado Plateau in the same time interval.

A formation is a mappable unit: a body of rock with distinctive features that can be recognized in the field with a magnifying glass. Most of the formations under discussion show a marked contrast in rock type and color with the units immediately above and below and can be easily identified from a distance. If a formation is dominated by a single rock type, that is reflected in its name—e.g., Wingate Sandstone or Navajo Sandstone. For more varied conglomerate rock structures such as the Chinle Formation, the noncommittal word "formation" is used. The rocks discussed here were deposited from about 250 to 170 million years ago.

In the Escalante region, the *Moenkopi Formation* is found only in the Circle Cliffs on the east side of Escalante Canyon. It is horizontal-bedded and is up to 500 feet thick. It was formed when streamborne silt and mud were deposited on floodplains or in tidal pools and mud flats on the edge of a shallow sea to the west. A layer of limestone containing fragments of ancient clams and snails records an interval when the shoreline lay farther east. The layers vary considerably in color, ranging from near white to red, yellow, brown, and dark brown. The Moenkopi Formation has been characterized as looking like a chocolate torte cake. It forms ledgy cliffs and steep slopes.

The *Chinle Formation* is horizontal-bedded and is up to 700 feet thick. It is found in the Circle Cliffs and along the lower Escalante River. The Chinle Formation was formed by streams depositing sand, gravel, mud, and silt in alluvial plains and river channels.

While this deposition was proceeding, wind carried in ash from volcanic eruptions to the southwest. As deposition continued, groundwater altered the ash to the clay mineral bentonite and dissolved uranium from the ash. Layers rich in bentonite weather to the frothy surface that is often described as "popcorn." The "popcorn" is found in the Purple Hills area of the Circle Cliffs.

The Chinle Formation contains a rainbow of colors—red, brown, purple, gray, and green—and forms steep and, when wet, very gooey muddy slopes. It often contains petrified wood.

A substratum of the Chinle Formation, the Shinarump Member, contains uranium ore. Uranium dissolved from the ash layers percolated through the porous sandstone of the Shinarump Member, where it was chemically precipitated by decomposed plant material. The plant material had been washed down streams and had collected in pockets and seams. Later, uranium miners looked for these pockets and seams. The presence of petrified wood often was an indicator that uranium deposits were near. The Shinarump Member is a dense, dirty white, medium-grained sandstone up to 150 feet thick. Parts of it contain river gravel and it can resemble concrete. Since the Shinarump Member is at the bottom of the Chinle Formation and is very resistant to erosion, it often stands out boldly as the top of the slopes and cliffs of the Moenkopi Formation.

Wingate Sandstone is found throughout the Escalante region. It is a cliff-forming, cross-bedded sandstone that is up to 350 feet thick. The Wingate was formed during a period of aridity and sand seas and its colors range from a light red to almost brown. This can vary considerably, and it is not unusual to see near-white Wingate Sandstone. This can make it hard to differentiate from Navajo Sandstone. Often the context it is in, immediately above the Chinle Formation and below the Kayenta Formation, is the clue to whether it is Wingate or Navajo. The Wingate forms vertical walls that have vertical cracks.

The *Kayenta Formation* records the last gasp of the Ancestral Uncompahgre Uplift. In a wetter period between the times of the Wingate and Navajo deserts, westward-flowing streams brought down final contributions of sand and silt. Repeated shifting of the channels and variation in the flow volumes scoured and filled the ancient streambeds to produce layers that persist for only short distances. Bed thickness and grain size decrease to the west as the current slackened. The formation, up to 400 feet thick, is reddish brown to dark purplish red in color and forms broken ledges and steep slopes. The Kayenta Formation is the friend of the backpacker, as it can provide wide benches that are easy to negotiate.

Navajo Sandstone is a cliff-forming, cross-bedded sandstone that is up to 1,250 feet thick. It is a dune deposit like the Wingate and it formed in a sand sea that not only covered the whole Colorado Plateau but extended well beyond. Navajo Sandstone is usually lighter in color than Wingate Sandstone, varying from bright white to red. It forms vertical walls, but the tops of the cliffs tend to be more rounded than Wingate cliffs.

Page Sandstone is a light-gray to red cliff-forming, cross-bedded sandstone that is up to 130 feet thick. It was formed after a considerable period of widespread erosion in the same environment as the Navajo Sandstone. Although it is a contemporary of the lower part of the younger Carmel Formation, it is so similar to the older Navajo Sandstone that the two were not differentiated by geologists until recently. Naturally, this similarity makes it difficult to tell the two apart.

The erosional surface between the Navajo and the overlying Page Sandstone is characterized by a thin layer of light-colored angular chert pebbles. It is necessary to locate this layer in order to identify the contact surface between the Navajo and the Page. Because of the general obscurity of the contact, references to Navajo Sandstone in the descriptions of the hikes will mean an undifferentiated Navajo Sandstone and Page Sandstone. The one exception is in Hike #8, where the Geologist's note points out the contact surface.

The *Carmel Formation* is horizontal-bedded and up to 300 feet thick. It was formed by a marine incursion into vast sand dunes during an arid period. Red to brown siltstone layers are intermixed with gypsum beds and limestone layers that often contain marine fossils. It forms sloping ledges that are often unstable to walk on.

Entrada Sandstone in the Escalante area is in a transition zone. It is usually cross-bedded and looks like a red to dark-red Navajo or Wingate sandstone. But, in some places, it has become interbedded with siltstone and mudstone that were deposited on coastal flats around lagoons. In these areas the Entrada has weathered into slopes and into "hoodoos," or "goblins," which are short towers or pinnacles. In the Escalante region Entrada Sandstone is 700 to 1,000 feet thick and is found only on the west side of Escalante Canyon. Good examples of Entrada Sandstone are Dance Hall Rock, the Sooner Rocks, and Devils Garden.

> **Note:** Throughout the manuscript the descriptions of the various formations have been shortened; for example, "a Wingate wall" instead of "a wall of Wingate Sandstone" or "walk along the Kayenta" instead of "walk along a Kayenta Formation ledge."

Man in the Escalante—The Prehistoric Period

No black is blacker than the window of an Anasazi Indian cliff dwelling. Stone the color of salmon flesh frames these small rectangles of thick, palpable emptiness, frames a darkness with the density of night on water, the river beneath a moonless sky.

Ellen Meloy, 1994

Little is known of the first arrival of prehistoric humans in the Escalante River region. Inconclusive evidence—fragments of Folsom projectile points and petroglyphs purportedly depicting woolly mammoths—place Paleo-Indians in the area at about 10,000 B.C. These Paleo-Indians were big-game hunters who roamed large areas while following seasonal migrations. They utilized stone tools and sharp sticks and lived in primitive shelters or caves. While the evidence is scanty in the Escalante area, it is known that Paleo-Indians occupied nearby sections of southern Utah and that woolly mammoths did wander the canyons of the lower Escalante.

Indians of the Desert Archaic Culture (5500 B.C. to A.D. 500) lived in Glen Canyon and its tributaries, specifically those to the north and east of the Escalante canyons. They evolved from the Paleo-Indians with their big-game hunting tradition to a people of cultural diversity. A hunter-gatherer tradition was born. Instead of meat being the main food staple, the gathering of nuts, roots, and berries predominated. Baskets, crudely woven at first, became more sophisticated, and pottery was soon introduced. Woven sandals and blankets and sewn animal-hide clothing and footwear were used. Atlatls, or spear throwers, gave way to the bow and arrow toward the end of the Desert Archaic Period.

The first Indians to definitely inhabit the Escalante River drainage date to the late Basketmaker II Period (approximately A.D. 400). The late date of Indian occupation compared to other areas of the Southwest was a function of the Escalante's remote location and a lack of need for its resources until burgeoning populations to the north and east forced Indian groups to seek new lands to settle. Certainly the canyons and upland areas of the Escalante were inviting. Large areas of tillable bottomland were abundant next to perennial streams. A plentiful supply of caves must have seemed a godsend.

Most important was the ecological diversity of the area. The dry, warm lowland canyons and the wet, cool highlands of the Kaiparowits Plateau allowed the Indians to exploit a wide variety of flora and fauna. Two distinct cultures were poised at about the same time to enter the new territory—the Fremont and the Anasazi.

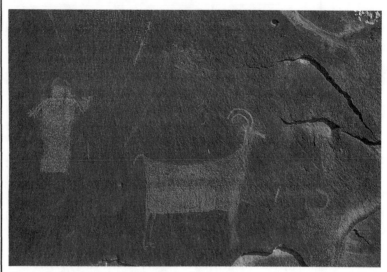

Petroglyph panel on the Escalante River.

The origin of the Fremont Culture is cloudy. Three hypotheses have been put forward by anthropologists. First, they were descendants of the Desert Archaic Culture people, hunter-gatherers from the Great Basin and the Colorado Plateau. Second, the Fremont were a breakaway Anasazi or Mogollon group from the Four Corners area. Third, the Fremont were bison hunters from the Great Plains who migrated to the area and adapted to the desert environment by borrowing techniques from the Anasazi.

The Fremont Culture developed differently from their Anasazi neighbors. They had communities of up to several hundred people, but they did not build the walled cities typical of the Anasazi. Instead, they built clusters of pithouses and utilized caves, which were improved with crude masonry walls.

Like the Anasazi, the Fremont cultivated corn, beans, and squash and built irrigation systems that stretched for miles. They made feather and hide blankets, finely tailored leather clothes, leather moccasins, and jewelry. Simple unpainted pots and finely woven baskets were used. Many small clay figurines have been found. Perhaps the best-known Fremont accomplishment was their rock art—extensive, varied, and often surrealistic in execution.

The earliest Fremont sites in the Escalante area are in Calf Creek Canyon. Pictograph panels found there date to the late Basketmaker II Period (approximately A.D. 500). The largest Fremont settlement was centered in Escalante Valley between the river and the Kaiparowits Plateau. A major site located just north of the town of Escalante consisted of a substantial multiroom dwelling that apparently was used year-round. Smaller sites were scattered throughout the valley.

Another Fremont stronghold was in Harris Wash, which was occupied from late Pueblo I to Pueblo III periods (A.D. 900 to 1200), with the highest use during the latter part of that period. During excavations in the late 1950s and early 1960s, archaeologists found forty-eight major sites in Harris Wash. Only two were well-defined habitations. The rest consisted of campsites under overhangs, lithic scatters, and rock art panels. A large number of storage cists or granaries suggests that Harris Wash was heavily populated. Analysis of pottery found in the canyon indicates that there was light use—perhaps during hunting or trading trips through the canyon—by Anasazi Indians.

It is known that the Fremont rarely went into Escalante Canyon proper except in the area near the present town of Escalante, but they did regularly traverse the base of the Kaiparowits Plateau to the Colorado River and frequented many of the side canyons.

The Fremont abandoned the Escalante area by A.D. 1250. Their collapse has been attributed to a long period of drought. The Fremont, though, were a tough people who had shown themselves capable of adapting to almost any condition. A more likely scenario is that Numic-speaking groups from the southwestern part of the Great Basin either forced the Fremont out or absorbed them into their own cultures. These Numic-speaking Indians—the Ute, Piute, and Shoshoni—are discussed later in this chapter.

Anasazi Indians were descendants of a Basketmaker culture that developed along the banks of the Colorado River and populated the Four Corners Region. The Anasazi were quick to assimilate innovations that originated in Mexico and Arizona. They developed a complex agricultural society: planting corn, beans, and squash, building irrigation systems, and domesticating turkeys and dogs. The arts flourished.

The hallmark of the Anasazi was their architecture. Extensive multistoried complexes of rooms built from shaped sandstone slabs held together with clay mortar and often plastered with mud are common, especially in areas east of the Colorado River. In the Escalante drainage the dwellings are smaller and less extensive, but many still exhibit the same fine craftsmanship.

The first Anasazi arrived in the Escalante area during the late Basketmaker II Period (approximately A.D. 500). Crossing the Colorado River from their homeland in the San Juan River area to the southeast and from northeast Arizona, the initial forays of these "Kayenta" Anasazis did not result in permanent habitations. The first area scouted was the Waterpocket Fold between the gap at Deer Point and the Escalante River. Archaeologists have found the oldest Anasazi sites there.

It was not until the late Pueblo I Period (A.D. 900) that substantial numbers of Kayenta Anasazi entered the Escalante region. Perhaps pressured by overpopulation, internal strife, or drought conditions, they left their traditional homelands to the east, crossed the Colorado River, and started exploring and exploiting the new environment. Over a period of many years they traveled up the main canyon of the Escalante and entered its tributary canyons on both sides of the river.

By the early Pueblo II Period (A.D. 1075) the Kayenta Anasazi had worked their way north to Boulder Valley, where they built the largest Kayenta village on the west side of the Colorado River. The village is now called the Coombs site and is located in the town of Boulder at Anasazi State Park.

Blessed with permanent water, an abundance of lumber for firewood and construction, arable land, and easy access to hunting on both the benches and in the canyons, Coombs village developed into a settlement that included more than eighty structures ranging from jacals and pithouses to numerous storage cists. The maximum population is thought to have been over 200 people. Visits by Fremont Indians, Anasazi from the Virgin River area to the southwest, and Anasazi from Mesa Verde and Chaco Canyon to the southeast have been documented.

Coombs village was abandoned after a fire devastated it about A.D. 1275. It is unclear whether the fire was the result of an accident, deliberate destruction by the Kayenta Anasazi before they vacated the village, or if it was started by hostile invaders. It is surmised that the Kayenta returned to their homelands near the San Juan River after vacating Coombs village. There is no evidence that any Kayenta Anasazi stayed in the Escalante area after abandonment of the village.

The highest Indian population in the Escalante area centered on the Kaiparowits Plateau. It was well suited for an agrarian people who depended on permanent water sources, tillable land, and a large quantity of wildlife. Peoples from two branches of the Kayenta Anasazi settled on the plateau: those coming from the San Juan River area worked their way up the tributary canyons of the Escalante to the Kaiparowits; and Virgin River Kayenta Indians, from what is now the Zion National Park area, came to the Kaiparowits from the southwest.

It is known that small groups from the Kaiparowits took periodic trips into the Escalante canyons, perhaps during the winter to escape the cold or during the spring and summer growing seasons. Routes were established between the Kaiparowits Plateau and most of the Escalante side canyons as well as into Llewellyn and Cottonwood gulches to the south.

By A.D. 1200 Anasazi flight from the Escalante region was un-

derway. Drought, internal conflict, lack of arable land, stream en-
trenchment, flash floods, a lack of wood, and outside aggressors
have all been cited as the reason for abandonment. It is known that
outlying groups started leaving first, working their way back to their
ancestral lands on the east side of the Colorado River. The last
Kayenta Anasazi to abandon the area were from Coombs village.

The use and exploitation of Escalante lands by both Kayenta
and Fremont Indians was extensive. There is virtually no side
canyon, slot, draw, bench, or high point that does not show evidence of use. Sometimes it is a lithic scatter where the Indians sat
fashioning stone implements while scouting the benches for game.
In other places one can find rows of Moqui steps leading to large
potholes in the deepest defiles. (Moqui steps are hand- and toeholds
Indians pecked into steep rock walls.) Pictograph and petroglyph
panels are almost ubiquitous along the river, in the side canyons, and
near the summits of the highest points in the area.

Contact between the Anasazi and Fremont was extensive and
peaceful. Although they ranged the same region, they assumed
different ecological niches: the Anasazi were primarily farmers who
preferred the Kaiparowits Plateau and the canyons of the Escalante,
while the Fremont, although also farmers, were primarily hunters
who most often remained on the upland areas near Escalante Valley
and below the Kaiparowits Plateau.

The Indian presence in the Escalante area does not end with the
Fremont and Anasazi. By A.D. 1300 Numic-speaking Indians from
the southwestern Great Basin had entered the general area. These
Ute, Piute, and Shoshoni Indians were not farmers; they were
hunters and gatherers who roamed far and wide without establishing permanent settlements. Archaeologists have identified some of
their temporary camps in the canyons near Boulder Valley, on the
north edge of the Aquarius Plateau, and along the northeast side of
the Kaiparowits Plateau.

It was not until Mormon settlers arrived in Escalante Valley in
the last half of the nineteenth century that first-hand knowledge of
the local Indians became written down. Almon Thompson of the
Powell survey of 1872 wrote of encountering a small tribe of Indians in Escalante Valley. Early pioneers told stories of meeting Piute
Indians hunting on the Aquarius Plateau and in Boulder Valley. A
small group that local Mormons called Escalante Indians lived in the
valley, raising goats, farming, trapping, and weaving. In 1918 the
few Escalante Indians left were moved to a settlement at Greenwich
on the northwest side of the Aquarius Plateau.

Before the Mormon settlers arrived in the Escalante area,
Athabascan-speaking Navajo Indians living on the east side of the
Colorado River had developed trails into the canyons of the Es-

calante and to the Kaiparowits Plateau where they herded their live-stock and hunted deer and bighorn sheep. Except for occasional problems with livestock theft, the settlers and Indians apparently got along fairly well.

It is certain that many of the trails used by the settlers had first been established by Indians. These included routes to the top of the Kaiparowits Plateau, the general route of the Boulder Mail Trail, and dozens of others.

Man in the Escalante—The Historic Period

What men had passed through this wilderness of rivers and canyons and left these names on the land?...Was there a history here to match the lavish beauty of the canyon?

C. Gregory Crampton, 1986

The present townsite of Escalante was discovered in August 1866 by a Mormon cavalry unit led by Captain James Andrus. He had been assigned the task of locating Indian trails between Utah's Dixie (extreme southwestern Utah) and the Colorado River to the east and hunting for a group of Indians who had been harassing and stealing from Mormon settlers as part of what was called the Black Hawk War. Andrus called the area Potato or Spuds Valley because of the many wild potatoes he found there.

The next white man to visit Potato Valley was Jacob Hamblin, the famous Mormon explorer and missionary to the Indians. He passed through the area in 1871 while trying to carry supplies to the mouth of the Dirty Devil River for John Wesley Powell's second Colorado River expedition. Thinking he was on the Dirty Devil River, Hamblin led his group down the Escalante River for about fifty miles. The trip was described as a terrible one and the group was finally stopped by quicksand and boulders. Hamblin looked in vain for a way out of the canyon before being forced to retrace his steps and return to his starting point in Paria.

After Hamblin's failure to reach the Dirty Devil River, Frederick Dellenbaugh and Almon Thompson, members of the second Powell expedition, were assigned the task of finding the Dirty Devil and getting supplies to Powell. They worked their way over what are now called the Escalante Mountains and dropped into Potato Valley.

Like Hamblin, Dellenbaugh and Thompson thought the stream running through the valley was the Dirty Devil River. They followed it downcanyon to the mouth of what they called Rocky Gulch (Harris Wash) and camped. Frederick Dellenbaugh wrote in his diary: "Prof. [Almon Thompson] and Dodds then climbed to where they could get a wider view.... Prof. perceived at once that we were not on the river we thought we were on, for by this explanation he saw that the stream we were trying to descend flowed into the Colorado far to the south-west of the Unknown [Henry] Mountain, whereas he knew positively that the Dirty Devil came in on the north-east. Then the question was, 'What river is this?' for we had not noted a tributary of any size between the Dirty Devil and the San Juan. It was a new river whose identity had not been fathomed." The

Wendy Chase and Diz on the Old Boulder Road.

Dellenbaugh-Thompson party then left Potato Valley by skirting
along the Aquarius Plateau. They eventually did find the Dirty Devil
River and joined Powell.

In 1875 Almon Thompson returned to Potato Valley while on a
mapping expedition. He ran into a group of Mormons from Panguitch who were interested in settling the valley. One of that group,
James Schow, described the meeting. His group was working on an
irrigation ditch when they noticed a billow of dust down on the Escalante Desert. Afraid that the dust signaled Indians and possible
trouble, they watched warily. The dust cloud approached Potato Valley, then disappeared over a hill. Waiting for nightfall, the Mormons
sneaked up the hill to where they could see that it was a company of
white men. They joined the group.

Thompson, having already designated the whole basin they
were in as the Escalante River Basin several years earlier, advised the
Mormons to name the new town Escalante. Franciscan friars Sil-
vestre Vélez de Escalante and Francisco Atanasio Domínguez were
the first white men known to have traversed the canyons of southern
Utah. They passed south of the Escalante River in 1776 while
searching for a route from Santa Fe to Los Angeles.

The first permanent white residents of Escalante arrived in July
1875. They quickly laid out the townsite and assigned farm and pasture lands. Their first houses consisted of cellars dug into the ground
topped with poles and branches covered with dirt. By the spring of
1876 the first log cabins had been erected and rough roads had been
built to the nearby canyons.

The town expanded quickly as others heard about the fine land in Escalante. Initially the primary industry was dairy farming. Over the years this was supplanted by sheep and cattle ranching. In 1880 the town had a population of 623; by 1923 it had risen to 1,010. Since then the town has decreased in population and at present has about 900 residents.

Equipment

As for backpacking, we all know the way it intensifies earthly gravity. Backpacking is awkward, ugly, monotonous, and lacks thrilling bodily sensations....Devoid of glamour, it is pure access.

Bruce Berger, 1990

It is not within the scope of this guide to provide comprehensive details on backcountry equipment. Books like Colin Fletcher's *The Complete Walker* cover backpacking thoroughly and at length. But, after many years of canyon hiking and guiding, I have found that desert camping presents some different problems than mountain hiking. The suggestions below are all tried and true techniques and will help you outfit yourself properly.

Backpacks: The standard external frame backpack works well on the nontechnical routes, but for those venturing off trail, a good internal frame pack is essential. Such a pack will not throw you off balance on the climbing sections and does not have the metal bracing that always seems to catch when you are butt-scooting down sandstone slabs. Most of the high-quality internal frame packs also come with a built-in fanny pack which will do you well for those quick trips up a side canyon.

Tents: Either freestanding or tie-down type tents work well in the desert. High winds are common in the Escalante. Make sure your tent can withstand winds in excess of eighty miles an hour. Except for the occasional campsite on the canyon floor, most of your camping will be on slickrock or desert cobble. Tent pegs will not work in these situations. Tie six-foot lengths of parachute cord to all of the tent hold-down loops—even on freestanding tents. The cords can be tied to rocks that, if moved, should be returned to their previous positions before breaking camp.

Mountaineers often wax or silicone the tent's zippers to keep them from freezing. In the desert environment, these products catch the sand, which can lead to non-functioning or prematurely worn-out zippers.

Stoves: Sand in the desert kills stoves. Experienced desert rats prefer either Svea or Optimus stoves. Though a tad heavy and clunky, they are simple, simmer well, and will not get clogged by blowing sand. Whatever type of stove you do carry, know how to fix it and bring a repair kit.

Wind will render even the best stove useless. Sandstone slab windbreaks tend not to work very well. Instead, bring a thick foil windscreen like the ones from Mountain Safety Research. It will solve the problem.

Any gas, whether it is Coleman fuel or gasoline, has a short shelf life. That quart of fuel you've been storing in the garage for a couple of years will clog your stove. Use fresh fuel for every trip.

Footwear: Heavy all-leather mountaineering-type boots are preferable for long trips with heavy loads unless you will be doing a lot of wading. Long-distance travel in the water will stretch most leather boots into oblivion. Many prefer composite boots made from both leather and synthetics—usually nylon and Gore-Tex. They are lighter and less expensive than the all-leather boots and seem to breathe better. Boots with nylon midsoles keep their shape better when wet than those made with leather.

Composite boots do have one drawback in sandstone country. The external stitching wears out quickly. This problem can be alleviated by coating all of the seams with Barge Cement, which will act as a sacrificial layer. It can be reapplied from time to time.

Camp shoes are essential. Tennis shoes are recommended. Often people bring sandals instead of tennis shoes for wading and camp wear. Sandals do not protect you as well as tennis shoes from cactus spines and jagged rocks. If your boots or feet fall apart, you cannot hike out in sandals. Tennis shoes give you an option. The smooth soles of tennis shoes also prove less damaging to the environment than lug-soled boots around camp, which lessens the impact.

Since it is a cardinal sin to wade barefoot, your tennis shoes can be used when you only have to cross a river a time or two; if you will be spending a lot of time wading, wear your boots. Changing from hot, heavy, or perhaps wet boots into tennis shoes at the end of the day gives your feet a chance to breathe and will keep you from getting prune foot.

The use of ankle gaiters will keep your socks clean by keeping the dirt and sand out. They work especially well when wading in rivers.

Rain gear: Rain suits are preferable in the backcountry. Ponchos flap around your legs and make it difficult and unsafe to negotiate steep rock faces or walk along narrow ledges.

Water containers: On most hikes you should have the capacity to carry at least six quarts of water. The smoke-colored Nalgene water bottles do not pick up and hold the taste of drink mixes or iodine like standard plastic bottles.

Carrying large quantities of water can be a trial. A Clorox-type bottle wrapped with a layer of duct tape is an inexpensive solution. The MSR Dromedary bags, though costly, are ideal. Lightweight water sacks are not dependable.

Insects: Gnats, mosquitos, and no-see-ums can be controlled with almost any commercial Deet-based insect repellent. Mosquito netting for the head can be a godsend, especially at night.

Deer flies are an entirely different matter; they are difficult to manage. These voracious insects can turn a summer sojourn into a nightmare. They are not only loud but also can bite through nearly anything. I remember one deer-fly-tainted trip on the Escalante River one summer with Kevin Shields. I still have the distinct picture of Kevin literally running upcanyon ahead of me, his back, legs, head, and pack completely covered with the little monsters.

Mosquito netting for the head, a loose long-sleeved shirt that can be cinched at the wrists, and Levi-type or baggy pants seem to work well. Some may prefer nylon wind pants, but they are hot during the summer when the deer flies are out. Deer flies like to congregate near water and seem to prefer direct sunlight, so it is usually possible to avoid them by hiding in the shade or traveling away from watercourses.

The Art of Travel

Our thighs were of marble, our kneecaps were missing, our calves were like rain-shrunk clothesline: we had spent two days working our way down the wrong canyon.

Bruce Berger, 1990

For those not familiar with desert travel, some advice is in order. The suggestions below do not include everything you need to know about hiking in the desert. They should be added to skills already attained in the woods or mountains.

Leave a complete and detailed itinerary with someone reliable. If you do not know anyone trustworthy, staple or tape your itinerary to your permit before you drop it into the trail register box. Better yet, get your hiking permit at the Interagency Office in Escalante. This gives personnel there a chance to discuss your proposed route. If you are reported missing, the first thing rangers check are the office permits. If the information is not there, they have to drive from one trailhead to the next, looking for your car or permit, a time-consuming proposition.

Those waiting for hikers to return home should realize that it is not uncommon for a hike to take longer than expected. Also, access roads that were initially dry and passable can be impossible to negotiate after heavy rains, leaving hikers stranded at a trailhead for a day or two.

Always carry the appropriate 7.5 series USGS topographic maps. Keep track of where you are on the map at all times. It is surprising how easy it is to get mixed up in a maze of canyons, washes, draws, and slots.

Watch your backtrail (Louis L'Amour rule 1; Star Trek rule 91). As you hike along keep an eye on where you have been by noting prominent landforms such as towers and pinnacles. This will help if you have to backtrack your route.

On steep slabs, stay on your feet and keep your weight over them. Your shoe soles have more friction than your britches!

When going down especially steep rock, pick a route that contains popstops. These are depressions, small ledges, trees, or bushes that will stop you if you should slip and start sliding.

Use a belay or a handline in any situation where a fall resulting in injury is possible. If an accident should happen, it may take several days for members of your group to make their way back to a trailhead and notify the sheriff in Escalante (call 911 or notify the Interagency Office). It may then take a couple of additional days for a rescue party or helicopter to reach you. Backcountry Escalante is not the place to test your mettle. The time spent setting up belays or handlines is trivial compared to the time and effort it takes to mount an evacuation.

Be aware of ball-bearing rock. This rock is found in Navajo Sandstone and consists of round, loose, marble-sized concretions that cover some sections of rock. Locally these are called Moqui marbles. They are as slippery as banana peels underfoot.

Watch out for those friable little sandstone ledges that can easily break underfoot.

If you are not comfortable climbing a steep pitch with your pack on, pull it up or lower it down on a rope.

When searching for routes up or down the cliffs, remember the canyoneering maxim that states "if it is green, it will go." This simply means that if you see an unbroken stretch of shrubbery going up a cliff, in all likelihood, you'll be able to make your way along the greenery. Be forewarned, however, that this is not 100 percent reliable.

Another axiom in canyoneering is that it is often nearly impossible to find a route down a cliff from its top. This is especially true with the higher walls. Make sure you can see the entire route down a cliff face before attempting it, even if it means skirting along the escarpment for some distance to get a good view. Binoculars work well here. There is nothing worse than getting most of the way down a wall, then finding that progress has been thwarted by a drop you could not quite see from above.

Most accidents do not occur on the steep routes. People are very careful and conservative when the challenge is the greatest. It is usually when the going is easy and you are not paying attention that accidents occur. A large percentage of accidents take place toward the end of the day when hikers are tired. Many accidents occur around camp or while taking the nighttime constitutional.

Wading can be a trial. Carry a walking stick—suitable poles can be found everywhere along the river—and probe for deep pools. Every group needs its sacrificial lamb while wading. The first person should not carry a camera. Wrapping gear in large plastic trash bags is recommended for those hiking along the river.

Be aware of punji sticks along the Escalante River. These are the short sharp ends of willow and tamarisk left by beavers. They are omnipresent and harmful if you fall on one.

Always—ALWAYS—carry enough water to get back to a known source. In this guide, a known source is defined as a water source that you were just at. Another known source is a perennial stream such as the Escalante River, Deer Creek, lower Death Hollow, or lower Coyote Gulch.

During periods of hot weather get an early start, rest during the midday heat, and resume travel during the cool evening hours.

Carry a well-equipped first-aid kit and know how to use its contents. It is inexcusable not to have taken at least an Advanced First-Aid and CPR course.

A scratched eye from a bush snapping back is one of the most common injuries seen along the river. Wear dark glasses or safety glasses.

Cellular phones used to summon emergency help can and have saved the lives of the injured in the backcountry. They usually do not work while in the canyons but do work from benches and other high points.

Those taking groups into the backcountry shoulder special responsibility. It is essential for leaders to scout the route before committing inexperienced and usually poorly equipped hikers to it. Water sources, sections of difficult terrain, times and distances, and campsites should be noted on the reconnaissance. There is nothing worse for a leader than to get to the middle of a hike and then find that skills are lacking. It is unconscionable—certainly negligent—for group leaders to be unfamiliar with the route.

Winds occasionally reach eighty miles an hour, especially in the lower Escalante canyon areas where three great rivers—the Escalante, San Juan, and Colorado—come together. When rain, sleet, or snow is added to the wind, miserable camping is assured. Make sure you and your equipment are up to the task.

Perhaps the most important thing you should remember while in the backcountry is that you are in it for the fun. If things do not go as planned, do not fret; the canyons will be waiting for you next time around. When in doubt, bow out. Keep this adage in mind when you think you are getting in over your head—whether you are contemplating a steep rock pitch or are having doubts about water availability.

None of the routes described in this book is worth injury, or worse. Think carefully about your actions and how they will affect others in your group. The litany in the canyons is that you should first be safe; second, protect the environment; and third, have fun.

Technical Canyoneering

Canyoneering, as it is called, is a sport in its infancy, just starting to be avidly practiced in the labyrinthine Southwest....But as with any young sport, the leading practitioners are still more or less improvising as they go.
David Roberts, 1996

There are many opportunities for technical canyoneering in the Escalante. Although this guide book does not detail routes through difficult technical canyons, it is imperative that safety issues and environmental concerns be addressed. This essay is not meant to be a primer on technical canyoneering; rather, it is meant to give canyoneers some ideas to think about.

The term "canyoneering" is ambiguous. If one hikes in the canyons, does that mean he or she is a canyoneer? or do you have to scale vertical walls and descend slots using ropes and technical climbing gear in order to properly use the appellation?

The first person to use the term "canyoneer" in print was Frederick Dellenbaugh of the Powell expedition down the Colorado River in 1872. The next time the term surfaced was among early river runners on the San Juan and Colorado rivers. A famed river runner from that period, Otis "Dock" Marsten, applied the term only to those who had "completed the traverse" of the Colorado River through the Grand Canyon. He considered those doing lesser rivers to be mere "river rats."

Others used "canyoneering" in a generic sense, applying the term to all who ran rivers. As river running became more sophisticated and a scale of difficulty developed for the sport, "canyoneering" disappeared from river lexicon and was increasingly applied to those who explored canyons on foot.

Today a canyoneer is defined as one who hikes in canyons. Technical canyoneering is the act of traveling through canyons using technical rock-climbing techniques such as rappelling, belaying, and ascending or descending rock walls using rock climbing equipment. Negotiating stretches of moving water by swimming or using flotation devices can also be added to the definition of technical canyoneering.

A slot canyoneer is a person who ascends or descends slot canyons, and a technical slot canyoneer is one who descends or ascends slot canyons using specialized canyoneering techniques and rock-climbing equipment.

Common usage defines a slot canyon as one whose walls are generally no farther apart than the distance of outstretched arms. Some argue with this definition and say that if you do not have to squeeze through it, it is not a slot canyon. The point is moot and not worth further discussion.

Perhaps the worst adventure a technical canyoneer can have is to drop into a canyon and be unable to continue down or climb back up. This does happen, and lives have been lost.

The most terrifying moment I had as a novice slot canyoneer was in the San Rafael Swell. I came to a deep pothole that appeared dry. It looked as though I would be able to climb back out of the pothole without much problem if the canyon below proved too difficult. I jumped down, only to find myself swimming; a fine dusting of sand covered the water, making the pothole look dry. Fortunately, I had a knife in my pocket and, after considerable effort, I was able to carve a couple of small handholds in the soft sandstone and extricate myself. I learned one of the basic lessons of technical canyoneering: you must always be prepared and able to reverse the route or escape the canyon.

Reversibility is the first option you should consider before heading down a canyon you have not been through before. Make sure you can climb up every drop you descend, or leave a rope at each drop. If the canyon proves too difficult, you can use mechanical ascenders or prussik knots to climb up the ropes.

If there are multiple drops, you may have to leave a lot of rope behind. I have been through canyons where we left a dozen or more ropes. After making it through the canyon, you can go through again and retrieve your ropes or rappel into the canyon, pull the ropes, and jumar out. Either method is time consuming, but that is the price one must pay for being a safe technical canyoneer.

Escapability means that there are breaks in the canyon walls that you can use to ascend to the rim. These include steep gullies, walls, and cracks that are easy to climb using standard rock-climbing techniques and equipment. Before descending a new canyon my partners and I spend considerable time walking the rim looking for such breaks. Often we will rappel into a canyon to see what it looks like. If the canyon looks exceptionally difficult, we hang ropes from the rim at strategic places to use for escape.

The primary reason the technical canyoneer must be familiar with the concepts of escapability and reversability is to be prepared if the canyon turns out to be more difficult than expected. Also, canyoneers must be ready for unanticipated conditions. These can take several forms: the conditions in the canyon are different from what was expected (e.g., high water, unexpected rock fall, flash flood, anchors have disappeared), equipment proves inadequate, or an injury necessitates evacuation.

A group of novice canyoneers found themselves in a difficult situation while trying to descend a slot canyon near Zion National Park. After entering the canyon and descending a couple of small drops, they encountered brutal conditions that were not expected. Escape routes were available and reversing the route was an option. The leaders, though, were apparently unfamiliar with the concepts of reversibility and escapability. Feeling they had no choice, the group continued downcanyon. Two of the trip members died. The others waited in the cold dark canyon for five days for a rescue.

Many years ago, I was with a group that was descending a technical slot in the White Canyon area. We reached a pour-off we could not climb back up. One of the new members of the team rappelled the pour-off with instructions to hike downcanyon and see if there was an escape route. We did not want to leave a rope at the drop if it was not necessary. A half hour later he returned and called up from below that there was an exit a short distance downcanyon. We all rappelled the drop and pulled the rope. As we walked downcanyon I asked him to show me the escape route. He pointed at a moderate slab. I suggested we walk to the far side of the canyon. What he had not been able to see from the canyon floor was that the moderate slab was topped by a featureless vertical cliff.

The group was now in trouble. As we worked our way downcanyon we all sweated the possibility that we were trapped. Luck was with us, however; we were able to complete the descent and an important lesson had been learned.

Statistically, the single most dangerous procedure a rock climber undertakes is the non-belayed rappel. A life dangles from the rope's anchors and often in canyoneering the anchors are "manky." Novice canyoneers often dismiss rappelling. After all, it seems easy to slide down a rope. It is simple until something goes wrong. Experienced rock climbers and mountaineers have been injured or killed on "simple" rappels. Letting your guard down can prove catastrophic. It is imperative that technical slot canyoneers know how to properly set up rappels, rappel over knots, deal with clothing caught in a rappel device, and ascend ropes using prussik knots or mechanical ascenders.

We use a technique called "LAMAR," or "Last Man At Risk," on most downclimbs and rappels. All but the last climber are belayed. Once the first climbers are down, they pull together on the rope from below to check anchors. The last man then rappels.

Substandard anchor placements are common in slots. It is essential that you back up and equalize anchors. On several occasions we have had "bombproof" chockstones "explode" after they were weighted.

Be exceptionally careful to rig your anchor so the ropes will pull easily. Use of rappel rings is critical here. I was descending a slot in Dirty Devil country, leaving ropes at each drop. Near the end of the day I was careless with my anchor on a long rappel, setting it too far back in the slot. Once down, I was unable to pull the ropes. The rappel had been down a narrow, twisting, smooth-walled chimney that my body could barely fit through. Reversing the route by using mechanical ascenders was nearly impossible. With almost no room to maneuver, it took me several hours of cursing and cramping to ascend the crack.

Entry into deep water from a rappel can be tricky and dangerous. The problem is in unclipping from the ropes while floating in turbulent water or being bombarded by falling water. The standard canyoneering technique is to lock your carabiners as usual at the start of the rappel. When you are close to the pool at the bottom of the rappel, stop, unscrew the threaded portion of the carabiners, then enter the water. This ensures that you will not be struggling in the water trying to unscrew a jammed or overtightened lock sleeve. Do make sure your rappel device is properly leashed so you will not lose it in a deep pool.

Jumping into deep pools sometimes seems the easiest way to descend a drop. I've been through slots with "experienced" canyoneers who blithely jumped into water of indeterminate depth and with possible obstructions lurking just under the surface. The first person down should always descend on a rope to check water depth and to see if there are hidden logs or other obstacles.

Groups have gotten into trouble in technical slots due to the inexperience of their leader, and deaths have resulted. There is a vast difference between going down a technical canyon with a peer—a person who has the same skills as oneself—and leading a group of novices. Trip leaders must recognize this. It is the leader who is responsible for watching everyone else in the group, for making sure things go smoothly, and for coordinating pack lowerings and rappels. The leader must be capable of recognizing and dealing with any and all hazardous situations that might arise. At all times he or she must be thinking about the safety of the group.

Equipment needs vary depending on the type of slot. Since most slots entail going downcanyon, ropes are most commonly used for rappels. Nine-millimeter climbing or static ropes work well. Dry ropes are preferred. Be careful when using ropes: they are easily abraded, cut, and ruined in the slots. Always carry an extra rope. It should be used for belays and can replace a trashed rope. Also, the extra rope can be cut up and used in place of sling material if you are desperate. Sometimes sling instead of rope can be left at short drops if the wall is less than vertical and you know you can "batman" up it. Brown or black sling is less visually intrusive than brightly colored sling.

Canyoneers with a death wish use old sling found at anchors. One canyoneering "expert" suggested that it is okay to use old sling and claimed that one way to check it is to see if there are burn marks on the sling from previous parties pulling their ropes. This is dangerous nonsense. Always use new sling and carry a lot more than you think you will need.

Wet canyons can be a trial. In some, wet suits may be necessary. Dry suits are not appropriate in canyoneering. If they rip, they can fill with water and will no longer provide protection from the cold. Polypropylene or comparable clothing is the only choice in slot canyons. It insulates when wet, which cotton does not.

When carrying gear through a wet slot, it is best to pack equipment in river-type dry bags and put them inside your pack. This will keep the dry bag from abrading and will keep everything dry.

Sit harnesses sold for rock climbing work fine in slots, though they do wear out quickly. In narrow slots where there are long stretches of chimneying, it is often difficult to carry a daypack on your back. Suspending it from your sit harness with a short length of webbing eases the problem.

The impact of canyoneers in slot canyons is at present minor. However, with the growing number of participants, an environmental ethic is needed. Perhaps of biggest concern is the overuse of bolts for rappel anchors in slot canyons. Many have criticized my anti-bolt stand, saying that bolts are an essential tool and that slots cannot be safely descended without them. The first technical slot I did was in 1968. Over the last twenty-eight years I have had the privilege of going through hundreds of technical slots in Utah, Arizona, California, Nevada, and Baja California. I have never used bolts.

I have seen bolts installed next to huge chockstones, trees, or other adequate natural features, places where bolts certainly were not essential. In many instances rappel bollards can be constructed out of smaller boulders piled high to fashion an acceptable anchor or rocks can be piled on top of a marginal boulder to reinforce it. Sometimes placing boulders in a chockstone position in a slot will do the trick. In other instances one may have to look far upcanyon to find a suitable anchor.

One correspondent told me that bolts were cleaner than leaving long pieces of sling in a canyon. Sling, though, can be removed by the next party; the bolts will leave a permanent scar. Of more importance, bolts do not last long when placed in soft sandstone, and they often fail in a wet environment. In Kolob Creek Canyon in Zion National Park unneeded bolts were installed below the high-water level, certainly making them of questionable value to those who came later.

Canyoneers usually do not know who installed a bolt, if they were qualified to do so, or how long ago the bolt was set. Often you end up with the problem we now see in Neon Canyon. At one rappel six bolts have sprouted. None are usable. A large natural arch next to the bolts works great as an anchor.

The bolt issue may be resolved in the future if lands in southern Utah do become wilderness. A part of the Wilderness Act of 1964 describes wilderness as areas "without permanent improvements." How this statement is interpreted is up to the individual agency involved, whether it be the U.S. Forest Service, National Park Service, U.S. Fish and Wildlife Service, or the Bureau of Land Management. Depending on each agency's recommendation, placing bolts in many canyon areas may become illegal.

If bolts are outlawed, it will certainly not spell the end of canyoneering; but it will force canyoneers to improve their skills and develop new techniques and equipment. I contend that most of the time bolts are used because the canyoneer is not skilled enough or is too lazy to descend the canyon "clean." Now is the time to work on canyoneering skills that do not include permanently defacing the rock.

You should never leave evidence of an anchor, usually sling material, where a hiker or tourist can see it. In slot canyons this often means at the first and last drops. The slings in the middle of the canyon will only be seen by slot canyoneers and therefore are not generally considered visually intrusive. There is no good reason a slot canyoneer cannot retrieve the sling at the first drop.

Sling left at the last drop should not be visible to the casual hiker enjoying the view from the canyon floor. Photographers find them to be a disaster. Someone placed unneeded bolts on the outside wall of the last drop in the East Fork of Choprock Canyon. The bolts, and the sling dangling from them, distract from the natural beauty of the hanging gardens on the wall below.

Technical slot canyoneering is in its golden age. The boundaries of difficulty are being pushed as different types of slots are discovered and new techniques are developed. We must take the time now to think about how we descend technical slots and canyons. Without care, we may be limiting the future of technical slot canyoneering. The number of quality slot canyons seems limitless now, but with the number of participants in the sport increasing, it will only take a generation or two before the slots have all been done. Once those "sheer terror" canyons become lined with bolts, they will become of interest to the novice and unqualified. Before you know it, that difficult slot you enjoyed will become a trade route for youth groups.

Too many technical canyoneers want to start with the hardest slot they can find and are willing to make the descent at any cost. Others seem to be into the sport for the wrong reasons. I talked to one young man after his descent of Quandary Canyon, a popular moderate-difficulty slot in the San Rafael Swell. He told me, condescendingly, that it was too easy. He did not mention how intensely beautiful the canyon was. I doubt he noticed or cared.

It is best to pay your dues by starting with easier slots and working up to the harder ones. It is the experience gained over many years that allows the technical canyoneer to analyze different situations and to react to them appropriately. Technical canyoneering can be challenging, rewarding, and fun when done safely and in an environmentally sound fashion. It is up to each of us to set the standards now so we can continue to enjoy the sport in the future.

Access

So now we come to Owl's house, as some of us have so many times before, searching for answers to questions of one sort or another. Will we find the answers here?

The Tao of Pooh

The towns of Escalante and Boulder provide access to the canyons of the Escalante. Escalante is the larger of the two towns and offers basic services including several gas stations and auto repair shops, cafes, two small markets, and lodging that runs from primitive to elegant.

Perhaps the most important stop on your way through Escalante is Escalante Outfitters, the local hiking and fishing supply store. Located in a large log building on the north side of Highway 12 in the middle of town, the Outfitters has become an institution. Barry and Celeste Bernards can provide you with everything you forgot to bring — or find that you need — including stove-repair kits, Coleman fuel and bottled gas for backpack stoves, clothing, tarps, T-shirts, hats, caps, visors, and a thousand other items. Their selection of USGS topographic maps for canyon country is the best I have seen in Utah.

The Escalante Outfitters and Bunkhouse is a favorite with hikers and bicycle riders. Small cabins fronted by an expanse of lawn, barbecue pits, a volleyball court, and a duck pond are the perfect place to meet or clean up and recover from your adventures. Large groups are welcome and reservations are accepted. The "Esca-latté" Coffee Shop, located at the Outfitters, features cappucino, homemade breakfast rolls and muffins, pizza, a salad bar, and beer on tap.

The Escalante Interagency Visitors Information Center combines the offices of Dixie National Forest, the Bureau of Land Management, and the National Park Service. The personnel there can provide information on road conditions, hiking, and camping, and they can issue backcountry permits. They also sell maps and books. The Center is located along Highway 12 on the west side of town.

The town of Boulder has limited services. There are two gas stations, a couple of small markets, several cafes, and two motels. Boulder is the home of Anasazi State Park, which contains the Coombs site, a large Anasazi town that dates back more than 700 years. It is open year around and is worth visiting.

Escalante Outfitters and Bunkhouse
310 West Main Street
Escalante, Utah 84726
801-826-4266
FAX: 801-826-4388
http://www.aros.net/-slickroc/escout
Hours: During the hiking season: Monday–Saturday, 7 a.m. to 8 p.m.; closed Sundays.
Winter: Monday–Saturday, 8 a.m. to 6 p.m.; closed Sundays.
Hours subject to change.

The Escalante Interagency Office—Visitor Information Center
P.O. Box 246
Escalante, Utah 84726
801-826-5499
Hours: From April to October the Interagency Office is open from 7:30 a.m. to 6 p.m., seven days a week. The rest of the year it is open Monday–Friday, 8 a.m. to 5 p.m. Hours subject to change.

National Park Service (Glen Canyon National Recreation Area)
P.O. Box 511
Escalante, Utah 84726
801-826-4315

Bureau of Land Management (Grand Staircase-Escalante National Monument)
P.O. Box 225
Escalante, Utah 84726
801-826-4291

Dixie National Forest (Box-Death Hollow Wilderness Area)
P.O. Box 246
Escalante, Utah 84726
801-826-5400

In case of emergency, call 911. This connects you with the Garfield County Sheriff in Panguitch. Their dispatcher will alert emergency medical technicians, Lifeflight, or search-and-rescue personnel in Escalante.

How to Use this Guide

The only right way to get to know this country (any country), the only way, is with your body. On foot. Better yet, on hands and knees. Best of all—after scrambling to a high place—on your rump. Pick out a good spot and just sit there, not moving, for about a year. (This is my own highest ambition.) Keep your eyeballs peeled and just sit there, through the hours, through the days, through the nights, through the seasons—the freeze of winter, the stunning glare and heat of summer, the grace and glory of the spring and fall—and watch what happens.

Edward Abbey, 1971

To get the most out of the guide and to help you understand the terminology, read this section carefully. The guide is divided into four main chapters, each representing an area that is accessed by one of the four main roads that cuts through the region. These are the Hells Backbone road, Highway 12, the Hole-in-the-Rock road, and the Burr Trail. Each chapter is prefaced with a general overview of the area, its main features, and a short history. This is followed by a road section that describes the roads used to access the individual hikes. The road section is followed by a description of the hikes.

Caveat: A guide book cannot keep up with all the changes that are happening in the Escalante. Some roads are being upgraded; others may be closed. Trailhead locations do change and trail registers are occasionally added. Changes in the newly designated Grand Staircase-Escalante National Monument are likely. Campfire, dog, group size, and other rules may also be revised. Please obey all signs. If you have questions, stop at the Interagency Office in Escalante.

Road Sections

The road sections direct you to the trailhead for each hike. The introductory paragraph tells you what type of vehicle can make it to the trailhead. Vehicle type is broken down into four categories:

Any vehicle is just that: Winnebagos, Cadillacs, cars towing trailers, etc.

Light-duty vehicles include most small cars: Toyota Corolla, Ford Taurus, Subaru, Nissan, VW Rabbit, etc.

High-clearance vehicles include Volkswagen bugs and buses, short-wheelbase vans, two-wheel-drive pickups, and mini-pickups.

Four-wheel-drive (4WD) roads are for true 4WDs, not for the smaller 4WD cars that do not have the necessary ground clearance.

Rain or snow can make any of the access roads impassable, even to 4WDs. On some roads short sections of deep sand will be encountered. Roads can change overnight. It is best to be wary. If in doubt, walk suspect sections of road first. Try not to drive any of the roads at night. A black cow on a black road on a black night cannot be seen. Roads that have washed out, sandy sections, and the occasional deer will all conspire against you. Play it safe.

The introductory paragraph informs you whether there is camping at or near the trailhead. This does not mean there is a campground; it simply means that there are short side roads, washes, or pullouts that can be used for camping. Do not make your own tracks to a campsite; there are plenty already. There may be restrictions in some areas; obey all signs. Car campers should not use campfires; stoves are preferred.

Next is the mileage list. It starts with a description of where the mileage starts. All mileage is cumulative. To some, the mileage lists may seem too detailed, but the extra landmarks are meant to reassure. When important side roads are reached, the mileage list for that road is included. At the trailhead, the number of the hike is printed in **bold type**. When compass readings are required, be aware that a compass may not point accurately while in a car.

There is a difference between a road and a track. A road, although dirt or gravel, is maintained by occasional grading. Tracks are not maintained and tend to be rougher than roads.

Shorter hikes, those that do not warrant their own heading, are described in the road sections. They are all worthwhile.

Historical details are added to the road sections and will tell you about the people and events that helped shape the Escalante area.

The road sections may seem complicated at first, though they are infinitely less confusing than being lost in a maze of roads. Signs have a habit of disappearing. Keep track of your mileage and follow the road sections assiduously as you drive along.

Route Descriptions
It is important to read the route descriptions carefully from beginning to end before you begin your trip. This will help you decide if the route is suitable for your group. The description of each hike is prefaced by a concise section that will tell you at a glance the pertinent parameters for that hike. These include:

Season: The recommended seasons noted for each hike are only suggestions. Weather extremes in canyon country are the norm. Be prepared to vary your itinerary as weather dictates. Below are some general guidelines.

Spring
February: Winter is starting to wind down by midmonth. Expect temperatures to vary from twenty to seventy degrees Fahrenheit.

The last big snows usually arrive during this month and can leave you stranded at the trailhead. There are few other hikers about.

March: The first glimmer of spring is tempered with unsettled weather and the chance for snow and rain. Temperatures vary from below freezing to eighty degrees. Trailhead access can be a problem. Spring break ushers in an influx of college students. The canyons start to get busy.

April: Spring is here and flowers start to bloom. Rain and high winds are common. Temperatures vary from freezing to ninety degrees. This is the most popular month for backpacking in the Escalante.

May: Spring flowers are in full bloom. This is the month the winds never seem to die. Plan on temperatures from just above freezing to 100 degrees by the end of the month. Short rains, and snow at higher elevations, are possible. Gnats, mosquitos, and biting flies along watercourses can be a nuisance.

Summer

June, July, and August: Summer is in full force. Bugs, temperatures over 100 degrees, and little moisture make it imperative that you select a hike with care. This is the time to explore the well-watered canyons and to avoid the routes that have long stretches of slickrock or bench walking. The rainy season starts in mid-July and lasts through September. Expect short intense rain- and windstorms. Flash floods are common.

Fall

September: August rains have reinvigorated the desert and the fall bloom has started; but temperatures are still hot, ranging from fifty to 100 degrees. Although the weather is usually stable, short intense rains and flash floods are common.

October and November: Nighttime temperatures start to drop as the season progresses and the days become shorter. Plan on a gamut of extremes from twenty to ninety degrees. Leaves are changing and the canyons are awash in color. This is my favorite time in the desert. Water is usually plentiful and the crispness of the nights is invigorating.

Winter

December to mid-February: Expect snowstorms and nighttime temperatures below zero degrees. The short days and fourteen-hour nights can be a trial, but you will see few hikers. Water is rarely a problem, making this a favored time to explore benchlands and normally dry canyons.

Roads have to be a consideration in winter. When snow-covered, they can be dangerous. When the days warm up, the roads turn into a slick clay and even 4WDs will have problems.

Flash floods occur in all of the canyons detailed in the guide. This becomes apparent when you see logs jammed well above the floor of a canyon. Stay out of narrow canyons when it is raining. If it starts raining while you are in a narrow canyon, get out immediately. The slickrock above the canyons does not hold water well. Often it takes only a couple of minutes of rain to send a wall of water through a canyon. Canyons can flash flood even though it is not raining on you. An ominous rumble from up the canyon may signify a flood. Scramble to high ground.

Time: For the most part, the times listed are the times it will take the average, fit, and moderately experienced person to do the described hike. A hike that is described for beginners to take three to four hours will take that long for them. A hike that takes ten to twelve hours for advanced canyoneers might take twenty hours for a novice. If you plan to do lots of exploring, photographing, or relaxing, add extra time to your itinerary. Due to the demanding nature of some of the hikes, it is prudent to carry extra food in case the trip takes longer than planned.

The suggested number of days a hike will take is just a recommendation. For most backpackers five to seven hours of walking a day is plenty. The times shown in parentheses ( ) every few paragraphs will help you plan your days and still allow you to determine your own agenda. These times are broad estimates; do not use them to compute actual hiking time between points.

Elevation range: The lowest and the highest elevations on the route.

Maps: The maps listed are all USGS 7.5-minute series topographic maps. There are many references to the maps in the route descriptions. **Maps must be carried on all of the hikes.** Maps noted in the road sections and in the preface for each hike are listed in the order they are used. As you move through the text, map changes are indicated by the name of the new map printed in **bold type.**

All of the maps listed in this guide are available from Escalante Outfitters. (Its address and phone number is in the "Access" chapter.) You can order the maps from the Outfitters or call ahead and have them reserve a set for you which you can pick up on your way through town. Escalante Outfitters also has most of the USGS 7.5-minute series maps for southern Utah. The cost is the same as from the USGS and the Outfitters can have the maps to you in a week instead of the couple of months it takes to get them from the USGS. The Escalante Interagency Office also carries maps of the area.

Many of the maps in the guide are based on the 7.5-minute maps and have been reproduced in their original size. They show only short stretches of the route and are designed to help locate the harder-to-find canyon exits, entrances, and water sources. It is up to you to fill in the missing pieces, which usually consist of long stretches of straight-ahead hiking where the likelihood of getting lost is reduced. Some may wish to pencil in the whole route on their maps before the start of the trip.

Water: Water should always be on your mind when hiking in the desert. **Always carry enough water to get back to a known source.** During periods of hot weather start hiking at first light, take a midday break, and resume hiking in the cool hours of the evening. In hot weather, water requirements go up; two gallons over a twelve-hour period may be realistic. The prophylactic use of electrolyte-replacement drinks like ERG and Gatorade is recommended. Those coming from cooler climates can take up to ten days to acclimate to the heat and should take it easy for the first few days. Alcohol and caffeine are diuretics and promote dehydration. Water loading, the intake of several quarts of water before you start to hike in the morning, works well and can reduce the amount of water you need to carry on your back.

Water sources, either springs or potholes, are described in the text and on the maps as small, medium, or large. This does not refer to their physical size but to the likelihood of finding water in them **during the recommended hiking seasons.** These descriptions are subjective and should not be taken as gospel. Small means the water source may dry up within days of a rain. Medium potholes should hold water for a week or two after a rain, and a medium spring runs most of the time but will dry up after long periods without moisture. Large potholes will be full even a month after a rain. Large springs will dry up only after prolonged drought.

Springs and potholes are shown on the maps and are described using abbreviations. A large spring or pothole is marked as **lsg** or **lph**. A medium spring or pothole is marked as **msg** or **mph**. A small spring or pothole is marked as **ssg** or **sph**.

All water should be treated or filtered, without exception. Giardia is a hard-shelled protozoan that can cause no end of bowel distress if you should happen to "get the bug." The latest medical research has shown that there are several effective methods for eradicating the pest:

Heat your water. Giardia, bacteria, and viruses are killed at a temperature of about 150 degrees. You just need to bring the water to a boil; you do not have to keep boiling it.

Use iodine. The 2 percent tincture of iodine liquid available at the grocery store works well. Use five drops per quart if the water is clear; use ten drops per quart if the water is cloudy. If the water is over 68 degrees, let it sit for thirty minutes before drinking. The colder the water, the longer you'll have to let it sit. The basic rule when using iodine is to either use a little and let it work for a long period of time or use a lot and wait for a shorter period. If you let the water sit overnight, you will just have to add one or two drops of iodine per quart. If the taste of iodine-treated water is objectionable, treat the water as prescribed, then take the lid off the water container. The iodine taste will somewhat dissipate. Some people get a sore throat from using iodine.

Iodine tablets such as Potable-Aqua and crystals of iodine (Polar Pure) work well but are expensive. Always use fresh iodine tablets; they lose their effectiveness after prolonged exposure to air.

Chlorine and halazone. These compounds are effective against viruses and bacteria. They will not kill Giardia.

Filters. A good filter can make dirty, scummy, muddy water palatable. The only filter I recommend for desert travel is the Katadyn Pocket Filter. It is initially expensive, and it is heavy, but the filter cartridge will last the average hiker a lifetime. The Katadyn is the only filter on the market that is easy to clean in the field. Hint: Before trying to filter muddy water, first strain it through a disposable coffee filter or let the sediment settle for a couple of hours.

Skill level: Do not kid yourself here. Have an idea of your capabilities. Realize that if you are not prepared mentally and physically for some of the routes you could get yourself and your party into serious trouble. For those new to the canyon country, start with shorter, easier hikes. Get a feel for the terrain, your reaction to it, and problems that off-trail hiking presents.

Difficulties in route finding can take several forms. Interpreting the guide and matching it with what you see admittedly can be confusing. Picking your way up or down steep ledges or in and out of canyon systems can be frustrating and time consuming. The 7.5-minute maps have contour intervals of forty feet. A thirty-five-foot cliff will not be shown on the map. After a 500-foot hike up a steep, loose, and troublesome slope it is not fun to find a twenty-foot cliff blocking progress. A hundred dead-end canyons were hiked in preparing this guide so you would not have to hike them.

A compass is essential when using the guide. Do not count on your innate sense of direction to get you through. A couple of sharp turns in a sinuous canyon and you will be confused. Inexpensive compasses work as well as expensive ones.

Some of the routes in the guide are technical, requiring the use of climbing ropes and other specialized equipment. **Unless you have extensive experience using this equipment, stay away from the technical routes.** Proper techniques can be learned by attending a climbing school.

The Yosemite Decimal System is used to describe the roughness of the terrain. This system has been used for years by hikers and climbers throughout the United States. The Yosemite Decimal System is divided into five classes:

1. Trail or flat walking. No objective dangers.

2. Off-trail walking. Some scrambling and boulder hopping. Steeper terrain.

3. Definite scrambling. Hands may be needed for balance. Exposure to heights possible.

4. Large hand- and foot-holds are used. A fall could have serious consequences. The use of a rope with beginners is often necessary. This is as difficult as the average, experienced, and fit hiker can handle. If you get to a section that looks too hard, do not do it. Climbing Class-4 routes with a heavy pack can make them very difficult. Many may wish to use a rope.

5. The fifth-class category, which is normally the start of roped climbing, is broken down into smaller segments: 5.0–5.14. Except for avoidable digressions, there are no problems over Class 5.4 in difficulty in the guide. If you are not familiar with roped climbing techniques, you should stay away from the fifth-class routes. There should be at least one person in your party who can lead the hard parts of a route without protection. Belay anchors and intermediate protection are often nonexistent in canyon country. Exposure heights are given in the description of the hikes when applicable. Example: (Class 5.1, 30') means there is a Class 5.1 move on a thirty-foot-tall wall, slab, or chimney. All ratings assume the use of tennis shoes or hiking boots. Specialized rock boots could substantially lower the ratings.

Special equipment: Each hike presents its own set of problems and may require some special equipment. When climbing ropes are mentioned, realize that old clothesline, ski rope, or nylon parachute cord is not adequate. Suitable climbing equipment and a knowledge of how to use it properly are essential.

Several of the routes require short stretches of swimming. Floating packs on a Therm-a-Rest does not work well, nor does stuffing your pack into a large garbage bag. They always seem to snag on something and rip at the wrong time. An automotive type inner tube works well and, though heavy, will ensure that your pack stays dry. Small bicycle pumps are adequate for inflating the tubes.

Hint: Use a valve-stem tool to remove the valve from the inner tube. Blow up the inner tube by mouth as much as possible, then use the pump. The tube can be filled quickly this way.

There are many hikes detailed in the guide that involve wading. Unless the wading is on smooth, sandy terrain, tennis shoes are not adequate. An old pair of lug-soled hiking boots is preferred. Sandals and neoprene booties do not provide enough support or protection.

Terminology: Each route description starts with a brief summary of the hike. Within the body of the text are several things to note. *Digressions* describe short side trips or note points of interest. *Alternate routes* are short variations that will take you to the same place as the standard route. They are used to describe ways around deep water or to avoid difficult climbing sections. *Rock-climber's notes* describe short, difficult side trips or variations that will be of interest to rock climbers. The *Historical notes* try to bring a sense of history to the hikes.

The Overland Route, presented at the end of the guide, describes a one-way route that parallels the course of the Escalante River but stays above the rim of the canyon. It starts on Highway 12 and ends at the Fortymile Ridge trailhead near Coyote Gulch. Along the way, the route takes you in and out of side canyons and along the benches in between. You can join the Overland Route at many places and can use it to design your own hikes.

LDC means Looking Downcanyon. *LUC* means Looking Upcanyon. *Heading* a canyon means walking upcanyon along one rim until it is possible to cross the top of the canyon and walk in the opposite direction along the opposite rim. A *dry camp* is one that is not near water. A *horse ladder* consists of wide steps chiseled into the sandstone by ranchers. *Moqui steps* are hand- and toeholds that Indians pecked into steep rock walls. They are common in the Escalante. A *cliff dune* is a sand dune that drops down a cliff.

Jump starting a day is a technique used when a waterless section is ahead. There are variations on the theme, but the idea is to eat dinner near water, then hike for a couple of hours before dark and dry camp. This can substantially reduce the amount of water you need to carry and can help ensure that you will get to water the next day.

Names for features are as historically accurate as possible. Some features are not named on the maps or in the literature but have a local name. When used, these are prefaced by (LKA)—Locally Known As. Features I have named are followed with an (AN)—Author's Name. Some object to the naming of landmarks and canyons; however, I have found it is easier for hikers to call a canyon by name rather than describe it. Example: Calling a canyon the Long Branch of Sleepy Hollow is infinitely easier than saying that it is the first little side canyon to the north below the hiker's maze that is between Dry Fork Coyote and Hurricane Wash in Coyote Gulch.

I
Box-Death Hollow Wilderness

The Box-Death Hollow area is located in the northwest corner of the Escalante drainage. It is bounded by Pine Creek on the west, the Aquarius Plateau and Boulder Mountain on the north, Highway 12 on the east, and the Escalante River on the south. Three major canyons cut through Box-Death Hollow: Pine Creek, Death Hollow, and Sand Creek. They all start in sub-alpine meadows and ponderosa pine and Douglas fir forests near the 9,000-foot level on Boulder Mountain and drop 2,500 feet over the course of many spectacular miles, ending at the Escalante River.

Those intervening miles contain some of the finest scenery in the region and are replete with ponderous, sheer-walled, flat-bottomed canyons, challenging narrows, iridescent pools, and idyllic campsites. While Pine Creek is an easy hike, both Death Hollow and Sand Creek are two of the most difficult hikes in the guide. The Boulder Mail Trail (BMT), an old pack trail, cuts through the area laterally. One of the few established trails in the Escalante area, the BMT allows one to sample the region and its hidden recesses.

The earliest arrivals in the Box Death Hollow area were Fremont Indians during the late Basketmaker II Period (about A.D. 500). Evidence—primarily rock art panels and pithouses—shows that they stayed near the present-day town of Escalante and along the Escalante River.

The Box-Death Hollow area was heavily used by Anasazi Indians during the Pueblo II and III periods (A.D. 900 to 1275). From their large base at what is now the Coombs site in the town of Boulder, the Anasazi fanned out to exploit resources on both the benches and in the canyons. Lithic scatters, granaries, and several cliff dwellings provide evidence of their passage.

The first white men to explore the Aquarius Plateau and Boulder Mountain were members of the St. George militia. They went up Pine Creek and ascended Boulder Mountain's west side in 1866. In 1872 Almon H. Thompson and Frederick Dellenbaugh of the second Powell survey traversed the Aquarius Plateau while searching for the Dirty Devil River. Thompson, impressed by the number of lakes on the plateau, is credited with naming the Aquarius for the waterbearer of the Zodiac. Mormon settlers, not aware of Thompson's designation, called the plateau Boulder Mountain for its many lava boulders.

Clarence Dutton, on a geological survey of the area in 1877, described the area: "The Aquarius should be described in blank verse and illustrated upon canvas. The explorer who sits upon the brink of its parapet looking off into the southern and eastern haze, who skirts its lava-cap or clambers up and down its vast ravines, who builds his camp-fire by the borders of its snow-fed lakes or stretches himself beneath its giant pines and spruces, forgets that he is a geologist and feels himself a poet."

Lower Pine Creek and the upper Escalante River provided fertile soil for the farms and ranches of the first Mormon settlers of the area in 1875. By 1879 the small valley that now contains the town of Boulder was being used as summer cattle range, and in 1887 the valley gained its first permanent inhabitant.

Initial access to Boulder from Escalante was along the Old Boulder road which paralleled the general route of present-day Highway 12. (See the "Highway 12 Area" chapter for details.)

The Boulder Mail Trail started as an Indian route from Escalante Valley to the Salt Gulch area and was initially called the Death Hollow Trail by stockmen. Ten miles shorter than the Old Boulder road, the BMT was improved by Mormon ranchers and was in constant use by the 1890s. Starting in 1902 the BMT was utilized during snow-free periods to carry mail between the towns of Escalante and Boulder. This lasted until 1935 when the Hells Backbone road was finished. (The BMT is described in Hike #3.)

The Bowington road was built in 1909 and provided access from Escalante to the Salt Creek area and to Boulder. Its course follows a horse trail first established by John Bowington (also spelled Boyington or Boynton). The road was abandoned after a couple of years when several sections washed out. (The Bowington road is described in Hikes #1 and 4.)

In 1933 the "upper road," now called the Hells Backbone road, was built by the Civilian Conservation Corps. Winding for nearly forty miles through what was then called Powell National Forest, the Hells Backbone road was the first automobile road to connect Boulder and Escalante; but it was not open in winter. The construction workers called the section of the road that crosses the head of Death Hollow the "Poison Road," declaring "one drop sure death." It was not until Highway 12 was completed in 1940 that the towns were permanently linked with a year-round automobile road.

Hells Backbone Road Section
Access to Hikes #1 through 3.
Access is from Highway 12.

Maps—Escalante, Wide Hollow Reservoir, Posy Lake, Roger Peak, and Boulder Town.

The Hells Backbone road starts at mile 60.2 on Highway 12 at the Hells Backbone road sign (shown as the main road going north from the east side of the town of Escalante on the **Escalante map**). The road is suitable for light-duty vehicles but may be impassable after recent rains. The road is closed in winter. There is camping along the road. See **Map One**.

0.0	—Signed Scenic Backway and Hells Backbone road to the left (N).
0.4	—Cross the Escalante River.
0.5	—"Y." Go right (NE).
2.0	—Cattle guard.
2.2	—Pine Creek is to the right. It was called Pleasant Creek by early explorers.
3.2	—Cattle guard.
3.4	—Pavement ends.
6.5	—(**Wide Hollow Reservoir map.**) Roundy Ranch on the right. It is shown and labeled on the map.
6.8	—Dixie National Forest sign.
7.0	—Cattle guard.
7.3	—Signed Box Death Hollow Wilderness—Lower Box Access to the right (NE). The trailhead is 0.3 miles down the track, which is sandy. (The trailhead is near a gaging station at elevation 6399 on the map.)
8.6	—A vague track on the left leads to Skull Spring. The name comes from cattle skulls found near the spring after one particularly difficult winter.
13.5	—(**Posy Lake map.**) "Y." Follow the signed Hells Backbone road to the right (E).
13.9	—Cattle guard.
14.1	—Signed Hungry Creek crossing. This was a place pack trains stopped to let their animals water and graze before the modern road was built.
14.7	—Signed Deep Creek crossing.
17.6	—Signed Blue Spring Creek and Blue Spring Creek trailhead.

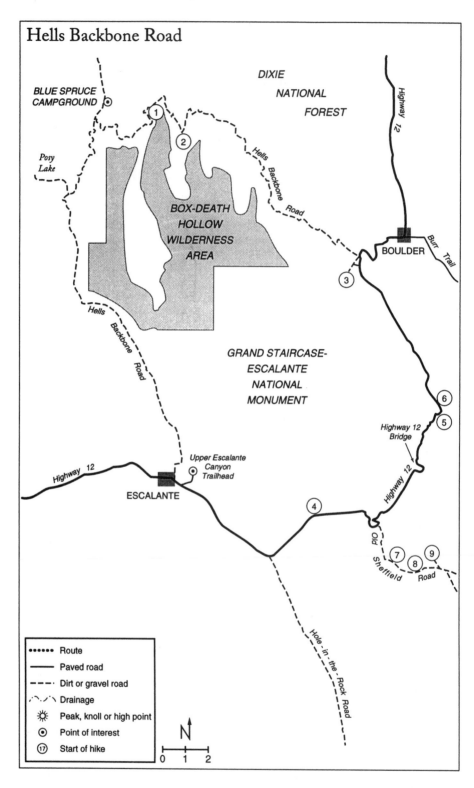

Hells Backbone Road

DIXIE

NATIONAL

FOREST

BLUE SPRUCE
CAMPGROUND

*Posy
Lake*

①

②

Hells
Backbone
Road

BOX-DEATH
HOLLOW
WILDERNESS
AREA

Highway 12

BOULDER

Burr Trail

③

Hells

Backbone

Road

GRAND STAIRCASE-
ESCALANTE
NATIONAL
MONUMENT

⑥

⑤

*Highway 12
Bridge*

Highway 12

Highway 12

Upper Escalante
Canyon
Trailhead

ESCALANTE

④

Old

Sheffield

Road

⑦
⑧
⑨

Hole - in - the - Rock Road

	Route
	Paved road
	Dirt or gravel road
	Drainage
☀	Peak, knoll or high point
⊙	Point of interest
⑰	Start of hike

N

0   1   2

Map One

17.8 —Signed Box-Death Hollow Wilderness—Upper Box Access on the right (E). Limited parking. The map shows a labeled Pack Trail. You are in Navajo Sandstone.

> **Digression:** A superb dayhike going down The Box of Pine Creek starts here. You will need to do a car shuttle. Leave a car at the Lower Box Access (mile 7.3 on the Hells Backbone road). Hike southeast down the hill to Pine Creek. Follow a good path along the creek, crossing it many times. Plan on one long day or two short days (7.5 to 12.5 hours). There is excellent camping and the stream has a perennial flow of water. Avoid this canyon during periods of high water or during spring runoff. Good rock jumpers may be able to get down the creek dry footed. Most will want to wear wading boots. This hike is in Box-Death Hollow Wilderness Area.

18.1 —"Y." Pine Creek sign. Follow the Hells Backbone road to the right (S).

21.3 —**(Roger Peak map.)** "Tee." Stay on the main road to the right (NE).

22.5 —Start of Death Hollow **Hike #1**. Signed Box-Death Hollow Wilderness—Death Hollow Access. Parking on the left. You are one-half mile south-southeast of Roger Peak (elevation 10,115 feet) and are in Navajo Sandstone.

23.4 —"Tee." Signed Sand Creek and Great Western Trail trailhead on left (NE). Stay on the Hells Backbone road to the right (SE).

23.6 —Cattle guard.

24.4 —Hells Backbone bridge. This is the second bridge built across the gap. The first, erected during initial construction in 1933, was replaced in 1960.

25.5 —This is approximately where you come out on Hikes #1 and 2 if you do complete loops.

27.1 —Start of Sand Creek **Hike #2**. Sand Creek sign. You are at a jeep road shown on the map that goes north, parallel to Sand Creek. You are in Navajo Sandstone.

29.4 —"Tee." Signed Bear Creek road. Cross signed Lake Creek. Stay on the Hells Backbone road.

38.3 —**(Boulder Town map.)** "Leaving Dixie National Forest" sign.

38.5 —"Tee." Track on the right (SW) leads to the Boulder Mail Trail trailhead and to the start of **Hike #3**. (This trailhead is more easily reached by way of Highway 12. See the Highway 12 Road Section for details.)

Side track to the Boulder Mail Trail trailhead and Hike #3

0.0 | —Go right (SW) down a track that is suitable for high-clearance vehicles. (The track is between "Home" and "Bench.")

0.4 | —"Tee." Continue straight ahead (S), across the Boulder airstrip. It was constructed in 1947.

0.5 | —Start of Boulder Mail Trail **Hike #3**. Signed Boulder Mail Trail trailhead. There is a trail register and good camping. You are at the "1" of the Jeep Trail shown just south of the landing strip on the Boulder Town map. You are on Navajo Sandstone.

End of side track

38.7 | —Highway 12. You are at milepost 84.0 on the highway.

Death Hollow—Hike #1

Season: If you plan to do this as a complete loop hike, the recommended seasons are late spring or early summer—after spring runoff—or early fall. Summer is too hot to do the complete loop.

If you do a one-way trip by exiting Death Hollow at the Boulder Mail Trail, or by hiking down the Escalante River to the Highway 12 bridge, or up the river to the upper Escalante trailhead near the town of Escalante, summer is fine.

Time: 35.0 to 52.0 hours. Five to eight days for the complete loop.

21.0 to 32.0 hours. Three to five days if you exit Death Hollow at the Boulder Mail Trail and go east.

22.5 to 34.0 hours. Three to five days if you exit Death Hollow at the Boulder Mail Trail and go west.

26.5 to 39.0 hours. Four to six days if you hike to the Escalante River and then either go east to the Highway 12 bridge or west to the town of Escalante.

Great latitude has been given in the times to allow for slow or large groups.

Elevation range: 5360' to 9040'.

Water: The first water in Death Hollow appears at the end of the first day, about eleven miles from the trailhead. The rest of Death Hollow and the Escalante River have perennial flows of water. Water is a problem on the return route. The text that follows notes water sources.

Maps: Roger Peak, Escalante, and Calf Creek.

Skill level:	Difficult route finding. Class 5.4 climbing with little exposure. The leader must be experienced with belay techniques and be capable of leading the climbing sections without protection. Lots of wading and swimming. This route is suitable only for experienced canyoneers who are in excellent physical condition. Low-impact camping skills are essential. **This route is not recommended for novice canyoneers, youngsters, or youth groups.**
Special equipment:	Wading boots, one inner tube for every two or three people, large garbage bags or river-type dry bags, and special dry bags for camera equipment and valuables. A forty-foot climbing rope is adequate.
Note:	This route has been designed for hardcore canyoneers who are in excellent condition. The return route is long, arduous, and has little water. Most will not want to do Death Hollow as a loop hike. Options include exiting at the Boulder Mail Trail (Hike #3) or, once at the mouth of Death Hollow, going up the Escalante River to the town of Escalante or downriver to the Highway 12 bridge.
	Death Hollow contains extensive patches of poison ivy that cannot be avoided. Be prepared.
Land status:	This route is in Box-Death Hollow Wilderness Area and Grand Staircase-Escalante National Monument.

Death Hollow, one of the most spectacular canyons in southern Utah, should be on every hardcore canyoneer's tic list. The operative words here are death and hardcore; this canyon is difficult throughout and many epics have unfolded in its deepest recesses. Luckily, no deaths have occurred; but it is just a matter of time. Death Hollow is not a canyon for the newcomer who may not appreciate what it offers. It is a canyon one aspires to, a reward for building skills and gaining experience over many seasons.

Death Hollow is a canyon of grand proportions. At its upper end huge white walls enclose a wide, forested valley. In the middle the walls taper into a relentless slot that proves challenging to traverse. The canyon ends with a serenity that fathoms the depths of beauty.

The route starts on the Hells Backbone road at the very top of Death Hollow Canyon high on Boulder Mountain and descends the canyon to the Escalante River. The river is followed downcanyon for a short distance to the Bowington road (a trail), which winds its way up the ridge that divides Death Hollow and Sand Creek. After crossing Slickrock Saddle Bench and the Boulder Mail Trail (BMT), the route leaves the Bowington road and follows a cross-country route back to the trailhead.

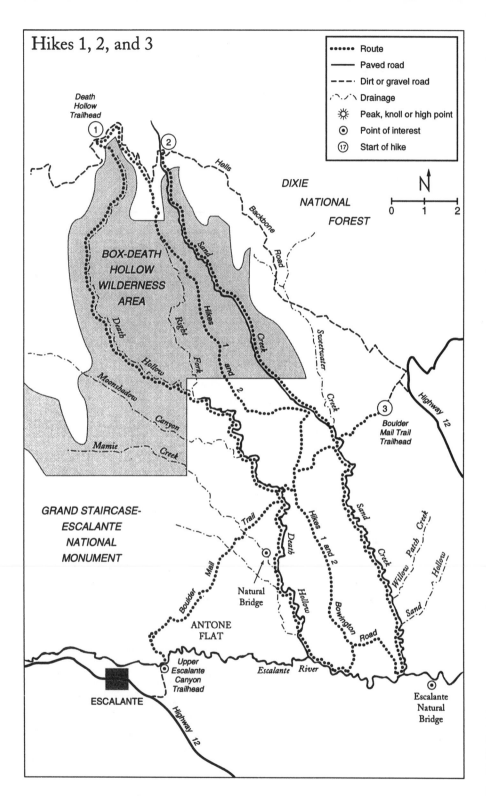

Hikes 1, 2, and 3

Legend:
- •••• Route
- —— Paved road
- – – – Dirt or gravel road
- ·–·–· Drainage
- ☼ Peak, knoll or high point
- ⊙ Point of interest
- ⑰ Start of hike

Death Hollow Trailhead
①
②

Hells

Backbone Road

DIXIE

NATIONAL

FOREST

N
0   1   2

BOX-DEATH HOLLOW WILDERNESS AREA

Sand

Death

Hollow

Right Fork

Hikes 1 and 2

Creek

Sweetwater

Creek

③
Boulder Mail Trail Trailhead

Highway 12

Moonshadow

Canyon

Mamie   Creek

GRAND STAIRCASE-
ESCALANTE
NATIONAL
MONUMENT

Trail

Mail

Boulder

Death

Hollow

Hikes 1 and 2

Sand

Creek

Willow Patch Creek

Sand Hollow

Natural
Bridge

⊙

Bowington   Road

ANTONE
FLAT

Upper
Escalante
Canyon
Trailhead

⊙

Escalante   River

ESCALANTE

Highway 12

Escalante
Natural
Bridge

⊙

Map Two

Into Death Hollow

(**Roger Peak map** and **Map Two.**) From the signed parking area cross the road and find a vague path that goes southeast down a steep hillside to the bottom of an east-running draw. The path, which passes through thick stands of ponderosa pine, Douglas fir, aspen, and manzanita, leads to the floor of Death Hollow. Intensely white cliffs of Navajo Sandstone topped with a thin layer of Page Sandstone appear on the left. Once in Death Hollow proper a Dixie National Forest trail register appears. You have now entered Box-Death Hollow Wilderness Area. (1.0 hour.)

> **Historical note:** There are two conflicting stories about the naming of Death Hollow. Old-timers tell the first story, and it is the most believable. They say that an early rancher named Death Hollow after some of his livestock fell off a steep section of the BMT as they descended into the canyon. The second story claims that Death Hollow was named for Washington Phipps, who had been killed by John Bowington on the Escalante River below Death Hollow. This story is recounted in Hike #7.

Down Death Hollow to the first water source

Hike down the wide canyon for many miles, cutting benches as you see fit. The canyon starts to narrow and the main streambed passes the right (W) side of an abandoned meander (elevation 7156). An hour below the meander, enter the first narrows, a short stretch that cuts through low Navajo walls and contains medium potholes. The narrows widen a bit. Look for a long, prominent, vertical brown streak on the slickrock to the left (LDC). It marks a spring, the first source of reliable water in Death Hollow. If the spring is not flowing well, make your way to the top of the brown streak. Large potholes dot the watercourse and there is excellent slickrock camping. (6.0–9.0 hours.)

Into the narrows

Fifteen minutes below the spring the real narrows begin. The first section contains several large potholes that require wading, stemming, or swimming. It is easy to pass this stretch on a bench to the right (LDC).

The canyon opens a little, then constricts again. You can either stay in the canyon or follow the left rim for a long distance before being forced back into the canyon.

The challenges mount. There are chockstones to negotiate and pools to swim or wade. It is important to belay the less experienced over the many small drops (up to Class 5.4, 12'). Packs can be lowered with a rope. The first major landmark, the Right Fork of Death Hollow, comes in on the left (NW). Its lower end contains large

Bob Bordasch and Joe Breddan in Death Hollow.

potholes and fine camping. You have now left Box-Death Hollow Wilderness Area and have entered Grand Staircase-Escalante National Monument. (3.0–5.5 hours.)

> **Digression:** The Right Fork is worth a visit. Pass the initial fall on the left (LUC). Large pools and delightful narrows lie above. (2.0–4.0 hours round-trip.)

Difficulties continue until you reach a series of beaver dams. (The dams start just as Death Hollow goes off the Roger Peak map onto the **Escalante map**.) The dams mark the end of the narrows and the beginning of the perennial flow of water in Death Hollow. (2.0–3.5 hours.)

The canyon opens

The character of the canyon changes dramatically and the way is lined with ponderosa pine, dogwood, birch, ferns, and flowers. Halloween walls, formed when bright orange iron seeps flow into the stream, provide sharp contrast to the green foliage and the white Navajo walls. A sulphur spring (shown on the map) trickles from a side canyon to the left (N). Its presence will be apparent to the nose. Thick stands of poison ivy prove irksome. Large groups will find few adequate campsites, though small parties can find nooks and crannies that will suffice.

The next landmark is a narrow side canyon that comes in on the right (W). It has a large ponderosa pine laying against its left wall 100 yards up from the confluence and the canyon is blocked by a pour-off after another 100 yards. There is fine camping suitable for large groups above the pour-off, which can be passed via a steep hill on the right (LUC). (The side canyon is the only canyon dropping from the west between "Death" and "Hollow" on the map.) (3.0–5.0 hours.)

> **Digression:** The side canyon is Moonshadow Canyon (AN). Huge potholes, some up to twenty-five yards across, line its slickrock floor. Above the campsite pass a fall by ascending a steep gully that cuts behind two abandoned meanders on the left (SW). It is easy to spend a day, or moonlit night, exploring this splendid canyon.

To the BMT

The BMT is tricky to find, so pay close attention to the map and to landmarks if you plan to exit there. Two hours of pleasant wading down the creek, past several large caves on the left wall, lead to a thin sandy campsite on the right that is partially tucked under a small overhang. Just past it, again on the right and a foot or two above stream level, is a fast-flowing spring that squirts vertically from the ground. (2.5–3.0 hours.) (**Map Three.**)

> **Historical note:** Shortly after World War II, Mac LeFevre, a rancher living on Salt Gulch near Boulder, carried a milk can full of trout across the BMT and released them at the squirter spring, stocking an otherwise fishless stream.

> **Digression:** The east section of the BMT, which leads to the Boul-

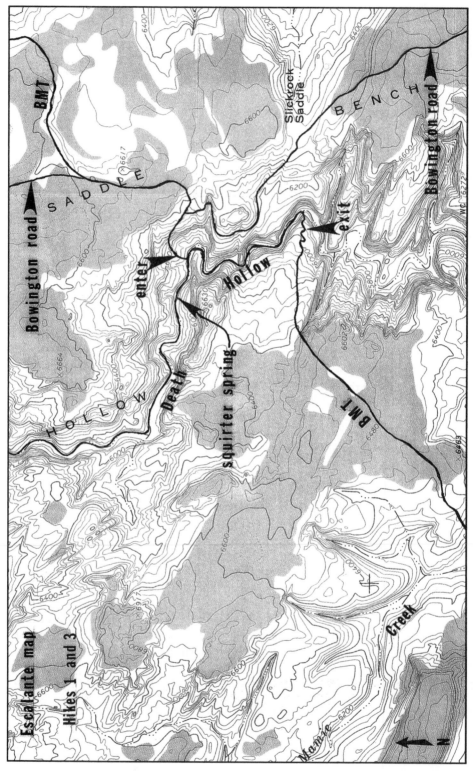

Map Three

der Mail Trail trailhead (described in the Hells Backbone Road Section), comes in on a tree- and brush-covered hillside to the left (NE) fifty yards below the squirter spring. If you can't find the BMT, look for an old telephone cable crossing the canyon above a large, wonderful, ponderosa-shaded campsite on a jut of land that forces the stream into a tight east-to-west bend. Backtrack for 100 yards. (The jut is located one-eighth mile east-northeast of elevation 6630.)

To Mamie Creek

Hike down Death Hollow for twenty-five minutes to the first break in the Navajo wall on the right (W). The BMT, marked with cairns, exits the canyon here. Many good campsites are in the area.

> **Digression:** You can follow the west section of the BMT to the upper Escalante Canyon trailhead near the town of Escalante. (See the Highway 12 Road Section for directions to this trailhead, and see Hike #3 for details on hiking the BMT.)

As you continue down Death Hollow, the first tamarisks and Russian-olive trees appear. Both are imported species. Mamie Creek, unexceptional at its mouth, enters on the right (W). (2.0–3.0 hours.)

> **Digression:** A hike up lower Mamie Creek is rewarding. Minor thrashing leads to a pool and large alcove. (1.0 hour round-trip.)

The final narrows

Forty-five minutes below Mamie Creek you will reach the lower narrows, the last impediment in Death Hollow. Pass a long string of pools on a thin ledge at water level on the left. If the water level is high, or if you are not comfortable traversing the ledge with a pack, you may have a short swim. Many consider these pools to be the prettiest in Death Hollow. Plan on extra time to swim, cavort, relax, and photograph these gems. (1.0–2.5 hours.)

To the Escalante

Hike down to the Escalante River. There are campsites near the confluence. (2.0–2.5 hours.)

> **Digression:** You can leave the standard route here and hike east up the Escalante River to the upper Escalante Canyon trailhead near the town of Escalante. (See the Highway 12 Road Section for directions to this trailhead.) It takes about four hours.

Down the Escalante

(**Calf Creek map.**) Finding the exit route out of Escalante

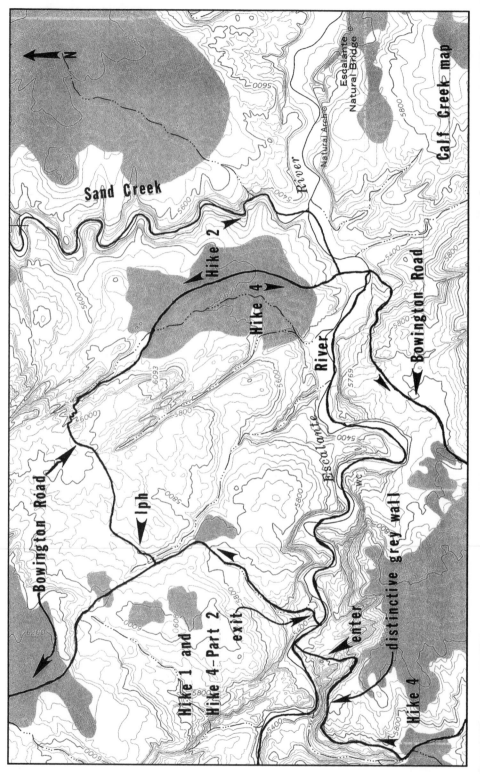

Map Four

Canyon is difficult. Pay close attention to your map. (**Map Four.**) Forty minutes downcanyon the river—going south-southeast—runs straight into a huge, vertical, distinctive gray wall and turns left (E). Ten minutes below the wall locate a large triangular-shaped overhang on river right that is about 100 feet above the river. A smaller overhang is to its left. You will leave the river here. The next reliable water source is about six hours away, at Sand Creek. Load up with water before leaving the river. (1.0 hour.)

> **Digression:** You can leave the standard route here and continue down the Escalante River to the Highway 12 bridge. (See the Highway 12 Road Section for directions to this trailhead.) It takes 2.0–3.0 hours.

The exit route

Go north up and over a low ridge that is directly across the river from the triangular-shaped overhang. Enter a sand-floored drainage lined with ponderosa pines. (The drainage is shown to the southeast of elevation 6084. The mouth of the drainage is immediately east of a marked 5400' elevation line. You cannot enter the drainage directly from the river due to a pour-off.) This exit route is also used in Part 2 of Hike #4.

At the upper end of the drainage is a long black streak that goes down the sloping white Navajo slickrock into a pond. Follow the drainage delineated by the black streak (N). Pass a couple of slickrock falls (Class 3) on the right (LUC). The drainage flattens a bit and ends in a sandy area below a gentle slickrock hill. A twenty-foot pinnacle is plainly visible near the top of a hill to the west.

Walk northeast for three minutes and intersect a small, northwest-running, ponderosa-lined canyon (shown to the east of elevation 6084). Many of the trees are dead. Follow the left (LUC) (SW) side of the canyon. In a couple of minutes the canyon divides. Follow the rim of the drainage to the left (NNW). This short canyon/gully ends at a sandy hill. Continue north-northwest across the sand for a couple of hundred yards and intersect the well-worn Bowington road (a trail) just before reaching slickrock. (0.5–1.0 hours.)

Along the Bowington road to the Boulder Mail Trail

Go left (W) on the Bowington road. It is heavily used by horse packers and its course is easy to follow; there are deep ruts as it runs along sandy sections and it is adequately cairned crossing the slickrock. The trail first goes generally northwest across slickrock for a mile, then turns north and winds around domes and along short escarpments. It takes about 1.5 hours of steady uphill hiking to reach Slickrock Saddle Bench, which is in the Carmel Formation.

The gradient eases as you continue north for an hour on Slick-

rock Saddle Bench to the Slickrock Saddle. (**Escalante map.**) Most
of this section is uphill through pinyon and juniper. The Slickrock
Saddle itself is easy to recognize. You drop off the Carmel and are
again surrounded by Navajo. Just before you reach the saddle, note
where the pioneer trail builders cut a ramp down a small cliff. Sand
Creek is visible to the east, Death Hollow to the west.

From Slickrock Saddle the trail traverses northwest near the rim
of Death Hollow on slickrock for about fifteen minutes. One hundred yards after the trail leaves the slickrock and drops onto the sand
the Bowington road joins the BMT. You are now fifty yards east of
the rim of Death Hollow. (3.5–4.5 hours.)

Go right (NW) on the BMT toward Sand Creek. In ten minutes
the trail divides. The BMT goes to the right (NNE); the Bowington
road goes to the left (NNW). At this juncture a small Navajo tower
(elevation 6617) is visible a short distance to the east. This junction
is difficult to see.

Follow the Bowington road. After fifteen minutes it takes you
across a wide shallow slickrock drainage that has two arms. After the
trail crosses another short pinyon-and-juniper area, it follows the
right (E) side of a small drainage and descends to Sand Creek. (You
are now at the "S" in Sand.) Sand Creek has a perennial flow of water and there is excellent camping under ponderosa pines. (1.0
hour.)

To the Hells Backbone road
The final push to the Hells Backbone road is very long and has a
lot of elevation gain. A jump start, if your schedule allows, is recommended. There will be no water until you reach the Hells Backbone
road. Load up at Sand Creek.

Exit Sand Creek to the left (LUC)(W) and make your way to
the top of the ridge that divides Sand Creek and Death Hollow.
There are many options. (**Roger Peak map.**)

Your goal is to follow the ridge north. After crossing elevation
7933 the ridge narrows in three places. The Right Fork of Death
Hollow is on your left (W); Sand Creek is on your right (E). After
passing the third narrow area (just north of elevation 8073), it is easiest to stay below the right side of the ridge at the 8,300-foot level
until you reach the Hells Backbone road (at mile 25.5). You can now
cache your pack and walk the road back to the trailhead. (6.5–9.5
hours.)

Sand Creek—Hike #2

Season: If you plan to do this as a complete loop hike the recommended seasons are late spring or early summer—after spring runoff—or early

fall. Summer is too hot to do the complete loop. If you do a one-way trip by hiking down the Escalante River to the Highway 12 bridge, summer is fine.

Time: 27.0 to 39.5 hours. Five to seven days for the complete loop.

16.0 to 25.0 hours. Three to four days if you hike down the Escalante River to the Highway 12 bridge.

Elevation range: 5320' to 8400'.

Water: There is a perennial flow of water in Sand Creek and the Escalante River. Water is a problem on the return route. The text that follows notes water sources.

Maps: Roger Peak, Escalante, and Calf Creek.

Skill level: Moderately difficult route finding. Class 4 climbing with little exposure. Lots of wading and a stretch or two of swimming, which is avoidable. This is an exceedingly difficult hike that is suitable only for experienced canyoneers who are fit. Low-impact camping skills are essential. **This route is not recommended for novice canyoneers, youngsters, or youth groups.**

Special equipment: Wading boots, one inner tube for every two or three people, large garbage bags or river-type dry bags, and special dry bags for camera equipment and valuables. A forty-foot climbing rope is adequate.

Note: This route has been designed for hardcore canyoneers who are in excellent condition. The return route is long, arduous, and has little water. Most will not want to do Sand Creek as a loop hike. The best option after reaching the Escalante River is to follow it down to the Highway 12 bridge.

Some may wonder if it is possible to hike up Sand Creek from the Escalante River and use it for the return journey after going down Death Hollow. A group of friends and I did it. The consensus: It is hell on earth.

Land status: This route is in Box-Death Hollow Wilderness Area and Grand Staircase-Escalante National Monument.

"Beauty and the Beast," Madame Villeneuve's tale, is an apt image for a hike down Sand Creek. Although the canyon has its moments of greatness, its beauty is shadowed by the difficulty of passage. This hike is a thrash. The route alternates between wading down a slippery boulder-choked stream or battling impenetrable stands of big sagebrush, willows, tamarisks, and wild rose bushes with their attendant thorns. Those are the disadvantages. The advantage is that you will have the canyon to yourself.

The route starts on the Hells Backbone road near the top of

Sand Creek, which is followed to the Escalante River. The return route is the same as that described in Death Hollow Hike #1 and follows the Bowington road to the Boulder Mail Trail (BMT) as it crosses Slickrock Saddle Bench. A cross-country route along the ridge that divides Death Hollow from Sand Creek leads back to the trailhead.

Down Sand Creek

(**Roger Peak map** and **Map Two.**) From the trailhead, hike south down Sand Creek into Box-Death Hollow Wilderness Area. You will be wading from the start so do not hesitate getting your feet wet. Deadfalls, slippery climbs out of the creek onto benches, and tree limbs hanging over the stream make for slow going. The canyon narrows as it enters the Navajo and the hiking becomes even rougher. There are few good campsites along the creek. After many miles the canyon opens into a park (near "Sand"). (4.5–7.5 hours.)

The Navajo walls give way to the limestones, siltstones, and sandstones of the Carmel Formation. Adequate campsites appear among large stands of big sagebrush. Again the canyon constricts and enters a short stretch of Navajo narrows that contain several small but idyllic pools (one-quarter mile southwest of elevation 6834). You are now in Grand Staircase-Escalante National Monument. (2.5–3.5 hours.)

As you exit the narrows look for colorful and carefully contoured towers and domes to the left (W). The Bowington road crosses Sand Creek here and there is excellent camping in the area (near the "S" in Sand on the **Escalante map**).

Twenty minutes below the Bowington road, Sweetwater Creek enters from the left (N). The flow of Sand Creek can nearly double. (**Calf Creek map.**) A couple of minutes downcanyon pass through a log fence, then under an old telephone cable high overhead. You are nearing the BMT, which enters from the left (N) at a shallow slickrock bowl. (The bowl is located by the red "8" on the map.) Lots of cairns mark the BMT. There is good camping in the area. (1.5–2.5 hours.)

> **Digression:** You can exit the canyon here and follow the BMT to the Boulder Mail Trail trailhead, which takes about an hour. (See the Hells Backbone Road Section for the location of the trailhead.)

> **Alternate route:** If you are averse to swimming through the narrows of Sand Creek, which are a short distance downcanyon from the BMT, they can be bypassed. From the confluence of Sand Creek and the BMT hike north up the slickrock bowl for 200 yards. Exit the bowl to the right (S). Hike along the rim of the canyon, pass behind a large dome (elevation 6236), cross a drainage, and return

to the rim of the canyon. You are now above the narrows. (The narrows start at "Creek" and continue south for one-half mile.) Reenter the canyon below the narrows. (2.0 hours.)

Through the narrows of Sand Creek

The willow bashing continues and the canyon narrows. An area of delightful slickrock and pools precedes the crux of Sand Creek. You will have to swim a long stretch of narrows. (2.5–4.0 hours.)

To the Escalante River

Continue downcanyon to the Escalante River. Good campsites are not plentiful until near the confluence. (4.0–6.0 hours.)

> **Digression:** You can leave the standard route here and hike east down the Escalante River to the Highway 12 bridge. (The location of the bridge is noted in the Highway 12 Road Section.) It takes 1.0–1.5 hours.

The Bowington road

(**Map Four.**) Hike up the Escalante River for ten minutes, hugging the wall to the right (LUC), and locate the Bowington road, which comes in on the right (N). The lower portion of this old road is easy to find. This may be the last water along the route until you reach Sand Creek, which is about six hours away. Load up with water here.

Follow the trail up the cliffs to the north. The route goes up a drainage shown one-eighth mile to the east of elevation 6093. Near the top of the drainage it cuts west across sand and slickrock before heading north toward Slickrock Saddle Bench. At this point pick up the description of the route to the Hells Backbone road described in Death Hollow Hike #1.

Boulder Mail Trail—Hike #3

Season: This route can be hiked any time of the year unless there is snow on the ground.

Time: 8.5 to 12.0 hours. Although very strong hikers can do this route in a day, there is so much to see and do along the trail that two or three days are recommended. Independent sources say the Boulder Mail Trail is sixteen miles long.

Elevation range: 5760' to 6640'.

Water: Water availability is a moderate problem on this route. Water is always available in Sand Creek and Death Hollow. Mamie Creek has medium potholes.

Maps: Boulder Town, Calf Creek, and Escalante. The Trails Illustrated map "Canyons of the Escalante" does a good job of showing the Boulder Mail Trail in its entirety.

Skill level: Moderate route finding. Class 2 walking. There may be a short stretch of wading in Death Hollow if water levels are high. This is a moderate hike with substantial elevation gain and loss. Low-impact camping skills are essential.

Special equipment: Wading shoes or boots.

Note: Poison ivy is unavoidable in Death Hollow. Be prepared.

Land status: This route is in Grand Staircase-Escalante National Monument.

Although the Boulder Mail Trail (BMT) does not form a loop, it is one of canyon country's premier routes. Easy walking along an established trail, adequate water sources, the incredible canyon of Death Hollow, and a picturesque natural bridge in Mamie Creek combine to make this hike a memorable experience.

By using the information in Hikes #1, 2, and 3 several loop trips can be devised. One suggestion is to follow the BMT into Death Hollow, descend Death Hollow to the Escalante River, and use the Bowington road to return to the BMT. Another is to hike down the Escalante River from the upper Escalante Canyon trailhead, exit at the Bowington road, and return to the start via the BMT.

The BMT starts near Highway 12, crosses Sand Creek, goes over Slickrock Saddle Bench, and drops into Death Hollow. It then goes down Death Hollow for a short distance, exits it, and crosses Mamie Creek and Antone Flats on its way to the upper Escalante Canyon trailhead near the town of Escalante.

To Sand Creek

(**Boulder Town map** and **Map Two.**) Hike southwest down the road for twenty minutes to a "Boulder Mail Trail" sign, which points to a closed track on the right (SW). (**Calf Creek map.**) Follow the track for five minutes. Look for several stacks of cairns on the left. They mark where the BMT leaves the track. Follow the cairned trail down small cliffs and across sand and slickrock to Sand Creek. There is good camping in the area. The first part of this hike is ideal for those with young children. (1.0–1.5 hours.)

To Death Hollow

The trail goes down Sand Creek, crosses it, and follows its right side for ten minutes. At a large burned-out log the trail exits the canyon on the right (W). (If you miss this turn you'll end up bush bashing beside the creek with no visible trail.) Halfway up the hill note the wire cable strung from poles and trees.

> **Historical note:** This old telephone line was installed in 1911 by the Forest Service to connect ranger stations in Escalante and Boulder. The ranger in Boulder let townspeople tie in with their own lines. The first telephone operator was Leander Shurtz who had been blinded as a child. Shurtz was renowned for being able to recognize each person's voice and was the modern version of the town crier, keeping everyone posted on the latest news. The line was used until 1955 when a microwave system replaced it.

The telephone line is your companion for the rest of the trip. It follows the BMT closely except when going up or down cliff faces. While going across benches it is usually visible.

From the top of the hill the trail leads southwest across Slickrock Saddle Bench to the rim of Death Hollow. (**Escalante map** and **Map Three.**)

> **Warning:** Fifty yards before reaching the rim of Death Hollow the trail divides. The Bowington road (a trail) goes to the left (SE). The BMT goes to the right (SSW). Make sure to stay on the BMT or you could find yourself in the wrong place with no water. This is a common mistake.

The 600-foot drop into Death Hollow starts as a cairned route down slickrock. As the angle of the rock increases, long stretches of constructed trail switchback to the canyon floor.

> **Historical note:** Lenora LeFevre, in her book *The Boulder Country and Its People,* tells of an adventure rancher John King had while riding this section of the BMT into Death Hollow in 1905. She writes: "Storms of sleet and rain had frozen on the trail leaving it a glare of ice. On the edge of the precipice John decided to walk and lead his horse. On the way down the slick narrow canyon trail both feet slipped from under him and off he went over the edge, hanging for dear life to the bridle reins which fortunately were new and strong. Clinching the wall of the chasm with his legs John gradually pulled himself up and over the sandstone to the trail while his horse stood braced against the pull. John promptly mounted his saddle horse and rode on down the steep trail refusing to think of what might have happened."

Ginger Harmon on the Boulder Mail Trail.

Poison ivy appears immediately. It is difficult to avoid. Death Hollow has a perennial flow of water and there is excellent camping in the area. (2.5–3.5 hours.)

To Mamie Creek

Walk and wade downcanyon for twenty-five minutes and locate the first break in the Navajo on the right (W). The BMT exits Death

Hollow here. Mamie Creek contains medium potholes that should be full after recent rains or during the spring. If in doubt, load up with water in Death Hollow.

The constructed trail zigzags up the cliff. Cairns and the telephone wire lead southwest across a long expanse of slickrock before making the short descent to Mamie Creek. There are medium potholes downcanyon and excellent camping in the area. (1.5–2.0 hours.)

> **Digression:** A half-hour stroll downcanyon leads to a splendid natural bridge. Upper Mamie Creek is lined with huge potholes, though they take an hour to get to.

To the trailhead

The trail goes down Mamie Creek for 100 yards, then exits on the right (W). An abundance of cairns mark the route. Follow the trail and the telephone wire across Antone Flat to an escarpment high above the town of Escalante. (2.0–3.0 hours.)

> **Historical note:** Antone Flat was named for Antone Woerner, who moved to Escalante in the 1880s.

The last section of the BMT goes across a large wide slickrock drainage, down a steep hill past the huge painted E that is visible from town, to Pine Creek. Follow the creek downcanyon (SSW) past a rancher's fields and through a short brushy canyon to the Escalante River. Follow the river upcanyon for a couple of minutes until you are out of Escalante Canyon. A marked trail leaves the river on the left (LUC)(S) and goes up a hill to the upper Escalante Canyon trailhead. The trail crosses private property. Stay on the trail. (1.5–2.0 hours.)

II
The Highway 12 Area

Utah Highway 12 starts in the town of Torrey and ends near the town of Panguitch to the southwest. The portion of the highway covered in this guide is from Escalante to Boulder. Highway 12 effectively cuts the Escalante region into two distinct areas: the mountain canyons that start on the Aquarius Plateau and the canyons of the lower desert region.

The Highway 12 area is a land of expansive views and endless slickrock. Travel and automotive magazines have rightfully called it one of the most scenic drives in America. For the backpacker and explorer, the highway provides easy all-weather access to the backcountry. The routes that start from the highway should be considered first when the weather is lousy and the dirt roads have turned to gumbo.

Indians of the late Basketmaker II Period (about A.D. 500) were the first to settle in the Highway 12 area. They left evidence of their occupancy in the form of pictograph panels high on the walls of lower Calf Creek Canyon.

Anasazi and Fremont Indians proliferated during the Pueblo II and III periods (A.D. 900 to 1300). The high benches now crossed by the highway supported an abundance of deer and bighorn sheep. Indians spent extended periods on vantage points chipping arrowheads and other stone tools; lithic scatters are found everywhere.

Cattlemen from towns to the north of Boulder were the first to use Boulder Valley, in 1879. The first permanent inhabitant settled there in 1887. It was about that time that Escalante ranchers started to graze their animals in Boulder Valley.

The first road between the towns of Boulder and Escalante was the Old Boulder road. It started as a rough trail that was slowly improved over a period of years to the point that wagons and, later, automobiles could use it. Starting from Escalante, the Old Boulder road crossed Big Flat and dropped to the Escalante River just below the mouth of Calf Creek. The road then went downriver for several hundred yards, exited the canyon, and followed a tortuous path up the cliffs to Haymaker Bench. After crossing the bench, the Hogback, and New Home Bench, the trail descended into Boulder.

The difficulties the pioneers had in traveling this road were

enormous. Early users planned on four to seven days from Escalante
to Boulder, camping en route. To negotiate the roughest sections,
wagons were unloaded or even taken apart. Bad weather often de-
layed passage. One pioneer woman, Sally May King, is quoted as
saying, "The man who found the route for this road should have a
medal, or else be killed." A companion then exclaimed: "Kill him,
damn him. That's what I say."

By 1914 an alternate route from Haymaker Bench across Dry
Hollow and Boulder Creek to lower Boulder had been established.
In 1924 this rough path was improved into a good wagon road. It
was called the Claude V. cutoff road, named for Claude Vincent
Baker, a Boulder rancher. This road shortened the trip from Escalante to Boulder by a day and became the standard route for several years. (Hike #6 follows a section of the Claude V. cutoff road.)

As the towns of Escalante and Boulder grew, both the Old
Boulder road and the Claude V. cutoff proved inadequate. In 1934
the Civilian Conservation Corps (CCC) started work on an all-
weather, one-lane "lower road" between the two towns. This road,
which became Highway 12, followed some sections of the Old
Boulder road but diverged from it by following lower Calf Creek
and then going directly up the steep cliffs to Haymaker Bench. A
one-lane bridge, which cost $5,000, was built across the Escalante
River. This road was a huge undertaking and was not finished until
1940. Widening and paving occurred in spurts and the present
paved configuration was not completed until the mid-1980s. The
original one-lane bridge across the river was replaced by a two-lane
bridge in 1995.

Harry Aleson and Georgie White— The First to Run the Escalante

Why are whitemen always discovering things and places that natives have known for ages? Just allow time enough, and there may come a day in the distant future when a whiteman reports the discovery of the Pyramids in a barren land once thought to have the name of:—E GIP TH.

Harry Aleson, 1959

It was an inauspicious beginning for the great river runners Harry Aleson and Georgie White. According to Aleson's notes, May 24, 1948, started normally. Harry and Georgie spent the morning visiting friends and buying groceries in Escalante. Their intent was to be the first to run the Escalante River. They would start at the Highway 12 bridge and paddle to the then still free-flowing Colorado River.

By mid-afternoon on that hot spring day they had provisioned their craft—a surplus seven-man U.S. Navy raft—and had set it in the river. But high water was not with them. Harry wrote: "We left directly — for Lees Ferry (?) Almost 40 feet after we started in a narrow, shallow pool — we were aground. So, out into the river (?), and pull — over the rocks, — and sandbars, — riffles, — on and off every few minutes until near dark. Whenever we could, we would sit on the opposite ends of the boat — and guide by foot. Believe we got about 4 miles in 4 hours."

Harry Aleson was born in 1899 in Waterville, Iowa, where he spent his formative years. In 1918 he enlisted in the U.S. Army Signal Corps and spent the World War I years in France. A plane he was in crashed, and his injuries, although not exceptionally debilitating, entitled him to a full pension.

After returning from France, Aleson finished high school and several years of college, then migrated to the Southwest while working as a geophysicist in the oil fields. In 1939 he was introduced to canyon country while on a boat trip on Lake Mead. That trip was the start of a thirty-year love affair with the Colorado River and its side canyons. Until his death in 1972, Aleson devoted most of his time to guiding river trips on the Colorado River and exploring this remarkable province on foot.

Harry Aleson was interested in all aspects of the canyons he visited. His extensive correspondence, now housed at the Utah State Historical Society library in Salt Lake City, provides an intimate view of those early explorations. Correspondence flew back and forth between Aleson and his peers, letters that often noted details on the discovery of a new canyon, arch, or bridge, a historical tidbit, or even a new row of Moqui steps or an Indian ruin. His friends included the legendary boatman Otis "Dock" Marston; Stella Ruess, Everett's mother; and then Arizona Senator Barry Goldwater.

Georgie White may have felt a bit out of place on the Escalante River. While Harry Aleson had spent a considerable amount of time exploring Glen Canyon and its tributaries, this was Georgie's first trip away from her first love, the Grand Canyon. Georgie de Ross was born in Chicago in 1911. After she married Harold White, the restless couple bicycled from New York to California in 1936, a remarkable feat at the time. During the war, Georgie joined the Women's Auxiliary Flying Squadron. In 1944 her daughter Sommona died in a bicycle accident. Devastated by the death, Georgie turned to the outdoor world for solace, joining the Sierra Club and participating in many of its outings.

In 1945 Georgie met Harry Aleson at one of his Grand Canyon slide shows. Their first adventure together was a float trip down the lower end of the Colorado River in the Grand Canyon—without a boat. The couple wore life vests and swam for eighty miles to Lake Mead.

Even with their butt-bumping start, Harry and Georgie decided to continue down the Escalante River. Aleson wrote: "The second day was tougher than the first — so the third — so the fourth. We battled the rocky, shallow places; many, many fast chutes of white water. We portaged many times."

On the fourth day their raft hit a boulder and flipped. Now in the water with their gear floating down the fast-moving river, Aleson and White "scrambled about in the churning water, hugging and puffing, choking, coughing, gagging,...grabbing things drifting by....We repacked, reloaded, and went on." Seven days from the start Harry Aleson and Georgie White finally reached the mouth of the Escalante River at Glen Canyon. Another day was spent on the Colorado River floating to their takeout point at Lee's Ferry.

A week after the trip, Harry wrote his friend Lou Fetzner: "I hereby predict that the Escalante Creek (?) run will be repeated but once in our lifetimes, and that only if you and I make it in 1949, for movies." Aleson and Fetzner did make that second trip, over eight days in late May 1949.

Aleson's third and final trip down the Escalante River was in June 1950. Instead of starting at the Highway 12 bridge, the third expedition began at the mouth of Harris Wash. It is interesting now to note that the group drove down Harris Wash to the river. Aleson was joined on this trip by Randall and Cyria Henderson, Georgie White, and Charles Lindsay.

Randall Henderson was the publisher of *Desert Magazine*. After the trip Henderson wrote an article about their adventures. In it he said: "We shoved out into the current—and 50 yards downstream the boat grounded in a rocky riffle. We got out to push and pull the rafts over the rocks—and never returned to the boats as passengers for eight days. The water that was expected to swell the stream flow as we continued our journey never appeared....The oars we carried were never unleashed until we reached the Colorado River."

Although the trip was exceptionally difficult for the five-person team, Henderson considered it a success. In summation he wrote: "Perhaps in a less colorful setting the arduous labor of this journey would have made it a grim, dismal experience. But not in Escalante Canyon. The red Wingate and the Navajo sandstone walls which towered above us fringed with the deep green of junipers and pinyon were ever-changing backdrops of fantastic sculpturing....In such a setting, with congenial companions—I never heard an unkind word, even when the going was very tough—we trudged along, dragging our boats and feeling that here was an experience which would leave pleasant memories long after the tired muscles had been forgotten."

The Escalante River is rarely in "nick" for a river run. Flow rates high enough to float a small boat only happen every four or five years. Often one must ride the crest of the spring runoff and hope it does not subside when partway down. Rafts are too large for this small river and most negotiate its tortuous course in kayaks or single-person inflatables.

The standard put-in for a run down the Escalante River is at the Highway 12 bridge and the normal takeout is via Crack-in-the-Wall to the Fortymile Ridge trailhead. Plan on seven to nine days for the trip. Familiarize yourself with other exit routes out of the canyon just in case things do not go as planned. The shortest optional exit is Fence Canyon to the Egypt trailhead.

It takes most river runners two trips over the course of a long day to carry their gear from the river to the Fortymile Ridge trail-head. If you are lucky, willing hikers may give a hand. A forty-foot rope will help pull boats up the cliff at Crack-in-the-Wall.

Highway 12 Road Section
Access to Hikes #4 through 9.
Provides access to the Hells Backbone road, Hole-in-the-Rock road, Old Sheffield road, and the Burr Trail.
Maps—Escalante, Dave Canyon, Tenmile Flat, Calf Creek, and Boulder Town.

Highway 12 is the major road cutting across Escalante country. All of the hikes presented in the guide either originate along the highway or from roads that branch from it. Since Highway 12 does have mileposts along it, they are used in this road section. (Mileposts are not used in any of the other road sections in this guide.) The road is paved and is suitable for all vehicles. Side roads lead to camping near the highway. Mileage starts at Escalante Outfitters in the town of Escalante. (See **Map Five**.)

59.7 —(**Escalante map.**) At Escalante Outfitters. Follow the highway east.

60.2 —Signed Hells Backbone road to the left (N). This road provides access to **Hikes #1 through 3**. See the Hells Backbone Road Section for details.

61.0 —Signed "Escalante Trailhead Jct" to the left (N). This road provides access to the upper Escalante Canyon trailhead.

Side road to the upper Escalante Canyon trailhead

0.0 —At Highway 12. Go north.

0.1 —Pass the cemetery on its right. Cattle guard. The road turns east.

0.3 —"Tee." Go left (NW).

0.5 —"Y." Go left (NW). The road ahead gets rougher. Light-duty vehicles may not be able to make it to the trailhead.

0.9 —Large, steep parking circle at the trailhead. The head of Navajo-walled Escalante Canyon is plainly visible to the north-northeast.

> **Digression:** A trail, starting at a hiker's maze, leads across private property (do not leave the trail) to the river. A trail register is located near the river. For those hiking down the river to the Highway 12 bridge, it will take 3.5 to 4.5 hours to reach the mouth of Death Hollow, 2.0 to 3.0 more hours to reach the mouth of Sand Creek, and another 1.0 hours to reach Highway 12.

End of side road

64.8 —(**Dave Canyon map.**) Signed Hole-in-the-Rock road to the right (SE). This road provides access to **Hikes #10 through 29**. See the Hole-in-the-Rock Road Section for details.

68.0 —(**Tenmile Flat map.**) Start of Big Flat Wash, the Escalante River, and the Bowington road **Hike #4**. Park off the road near the mile 68 signpost. You are at the red 20 in the upper left corner of the map and are in the Carmel Formation.

69.4 —Top of a hill. A track to the left (E) marks the start of a section of the Old Boulder road, which diverges from Highway 12.

> **Digression:** For those wishing to hike this section of the Old Boul-

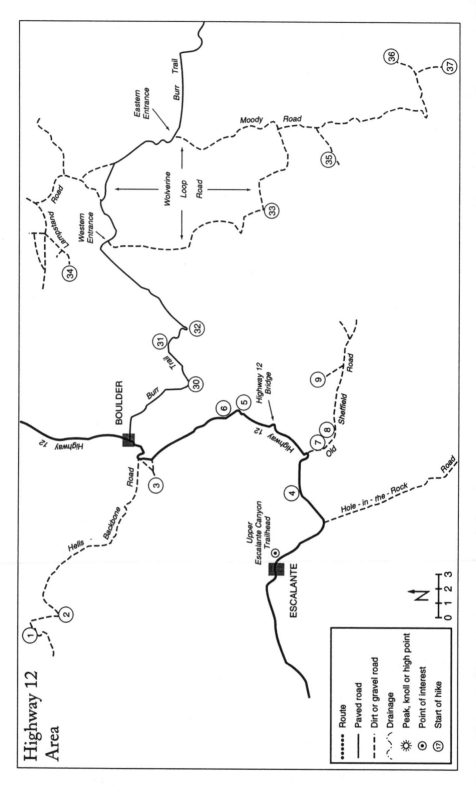

Highway 12
Area

Map Five

der road, park off the track near the highway. Follow a track to the right (E). In short order the track descends a steep cliff. The way is easy to follow and ends at mile 73.1 on Highway 12. Plan on 1.5 to 2.0 hours one-way. This is a delightful and easy hike suitable for most.

69.8   —Head of Rocks Scenic Overlook on the left. Great views.

70.5   —Old Sheffield road to the right (SE). This road provides access to **Hikes #7 through 9**. See the Old Sheffield Road Section for details.

72.4   —**(Calf Creek map.)** Across the Camel's Back (LKA).

73.6   —Bowington Overlook to the left.

74.3   —Cross the Escalante River on the Highway 12 bridge. There is parking and a trail register on the far (W) side of the bridge on the left.

> **Digression:** Although no loop trips start at this trailhead, it is a popular starting point for visiting both upper and lower Escalante Canyon areas. There is private property both up- and downcanyon. For those going upcanyon, cross the river and follow its left (LUC) (S) side. It takes about an hour to reach the mouth of Sand Creek.
>
> For those going downcanyon, follow a trail under the Highway 12 bridge, cross a wood footbridge over Calf Creek, and hike along the left (LDC)(N) side of the river. "Trail Easement" signs lead you across private property. Please stay on the trail. It will take about an hour to reach the mouth of Phipps Wash, which comes in on the right (S). Hike #7 details Escalante Canyon below Phipps Wash.

75.1   —Cross Calf Creek.

75.5   —Signed Calf Creek Recreation Area to the left (W). This fee-for-use campground has outhouses, trash barrels, and drinking water. A campground host is available during the busy season.

> **Digression:** A trail suitable for most people starts at the campground and follows Calf Creek upcanyon to the spectacular 126-foot-high Lower Calf Creek Falls. This is the perfect and recommended hike for those who have little time to spend in the area. (2.5–4.5 hours round-trip.)

77.0
+ 50 yards   —Start Middle Boulder Creek **Hike #5**. There is parking before a barb-wire fence on the right (E). You are one-quarter mile north of the "h" in Bench and are in Navajo Sandstone. You are on Haymaker Bench, which was named for early rancher Charley Haymaker.

> **Digression:** The Old Boulder road crosses this parking area and descends to the Escalante River. To follow it, go south through a wire gate. The old road goes generally south and is not too difficult to follow. It enters Escalante Canyon several hundred yards below

the Highway 12 bridge. This is a pleasant stroll. (1.5–2.5 hours one way.)

77.5 —Start of Upper Boulder Creek and Dry Hollow **Hike #6**. Small parking area on the right. You are one-eighth mile west-southwest of elevation 5863 and are in Navajo Sandstone.

79.1 —Start of a section of the highway called the Hogback. Calf Creek is to the left (W) and Dry Hollow is to the right (E).

80.0 —Start of a section of the highway called New Home Bench. Early settlers to Boulder wanted to build homes on this bench but a planned aqueduct proved to be unfeasible and the idea was dropped.

81.4 —Track to the left (W) goes a couple of hundred yards to the Upper Calf Creek Falls trailhead. Be careful of the deep sand at the parking circle at the end of the track. There is a trail register and good camping. You are just south of the "e" in Home and are in Navajo Sandstone.

> **Digression:** A popular hike starts here. Simply follow a heavily cairned trail down a steep slope to Upper Calf Creek Falls. There is a lot to explore. This area has become impacted by careless hikers. Stay on the trails! (2.0–3.0 hours round-trip.)

83.3 —**(Boulder Town map.)** Track to the left (SW) goes to the Boulder Mail Trail trailhead, which provides access to **Hike #3**.

Side track to Boulder Mail Trail trailhead and Hike #3

0.0 —At Highway 12. Follow the track southwest. This track is suitable for high clearance vehicles.

0.4 —"Tee." The Boulder Airstrip and UFO Landing Site is straight ahead. Go left (S).

0.5 —Start of Boulder Mail Trail **Hike #3**. Signed Boulder Mail Trail trailhead. There is a trail register and good camping. You are at the "l" of the Jeep Trail shown just south of the landing strip on the Boulder Town map and are on Navajo Sandstone.

End of side track

84.0 —Signed Hells Backbone road to the left (W). This road provides access to **Hikes #1 and 2**. See the Hells Backbone Road Section for details. (You are one-quarter mile north-northeast of elevation 6776.)

85.1 —Enter the town of Boulder.

87.1 —Signed Burr Trail (a road) to the right (E). This road provides access to **Hikes #30 through 37**. See the Burr Trail Road Section for details.

87.8 | —Anasazi State Park on the right.

Big Flat Wash, The Escalante River, and the Bowington Road—Hike #4

Season: Part 1—Spring, summer, or fall.
Part 2—Any.

Time: Part 1—5.0 to 7.5 hours.
Part 2—6.5 to 10.5 hours. This is a fine short backpack trip.

Elevation range: 5320' to 6120'.

Water: Water availability is not a problem on these hikes. The Escalante River has a perennial flow of water. Medium potholes may be found along the slickrock.

Maps: Tenmile Flat and Calf Creek.

Skill level: Part 1—Moderate route finding. Class 3- scrambling. Lots of wading. This is a moderate dayhike.
Part 2—Difficult route finding. Class 3 + scrambling. You will wade across the Escalante River twice. This is a moderately strenuous hike with substantial elevation gain and loss. If done as a backpack, low-impact camping skills are essential.

Special equipment: Part 1—Wading boots.
Part 2—Wading shoes.

Land status: These hikes are in Grand Staircase-Escalante National Monument.

Kenophobes, cremnophobes, and ergasiophobes must be wary on this hike. You cannot have a fear of hiking across wide open spaces, negotiating precipices, or working hard to cover the exceptional terrain offered on this route. Designed for intermediate hikers willing to push their skills just a tad, this route blends bench walking, river wading, cliff climbing, and slickrock sauntering.

The hike comes in two parts. Part 1 starts on Highway 12 and follows Big Flat Wash to the Escalante River. The route then goes a couple of miles down the river and returns to the trailhead by following a short stretch of the historic Bowington road.

Part 2 crosses the Escalante River where you first intersect it and follows an inspiring cross-country route that traverses long sweeps

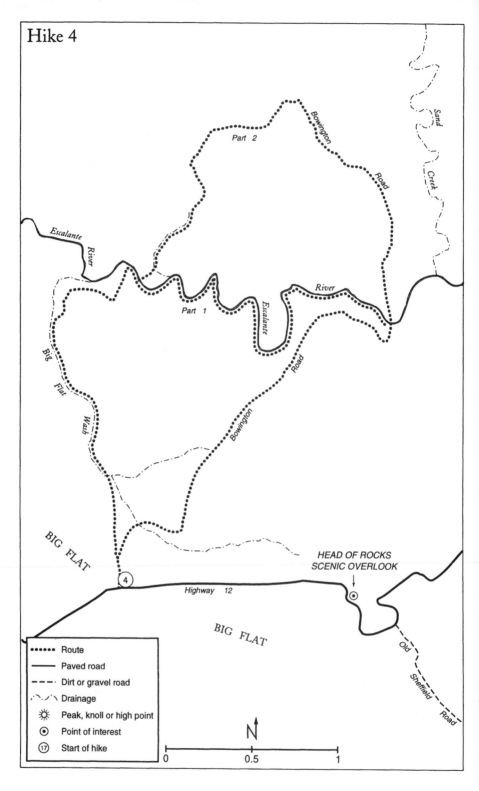

Hike 4

Part 2

Bowington Road

Sand Creek

Escalante River

Part 1

River

Escalante

Big

Flat

Wash

Bowington Road

BIG FLAT

HEAD OF ROCKS
SCENIC OVERLOOK

4

Highway 12

BIG FLAT

Old

Sheffield

Road

Route
Paved road
Dirt or gravel road
Drainage
Peak, knoll or high point
Point of interest
17   Start of hike

N

0   0.5   1

Map Six

of slickrock before intersecting the Bowington road, which is followed back to the trailhead.

Part 1: To the Escalante River

(You immediately leave the **Tenmile Flat** map and go onto the **Calf Creek map. Map Six.**) From milepost 68 walk northwest for 100 yards and enter a shallow dirt-lined wash. Follow its course downward. (Big Flat Wash is not named on the map. It runs generally north between "Big" and "Flat.") Within twenty minutes the wash enters Navajo Sandstone and slowly deepens into a modest canyon. After passing several small pour-offs, the drainage abruptly plummets into a deep gorge. A squat ten-foot tower is to the right (LDC). (**Map Four.**) The upper walls of Escalante Canyon are visible downcanyon.

Scramble up to a wide ledge on the right (LDC)(E) side of the gorge and follow it downcanyon for a couple of hundred yards until you see a ten-foot-tall pinnacle on top of the slickrock to the right (E). Clamber up to the pinnacle. Now look northeast up a wide, shallow slickrock drainage and locate a short, squat balancing rock on the skyline. From the balancing rock walk several yards to the edge of Escalante Canyon. Look east. A quarter mile away is a steep boulder-filled gully leading down to the river. Traverse along a ledge to the top of the gully.

Follow a cairned path down the left side of the gully. Partway down, the path crosses the gully, then descends to the river. Several short obstacles prove easy to overcome (Class 3-). (1.5–2.5 hours.)

Down the Escalante River

Walk and wade downriver, cutting meanders as necessary. Your goal is to exit the canyon via the Bowington road, which starts at the mouth of a small side canyon on the right in about 1.5 hours. (The small side canyon is shown one-quarter mile east of elevation 5769. Do not confuse it with a larger drainage that is a couple of hundred yards to the east.) Unfortunately, landmarks are limited, so do keep track of your progress on the map.

A quarter mile before reaching the mouth of Sand Creek look for the Bowington road cutting diagonally up a hillside on the left (LDC)(N). (It is easier to see the Bowington road coming down the north wall of the canyon than it is to see it going up the south wall. If you miss the road, you will meet the mouth of Sand Creek. Backtrack for ten minutes.) From the base of the road walk south to the river. (1.5–2.0 hours.)

Digression: Escalante Natural Bridge is a short stroll downcanyon on the right (S). It is worth a visit. (1.0–1.5 hours round-trip.)

Up the Bowington road

Cross the river and start to enter a short canyon to the south. Cottonwoods and several large Russian-olive trees block its mouth. The Bowington road starts on the right (W) just as you enter the canyon.

> **Historical note:** Several names are etched on the canyon walls near the road. O. (Orlow) H. Griffin was the son of Charles E. Griffin, who moved to Escalante in 1879. Orlow scratched his name on the rock on March 15, 1911. Other names along the trail include Emerson Porter (Oct. 3, 1922) and Mazle Alvey.

Short constructed sections and cairns along the slickrock make route finding easy as the trail cuts up the Navajo escarpment. After traversing a short sandy hill, a large area of rolling slickrock is encountered. A few cairns lead southwest across the slickrock. Near the top of the cliffs the trail turns into an often used off-road vehicle track. Follow this track as it crosses nondescript benchlands before winding its way back into Big Flat Wash. It is followed back to the trailhead. (If you lose the trail, simply hike southwest and intersect Big Flat Wash.) (2.0–3.0 hours.)

Part 2: To the Bowington road

(Calf Creek map.) Start at the bottom of the steep gully where you first encounter the Escalante River. Cross the river once, then hike downstream for 100 yards. Exit the canyon through a break in the Navajo to the left (N). (If you go too far downriver, around the first corner, the canyon walls rise and there is no possible exit.) You will find yourself in a sand-floored drainage lined with ponderosa pines. At its upper end is a long black streak that descends the sloping white Navajo slickrock into a pond. (The drainage is shown to the south-southeast of elevation 6084. The mouth of the drainage is immediately east of a marked 5400' elevation line.)

Follow the drainage delineated by the black streak (N). Pass a couple of pour-offs on either side (Class 3). The drainage flattens a bit, goes over a short rise, flattens again, and ends in a sandy area below a gentle slickrock hill. A fifteen-foot pinnacle is plainly visible near the top of a hill to the west.

Walk northeast for three minutes and intersect a small, northwest-running, ponderosa-lined canyon (shown to the east of elevation 6084). Many of the trees are dead. Follow the left (LUC)(SW) side of the canyon. In a couple of minutes the canyon divides: the main canyon veers right (NNE); the short left arm is to the northwest. (Up to this point you have been following the same exit route described in Hike #1.)

Cross the canyon and enter the drainage on the right (NNE).

Follow it for a couple of minutes, passing a string of large potholes along the way. This is an excellent place to camp.

Above the potholes the canyon turns into a wash. A large slickrock sheet is to your left (LUC). Immediately start looking for a cairned trail that crosses the wash and cuts up a sandy slope on the right (E). (If you go too far upcanyon, the drainage fizzles out below an escarpment.) (0.5–1.0 hours.)

Along the Bowington road

This trail is the Bowington road. Recreational horseback riders still use the trail, making it easy to follow as it winds east, then south across sandy benches and around, down, and through a maze of domes, draws, and defiles. (At one point the trail skirts along the right (LDC)(W) side of a canyon shown one-eighth mile to the northeast of elevation 6093.)

As the trail makes its final descent to the Escalante River an unnamed arch becomes visible high on a wall downcanyon. Across the river to the south a diagonal cut across the cliff-face marks the Bowington road as it exits the canyon. From the base of the trail hike south across the flats to the river. (1.0–1.5 hours.)

Back to the trailhead

Now join the standard route as it winds its way up the Bowington road to the trailhead. (2.0–3.0 hours.)

Middle Boulder Creek—Hike #5

Season:	Spring before or after spring runoff, summer, or fall.
Time:	4.5 to 6.5 hours. One moderate day. This is a great area to hang out in. A two-day trip is recommended.
Elevation range:	5280' to 6040'.
Water:	Water availability is not a problem on this hike. Boulder and Deer creeks have perennial flows of water.
Maps:	Calf Creek and King Bench.
Skill level:	Moderate route finding. Class 3- scrambling. During periods of high water there is a lot of wading. This is a moderately strenuous route. If done as an overnight trip, knowledge of low-impact camping techniques is essential.
Special equipment:	Wading boots may be necessary.

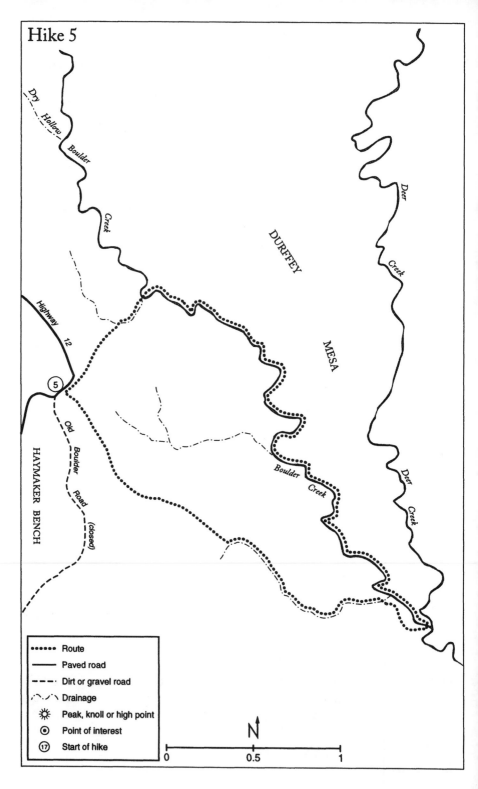

Hike 5

Dry Hollow

Boulder

Creek

DURFFEY

MESA

Deer

Creek

Highway 12

⑤

HAYMAKER BENCH

Old Boulder Road (closed)

Boulder Creek

Deer Creek

•••••• Route
——— Paved road
– – – Dirt or gravel road
⌒⌒⌒ Drainage
☀ Peak, knoll or high point
⊙ Point of interest
⑰ Start of hike

N↑

0   0.5   1

Map Seven

Land status: This hike is in Grand Staircase-Escalante National Monument.

Boulder Creek, named by Almon Thompson of the Powell surveys for the black lava boulders that line its floor, is my single favorite canyon in the Escalante. The main attraction—beyond easy access from a paved road, idyllic swim holes, and fine camping—is the bucolic ambience of the canyon. This is the perfect place to spend a day or two reading, relaxing, or exploring and photographing the extensive slickrock benches on the east side of both Boulder and Deer creeks.

The route starts on the Hogback section of Highway 12 and descends a cattle trail to Boulder Creek, which is followed to its confluence with Deer Creek. A steep, unnamed canyon that starts near the confluence leads back to the trailhead.

To Boulder Creek

(**Calf Creek map** and **Map Seven.**) Hike several hundred yards northeast over a sandy hill and down into a wide, steep, east-running drainage (shown to the east of elevation 5863). Follow it down until you are on a cliff above Boulder Creek. (**Map Eight.**) Cut left a few paces and descend the remnants of a constructed cattle trail to the canyon floor. (0.5 hours.)

Rock climber's note: A short technical slot leads to Boulder Creek. From the trailhead go through a gate in the barb-wire fence. Hike east-southeast into a shallow drainage (shown one-half mile south of elevation 6228). Go downcanyon past a string of large reed-filled potholes. The canyon narrows into a stunning slot. There are several potholes to stem or wade. One of them may be difficult to exit on its far end if water levels are low and you are not able to chimney across it. Be wary!

The last drop is into a huge pothole. Slide five feet into the water and swim across. As always, lower the first person with a rope to check water depth. The slot can also be passed on the right (LDC) by a difficult and exposed climb (Class 5.1, 40'). Pass the next narrow section on the left, then descend a short slab to Boulder Creek. (1.0–1.5 hours.)

Down Boulder Creek

Hike and wade downcanyon. Short stretches of willow thrashing are interspersed with small but delightful pools cut into corrugated slickrock. Good camping and larger swim holes are found near the confluence of Boulder and Deer creeks. (**King Bench map.**) (1.5–2.5 hours.)

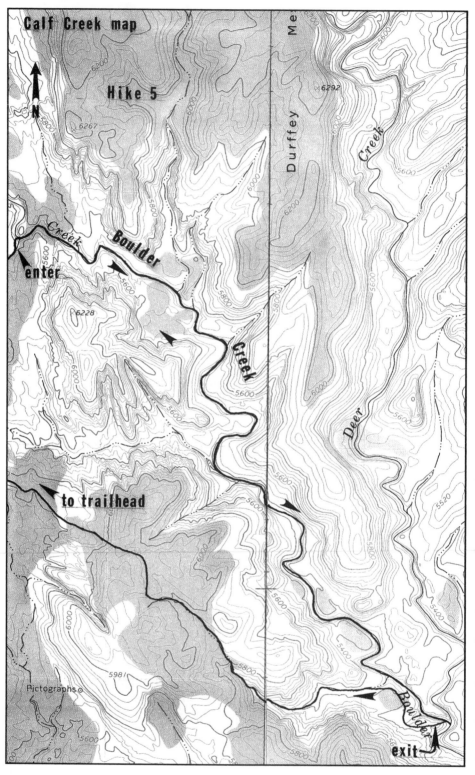

Map Eight

Exit Boulder Creek

From the confluence, hike up the left (LUC)(W) side of Boulder Creek for fifty yards and climb a short slab dotted with worn Moqui steps. Scramble a couple of hundred feet up to the top of the first cliff band. Follow a wide terrace west along the rim of Boulder Creek for fifteen minutes to the first canyon that comes in on the left (W) (shown one-half mile north of elevation 6065).

Follow this steep canyon up through a sharp right-hand turn to its apparent end at a fall. (**Calf Creek map.**) Pass the fall in a gully to the left (LUC), then drop back into the canyon.

The canyon continues to circle to the right, then steepens and narrows. Pinyons, junipers, and buffaloberry bushes line the drainage. Near its head, the canyon divides several times. Stay in the main canyon until it becomes impossible to tell which canyon is the main one. Exit the canyon completely, then make your way northwest to the top of a ridge. Discrepancies here will not matter. Highway 12 and the trailhead will be visible to the west. (2.5–3.5 hours.)

Upper Boulder Creek and Dry Hollow—Hike #6

Season:	Spring before or after spring runoff, summer, or fall.
Time:	4.0 to 6.0 hours.
Elevation range:	5400' to 6120'.
Water:	Water availability is not a problem on this hike. Boulder Creek has a perennial flow of water. Dry Hollow has a seasonal flow.
Map:	Calf Creek.
Skill level:	Easy route finding. Class 2 walking. During periods of high water there will be some wading. This is a moderately easy dayhike.
Special equipment:	Wading boots. There are wild rose bushes on this route; some may wish to wear long pants.
Land status:	This hike is in Grand Staircase-Escalante National Monument.

The newcomer to the Escalante is faced with a daunting task—figuring out which hike to do first! If you have little canyon experience and are looking for a short hike with little chance of getting lost, this is the one. Short stretches of off-trail hiking combine with a lovely creek and the historic Claude V. cutoff road to provide an exemplary canyon experience. This is one of the finest and funnest short dayhikes in the region.

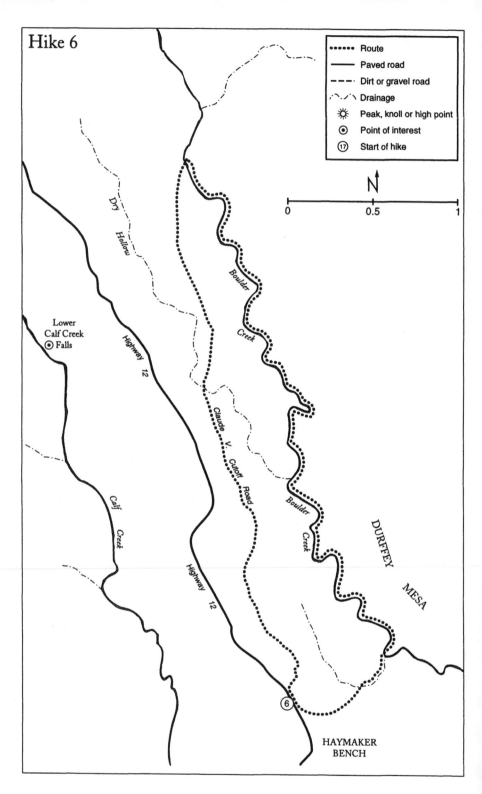

Map Nine

The hike starts on the Hogback section of Highway 12, drops to Boulder Creek, and then follows it upcanyon until near the town of Boulder. The Claude V. cutoff road, an abandoned wagon road, leads back to the trailhead. Although Boulder Creek has been damaged by cattle, the stretch along the old wagon road more than makes up for this.

To Boulder Creek
(**Calf Creek map** and **Map Nine.**) Before you start, look north and locate a road cut on the hillside. You will come down that road at the end of the hike.

Descend a hillside to the east into a wide steep drainage. Follow it down until you are on a cliff above Boulder Creek. Cut left a few paces and descend the remnants of a constructed cattle trail to the canyon floor. (The lower portion of this route into Boulder Creek is also used in Hike #5.)

Up Boulder Creek
Walk and wade upcanyon along sandy benches and through short stretches of willows and wild roses. In forty-five minutes the canyon divides at a sharp corner. The narrow, hard-to-see entrance to Dry Hollow is to the left (W). Boulder Creek, which you will follow, is to the right (NNE).

The canyon slowly widens. After an hour cross a barb-wire fence that stretches across the canyon. Five minutes upcanyon spot a two-strand power line that crosses the canyon. It marks the exit. (2.5–3.5 hours.)

The wagon road
Hike southwest up a steep hillside strewn with lava boulders until you are under the power lines. Follow them uphill (S) to the top of a rise. You will intersect the Claude V. cutoff road here. Dry Hollow and Highway 12 are visible to the south.

> **Historical note:** The Claude V. cutoff road was built in 1924 as a shortcut for those going from Escalante to lower Boulder town. Although primarily traveled by wagons, pack animals, and cattle, automobiles were occasionally used. (See "The Highway 12 Area" chapter for more details on this road.)

Hop a log fence and follow the road to the floor of Dry Hollow. The road is adequately cairned as it crosses sandy areas. If you lose the road, simply follow the course of the power lines.

The road from the bottom of Dry Hollow up the cliffs to the southwest back to the trailhead no longer follows the power lines. If you miss the road, which is easy to do in the thick vegetation of the canyon bottom, cross the stream and hike downcanyon for a couple of hundred yards, then cut west up the hill. You will intersect the road. Near the top, follow cairns up a wide slickrock drainage. At the top of the drainage intersect a track that crosses a sandy pinyon-and-juniper-studded flat and join the final segment of the road that was visible at the start of the trip. (1.5–2.5 hours.)

Old Sheffield Road Section
Access to Hikes #7 through 9.
Access is from Highway 12.
Maps—Tenmile Flat and Red Breaks.

The Old Sheffield road starts at milepost 70.5 on Highway 12 (located at elevation 6001 on the **Tenmile Flat map**). The road is suitable for high-clearance vehicles. There are campsites along the road. (See **Map Five**.)

0.0	—At Highway 12. Go southeast onto the Old Sheffield road.
0.8	—Start of Little Spencer Flat.
1.2	—"Tee." Stay with the main road to the right.
1.7	—Cattle guard.
1.9	—Along a side-cut. The head of Phipps Wash is to the left (NE).
2.0	—Start of Phipps Wash **Hike #7**. Parking is available along the road. You are at the "L" in Sheffield and are in the Carmel Formation.
2.4	—Beehive dome next to the road on the left.
2.7	—Cross a culvert at the bottom of a hill.
2.8	—Start of Big Horn Canyon **Hike #8**. A squat, flat-topped, vertical-walled tower is visible 300 yards to the south-southeast. (It is shown as elevation 5844.) You are in Navajo Sandstone. There is limited parking. Cattle trucks frequent this road. Park off of it.
3.8	—Top of a hill. The three major summits of the Henry Mountains are visible in the far distance.
4.3	—Start across Big Spencer Flats.
4.6	—A solitary sandstone peak is visible to the right (S). A couple of Class 4 routes go to its summit.
5.4	—(**Red Breaks map**.) "Tee." The track to the left (N) goes to the start of **Hike #9**.

Side track to the Escalante River and the Sand Slides Hike #9

0.0 —At the "Tee." Go left (N). (This track is not shown on the map.)

0.9 —Start of the Escalante River and the Sand Slides **Hike #9**. At a parking circle near a drill pipe. There is adequate parking and camping. You are near elevation 5701. The white slickrock is Navajo Sandstone.

End of side track

5.8 —"Y." The Old Sheffield road goes to the left (E). The track turns sandy. You can probably continue driving for another one-half mile.

> **Historical note:** The Charles Hall road to Halls Crossing replaced the difficult Hole-in-the-Rock road. The standard Hall road went from the town of Escalante down Harris Wash; however, when first scouted and laid out by Charles Hall, the road followed the approximate route of the Old Sheffield road across Spencer Flat, descended the Sand Slide to the Escalante River, and went downcanyon to the mouth of Silver Falls Creek.

Phipps Wash—Hike #7

Season: Spring, summer, or fall.

Time: Part 1—4.0 to 5.5 hours.
Part 2—6.5 to 8.5 hours. A long dayhike or a pleasant two-day backpack. Add a couple of hours to visit Phipps Arch, Maverick Natural Bridge, and Bowington Arch.

Elevation range: Part 1—5240' to 6000'.
Part 2—5160' to 6000'.

Water: Water availability is not a problem on these hikes. There is a perennial flow of water in lower Phipps Wash and in the Escalante River. Deer Canyon contains large springs.

Maps: Tenmile Flat and Calf Creek.

Skill level: Part 1—Moderate route finding. Class 4+ climbing with exposure. The leader must be experienced with belay techniques and be capable of leading the climbing section without protection. This is a moderately strenuous hike.
Part 2—Moderately difficult route finding. There is one long cross-country section. Class 3+ scrambling. Some wading. This is a long dayhike or a moderate backpack trip. Overnighters must be familiar with low-impact camping techniques.

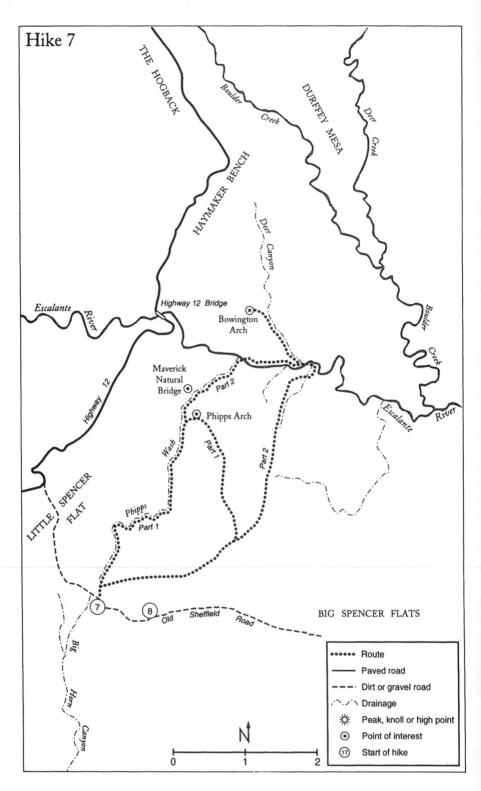

Hike 7

THE HOGBACK

Boulder Creek

DURFFEY MESA

Deer Creek

HAYMAKER BENCH

Deer Canyon

Escalante River

Highway 12 Bridge

Bowington Arch

Boulder Creek

Maverick Natural Bridge

Part 2

Escalante River

Highway 12

Phipps Arch

Wash

Part 1

Part 2

LITTLE SPENCER FLAT

Phipps

Part 1

⑦

⑧ Old Sheffield Road

BIG SPENCER FLATS

Big Horn Canyon

••••• Route
——— Paved road
- - - Dirt or gravel road
·–·–· Drainage
☼ Peak, knoll or high point
⊙ Point of interest
⑰ Start of hike

N

0   1   2

Map Ten

Special equipment:	Part 1—An eighty-foot climbing rope is essential.
	Part 2—Wading shoes or boots. No rope is needed.
Land status:	These hikes are in Grand Staircase-Escalante National Monument.

When we speak of "running the gamut" in canyoneering, we mean a route that has a lot of variety—benchlands, towers, arches, bridges, water, forests, tapestry walls, and more. The word gamut, though, started in the eleventh century as a musical term that defined a specific scale: ut, re, mi, fa, sol, la. The Phipps Wash hike cheerfully encompasses both definitions—it is long on variety and there is a melodic quality throughout. Enjoy.

The hike comes in two parts. Part 1 starts on the Old Sheffield road and goes down Phipps Wash, through Phipps Arch, and returns to the trailhead via a cross-country route.

Part 2 continues down Phipps Wash, detours by Maverick Natural Bridge, and goes to the Escalante River. After following the river downcanyon for a short distance, the route detours to Bowington Arch in Deer Canyon. It returns to the trailhead by way of a cross-country route.

Part 1: Down Phipps Wash

(**Tenmile Flat map** and **Map Ten.**) From the parking area hike northeast for 100 yards to the end of a wide point. Make your way down the right side of the point, cross a fence that is on the left, and go north into the shallow head of Phipps Wash. Follow one of several small washes downcanyon. They slowly converge and the wash deepens. Pass the first fall on the left (LDC)(N). The second drop comes up abruptly and consists of a large red-and-white-banded Navajo slickrock slab that you walk down. Remember this slab. It will be an important landmark on the return trip. In the distance, Phipps Arch is visible in an area of dark red domes to the northnortheast. Unless the light is right, the arch appears to be a large cave.

Follow the drainage down the slab. Near its base look over your left shoulder (WNW). Note a white Navajo tower and a pinnacle to its right on the skyline. These features will be helpful on the return trip.

The third drop is into the main part of Phipps Wash. Pass the fall on the left (N) by scrambling down ledges. You may intersect an old constructed cattle trail near the floor of the canyon. A minute or so downcanyon note a large cowboy glyph on a varnished wall to the right (LDC)(S).

Historical note: Three men etched their names on the wall in 1899. William Alvey, John Justet, and William Osborn were all early inhabitants of Escalante.

In another couple of minutes the North Fork of Phipps Wash comes in on the left (N). Again, note a cowboy glyph on the right from John Justet (April 15, 1899). (1.0–1.5 hours.)

Phipps Arch is a bit tricky to locate. Pay attention to the following details. Ten minutes downcanyon, the first side canyon enters on the right (E).

> **Digression:** The side canyon, lined with boxelder trees, ends in an impressive alcove. (0.5 hours round-trip.)

Continue downcanyon for five minutes. The second side canyon, which contains a large alcove, comes in on the right (E). Phipps Wash narrows and a riparian habitat develops. Cottonwoods, boxelders, Russian-olive trees, coyote willows, rabbitbrush, and virgin's bower vines choke the canyon, but a good path makes the hiking easy. The canyon deepens as it cuts through the Navajo into the slope- and ledge-forming Kayenta Formation. Springs and fine campsites appear now and again.

Thirty minutes from the second side canyon, the third side canyon enters on the right (SE). This marks the start of the trail to Phipps Arch. **(Calf Creek map.)** (1.0 hour.)

For those doing Part 2, the hike up to the arch is a digression. Leave your backpack at the base of the trail. Those doing Part 1 will not return to Phipps Wash.

To Phipps Arch

The trail starts on a slickrock hill on the downcanyon (N) side of the mouth of the side canyon. Follow a heavily cairned trail northeast up steep slickrock (Class 3) to the arch. (The arch is shown on the map.) (0.5 hours.)

> **Historical note:** The arch was named for Washington Phipps, a rancher who was killed by John F. Bowington in November 1878. Phipps and Bowington ran a herd of horses in Escalante Canyon. Locals report that the two men were good friends for a time, but something came between them. They split their camp: Bowington lived on the upper Escalante River; Phipps stayed on the lower Escalante near Phipps Wash. One day, Phipps, in a belligerent mood, approached Bowington and threatened him with a club. After warning him to stop, Bowington shot and killed Phipps. Bowington turned himself in to the local sheriff and was later acquitted.

Back to the trailhead

Walk through the arch, then go north for 200 yards to a short steep slickrock gully that drops from the wall on the right. Scramble up the gully (Class 3+) to a small saddle. Climb southeast up a steep slab (Class 4+, 40', belay), cross the top of a dome, and scramble

Phipps Arch.

down its far side (Class 4, 35', belay). Select a route east across astounding slickrock to the rim of the canyon. If this route is too difficult, simply reverse the hike back to the trailhead.

Look south. You can barely see the top of the white Navajo tower mentioned at the start of the hike. (**Tenmile Flat map.**) Find your own route toward the tower. If you go straight toward it, the way is arduous due to a series of deep washes and small canyons.

You will be better off finding high ground to the east and going over the heads of the washes and canyons. Near the tower you can see the red-and-white-banded Navajo slickrock slab you descended earlier. Follow upper Phipps Wash to the trailhead. (1.5–2.5 hours.)

Part 2: To the Escalante River

(**Calf Creek map.**) Start at the base of the trail to Phipps Arch. Fifteen minutes downcanyon a side canyon comes in on the left (W).

> **Digression:** This narrow tree-lined canyon contains Maverick Natural Bridge. (The bridge is incorrectly marked on the Calf Creek map. It is located in a west-running side canyon that starts between "Phipps" and "Wash.") (0.5 hours round-trip.)

It takes another thirty minutes to reach the Escalante River. There is good camping in the area. (1.0 hours.)

To Deer Canyon

Follow a trail downcanyon along the right side of the river until it encounters a wall, which forces you to cross. Deer Canyon (LKA) comes in on the left (NW) in ten minutes. There is good camping in the vicinity. (Deer Canyon is not named on the map. It contains the labeled Bowington Arch. Do not confuse Deer Canyon with Deer Creek.) (0.5 hours.)

> **Digression:** A path leads northwest up Deer Canyon. This is the type of hidden canyon Zane Grey was so enamored with in his western adventures—a pastoral, spring-lined glen filled with slender pinnacles, imposing towers, huge alcoves, and an abundance of cottonwoods. Pass a large pool and a lush hanging garden on its left side. Above the pool the canyon divides. Stay on the path as it enters the canyon to the left (W). After passing an indent in the wall that is to the left, the trail enters a short side canyon to the left (W). Bowington Arch is visible at the head of the canyon. (1.0–1.5 hours round-trip.)

Out of Escalante Canyon

From the mouth of Deer Canyon go down the Escalante River for two minutes and cross. You will exit the canyon here. Water is not available until back at the trailhead. Load up here.

Hike south-southeast to the foot of the Kayenta cliff. Locate a short section of constructed cattle trail built with logs. This is the only possible way up the cliff in this vicinity. You may have to do some scouting along the wall to find this break. The cattle trail ends in a shallow drainage at the top of the first short cliff. (The drainage is to the north-northeast of elevation 5682). Look southwest. The red slope-forming Kayenta is topped by a wide white Navajo tower. Your goal is to pass the tower on its right (W) side by scrambling up the steep Kayenta slopes. As you near the west side of the tower you will see a short roosterhead-shaped pinnacle behind the tower. Make your way to the pinnacle. Follow a bumpy ridge that divides two small canyons south-southwest to the top of the cliffs. There is one tricky downclimb (Class 3 + , 60') along the ridge. (1.0–1.5 hours.)

Back to the trailhead

Change course to due south. Follow the top of a gentle, sandy, pinyon-and-juniper-covered ridge for twenty-five minutes to a large area of white undulating Navajo slickrock. You can now see the escarpment you started on. (**Tenmile Flat map.**) The second drop described at the start of the hike (the red-and-white-banded slab) will also be visible.

Cross broken ground toward the second drop. Skirt washes and small canyons as necessary. You will lose sight of the second drop; but, as you near the escarpment, the white Navajo tower and pinnacle will appear. Follow upper Phipps Wash back to the trailhead. (2.0–3.0 hours.)

Big Horn Canyon—Hike #8

Season:	Any.
Time:	5.0 to 7.0 hours.
Elevation range:	5160' to 5960'.
Water:	There is no reliable water along this route. Bring your own drinking water.
Map:	Tenmile Flat.
Skill level:	Moderate route finding. Class 3- scrambling. This is a moderate dayhike.
Special equipment:	None.
Land status:	This hike is in Grand Staircase-Escalante National Monument.

When I first started exploring Big Horn Canyon and its environs I found I had stumbled onto a real gem. This rarely visited area contains a diversity of landforms that are unique in the Escalante area—yellow-walled narrows, an area of sand dunes, a singular slot

Ginger Harmon in the exit canyon.

with distinctive horizontal banding, and a peculiar area of "staccato" slickrock (gray rock laced with red intrusions). Although a little long on slogging, the features encountered make this a worthwhile hike.

The route starts on the Old Sheffield road and descends Big Horn Canyon to Harris Wash. An unnamed canyon and a short cross-country stretch through an area of domes leads back to the trailhead.

To Harris Wash

(**Tenmile Flat map** and **Map Eleven.**) From the trailhead go south-southeast, passing the flat-topped dome mentioned in the road section (elevation 5844) on its right (W) side. Enter a shallow wash and follow it downcanyon. In fifteen minutes you reach a fall. Pass it on its left side via a steep slab (Class 4, lots of exposure) or go up and around to the left and descend a gully.

The farther downcanyon you go, the better it gets. Textures and colors are the attraction. Short narrows in the Navajo are interspersed with sandy areas. The occasional drops are all easy to bypass. Colors become kaleidoscopic before the canyon withers into an endless Navajo corridor that empties into Harris Wash. A hanging fence marks the junction. (**Map Twelve.**) (1.5–2.0 hours.)

Down Harris Wash

Hike down Harris Wash. Although this section is not particularly interesting, it is fun to contemplate wagonloads of Mormon pioneers and caravans of supply-laden mules going down the wash on their way to Halls Crossing.

The walls slowly rise and are dominated by Navajo Sandstone topped with thin layers of Page Sandstone and Carmel Formation limestones. Thirty-five minutes from the mouth of Big Horn Canyon a wide side canyon enters on the right (W). This is Cottonwood Wash. Now keep an eye to the right (SW). The first time you clearly see some of the Kaiparowits Plateau through a break in the canyon wall marks the start of the exit route. This is twenty minutes below the mouth of Cottonwood Wash and is 150 yards before the wide mouth of Halfway Hollow, which enters on the right (W). (1.0–1.5 hours.)

> **Geological note:** This is the perfect viewpoint for figuring out Page Sandstone. Look west at the cliffs. On top you can see a thin brown layer of limestone (the Judd Hollow Member of the Carmel Formation). About forty feet below the limestone is a light-colored horizontal band. Above the band is the Harris Wash Tongue of Page Sandstone; below the band is Navajo Sandstone.

Out of Harris Wash

The exit canyon (shown one-quarter mile west of elevation 5579) starts as a wide sandy wash to the left (N). Within a quarter mile the wide wash enters a slot.

> **Digression:** You cannot get all the way through this short slot, but it is worth going up as far as possible if there is not too much water. Photographers favor this exceptional and unique slot.

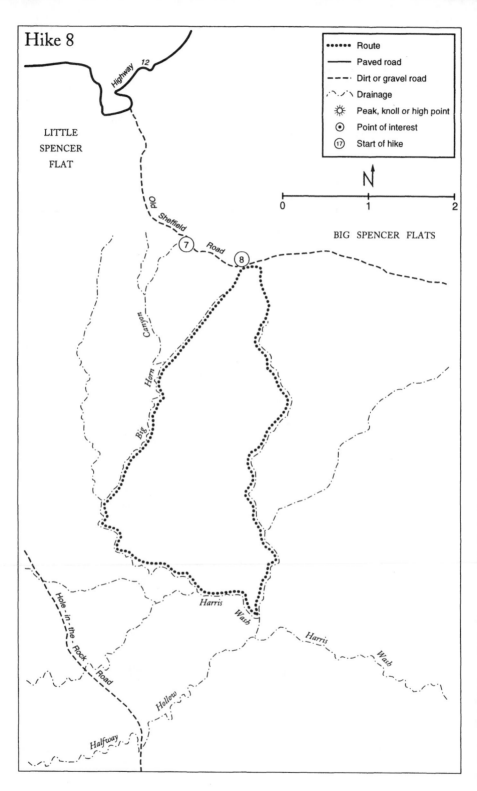

Map Eleven

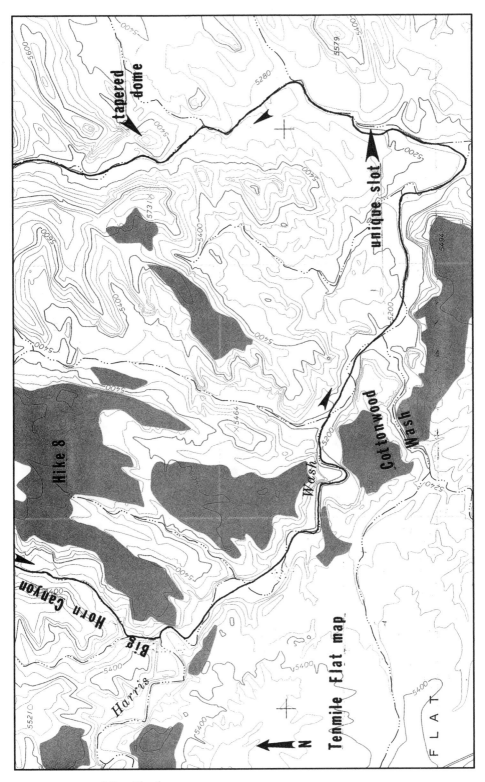

Map Twelve

The exit canyon.

Pass the slot on the left (LUC) by scrambling up a slickrock slab. Make your way along the rim to the top of the slot.

Look north. You will see two distinct tapered domes. (The dome to the left is located a quarter mile to the east of elevation 5731.) Follow the wash until you pass the left dome on its left (W) side. Once past the dome, a long stretch of sand dunes will be to your left.

Follow the wash north-northeast below the dunes. After rounding a corner, the largest sandstone peak in the area will be visible to the northeast. To its left is a mesa with a prominent cave in its middle. Follow various washes and small canyons and pass the prominent cave mesa on its left (W) side. On the way to it you will cross a long stretch of what I call "staccato" rock. Unique and dramatic.

To the trailhead
From the left side of the prominent cave mesa look north. You will see a pointed white dome (elevation 6150) on the far side of a small mesa. Pass the small mesa on its left (S) side. You will intersect an abandoned road that is now occasionally used by off-road vehicles. Follow it to the left (NW) until it ends. Now make your way northwest over a small rise. The trailhead should be visible. Descend a cliff band (several options) back to the start. (If you should get mixed up during any portion of the exit route, simply head north. You will intersect the Old Sheffield road.) (2.5–3.5 hours.)

The Escalante River and the Sand Slides—Hike #9

Season:	Spring, summer, or fall.
Time:	Part 1—10.0 to 14.5 hours. Two to three days. Part 2—12.0 to 16.5 hours. Two to three days.
Elevation range:	Part 1—5000' to 5720'. Part 2—4800' to 5720'.
Water:	Water availability is a problem on these hikes. The Escalante River has a perennial flow of water. The cross-country route back to the trailhead has no water.
Maps:	Part 1—Red Breaks and King Bench. Part 2—Add Silver Falls Bench.
Skill level:	Part 1—Moderately difficult route finding. There is one long cross-country section. Class 3+ scrambling. If the Class 5.0 climb up the "ladders" is planned, the leader must be experienced with belay techniques and be capable of leading the "ladders" pitch without protection. There is a lot of exposure. Lots of wading. This is a moderate hike. Knowledge of low-impact camping techniques is essential. Part 2—Moderately difficult route finding. There is one long cross-country stretch. Class 3+ scrambling. Lots of wading. This is a moderate hike. Knowledge of low-impact camping techniques is essential.

Hike 9

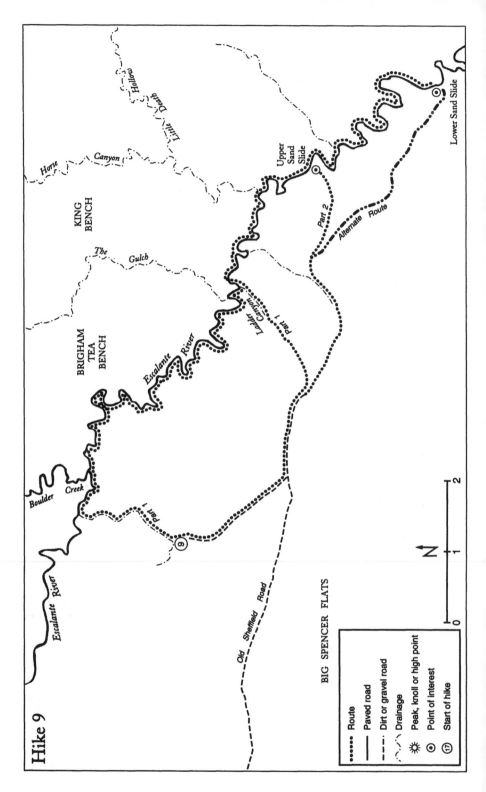

Map Thirteen

Special equipment: Part 1—Wading boots. If you plan to do the "ladders" route, a sixty-foot climbing rope is essential.

Part 2—Wading boots. No rope is needed.

Land status: Part 1—This hike is in Grand Staircase-Escalante National Monument.

Part 2—This hike is in the monument and in Glen Canyon National Recreation Area.

Often the dream of a Homeric "Lotus-land" appears to me while in the backcountry and fights to overwhelm my native instinct to return to the real world. Should I ever eat from the lotus tree and disappear into a world of idleness, this is the area where you'll find me. Interesting route finding, easy wading along the Escalante, a surfeit of historic sites, and an abundance of distractions can keep you occupied for a long time.

The route comes in two parts. Part 1 starts on Big Spencer Flats near the Old Sheffield road and descends an unnamed canyon to the Escalante River. The river is followed down to the mouth of The Gulch. A cross-country route leads back to the trailhead.

Part 2 continues down the Escalante River until you are between Horse Canyon and Harris Wash. You then exit Escalante Canyon by way of either the Upper or Lower Sand Slide. Cross-country routes take you back to the start.

Part 1: To the Escalante River

(**Red Breaks map** and **Map Thirteen.**) From the drill pipe, hike north-northeast down a sandy track across Big Spencer Flats. At the north end of the flats the track goes up to a break in a low Navajo ridge, then turns left (W), and ends in 100 yards. Leave the track before it ends—at the corner—and go northeast through the break into a shallow bowl that contains a tiny drainage (shown to the north-northwest of elevation 5770). Follow the drainage down-canyon as it slowly enlarges and deepens. Obstacles are minor until you reach a high fall where the reddish Navajo gives way to yellow sandstone below. (**King Bench map.**)

It will take some effort and scouting to get around both this fall and a couple more below it. The wash suddenly narrows into a slot lined with potholes. Immediately beyond these is an impassable fall. Backtrack 100 yards to the start of the slot and exit the canyon to the right (LUC)(N) via either of two steep gullies. The upcanyon gully is the easiest.

At the top of the gully you can see the Escalante River. A deer trail that starts 100 yards uphill to the left leads down a cliff to the river. (1.5–2.5 hours.)

The Sheffield cabin.

To Boulder Creek

Following a good trail, walk and wade down the Escalante River. Boulder Creek enters from the left (W). Its mouth is blocked by vegetation and can be hard to see. There is poor camping in the immediate area. If the river is muddy, obtain clear water from Boulder Creek. (1.0 hour.)

To The Gulch

Boulder Creek can nearly double the flow of water in the Escalante River, especially during spring runoff and after big rains. Lava rocks washed down Boulder Canyon from Boulder Mountain make the river crossings harder. Fifteen minutes below the mouth of Boulder Creek cross a barb-wire fence. A wall to the right bears a cowboy glyph from Bille D. Wooley and J. H. Barney dated February 30, 1907. Both were area stockmen.

Four minutes past the fence, and 100 yards after crossing the river once, locate an inconspicuous cattle trail going up the slickrock to the left (N). A wood fence partway up is easier to see than the trail.

> **To the Overland Route:** To intersect the section of the Overland Route that runs between Highway 12 and Silver Falls Creek, hike up the cattle trail to an old line shack. Join the Overland Route at this point. Note that the location of the line shack is shown correctly on the USGS map, but the trail to it is not accurate. Instead of going down a point to the southeast of the shack, the trail goes down the point to the southwest.

Continue down the river. A side canyon to the north (shown to the southwest of elevation 5441) a couple of minutes past the bottom of the cattle trail contains a large spring. The canyon below narrows considerably. This is the narrowest section of the Escalante River. Past the narrows and after rounding a corner with a huge sand beach, look for an unapproachable cliff dwelling on a wall to the right (N). Several minutes below the dwelling cross a barb-wire fence.

Digression: Just before the fence, to the north, is a constructed cattle trail that leads to Brigham Tea Bench.

(Red Breaks map.) The next landmark worthy of note is a side canyon that comes in on the right (SW) in two hours. Its mouth, a narrow defile, leads into a short canyon that contains a large spring. (The canyon is located to the south of elevation 5355.)

An hour downcanyon The Gulch enters from the left (NW). Its mouth is a bit hard to see. There is poor camping in the area and The Gulch may or may not have clear water. **(Map Fourteen.)** (3.5–5.0 hours.)

To the ladders exit

After recent rains red water from The Gulch will cloud the Escalante River, making the going more hazardous, though the silt brought down the creek does help smooth out the floor of the stream. More petrified wood also becomes evident.

Ten minutes below the mouth of The Gulch a side canyon enters on the right (S). A thick stand of cottonwoods hides its mouth. This is the "ladders" canyon (shown one-half mile south of elevation 5365). There are now two choices for exiting Escalante Canyon. The first is easier and safer. The second, presented as a rock climber's note below, is the "ladders" route. It is dicey but fun. Whichever route you choose, load up with water before leaving the river.

From the mouth of the "ladders" drainage go downcanyon for a couple of minutes, crossing the river twice. Immediately before a sharp right corner (shown one-half mile south-southeast of elevation 5365) ascend a steep gully to the east. (If you go too far downcanyon, you will intersect a barb-wire fence. Backtrack for ten minutes.)

From the top of the gully find a break in the upper cliffs a couple of hundred yards to the east. You may find a faded row of Moqui steps on a short slab (Class 3 +). Follow the rim of the "ladders" canyon to its head near the ladders. Now follow the shallow canyon southwest through the cliffs (there are a couple of options) to a large plain. (You will end up near elevation 5520.) (1.5–2.5 hours.)

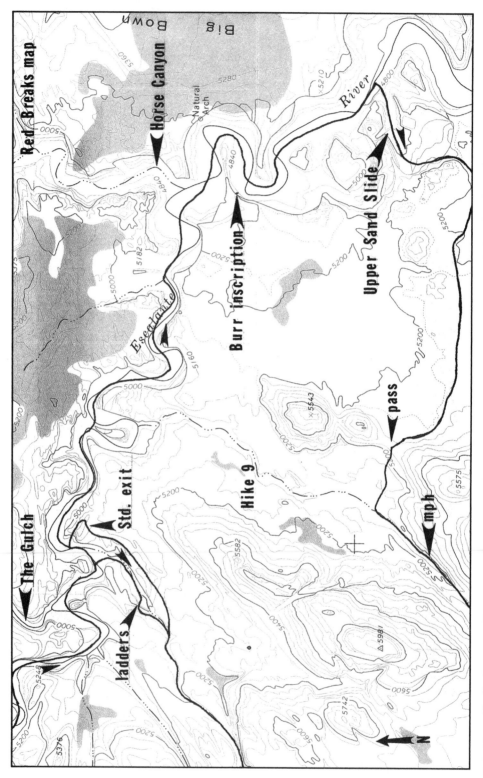

Map Fourteen

Rock climber's note: Hike south up the "ladders" canyon until near its head. You will plainly see two aluminum ladders on a wall to the right. Climb the ladders (Class 5.0, 35'), then join the standard route.

Warning: The ladders were installed by a youth group several years ago. You must decide if they are safe or not. If you deem them unreliable, use the standard route. Belays must be used. It is possible that the ladders will be removed in the future.

To the trailhead

To the southwest is a long, low cliff band. Hike west across the plain parallel to the cliff until you intersect the Old Sheffield road, which at this point is a sandy track. You can now either follow the road or cut away from the track and head directly for the trailhead. Since the track is very sandy, it is not easy to walk it, although it is reassuring. (2.5–3.5 hours.)

Part 2: To Horse Canyon

(Red Breaks map.) From the mouth of the "ladders" canyon continue downriver. The next stretch has easy walking and is remarkable for its stunning tapestry walls. Horse Canyon, with its wide and plainly visible mouth, enters on the left (NE). This marks the start of the dark red, slope- and ledge-forming Kayenta Formation. There is good camping near the canyon's mouth, which usually has clear water. (2.0–2.5 hours.)

To the Upper Sand Slide exit route

One turn below Horse Canyon note an arch on the skyline to the left. After rounding a long peninsula (elevation 4840), look for the inscription "JA Burr 1891" on a wall to the west.

Historical note: The story of John Atlantic Burr is recounted under the historical note in the Burr Trail Road Section.

Several minutes past the Burr inscription note a sand dune and an abandoned meander to the right (located one-quarter mile west of elevation 5210). This dune is not significant, except that you do not want to confuse it with the next dune downcanyon, which is important.

Ten minutes below the first dune, keep a lookout for a second sand dune dropping from the right (SW). A tower divides the dune, and from the canyon floor you cannot see its top. (The dune is located one-half mile south of elevation 5210 at the second "r" in River.)

This dune, locally known as the Upper Sand Slide, was part of a historic trail and is used as the exit route. The Lower Sand Slide exit route is presented as an Alternate route below.

Exit Escalante Canyon via the Upper Sand Slide

Sweat up the dune and exit at its highest point.

Historical note: Before topping the dune, look 150 yards to the left (E). You will see the original wagon trail cutting along a wall. The last eight feet, now a vertical wall, was once filled with riprap. Near the drop are extensive cowboy glyphs dating from 1902.

Walk west over a rise. Before you (W) is a large, pink, pointed dome (elevation 5932). To its right (N) is a smaller dome, and to its right a larger dome (elevation 5543). Go to a pass between the pink, pointed dome and the smaller dome. Drop southwest into a southwest-running drainage that cuts between several large domes (elevations 5932 and 5981). (1.0–1.5 hours.)

To the trailhead

Hike up the southwest-running drainage. It contains a string of medium potholes and there is good camping in the area. This short drainage passes through the large domes and fizzles in the sand. You are now on a plain that gently rises to the west-northwest. On either side are lines of Navajo domes.

Head west-northwest up the plain between the cliffs for a couple of miles. Your goal is to intersect the Old Sheffield road. (It is labeled on the map.) You will not miss it. Now join the last part of Part 1 and return to the trailhead. (3.0–4.0 hours.)

Alternate route: From the base of the Upper Sand Slide go downriver for a half hour. A huge pasture on the right (at elevation 4760) with a short steep-walled side canyon on its west side is Sheffield's Bend, the site of the Sheffield cabin. The cabin's chimney, which is all that remains, is located near the mouth of the side canyon next to a large reed-lined spring. At the back of the canyon a long, worn row of Moqui steps leads up a steep prow that divides Sheffield's Alcove. Fun to view from a distance, the steps are too steep to climb.

Historical note: Sam Sheffield moved from Colorado to Boulder in 1889. He is credited as being the first white man to plant corn in Boulder Valley and with discovering the Coombs site. It is unclear when Sheffield built the cabin. In 1895 Sam Sheffield's sister Josepha, her husband Cal Gresham, and their four children lived on the bend.

Continue down the river. **(Silver Falls Bench map.)** The Lower Sand Slide is about two hours from the Sheffield cabin site. It climbs a wall to the southwest. You will not miss this intimidating obstacle! (It is located one-quarter mile south of elevation 5162AT.) (2.0–2.5 hours.)

Digression: A cattle trail that goes northeast up to Big Bown Bench starts across the river from the Lower Sand Slide. It is immediately north of a side canyon shown to the east of elevation 5162AT.

Make your way up the Lower Sand Slide to a log fence at its top. Hike west to the top of a rise. In the distance you will see a pink, pointed dome (elevation 5932 on the **Red Breaks map**). Behind it and to its right is a flat-topped dome (elevation 5981). Your goal is to hike across rolling terrain to the right (N) side of the pink, pointed dome. As you get closer to it, you will see a small dome on its right (N) side and to its north a large dome (elevation 5543). Enter a pass between the pink, pointed dome and the smaller dome. Join the standard Part 2 route here. (1.5–2.5 hours.)

III
Hole-In-The-Rock—The Western Escalante

The western Escalante region is bounded by Highway 12 on the north, the Escalante River on the east, Lake Powell on the south, and the Kaiparowits Plateau on the west. The Hole-in-the-Rock road cuts through the area and provides access to the many canyons that begin in the shadow of the massive Straight Cliffs. Although the region is dominated by Escalante Canyon, it is the side canyons that are the real attraction. Varying from the lush flat-floored Harris Wash and the vertiginous-walled splendor of Coyote Gulch to the narrowest of crevices like Brimstone Gulch and Egypt 3, these canyons provide canyoneers of all ability levels ample opportunities for exploration.

The lower portions of the Escalante were home to the first influx of Anasazi Indians during the late Basketmaker II period (approximately A.D. 500). Over a period of centuries they slowly made their way up the main canyon and eventually visited or occupied nearly every side canyon and small drainage in the area. Many Anasazi found the high plateau country of the Kaiparowits to their liking and it became the most densely populated region outside the San Juan River basin.

Later, Piute Indians, who subsisted on hunting and gathering, settled in the region. Starting in the mid-1800s, Navajo Indians crossed the Colorado River and herded their sheep throughout the area, leaving behind many constructed trails that backpackers still use.

The western Escalante was partially opened by the early Mormon settlers who grazed their animals on the abundant grass that used to cover the now nearly barren hills. It was not until members of the Hole-in-the-Rock expedition built a wagon road below the Straight Cliffs from Escalante to the Colorado River that the area was truly revealed.

The number of livestock that ranged the area increased dramatically, rising to a high of 20,000 head of cattle and 60,000 sheep near the turn of the century. Overgrazing became a serious problem. It was during this time when the ranchers were seeking every available morsel of feed for their animals that most of the livestock trails leading to remote benches or canyons were built. Cattlemen often said that to find the easiest path from the canyon to its rim, they would simply put a hay bale on top. The cows would find the best way.

The Hole-in-the-Rock road has slowly improved over the years, and although it is no longer the adventure to travel that it once was, it still leads into terrific country.

The Hole-In-The-Rock Expedition

Monday, Oct. 20th, 1879. Spent most of the day in loading my wagons, and in the evening sold my house and lot to Geo. Lovell for a span of mules and harness and $100.00 in money.
Tuesday, Oct. 21st, 1879. Started in the afternoon for [the] San Juan....

From the journal of Platte D. Lyman

Although many are familiar with the epic Hole-in-the-Rock expedition, it is important to describe it in a historical context. According to Mormon belief, the story starts in ancient times on the American continent with the prophet and historian Mormon, who, some time after the resurrection of Christ, inscribed the history of his people along with the words of many ancient prophets and Jesus Christ onto golden plates. The plates were passed to Mormon's son Moroni, who added to them and then hid them in a hill in what is now upstate New York.

It was on this hillside, on September 1, 1823, that Moroni came as an angelic being to Joseph Smith and showed him the golden plates, later giving him the power to translate them. This was the start of the Mormon religion. Smith was able to gather followers for his new religion but, because of some of the Mormon claims and beliefs, there was a strong anti-Mormon backlash. The Mormons found themselves castigated by their neighbors.

This started a twenty-five-year search by the followers of Joseph Smith for a home free from persecution. Their first stop was in Kirtland, Ohio. After several years they moved to Far West, Missouri, a town that, according to Mormon doctrine, was their Zion. Doctrine or not, the Mormons soon were forced out by unsympathetic townspeople.

The next move was to Nauvoo, a town founded by the Mormons in Illinois. It was near there that Joseph Smith was killed in 1844 after offending locals by ordering a local opposition printing press destroyed. Now under the leadership of Brigham Young, the Mormons moved to Council Bluffs, Iowa.

Council Bluffs, and Winter Quarters, Nebraska, near present-day Omaha, were to be used as staging areas for the last segment of the Mormon pilgrimage—crossing the Great American Desert to Utah's Great Salt Lake. This portion of the odyssey—from Council Bluffs to the Great Salt Lake—took two years, from 1846 through 1847. It involved 14,000 people as well as wagons, horses, cattle, and miscellaneous livestock.

Salt Lake was not Zion, but it did have several distinct advantages over the other towns the Mormons had lived in. The area between the Great Salt Lake and the Wasatch Mountains to the east had been explored. The famous trapper Jedediah Smith, and others, had written of the fertile valley. Although a branch of the Old Spanish Trail cut near the area, it was still remote and only sparsely inhabited.

Brigham Young realized that the Mormons would have to colonize as much of their new land as possible. There were several reasons for this. First, the federal government wanted to control the land, not because it needed it, but because it did not want the Mormons to dominate it. Young wanted the Mormons to take possession quickly before the government could formalize its opposition. Second, the land in Utah was sparsely populated and was considered free for the taking. The third factor was the burgeoning Mormon population. Finally, Young understood that by establishing settlements throughout the country, he could create a buffer to hold back the gentiles, or non-Mormons.

Colonization in southern Utah was very successful, although not necessarily for the reasons the settlements were initially established. Called "missions," settlement efforts were organized and financed by the Mormon church.

The first sizeable mission was the Iron Mission of 1850, which established the towns of Cedar City and Parowan. There were good iron-ore deposits in the area and an abundance of juniper (which they called cedar), which was turned into the coke used to fire iron smelters. Unfortunately the Iron Mission was not successful in making quality pig iron; there was a problem with the smelting process that was never solved. Nonetheless, the new settlers were able to farm and to utilize the rangelands in the area.

The second was the Cotton, or Dixie, Mission of the late 1850s, which was centered around the town of St. George. The Cotton Mission was formed in response to the Civil War to produce cotton and grapes for wine. Brigham Young thought that the land in the Virgin River Basin would be good for these crops. Unfortunately the Dixie Mission was not economically successful; but, like the Iron Mission, it did open a large area to farming and ranching. The settlements of Kanab and St. George were results of the Dixie Mission.

The Iron and Dixie missions were located on the west side of the Colorado River. The land to the east, between the Uncompahgre and San Juan mountains in Colorado and the Colorado River in Utah, was largely uninhabited. The gold and silver booms in Colorado brought a trickle of prospectors and ranchers into the desert country to the east of the river. The only other residents were Indians and outlaw whites. Although lightly populated with settlers, Brigham Young knew that it was just a matter of time before non-Mormons could gain control of this vital region. A buffer of Mormon settlements would slow or stop the encroachment.

Brigham Young envisioned a colony in the San Juan River drainage. Scouting reports from the area were promising and Young needed a solid settlement to provide a toehold in the new country. Before Young was able to act on his dream, however, he died. Leadership of the Mormon Church was passed to Apostle Erastus Snow, and in 1877 he ordered a mission to explore the country.

The initial San Juan Mission could be considered a reconnaissance party. It consisted of twenty-six men, two women, eight children, and a small herd of cattle. The explorers, led by Silas S. Smith, left Paragonah in April 1879. Going south, they passed through present-day landmarks of the Sevier River Valley including the towns of Hillsdale and Alton, Horse Rock Spring, and Jacobs Pool before crossing the Colorado River at Lee's Ferry.

They continued south to Moenkopi, then turned north and east through Navajo Indian country, passing Red Lake, Cow Spring, Cave Spring, Kayenta, and Montezuma. The settlers finally arrived in Bluff, their final destination, about the first of June, having covered 500 miles. Several months were spent exploring the surrounding country, laying out a townsite, clearing farmland, and building houses. Some of the expedition members returned to Paragonah, following the northern route of the Old Spanish Trail.

After the explorations by the San Juan Mission members, it was decided that a new route was needed—the original route was too long, did not have reliable water, and was threatened by hostile Indians. The northern route of the Old Spanish Trail via Salina Canyon, Green River, and Moab was well traveled, but it was 450 miles long. By comparison, a direct line between Cedar City and Bluff was only 205 miles.

Andrew P. Schow, Reuben Collett, and Charles Hall, all residents of the new town of Escalante, were given the task of finding a route across the Escalante Desert and the Colorado River. Hall traveled to the rim of Glen Canyon by himself and is credited with the actual discovery of the Hole-in-the-Rock. He was able to look up Cottonwood Wash on the east side of the river and, seeing no problems, stated in his report to church leaders that, "It would be something of a problem to get wagons down to the river, but once down and across, it would be a simple matter to move on to the San Juan, about sixty miles away."

Schow and Collett conducted their own survey of the country. They hauled a small boat on a two-wheeled cart to the escarpment overlooking Glen Canyon at Hole-in-the-Rock. Following the rim north for a couple of miles, they discovered a route to the Colorado River near what is now called the Jackass Bench Trail. After ferrying across the river, they hiked several miles up Cottonwood Wash. Finding no major impediments, Schow and Collett returned to Escalante and reported favorably on the route.

Mission members were anxious to head for the San Juan town-site as quickly as possible in order to have enough time to prepare for spring planting. Expecting the trek to take six weeks, the October 1879 start did not seem too late in the season. Many small groups of settlers were instructed to meet in the desert east of Escalante. A good wagon road had been established as far as Tenmile Spring, which is in Harris Wash. This was to be the first camp of the trek. Because of a scarcity of feed for their animals, some of the late-arriving settlers went down Harris Wash to the Harris Ranch on the Escalante River.

The pace of the expedition slowed after the wagon road ended. Cattle trails were followed, but considerable energy was required to cross the many small washes along the route. Twentymile Spring (now called Collett Wash) was the second camp, and Coyote Holes was the third. Each camp was about a day's journey, or ten miles, apart. Water and feed were problematic, but the expedition proceeded smoothly.

The fourth camp was at Fortymile Spring near Dance Hall Rock. This was the eventual meeting place for all the settlers. Wagons started to assemble there in mid-November. By the time the whole entourage had gathered, it consisted of 250 settlers, 1,800 head of livestock, and eighty-three wagons.

Trip leaders soon realized that the explorations by Hall, Schow, and Collett of the country to the east had not been thorough. An easy traverse of the Colorado River could not be found. In trouble, the expedition ground to a halt even as more settlers arrived.

Several scouting parties were sent out, but all found the country nearly impassable. Unfortunately, the trail back to the town of Escalante was now snowed in. Though retreat was considered, it was not thought to be a viable option. The wagons could not make it through the snow and the livestock most likely would be lost as well. The Hole-in-the-Rock route was chosen simply because it was the lesser of many evils.

From Fortymile Spring to Fiftymile Spring the going was exceptionally difficult. Unfamiliar with side-cuts and switchbacks, the pioneers excavated dugways across washes and small canyons.

The group divided at Fiftymile Spring. Those working to widen the Hole-in-the-Rock for passage moved close to the canyon edge. The others stayed near the spring. A smaller group was sent across the river to prepare a long dugway out of Glen Canyon into Cottonwood Canyon.

For two months the settlers worked at building the road down to the river. The obstacles were enormous. The first section of the Hole-in-the-Rock was a vertical fifty-foot-tall solid rock slit too thin for a man to squeeze through. During initial construction, the men hung from ropes while working with picks or drilling holes for dynamite.

Lower down, one section of the road was constructed by cantilevering it out over a steep ramp with oak supports placed in drilled holes. This was named Uncle Ben's Dugway after its engineer, Benjamin Perkins. Other sections were widened and most of the ramp was smoothed with fill.

At the end of January 1879 the wagons were lowered through the Hole-in-the-Rock. Though much subsequently has been made of getting the wagons down, most were at the Colorado River by the end of the first day. After cross-locking the wheels with chains to keep them from turning, ropes from the rear axle were run around a juniper post embedded in the ground. The men then belayed the wagons down the initial chute.

Nathaniel Z. Decker described the descent: "...putting mother and us five children out, he [Decker's father] seated himself on the front wagon and started. Down they went in a flash and landed in the soft ground at the end of the slick rock slide...but one big mule was dragged and seriously hurt. How mother and the rest of the kiddies got down without harm; I suppose they were too scared to get hurt. I could scarcely keep my feet under me it was so steep and slick..."

Once they were across the river the hardships were hardly over. Road workers had already blasted a 250-foot-high ramp from the river up a sheer cliff to Cottonwood Canyon. A short, easy traverse up Cottonwood Canyon ended at Cottonwood Hill where difficult country slowed the expedition. The Little-Hole-in-the-Wall, another steep slope almost as severe as the original Hole, went out of Cottonwood Canyon to Little Mesa.

After crossing Little Mesa, the trail builders forced a passage to the top of Grey Mesa. Another dugway was built down its north side, and easy terrain led to Lake Pagahrit, which was formed by a natural dam in Lake Canyon.

Clay Hills Pass was the next problem. A three-mile-long trail was excavated down the thousand-foot-tall mud cliff, causing a week-long delay. Comb Ridge, a steep sandstone cliff near the San Juan River, was the last major problem. A road was blasted up the precipice, which is now called San Juan Hill. After planning for a six-week trek, the expedition finally arrived in Bluff six months later, in April 1880; however, no lives were lost and three babies were born.

Contrary to popular belief, the expedition was not cut off from help. Money to support the expedition was raised throughout Mormon country. Great interest was shown by outsiders and newspapers reported on progress. Food and dynamite were brought in from Escalante. Townspeople from neighboring communities gave assistance and watched the proceedings.

Modern-day hikers can only get a taste of what the Hole-in-the-Rock was really like. Several large boulders now choke the upper sections and the fill that smoothed the ramp has long since washed away. A careful search, especially ten to twenty feet above the present floor, will reveal signs of the old trail.

Hole-In-The-Rock Road Section
Access to Hikes #10 through 29.
Access is from Highway 12.
Provides access to the Harris Wash road, Egypt road, Early Weed
 Bench road, Dry Fork Coyote road, Red Well road, Hurricane
 Wash trailhead, and the Fortymile Ridge road.
Maps—Dave Canyon, Tenmile Flat, Seep Flat, Sunset Flat, Basin
 Canyon, Big Hollow Wash, Sooner Bench, and Davis Gulch.

The Hole-in-the-Rock road starts at mile 64.8 on Highway 12 (located at elevation 5740 on the **Dave Canyon map**). The road is suitable for high clearance vehicles to mile 50.8. From there to the Hole-in-the-Rock is for 4WDs only. This is a long, rough road. Make sure to carry plenty of gas and water. There is camping near the road. (See **Map Fifteen**.)

> **Note:** The Hole-in-the-Rock road traverses the area under the eastern escarpment of the Kaiparowits Plateau. The many names used to describe the Kaiparowits Plateau often are confusing to the first-time visitor. The whole upland area is commonly called the Kaiparowits Plateau even though the actual plateau is several miles to the west of the near-vertical cliffs facing you as you drive down the Hole-in-the-Rock road. The near-vertical cliffs are called the Straight Cliffs, though the section between Escalante and the Collet Top road (at mile 13.7) is also called the Escalante Rim. Beyond Collet Top, the highlands above the Straight Cliffs are named Fiftymile Mountain. Throughout the guide I have used the names Fiftymile Mountain and the Kaiparowits Plateau interchangeably.

0.0 —On Highway 12 at the start of the signed Hole-in-the-Rock road. Go southeast.

3.3 —(**Tenmile Flat map**.) "Tee." Signed road to Cedar Wash on the right (S). This road goes to Cedar Wash Arch and Covered Wagon Natural Bridge.

Side road to Cedar Wash Arch and Covered Wagon Natural Bridge

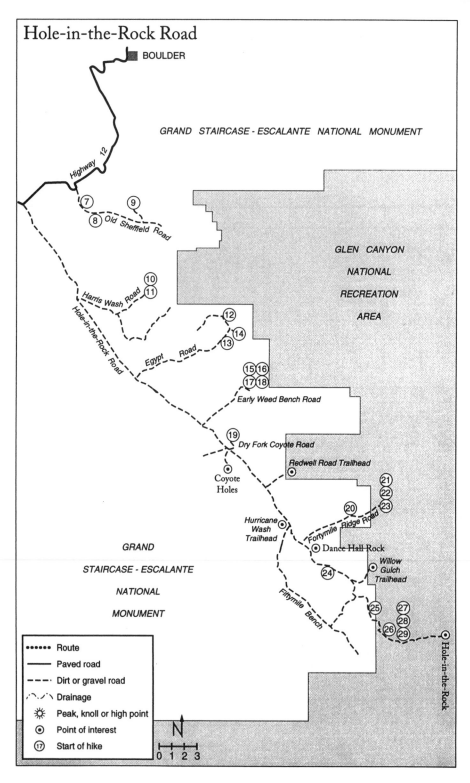

Hole-in-the-Rock Road

BOULDER

GRAND STAIRCASE - ESCALANTE NATIONAL MONUMENT

Highway 12

GLEN CANYON

NATIONAL

RECREATION

AREA

⑦
⑨
⑧ Old Sheffield Road

⑩
⑪
Harris Wash Road

Hole-in-the-Rock Road

⑫
⑭
⑬
Egypt Road

⑮⑯
⑰⑱
Early Weed Bench Road

⑲
Dry Fork Coyote Road

Redwell Road Trailhead

Coyote
Holes

㉑
㉒
㉓

⑳
Fortymile Ridge Road

Hurricane
Wash
Trailhead

GRAND

STAIRCASE - ESCALANTE

NATIONAL

MONUMENT

Dance Hall Rock

Willow
Gulch
Trailhead

㉔

Fiftymile Bench

㉕
㉗
㉘
㉖㉙

Hole-in-the-Rock

Route
Paved road
Dirt or gravel road
Drainage
Peak, knoll or high point
Point of interest
⑰ Start of hike

N

0 1 2 3

Map Fifteen

0.0	—Go right (S).
0.3	—Cross Alvey Wash.
0.9	—(**Dave Canyon map.**) Cattle guard.
2.1	—Water tank on hillside to the right (W).
2.9	—Wire fence starts next to the track on the right.
3.4	—Vague track enters on the left (NE). Park here. Hike southeast over a low hill for a couple of minutes to the rim of a white-walled canyon. Cedar Wash Arch is located in a fin on the north side of the canyon.
4.4	—Cattle guard.
4.7	—Outside of a bend. A vague track goes west down the hillside on the left. Hike down the track into a ravine to Covered Wagon Natural Bridge.
10.9	—Road turns to pavement.
13.9	—Escalante.

End of side road

4.0	—Cattle guard.
4.2	—Signed Tenmile Wash. The upper part of Tenmile Wash is called Alvey Wash. Tenmile Spring, a short walk downcanyon, is considered the start of Harris Wash.
	The Hole-in-the-Rock expedition used Tenmile Spring—which is ten miles from Escalante—for their first campsite. Expedition member George Decker wrote in his diary: "Moved to 10 Miles Gulch, feed scarce, water up." A wagon road developed by ranchers ended at Tenmile Spring. A single-track trail continued on. The going started to get rough.
4.3	—Corral on right.
7.3	—Deadman Ridge is a small hill to the right (W). Myron Shurts, a local rancher, was struck and killed by lightning on the ridge in 1912.
7.9	—Cattle guard.
10.5	—(**Seep Flat map.**) "Tee." Signed Harris Wash road on the left (SE). This road provides access to **Hikes #10 and 11**. See the Harris Wash Road Section for details.
11.5	—Across Seep Flat. Water seeps from the base of the Straight Cliffs onto the flats.

12.1	—"Tee." Signed Devils Garden road on the right (S). The first documented visit to this wonderful area was by Jack Sumner, a member of the Thompson-Dellenbaugh expedition in 1872. There is no evidence that the Hole-in-the-Rock trekkers saw the area. Strange "hoodoo" shapes and Metate Arch make this a great place to wander. Escalante schoolteacher Edson Alvey named both Devils Garden and Metate Arch. There are picnic tables, grills, and an outhouse. No overnight camping.
13.7	—"Tee." Signed Collet Top road on the right (SE).
14.2	—Signed Twenty Mile Wash. A spring a short distance up the wash marked the second camp for the Hole-in-the-Rock expedition. Again, George Decker: "Up to 20 Mile Gulch, feed good water bad." The trekkers had to dig in the sand to procure sufficient water.
14.3	—Cattle guard.
16.5	—(**Sunset Flat map.**) "Tee." Signed Egypt road on the left (NE). This road provides access to **Hikes #12 through 14** and to the Twentyfive Mile Wash trailhead. See the Egypt Road Section for details.
16.6	—Garfield County/Kane County line.
17.0	—Cross Rat Seep Hollow. The name comes from a small seep in the hollow that was often full of dead rats.
17.3	—Onto Sunset Flat. Local ranchers named this large, flat area. The jutting bench to the right (SE) that drops off the Straight Cliffs almost to the Hole-in-the-Rock road is called White Point.
19.8	—"Tee." Track to the left (E). Sign states "Caution 4 Wheel Drive Only." This track provides alternate, and rough, access to the Early Weed Bench trailhead.
23.5	—(**Basin Canyon map.**) Signed Cat Pasture. Cat Pasture, named for an abundance of bobcats that used to inhabit the area, is to the left (NE).
23.6	—"Tee." Signed Early Weed Bench road on the left (ESE). This road provides access to **Hikes #15 through 18**. See the Early Weed Bench Road Section for details.
23.8	—Cattle guard. Corral on the right.
24.0	—Cattle guard. Cat Well is to the left. The wash to the left (N) is the head of Dry Fork Coyote.
25.9	—(**Big Hollow Wash map.**) Four-way junction. Signed Dry Fork track to the left (E). This track provides access to **Hike #19**. See the Dry Fork Coyote Road Section for details.

A large bench below the Straight Cliffs to the south is called Fiftymile Bench.

The track to the right (SW) goes to Batty Pass Caves. A sign at its start states "Dead End Road." Follow the main track for 2.3 miles to a junked car on the left. Three large caverns on a ledge to the left were excavated in the mid-1950s by Bill and Cliff Lichtenhahn. The brothers filled the caves with machinery that they used to cut and polish rock and to build lapidary machines for others. The partially completed hull of a boat they planned to use on Lake Powell sits in one cave.

26.0	—"Tee." Track to the right (S) goes to Coyote Holes. High-clearance vehicles can follow the track for 1.1 miles, past a corral and windmill, to a washout. 4WD vehicles can continue for about another mile to Coyote Holes at the end of the track. It is now a dry wash lined with tamarisks. This was the location of the Hole-in-the-Rock expedition's third camp. They had to dig for water at the Holes.
28.2	—Cattle guard.
28.8	—Cross Big Hollow Wash. The USGS Board on Geographic Names named it Big Hollow Wash because, "The dry drain or hollow was the widest (biggest) at the point of crossing in the days of wagon travel."
30.2	—"Tee." Short track to the left (E) goes to Liston Seep, named for a large extended family who moved to Escalante in the 1880s.
30.7	—"Tee." Signed Red Well track on the left (NE). See the Red Well Road Section for details.
31.0	—Cattle guard. Track to the left goes to a line shack and Red Well.
32.9	—"Tee." Signed 4WD track to Chimney Rock on the left (NE).
33.6	—Cattle guard. Line shack at Willow Tank is to the left.
33.8	—Signed Hurricane Wash trailhead by the side of the road on the right. See the Hurricane Wash Trailhead Road Section for details.
34.1	—"Tee." Signed "50 Mile Bench" track to the right (SW). This road is very steep and is not recommended for access to Fiftymile Bench. Use the Sooner Slide road (at mile 43.4) instead.
34.8	—(**Sooner Bench map.**) Cross the south fork of Hurricane Wash. A section of the original Hole-in-the-Rock road cuts across the switchbacks.
36.1	—"Tee." Signed "40 Mile Ridge" track to the left (NE). This track provides access to **Hikes #20 through 23**. See the Fortymile Ridge Road Section for details.

36.8 —"Tee." Signed Dance Hall Rock track to the left (E). Dance Hall Rock was used by Hole-in-the-Rock members for dances while they were camped at Fortymile Spring. The hall, and the surrounding domes, are carved from Entrada Sandstone. The area is perfect for wandering and exploring.

37.0 —Cattle guard.

37.5 —"Tee." Signed "40 Mile Spring" track to the left (E). A spring, nestled in an Entrada Sandstone bowl, is 1.1 miles down the track.

The Hole-in-the-Rock expedition, finding the best water they had encountered since leaving Escalante at Fortymile Spring, tarried here for three weeks while a scouting party explored the route ahead. This pause in the trek allowed new members to catch up to the main group. Boredom was relieved by hiking up the wash to Dance Hall Rock. Forage for livestock was a major problem and pastures ranging from the Escalante River to the base of the Straight Cliffs were sought out.

The road ahead, as you will see, became much harder to negotiate. Large washes and deep draws hindered progress. Trip member Platte DeAlton Lyman wrote in his diary: "We drove 10 miles [from Fortymile Spring] over the roughest country I ever saw a wagon go over and camped at the 50 mile spring."

39.5 —Signed Carcass Wash. A monument on the right tells the story of a tragedy that occurred here in June 1963. A group of Explorer Scouts from Salt Lake City were being shuttled to the Hole-in-the-Rock, where they were to take a river trip through Glen Canyon. The truck they were in lost control and rolled down the hill. Thirteen young men lost their lives and twenty-six were injured in the accident.

40.6 —Start of Fortymile Creek and Willow Gulch **Hike #24**. Signed Sooner Wash. A vague track to the right provides parking. You are at elevation 4265 and are in Entrada Sandstone.

40.8 —"Tee." Track to the right (W) goes to the Sooner Rocks. The Sooner Rocks, Sooner Bench, and Sooner Slide were named for a young homesick sheepherder who said he would "sooner be home than out in this forsaken region."

41.5 —"Tee." Track to the left (ESE) goes to the Willow Gulch trailhead. This trailhead provides the shortest access to Willow Gulch and Broken Bow Arch. The trailhead is located at the end of a road that starts at elevation 4323. The track is suitable for high-clearance vehicles and is 1.4 miles long. It ends at a turnaround and parking area.

Follow a path north down a hill past a small tower that looks like a graduation cap, or mortar board. Traverse along a sand dune and descend into the canyon. It takes about 1.5 hours to reach the arch.

42.1   —Cattle guard.

42.4   —Cross Cottonwood Wash.

43.1   —Cross the north fork of Willow Gulch.

43.4   —"Tee." Signed "50 Mile Bench" track to the right (SW). This track goes up Sooner Slide to Fiftymile Bench. It is suitable for high-clearance vehicles.

44.3   —Cross the south fork of Willow Gulch.

45.4   —Cattle guard. Cave Point is to the right (SW). The caves are in Entrada Sandstone.

45.7   —Start of Fiftymile Creek **Hike #25.** "Tee." There is a track and parking to the right (SW) just before the bottom of a hill. The track itself goes to beautiful Cave Spring. You are at elevation 4237 and are in the Carmel Formation.

47.2   —Signed Glen Canyon National Recreation Area boundary.

47.6   —"The Soda" sign. This is labeled as Soda Spring on the map. The spring is a short distance downcanyon.

       Three springs have been claimed as the Fiftymile Spring used by the Hole-in-the-Rock expedition. Evidence is inconclusive about which was actually used. This is the first possibility.

48.1   —"Y." Follow the main road to the left. The short road to the right goes to Fiftymile Spring, which is called The Sodie by locals. It is the second spring that may have been used by the Hole-in-the-Rock expedition. Fiftymile Spring flows from an overhang in a small canyon a quarter mile to the left of the end of the road. A historic line shack here was burned by an arsonist in 1996. Several rows of Moqui steps lead up the cliffs behind the cabin site and cowboy glyphs dating from the early 1900s can be found on the Entrada Sandstone walls.

49.1   —(**Davis Gulch map.**) Cross Fiftymile Creek. The third spring that may have been used by the Hole-in-the-Rock expedition is a short walk up the wash. It has the largest flow of the three springs and is considered the most likely camp by local historians. The expedition, finding no water near the Hole-in-the-Rock, divided: half stayed at this spring, the other half camped at the top of the Hole-in-the-Rock. Blizzards, a lack of food and forage, and a paucity of wood for fuel became major problems. The expedition stalled here for two months while the route was built down the Hole-in-the-Rock to the river and a dugway was excavated up a 250-foot cliff on the opposite side.

49.2 —Start of Sixty Point and Twilight Canyon **Hike #26**. There is a small pullout on the right. You are at elevation 4424 and are in the Carmel Formation.

50.4 —Cattle guard.

50.6 —Start of Llewellyn and Cottonwood Gulches **Hike #27** and Davis Gulch **Hike #28**. The road crosses a short stretch of slickrock at the bottom of a hill. This marks the start of Davis Gulch. Parking is available on the flat 100 yards past the gulch. You are at elevation 4315 and are on Navajo Sandstone.

50.7 —A very faded track (no longer open to vehicles) on the left marks the start of the now abandoned Clear Creek Trail.

50.8 —Start of Clear Creek and the Cathedral in the Desert **Hike #29**. End of the two-wheel-drive road. 4WDs only past this point. From here it takes two hours to walk to the Hole-in-the-Rock. Many ride mountain bikes. Garfield County has proposed repairing the last section of road to the Hole-in-the-Rock, making it accessible to high-clearance vehicles. Check locally for current conditions. You are a quarter mile northeast of elevation 4315 and are on Navajo Sandstone.

51.6 —Hole-in-the-Rock Well is on the right.

52.9 —At the bottom of a slickrock hill.

53.4 —"Tee." A vague track marked with an orange "No Vehicle" sign on a flexible post marks an alternate start to Hike #29. This is one-eighth mile east of elevation 4422.

55.7 —Turnaround at the Hole-in-the-Rock.

Hole-In-The-Rock—The Story Continues

The story of the Hole-in-the-Rock does not stop with the initial expedition. Mormon pioneers continued to use the road for another year, until Charles Hall established the Harris Wash/Silver Falls Creek/Muley Twist Canyon route to the Colorado River. In 1881 William Hyde opened a trading post at the Hole-in-the-Rock that was frequented by Navajo and Piute Indians crossing the river from the east to the fertile grazing lands on the Escalante Desert and the Kaiparowits Plateau. It is not known how long Hyde stayed, perhaps just a year or two.

The next phase of use began with the discovery of gold in Glen Canyon. In October 1871 three men who were bringing supplies to the second Powell expedition found gold in Kane Creek and other Colorado River tributaries. John Wesley Powell, though, was not interested in gold and his men's finds went unnoticed.

It was not until Cass Hite, the founder of Dandy Crossing near what is now Hite Marina, discovered gold in northern Glen Canyon in the fall of 1883 that word got out. The gold rush that followed Hite's find was short and not very productive. While gold was plentiful, it was as fine as flour, making it exceptionally difficult to separate from the river sand.

J.R. Neilson arrived in Escalante in 1888. There he built a thirty-eight-foot double-decked boat that he hauled in pieces through the Hole-in-the-Rock to the Colorado River. After assembling it and loading it with mining equipment, he floated down-canyon, trying placer mining on benches above the river. The enterprise was not successful and the boat was abandoned near Lees Ferry.

Robert Brewster Stanton launched the most ambitious mining enterprise in Glen Canyon. Stanton had been through both Glen Canyon and the Grand Canyon in 1889 while scouting a potential railroad route along the river. The route was not feasible; but, after talking to Cass Hite, Stanton became excited about the gold mining possibilities.

In 1897 Stanton and a group of financiers formed the Hoskaninni Mining Company. They quickly staked 145 placer claims encompassing 19,000 acres along the length of Glen Canyon,

Ginger Harmon on the Jackass Bench Trail.

from a couple of miles above Hite to Lees Ferry. Their plan was to build a special dredge that could isolate the flour gold. A dam built near the mouth of the Dirty Devil River was to provide water and electricity to power the dredge. Once the infrastructure was in place, the dredge would slowly make its way downcanyon. To that end, a dredge was carted to the river in pieces and assembled at Camp Stone, which was a couple of miles upcanyon from Bullfrog Basin.

While the dredge was being assembled, Stanton sent Nathaniel Galloway and twenty-six laborers to the Hole-in-the-Rock to improve the ramp at the top and to reconstruct the lower section. This was to be a major resupply route for the dredging operation. Galloway and his crew are responsible for the long series of platform steps along the first quarter mile of the ramp.

Simultaneously, Galloway and his crew improved the Jackass Bench Trail, an old livestock path that starts a mile north of the Hole-in-the-Rock and descends steep slickrock onto the now inundated Jackass Bench. This steep, dangerous trail was first used by scouts on the Hole-in-the-Rock expedition. Galloway abandoned the trail after losing nine pack animals in falls.

Meanwhile, Stanton had started his dredging operation, which was a failure. The gold was too fine to separate from the sand. After gleaning a couple of hundred dollars worth of gold from the river, the Hoskaninni Mining Company went bankrupt. The dredge sat along the river for many years, its beams and metal parts slowly stripped by other miners. It is now under Lake Powell.

In 1900 Henry N. Cowles and Joseph T. Hall (no relation to

Charles Hall) opened an Indian trading post near the river at the foot of the trail. It thrived for several years before they abandoned it.

The road from Escalante to Hole-in-the-Rock slowly improved over the years and by the mid-1950s it was graded regularly. Now the grader stops near the head of Davis Wash and the last several miles are passable only by four-wheel-drive vehicles, although the road may be upgraded in the near future.

The Hole-in-the-Rock route takes about an hour to explore. As you descend remember that during the original expedition the steep cliffs and drops that are now troublesome were filled with riprap. The large boulders blocking the way in places are recent products of erosion.

The hike to Lake Powell via the Jackass Bench trail provides access to the lake away from the swarms of tourists at Hole-in-the-Rock. Hike northeast to the rim of the canyon, then follow it north. The sheer wall gives way to a long sloping maze of slickrock sheets and domes that drop to the lake. Continue along the rim for a couple of minutes until you are forced to descend a steep slickrock hill. A line of cairns leads east down to the lake. (The trail starts one-quarter mile northwest of elevation 4252T on the Davis Gulch map and ends one-eighth mile south-southeast of elevation 4164T on The Rincon map.) Most of the constructed portions are near the lake. Do not panic if you miss the trail; there are many potential routes down the slickrock. Benches can be used for camping. (3.5–5.0 hours round-trip.)

Local rancher Hy Roundy used the Jackass Bench trail in 1919 while leading a group of miners to oil seeps a short distance above the mouth of the Escalante River in Glen Canyon. He described the slickrock portions of the trail as, "like being on ice" for his saddle stock. At the base of the trail—which is now under water—Roundy recounted that the horses had to jump onto a steep sand dune. Some made the jump without falling; others landed on their sides. None were seriously hurt.

Harris Wash Road Section
Access to Hikes #10 and 11.
Access is from the Hole-in-the-Rock road.
Maps—Seep Flat, Sunset Flat, and Red Breaks.

The Harris Wash road starts 10.5 miles down the Hole-in-the-Rock road at the "7mi. Harris Wash" sign (located at elevation 5386 on the **Seep Flat map**). The road is suitable for light-duty vehicles. There are few campsites along the road. (See **Map Fifteen**.)

0.0	—At the Hole-in-the-Rock road. Go southeast.
0.3	—"Tee." Stay with the main road to the right (E).
2.5	—Cattle guard and a "Y." Go left (N). You will now cross a corner of the Sunset Flat map.)
5.1	—(**Red Breaks map.**) Corral and good camping on the right.
5.8	—Start of Red Breaks Canyon **Hike #10** and Harris Wash **Hike #11**. At the Harris Wash trailhead and trail register. There is a limited amount of camping. You are at the end of the two-wheel-drive road, a half mile northeast of the corral and spring near elevation 5059. You are in the Carmel Formation.

> **Historical note:** Harris Wash was called False Creek or Rocky Gulch by Almon Thompson, a member of the Powell survey of 1872. He initially thought it was the Dirty Devil River. The canyon was later named for Llewellyn Harris, an immigrant from Wales who was an Indian scout, missionary, and homesteader. Harris brought his family to Escalante in 1878. He later built a house at the head of the wash.
>
> After the Hole-in-the-Rock expedition of 1876, Charles Hall, a scout on that trek, found a better though longer route from the town of Escalante to the Colorado River. The route became a popular wagon road that went down Harris Wash, up Silver Falls Creek, and across Circle Cliffs Basin to the Waterpocket Fold. It then went down Muley Twist Canyon into Halls Creek and crossed the Colorado River at Halls Crossing. In 1920 the Ohio Drilling Company improved the old wagon road through Harris Wash and up Silver Falls Creek to Wagon Box Mesa in Circle Cliffs Basin, making it passable for trucks. The road was closed after the area was included in Glen Canyon National Recreation Area.

Red Breaks Canyon—Hike #10

Season:	Any.
Time:	5.0 to 6.5 hours.
Water:	There may be no water along the route. Bring your own drinking water.
Elevation range:	4960' to 5800'.
Map:	Red Breaks.
Skill level:	Moderate route finding. Class 5.3 climbing with little exposure. The leader must be experienced with belay techniques and be capable of

leading the climbing sections without protection. Except for the climbing sections, this is a moderate hike.

Special equipment: After recent rains wading shoes may be necessary. A forty-foot rope is necessary.

Land status: This hike is in Grand Staircase-Escalante National Monument.

William Strunk in his popular book *Elements of Style* says that the word "nice" is "a shaggy, all-purpose word, to be used sparingly." Yet no other word as accurately describes the hike into Red Breaks. It is not quite a great hike; it is a "nice" hike. Yet, when friends come out to visit, this is often the route we do.

The hike starts at the Harris Wash trailhead, ascends a narrow canyon, crosses a slickrock ridge, and descends another canyon back to the start.

Up Red Breaks Canyon

(**Red Breaks map** and **Map Sixteen.**) From the trail register follow the track across (not down) Harris Wash. Within a couple of minutes the track crosses a sandy wash that comes in on the left (N). This is Red Breaks Canyon. (Red Breaks Canyon is not named on the map. Its mouth is at the "W" in Wash.)

Follow the rabbitbrush-lined wash upcanyon. The colorful Carmel hills give way to a low-walled Navajo inner gorge. Pass a fall on the right (LUC) by ascending a broken slab (Class 5.0, 20'). Above the fall the canyon divides. Stay with the main channel to the right (NE).

The canyon again narrows, and after recent rains there may be some shallow wading or strenuous stemming. A couple of chockstones wedged in the narrows are irksome (Class 5.3, 15'). The canyon alternates between short stretches of narrows and open areas. Several side canyons enter, but all are above streambed level and are barely noticeable.

Finally, the canyon does divide. The left fork (NW) narrows quickly and ends at a large pothole. The right fork (NE) has a short pour-off that drops into a medium pothole. (2.0–2.5 hours.)

Climb north up a steep slab between the forks (Class 4-), then follow the left rim of the right (E) fork until it is possible to drop back to the canyon floor. Before descending, note a prominent dome (elevation 6015) in the distance at the top of the canyon. The canyon floor widens into a shimmering expanse of slickrock and a string of medium potholes. Nearby domes and buttresses shadow the curving patterns of cross-stratified Navajo sandstone—a photographer's heaven.

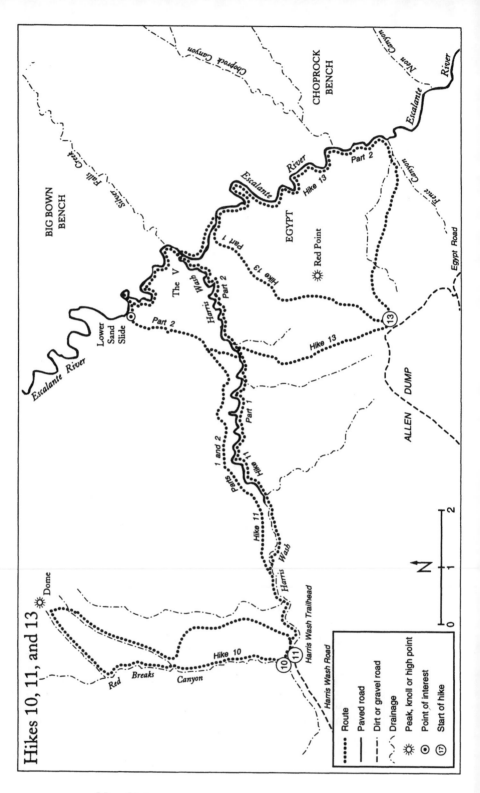

Hikes 10, 11, and 13

BIG BOWN BENCH

CHOPROCK BENCH

Choprock Canyon

Neon Canyon

Escalante River

Escalante River

Silver Falls Creek

The V

Lower Sand Slide

Part 2

Part 1

Part 2

Harris Wash

Hike 13

Part 2

EGYPT

Red Point

Hike 13

Part 2

Neon Canyon

Egypt Road

(13)

Hike 13

ALLEN DUMP

Parts 1 and 2

Part 1

Hike 11

Hike 11

Harris Wash

Dome

Harris Wash Trailhead

Red Breaks Canyon

Hike 10

(10) (11)

Harris Wash Road

Route
Paved road
Dirt or gravel road
Drainage
Peak, knoll or high point
Point of interest
Start of hike

N

0   1   2

Map Sixteen

Exit Red Breaks Canyon

A hundred yards before reaching the prominent dome, exit the canyon to the right (S), hike through a pass in a low slickrock ridge (shown to the northeast of elevation 5887), and drop into a south-running canyon (shown to the west of elevation 5623). (1.5–2.0 hours.)

> **Digression:** The dome, easily climbed on its west side, provides a platform for viewing a large part of the surrounding country. Visible are the Henry Mountains, Waterpocket Fold, Navajo Mountain, and the Kaiparowits Plateau.

Down the canyon

Follow the wide, wavy canyon down until it intersects Red Breaks Canyon at a twenty-foot drop. Exit the canyon to the left and follow an intermediate ledge downcanyon. You can now either exit the canyon completely and hike to Harris Wash along a bumpy ridge or reenter the main canyon and retrace your steps. Avoid the difficult climb at the initial fall by following a cattle trail along the right (LDC) rim. (1.5–2.0 hours.)

Harris Wash—Hike #11

Season:	Spring, summer, or fall.
Time:	Part 1—9.0 to 12.0 hours. Two days. Part 2—13.0 to 17.0 hours. Two to three days. There is a lot to explore along Harris Wash. Adding an extra day is advised.
Water:	Water availability is a minor problem on this route. Lower Harris Wash has a perennial flow of water. The route back to the trailhead is dry.
Elevation range:	Part 1—4750' to 5100'. Part 2—4650' to 5200'.
Maps:	Red Breaks and Silver Falls Bench.
Skill level:	Part 1—Easy route finding. Class 5.0 climbing with little exposure or Class 3- scrambling with lots of exposure. (See the text for details.) The leader must be experienced with belay techniques and be capable of leading the climbing section without protection. Lots of wading. Except for one climbing section, this hike is suitable for most. Familiarity with low-impact camping skills is essential. Part 2—Easy route finding. Lots of wading. This hike is suitable for most. Familiarity with low-impact camping skills is essential.

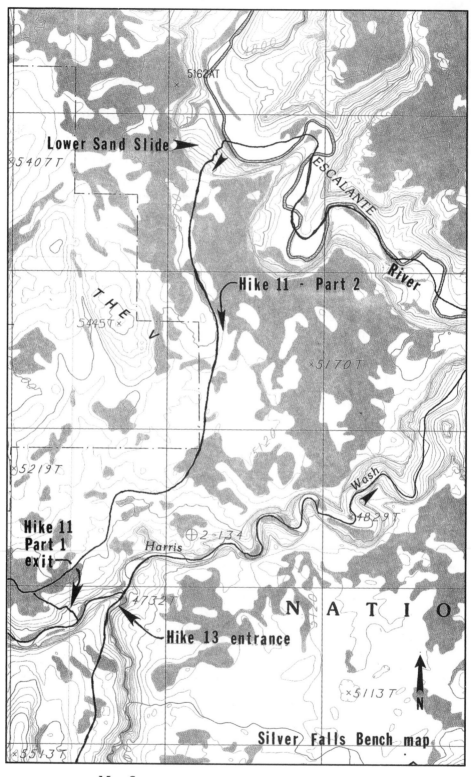

Lower Sand Slide

ESCALANTE

River

Hike 11 - Part 2

T H E

V

Wash

Hike 11
Part 1
exit

Harris

Hike 13 entrance

N A T I O

N

Silver Falls Bench map

Map Seventeen

Harris Wash.

Special equipment: Part 1—Wading boots. A forty-foot climbing rope is essential. Part 2—Wading boots. No rope is needed.

Note: Harris Wash, popular and pretty, is often crowded. Easy access attracts the hordes. During the busy season—March to June—do not expect solitude. If possible, plan your trip for the fall months when the crowds have subsided. You must carry out your toilet paper while in Harris Wash.

Land status: These hikes are in Grand Staircase-Escalante National Monument and Glen Canyon National Recreation Area.

Harris Wash is one of the most favored canyons in the Escalante area. Easy walking along a lively creek, plenty of diversions, no cattle in the main canyon, and fine camping in a pastoral setting blend to make these hikes especially suitable for the less experienced canyon explorer, the less physically inclined, or for families with children.

The route comes in two parts. Part 1 starts at the Harris Wash trailhead and goes most of the way down Harris Wash. It exits the canyon and follows the north rim of the canyon back to the trailhead.

Part 2 continues down Harris Wash to the Escalante River. After a short stroll upriver, a historic trail is used to exit the canyon. A cross-country jog across a bench called The "V" takes you to the north rim of Harris Wash, which is followed back to the trailhead.

Part 1: Down Harris Wash

(**Red Breaks map** and **Map Sixteen.**) From the trail register, walk down the road through a tunnel of Russian-olive trees to Harris Wash. These trees, with their silvery leaves and thorn-studded branches, are not related to olive trees but to oleasters. Russian-olives were introduced from Russia as an ornamental shade tree in the late 1800s. Like tamarisks, they quickly spread along watercourses throughout the Southwest.

Harris Wash, wide and dry in its upper reaches, quickly enters Navajo Sandstone and slowly narrows as you head downcanyon. An old track makes the walking easy. By the time you reach a hiker's maze through a fence the wash has become a splendid canyon. Cattle were the bane of Harris Wash until 1992 when the canyon below the fence was closed to grazing. Although cow pies and other cattle signs still exist, the canyon has started to recover from its 100 years of abuse.

Below the fence a riparian habitat develops and water starts flowing. A Glen Canyon National Recreation Area boundary sign a mile downcanyon gives you the opportunity to orient yourself on the map. (The boundary is shown by a heavy red vertical line to the west of elevation 5054.) A short side canyon to the left (N) is worth a visit.

> **Historical note:** Downcanyon you will see many caves along south-facing walls. Fremont Indians used these caves during the Pueblo II and Pueblo III periods (A.D. 900 to 1200). Unlike the Fremont sites near the town of Escalante, which were permanent settlements, these were transitory camps, used seasonally to escape harsh winters and during the summer months for growing corn, beans, and squash. Round masonry structures in several caves were used to store produce. Alluvial deposits that once provided fertile platforms for growing crops have eroded, leaving the creekbed ten to twenty feet lower than during the period of Indian occupation. The Indians chipped rows of steps up the steep walls of the canyon to simplify getting to the benchlands where they hunted deer and bighorn sheep. Fun to view from a distance, the steps have been worn by the elements and are dangerous to climb.

Three major side canyons come in on the right (LDC) as you work downcanyon. Your goal is to exit Harris Wash between the second and third canyons, so do keep track of your progress. The first is a short canyon on the right (SE) immediately before a "gate"—the narrowest part of Harris Wash. (It is located at the "H" in Harris.) (2.0–2.5 hours.)

The second canyon coming in on the right (SSW) has two forks divided by a massive prow. (It is at the "l" in Jeep Trail.) You are now nearly off the **Red Breaks map.**) (2.0–2.5 hours.)

The exit route from Harris Wash is by way of a break in the canyon wall to the north a quarter mile before reaching the mouth of the third side canyon. (The side canyon is shown at elevation 4732T on the **Silver Falls Bench map. Map Seventeen.**) Most will find it easiest to locate the mouth of the third side canyon, then backtrack to the exit.

Scramble up moderate slickrock to a wide ledge under the final cliff band. Walk upcanyon (NW) along the ledge until you are near its end. Ascend a right-curving crack on a moderate slab to the top of the cliff (Class 5.0, 25', belay as necessary). A log leaning against the wall can help on the hardest part, which is the first eight feet.

> **Alternate route:** An easier but much more exposed route is available. From the top ledge, walk downcanyon a hundred yards, drop about fifty feet, then cut diagonally across a steep slab (Class 3-). Although easier, this route is not suitable for inexperienced slickrock hikers.

This is the last reasonably easy exit from the canyon. (1.0–2.0 hours.)

Back to the trailhead

Make your way north up to the rim of Harris Wash, then follow the rim west. Although you may think you have seen Harris Wash in its entirety while hiking along its floor, most will be amazed at what you have missed. Rows of Moqui steps, perhaps a cliff dwelling or two, and delightful views of the sinuous curves of the canyon make the rim walk enchanting. You can stay within a couple of hundred yards of the rim. (**Red Breaks map.**) After reaching the Carmel Formation either find a way into Harris Wash or follow a cattle trail that deposits you in the canyon near the start. (4.0–5.0 hours.)

Part 2: To the Escalante River

(**Silver Falls Bench map.**) From the mouth of the third side canyon continue down Harris Wash. The walls rise and the canyon narrows. Good campsites appear near the confluence with the Escalante River. (1.5–2.0 hours.)

Up the Escalante River

Hike up the Escalante River. Pass the mouth of Silver Falls Creek. It is the large canyon that comes in on the right (LUC)(NE) in fifteen minutes. The walls along the left (LUC) side of the river are vertical for a couple of miles until a huge sand dune to the left (SW) breaks the symmetry. This is the Lower Sand Slide, which was part of a historic wagon route. You will not miss it. (The dune is one-quarter mile south of elevation 5162AT.) Battle your way up the dune and through an old log fence at its top. This exit is also used in Hike #9. (1.5–2.0 hours.)

To the rim of Harris Wash
Travel cross-country south across The V, an area of gentle hills, to the rim of Harris Wash. (1.0 hour.)

> **Historical note:** The V was named by early ranchers for the V-shaped point of land formed at the junction of Harris Wash and Escalante Canyon.

Follow the Part 1 route along the rim of Harris Wash back to the trailhead. (4.0–5.0 hours.)

Egypt Road Section
Access to Hikes #12 through 14.
Access is from the Hole-in-the-Rock road.
Maps—Sunset Flat and Egypt.

The Egypt road starts 16.5 miles down the Hole-in-the-Rock road at the "Egypt 10 mi." sign (shown as a Jeep Trail at elevation 5269 on the **Sunset Flat map**). The road is suitable for high-clearance vehicles. There are fine campsites along the last three miles of the road. (See **Map Fifteen**.)

0.0 —At the Hole-in-the-Rock road. Go northeast.

2.8 —Four-way intersection. Proceed straight ahead (E) on the main road.
The track to the left (N) leads to Twentyfive Mile Corral. The wash above the corral is called Twentymile Wash; below the corral it is called Twentyfive Mile Wash. (The next 4.6 miles of the Egypt road are not shown on the map.)

3.3 —Signed "25 Mile Wash trailhead" parking area on the right.

> **Digression:** Twentyfive Mile Wash provides cattle-trashed access to the Escalante River. It takes four hours to get to the first water source (may be dry in the summer), which is in an area of beaver ponds (north of elevation 4844T on the Egypt map). Fox Canyon is reached after another hour. (Fox Canyon is not named on the map. It is located one-half mile northwest of elevation 5009T.) See Hike #15 for details on Twentyfive Mile Wash from Fox Canyon to the Escalante River.

3.4 —Cross Twentyfive Mile Wash. This can be troublesome after recent rains. The gray-and-red slope-forming hills you are driving through are in the Carmel Formation. They are topped by a short red Entrada Sandstone cliff.

3.8 | —Old wood rip-gut fence to the right. These are also called buck, or stake and rider, fences.

6.5 | —Down a narrow side-cut on a hill.

6.6 | —Across the head of a small canyon that is to the right (S). This is the first canyon head you will cross (shown to the east of elevation 5320.)

7.9 | —(**Egypt map.**) Across the head of a canyon that is to the right (SE). This is the second canyon head you will cross (shown one-quarter mile southeast of elevation 5483T). A large slickrock sheet at the head of the canyon provides a place to park. The road ahead gets rougher. (The Egypt road is shown on this map.)

8.8 | —At the top of a small rise. An incongruous, bottom-heavy, white pinnacle is visible on a red hillside to the left (NW). Go down a gentle hill.

8.9 | —Bottom of the hill. The top of Egypt 3, the third canyon head you pass, is on the right (SE). It presents itself as a rock-strewn gully.

9.0 | —Start of Egypt 3—The Slot **Hike #12**. At a silver culvert that goes under the road. A vague track on the left provides parking. You are a quarter mile west-southwest of elevation 5651T and are in the Carmel Formation.

9.4 | —"Y." Go right (E). The road to the left goes to the start of **Hike #13**.

Side road to Lower Harris Wash Hike #13

0.0 | —At the "Y." Go left (N).

1.1 | —Start of Lower Harris Wash **Hike #13**. Stock pond on the right (NE). There is no trail register, though you can register at the Egypt trailhead. The stock pond is shown to the west-northwest of elevation 5735T. You are in the Carmel Formation. Although this is the start of the hike, keep driving!

1.8 | —Deep gorge to the right (N) (shown to the east of elevation 5921T). You will hike along its right side at the start of Hike #13. Now that you have seen part of the route, return to the stock pond.

> **Historical note:** Allen Dump, the high area to the west of the stock pond, was named for the Philo Allen family. Allen is credited with bringing the first cattle into the area in 1875. Before moving his family to Utah and to Escalante, he was a bodyguard to the Mormon prophet Joseph Smith.

End of side road

9.9 —Start of Fence Canyon, the Escalante River, and Twentyfive Mile Wash **Hike #14**. At the Egypt trailhead and trail register. There is plenty of camping in the area. The parking circle is located one-quarter mile southwest of elevation 5257T. You are on a thin layer of Carmel Formation limestone. To the north-northeast are the three peaks of the Henry Mountains. They are, from left to right: Mt. Ellen (11,506'), Mt. Pennell (11,132'), and Mt. Hillers (10,737').

> **Historical note:** The bench to the east was named Egypt for its imagined similarity to the deserts of North Africa.

Egypt 3—The Slot—Hike #12

Season:	Any. Recent rains will make this hike a difficult undertaking.
Time:	4.5 to 6.0 hours. Add more time if your group is large.
Water:	There may be no water along this route. Bring your own drinking water.
Elevation range:	4800' to 5600'.
Map:	Egypt.
Skill level:	Moderate route finding. Class 5.0 climbing. The leader must be experienced with belay techniques and be capable of leading the climbing sections without protection. There may be some wading. This hike is suitable only for the athletic. The slot you descend is so narrow that overweight hikers cannot squeeze through it. **This slot is not appropriate for claustrophobes, novice slot canyoneers, youngsters, or youth groups.**
Special equipment:	Wading boots and a forty-foot rope are needed. Use the smallest daypack you can; a large pack will be difficult to maneuver through the narrowest sections.
Land status:	This hike is in Grand Staircase-Escalante National Monument.

Thirteenth-century Italian poet Dante Alighieri wrote *"lasciate ogni speranza, voi ch'entrate"* (abandon all hope, ye who enter). Dante was, of course, referring to the underworld. I hope that you will not abandon all hope as you descend Egypt 3, one of the tightest and longest slots in the area.

The route starts high on Egypt and descends a seemingly endless slot that ends near Twentyfive Mile Wash. A cross-country route over a marvelous slickrock ridge climaxes the trip.

Down Egypt 3

(**Egypt map** and **Map Eighteen.**) Drop south off the road to the floor of the wash. Saunter downcanyon. Pass a large pour-off at the top of the Navajo on the left (E) and find a route down steep slickrock into the canyon below. If you have problems getting into the canyon, this route is not for you.

Long stretches of tight narrows with high vertical walls are interspersed with open areas where the walls lay back at a reasonable angle. At these junctures it is possible to exit the canyon. There are many small obstacles to overcome, though none are difficult (Class 5.0) or have much exposure. In a couple of places a handline or belay will reassure the less experienced. The amount of wading depends on the season and how soon after rains you descend the canyon.

The exit

Near the end of the canyon the slot opens for a stretch before plunging into the final slot, which contains several small natural bridges near its top. Do not continue farther down the canyon. The obstacles below are overwhelming. (3.0–4.0 hours.)

> **Digression:** Twentyfive Mile Wash is now a quarter mile away and can be most easily reached by following the canyon's right (LDC) rim.

> **Rock climber's note:** The final section of slot, below the bridges, can be descended. A full-length climbing rope tied to one of the natural bridges provides an anchor for a thirty-five-foot rappel. Retrieve the rope on the way back. Short obstacles and deep wading or swimming through an intimidating stretch of narrows leads to the end of the canyon at Twentyfive Mile Wash.

Back to the trailhead

From the natural bridge scramble east up slickrock for 100 yards to the crest of a ridge. Another deep slot will be visible a quarter mile to the east. Follow the ridge north-northeast between the two slots (over elevations 5004T, 5201T, and 5281T). The ridge dies in a maze of domes, towers, and striking slickrock. Wend your way north-northeast back to the Egypt road (many options). (1.5–2.0 hours.)

Lower Harris Wash—Hike #13

Season: Part 1—Any.
Part 2—Spring, summer, or fall.

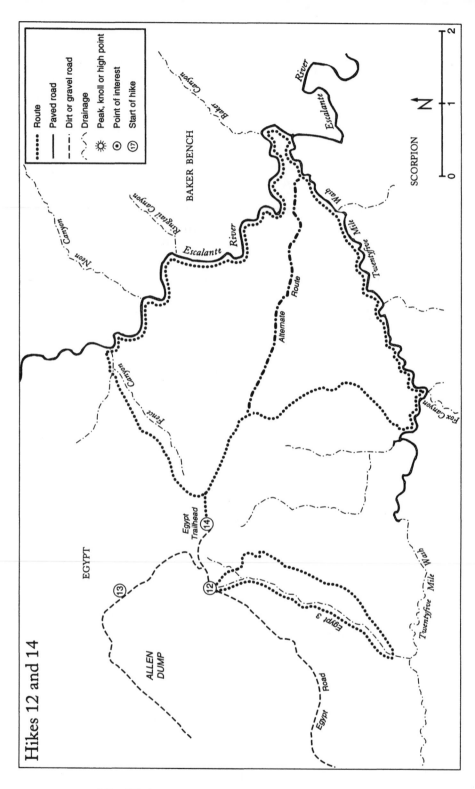

Map Eighteen

Mike Sutak and Wendy Chase in Egypt 3.

Time: Part 1—6.5 to 9.5 hours. This can be done as a long dayhike or a pleasant two-day hike.

Part 2—10.0 to 14.5 hours. Two days. Add another day if you plan to explore side canyons.

Water: Water availability is not a problem on this hike. There is always water in Harris Wash and along the Escalante River.

Elevation range:	Part 1—4650' to 5880'. Part 2—4540' to 5860'.
Maps:	Egypt and Silver Falls Bench.
Skill level:	Moderate route finding. Class 3 + scrambling. There is a lot of elevation loss and gain. Lots of wading. This is a moderately strenuous hike. If done as an overnighter, low-impact camping skills are essential.
Special equipment:	Wading boots.
Land status:	This hike is in Grand Staircase-Escalante National Monument and Glen Canyon National Recreation Area.

A mundane start on a boring plain leads to an unexpected expanse of peerless slickrock, striking views of the upper Escalante drainage, and entrance into a redoubtable canyon. Although the route is tiring, the toil is worth the effort.

The route comes in two parts. Part 1 starts on Allen Dump, a high bench to the northwest of Egypt, and descends a rambunctious ridge into lower Harris Wash. A short stroll down the Escalante River leads to an old cattle trail that takes you out of the canyon. A steep scramble up an imposing wall ends the hike.

Part 2 continues down the Escalante River to Fence Canyon. After exiting at Fence Canyon, the route crosses a corner of Egypt and ascends a slickrock rib to the top of an escarpment. A short stroll leads back to the trailhead.

Part 1: To Harris Wash

(**Egypt map** and **Map Sixteen.**) Hike north-northwest across a juniper-and-pinyon plain until the deep gorge mentioned in the road section is in view. Follow its course northwest. Stay on the plain; do not drop to the rim of the canyon. The plain ends at a steep Navajo slab. Descend it, then cross the top of, or go around, a squat, flat-topped butte (elevation 5728T on the **Silver Falls Bench map**). You are now between two canyons. Descend slickrock to the left (W) rim of the canyon to the right (NE) (shown one-quarter mile east of elevation 5513T) and follow its rim down until you are above Harris Wash. A steep slab at the junction of Harris Wash and the side canyon is studded with faded Moqui steps. (**Map Seventeen.**) They lead into Harris Wash (Class 3 +). (2.5–3.5 hours.)

Down Harris Wash

Hike and wade downcanyon. Near the Escalante River Navajo Sandstone gives way to the Kayenta Formation. Good camping can be found in Harris Wash, at the confluence, and along the Escalante River. (1.5–2.5 hours.)

The exit route

Follow a troublesome path along the right side of the Escalante River (or wade) as you make your way downcanyon. In fifteen minutes a short drainage comes in on the right (SW). Past the drainage the thrashing ends and a good trail cuts across a wide bench. Within a couple of minutes of starting across the wide bench a sandy slope to the right (SW) marks the exit route out of the canyon. (The sandy slope is north of an abandoned meander shown as elevation 5056T.) Make your way up the slope toward the middle of the abandoned meander. Near its Navajo base intersect a constructed cattle trail and follow it to the north side of the abandoned meander. A sand dune to the southwest takes you out of the canyon.

To the trailhead

From the top of the dune go southwest for a couple of minutes until a dominant escarpment to the south-southwest becomes plainly visible. Though most of the walls of the escarpment are rounded, there is one large vertical wall (north-northwest of "Red" at elevation 5933). Make your way southwest across broken slickrock, sagebrush, and sand and ascend steep slickrock (Class 3-) just to the right (W) of the vertical wall. From a distance this prow looks intimidating, but once you are on it the angle of the rock is less than it first appeared.

From the top, a short stroll southeast takes you to Red Point, which has a bench mark on its summit. A southerly course takes you back to the stock pond. (**Egypt map.**) (2.5–3.5 hours.)

Part 2: To Fence Canyon

(**Silver Falls Bench map.**) From the base of the Part 1 exit route, continue hiking and wading down the Escalante River.

> Digression: Hike #35 describes some of the side canyons that enter the Escalante on the left (LDC). Choprock Canyon is especially worth exploring.

You will leave the river at Fence Canyon, the first major side canyon on the right (W). (**Egypt map.**) (3.0–4.5 hours.)

To the trailhead

Water is not available after leaving the river. Load up here. Hike up Fence Canyon (W). It divides in a quarter mile. Follow a trail up the point that divides the two canyons. Look west-northwest at a slickrock escarpment that has a couple of wide ribs dropping from its crest. Hike up the rib that plainly goes all the way to the top (located between elevations 5855T and 5132T).

You are now on the boring plain you started on. Walk a mile south-southwest back to the trailhead. (2.5–3.5 hours.)

Fence Canyon, The Escalante River, and Twentyfive Mile Wash—Hike #14

Season:	Spring, summer, or fall.
Time:	13.0 to 20.0 hours. Two to three days. Add another day if you plan to explore side canyons.
Water:	Water availability is a minor problem on this hike. Fence Canyon and the Escalante River have perennial flows of water, and Twenty-five Mile Wash has large springs. The cross-country route back to the trailhead is dry.
Elevation range:	4500' to 5650'.
Map:	Egypt.
Skill level:	Moderate route finding. There is one long cross-country stretch. Class 2 + walking. Lots of wading. This is an easy hike. Familiarity with low-impact camping techniques is essential.
Special equipment:	Wading boots.
Land status:	This hike is in Grand Staircase-Escalante National Monument and Glen Canyon National Recreation Area.

"Omne ignotum pro magnifico" is a joyful Latin expression every canyoneer should become familiar with. It means, "everything unknown is assumed to be grand." And what a fine sentiment that is when you arrive at a new trailhead and are faced with fresh terrain. Sometimes I get a little nervous. Can I find the way or will I wander around forever trying to find the route? But, whatever happens, I know that what is ahead will indeed be grand! The route goes from the Egypt trailhead, down Fence Canyon, to the Escalante River. The river is followed downcanyon to Twentyfive Mile Wash, goes up it, and finishes with a cross-country hike across Egypt back to the trailhead.

To Fence Canyon

(**Egypt map** and **Map Eighteen.**) Before you embark on your

Rob Roseen in the Golden Cathedral.

adventure take a short walk from the trail register to the end of the road and to the edge of the cliff. From there you can see most of the route into Fence Canyon. A horse and cattle trail starts at the trail register and zigzags northeast down a Navajo slickrock slab. Steps have been chiseled into the rock.

Look northeast across a sandy plain below the slab. The main fork of Fence Canyon starts as a shallow wash below the slab and, as it gets deeper, it features several small linear sandstone ridges. To the left (N) of the main fork, near the river, are the dark red walls of the north fork of Fence Canyon. The two forks join at the point of a wide "Vee." The trail follows the left (LDC)(N) side of the main fork of Fence Canyon until near the point of the "Vee." The trail is not maintained and is often hard to locate as you cross the plain. If you do lose it, do not worry. You know where you are headed.

Near the point of the "Vee" you will intersect a well-defined and heavily cairned trail. It follows the north rim of the main canyon and includes a stretch of an old cattle trail as it drops off the point. A short stroll takes you down to the Escalante River. You have descended the Navajo and Kayenta formations and are now in Wingate Sandstone. There is fair camping in the area. Better camping can be found a quarter mile down the Escalante River on the right. (2.0–3.0 hours.)

> **Historical note:** A couple of hitching posts and a small concrete foundation near the river are all that remain of a line shack that was burned to the ground in April 1990 by an arsonist. On the same day this line shack flared, another one at the mouth of Silver Falls Creek was torched. Twenty-one head of cattle were killed a short distance upriver. Although a $10,000 reward was posted, the perpetrators were never found.

> **To the Overland Route:** To intersect the section of the Overland Route that runs between Choprock Canyon and Twentyfive Mile Wash, cross the Escalante River and hike east to the base of the Wingate wall. Follow it upcanyon (N) for several minutes to the dilapidated remains of a pole corral that uses the Wingate cliff as one wall. Ascend a moderate (Class 3+) slab behind the corral to the top of the Wingate. Follow it downcanyon. (Do not go too far above the Wingate or you may intersect a horse trail that will take you to the wrong place.) See the Overland Route description for details on getting into Neon Canyon, the first side canyon to the south.

Down the Escalante River to Neon Canyon

Start wading immediately. The first side canyon on the left (NE) is Neon Canyon, named for its shimmering, iridescently varnished walls. (Neon Canyon is not named on the map. It is shown to the west of elevation 5270T.) (1.0–1.5 hours.)

To Ringtail Canyon

Hike downriver from the mouth of Neon Canyon. The first canyon encountered on the left (NE) is Ringtail Canyon (AN). (Ringtail Canyon is not named on the map. It is shown to the northwest of elevation 4988T.) (1.0–1.5 hours.)

Digression: This short narrow slot is reminiscent of Brimstone Gulch, but is even darker. It is worth checking out. (0.5 hours round-trip.)

Ringtail cats are rarely seen in the Escalante area, but they have been observed in the pitch-black depths of this canyon. Ringtails are closely related to raccoons and have a similar banded tail. Subsisting on berries, eggs, small rodents, insects, birds, bats, and lizards, they are active at night and build their dens in trees or in the cracks of cliffs.

To Baker Canyon

Baker Canyon is the next canyon to the left (N) as you continue down the river. (Baker Canyon is not named on the map. It is shown at elevation 4468T.) (2.5–4.0 hours.)

Digression: Baker Canyon is cottonwood-lined and boulder-clogged in its lower reaches and ends at a fall. (0.5 hours round-trip.)

To Twentyfive Mile Wash

A half hour below Baker Canyon, Twentyfive Mile Wash comes in on the right (W). There is no camping at its brush-choked mouth, but good sites appear upcanyon. (0.5–1.0 hours.)

Up Twentyfive Mile Wash

Proceed up Twentyfive Mile Wash. It has a large flow of water and, although there is a trail, beaver dams have formed ponds that may force you to wade.

Alternate route: This route takes you out of Twentyfive Mile Wash near its mouth and back to the Egypt trailhead. Walk upcanyon. Fifteen minutes from the mouth of the canyon pass an arc (arcs are arches that have not quite broken through) that is on the right wall. A second arc appears around the corner. It has an unapproachable cliff dwelling under it. A hundred yards past the dwelling is a low point of land that forces the streambed against the left wall (shown one-quarter mile south-southeast of elevation 4951T). Find a short slot/ramp on the right (LUC)(W) that allows access to the top of the low point. Make your way west through the Wingate, then turn north and find a route to the top of the Kayenta (many options). Travel generally west below a long ridge of rounded Navajo slickrock that is to the left (S) until the ridge ends at a wide side canyon that drops to the Escalante River. (The highest point on this ridge is elevation 5175T.) Scramble north over the ridge. From the top of the ridge, the long Navajo escarpment that contains the Egypt trailhead will be visible to the west-northwest. Cross a broken plain and follow the horse trail back to the trailhead. (3.0–4.5 hours.)

Twentyfive Mile Wash

Twentyfive Mile Wash contains several interesting side canyons that are worth exploring.

> **Digression:** The first canyon on the left (SE) (shown to the east of elevation 4915T) contains a short set of narrows and can be used as an exit out of the canyon onto the area known as Scorpion (see Historical note, Early Weed Bench Road Section).

As the main canyon widens, the Wingate walls are supplanted by the less severe Kayenta Formation.

The first canyon on the right (NW) (at elevation 4523T) signals the end of the Kayenta and the start of the Navajo. The canyon walls become more interesting. A hard-to-spot arch is hidden in the folds of the Navajo wall to the left.

The next side canyon to the left (S) (between elevations 5124T and 5013T) is a real gem. About an hour upcanyon two canyons that are a minute apart now come in on the left (LUC). The first canyon is short and comes in from the southeast. The second canyon (LKA Fox Canyon) (shown to the west of elevation 5009T) comes in from the west. Fox Canyon is the standard route out of Twentyfive Mile Wash to the Early Weed Bench trailhead. (**Map Twenty.**)

The exit route

Fifteen minutes past the mouth of Fox Canyon is a Glen Canyon National Recreation Area boundary sign. Exit the canyon to the right (N) as soon as you can (several options) once past the sign. The cross-country hop back to the trailhead has no reliable source of water. Load up before leaving Twentyfive Mile Wash. (3.5–5.0 hours.)

> **Note:** Although a canyon system to the west of the exit route (at elevation 4652T) looks appealing on the map, it is brutal to negotiate; beaver ponds have turned it into a marshy, reed- and tamarisk-choked horror.

Work your way generally northwest over a neverending line of slickrock hills and dales to the foot of the Egypt escarpment. Follow the horse trail back to the trailhead. (2.5–4.0 hours.)

Early Weed Bench Road Section

Access to Hikes #15 through 18.
Access is from the Hole-in-the-Rock road.
Maps—Basin Canyon, Big Hollow Wash, and Egypt.

The Early Weed Bench road starts 23.6 miles down the Hole-in-the-Rock road at the "Early Weed Bench 6 mi." sign (shown as a Jeep Trail to the northwest of elevation 4865 on the **Basin Canyon map**). The road is suitable for high-clearance vehicles. There are few campsites along the road. (See **Map Fifteen.**)

0.0	—At the Hole-in-the-Rock road. Go east-southeast.
0.2	—"Y." Go left (N). After heavy rains the wash can be troublesome. You will now cross a corner of the **Big Hollow Wash map**.
1.0	—(**Egypt map.**) You are in the Carmel Formation. The sandstone cliffs to the left (N) are Entrada Sandstone.
4.4	—"Tee." Stay with the main road to the right (E).
4.8	—Start of Twentyfive Mile Wash, the Escalante River, and Scorpion Gulch **Hike #15**. Early Weed Bench parking area and trail register. There is good camping another quarter mile along the road. The trailhead is one-eighth mile north of elevation 5453T. You are in the Carmel Formation.
5.1	—Start of Spooky and Peek-a-boo Gulches—The Long Loop **Hike #16**. Cross the head of a Navajo-walled canyon that goes south. There is a parking area 0.1 miles farther along the road. You are one-quarter mile east of the Early Weed Bench trailhead and are in the Carmel Formation.
5.2	—Large parking and camping area on the left.
5.3	—Start Upper Brimstone Gulch—The Slot **Hike #17** and Scorpion Gulch and the Scorpion Horse Trail **Hike #18**. End of the road. There is good camping in the area. You are at the end of the road shown one-quarter mile southwest of elevation 5524T and are in the Carmel Formation.

Historical note: Early Weed Bench was named by ranchers who noticed that since the bench tips to the south it warms up quickly in the spring, allowing the plants to bloom earlier than in other areas. The name Scorpion refers to the benchlands lying between Twenty-five Mile Wash and Coyote Gulch. Scorpion is referred to simply as "Scorpion"; it is not succeeded by Flats or Bench. The name derivation is twofold. First, the area is ideal scorpion habitat. Second, from the end of the road, look east. In the background, with only its upper half visible, is Scorpion Point, a flat-topped slickrock mesa (elevation 5460 on the Scorpion Gulch map). On its right side is a small pointed dome; to its right is a small dark pinnacle, the tail of the scorpion.

Twentyfive Mile Wash, The Escalante River, and Scorpion Gulch—Hike #15

Season:	Spring, summer, or fall.
Time:	Part 1—9.0 to 13.5 hours. Two to three days. Part 2—21.5 to 31.0 hours. Three to five days.
Water:	Water availability is a minor problem on this hike. The Escalante River has a perennial flow of water. Twentyfive Mile Wash and Scorpion Gulch have large springs. The cross-country route back to the trailhead is dry.
Elevation range:	Part 1—4440' to 5400'. Part 2—4240' to 5400'.
Maps:	Part 1—Egypt. Part 2—Add Scorpion Gulch.
Skill level:	Part 1—Moderately difficult route finding. There is one long cross-country stretch. Class 3 scrambling. Lots of wading. This is a moderately strenuous route. Familiarity with low-impact camping skills is essential. Part 2—As above, but with Class 4- climbing.
Special equipment:	Wading boots.
Note:	Those doing Part 2 will encounter thick stands of unavoidable poison ivy in lower Scorpion Gulch.
Land status:	These hikes are in Grand Staircase-Escalante National Monument and Glen Canyon National Recreation Area.

This loop combines the finest stretch of the Escalante River with two impressive canyons—Twentyfive Mile Wash and Scorpion Gulch. Ceaseless Wingate walls, rows of Moqui steps, the Harry Aleson inscription, access to the Moody canyons, idyllic pools in Scorpion Gulch, and other assorted delights and distractions add panache to an already great hike.

The hike comes in two parts. Part 1 starts at the Early Weed Bench trailhead and goes down Fox Canyon into Twentyfive Mile Wash, which is followed to the Escalante River. A short walk along the river leads to a sand dune that takes you out of the canyon. A cross-country route goes across the north end of Scorpion back to the trailhead.

Part 2 continues down the Escalante River to Scorpion Gulch. It then goes up Scorpion Gulch and across the middle part of Scorpion back to the trailhead.

Part 1: Down Fox Canyon

(**Egypt map, Map Nineteen,** and **Map Twenty.**) From the trail register walk northwest along the road to the "Tee" mentioned at mile 4.4 in the Egypt Bench Road Section. Turn right (N) and hike to the edge of the escarpment. A slickrock bowl below you marks the top of a canyon dropping to the northeast. Descend a steep Navajo slab into the bowl. A small inner gorge develops. Stay along its left side until you are on a prow overlooking the vertical walls of Fox Canyon (LKA). (Fox Canyon is not named on the map. It is located to the northeast of elevation 5053T.) A path on a bench below a steep slab (Class 3) is visible to the east-northeast. Follow the path into Fox Canyon and down it to Twentyfive Mile Wash. (1.5–2.5 hours.)

To the Escalante River

You have intersected Twentyfive Mile Wash a short distance below the Glen Canyon National Recreation Area boundary. Good campsites along the stream abound. You may encounter short stretches of wading. A host of side canyons are interesting to explore. They are detailed in Hike #14. Although camping is nonexistent at the mouth of Twentyfive Mile Wash, there is fine camping a short distance down the Escalante River. (3.5–5.0 hours.)

To the Overland Route: Warning! This route is technically difficult and has lots of exposure. Experienced rock climbers only. To intersect the section of the Overland Route that runs between Twentyfive Mile Wash and Scorpion Gulch, hike down the Escalante River from the mouth of Twentyfive Mile Wash for a couple of hundred yards, then cross the river. Skirt along the base of the cliff to a break in the wall. The first ten feet are the hardest (Class 5.5, 10'), but climbing a cottonwood tree can ease the difficulty. The steep gully above has Moqui steps. Pass a crack near the top by using an exposed set of Moqui steps to the left (Class 5.2, 60'). Hike across a wide terrace and climb a sloping ramp (Class 4+) that has Moqui steps near its top to the rim.

To the exit route

Head down the river for several minutes. The exit route out of the canyon goes up the first sand dune encountered on the right (W). (The dune is located one-eighth mile northwest of elevation 4538T.) There is no water on Scorpion. Load up before leaving the river.

At the top of the dune work southwest along the Kayenta ledges that parallel Twentyfive Mile Wash until a side canyon to your right (W) forces you south. Make your way to a high point at the top of the canyon. Follow a compass course west-southwest across Scorpion. Make sure to stay far enough south to avoid the drainages that

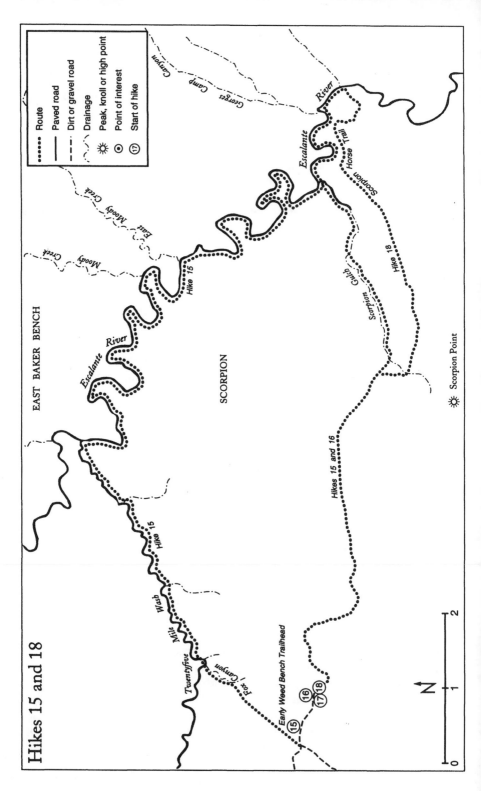

Map Nineteen

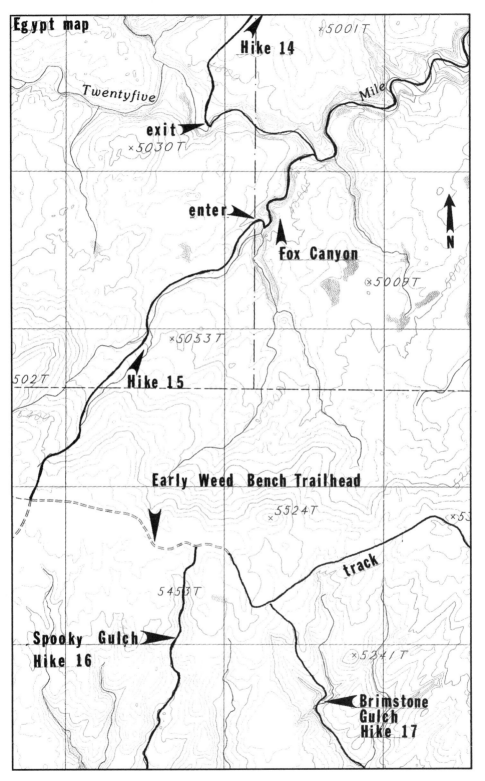

Map Twenty

drop north into Twentyfive Mile Wash. One of those canyons (shown to the north of elevation 4950AT) contains large potholes, though the canyon is difficult to get into (Class 4+). The closer you get to the escarpment leading to the Early Weed Bench trailhead, the more familiar things should look. Do not worry too much about hitting the trailhead right on, as this can be hard to do. (4.0–6.0 hours.)

Part 2: On down the river

(**Egypt map.**) Instead of exiting the river at the sand dune, continue downcanyon. The hiking varies between stretches of wading and making your way across benches behind thick stands of willow and tamarisk. A cave high on a wall to the left (N) just past the first corner (at the edge of the map) contains an inscription by Harry Aleson and the date May 27, 1949, which was during his second raft trip down the Escalante River. See the "Harry Aleson and Georgie White—The First to Run the Escalante" chapter for details.

> **Rock climber's note:** A steep row of Moqui steps a short distance upcanyon from the cave leads to East Baker Bench (Class 5.4, 50').

(**Scorpion Gulch map.**) As you head downcanyon toward Moody Creek you can look for three Moqui-step exits out of the canyon. Two go south up to Scorpion; the other goes north up to East Baker Bench.

> **Rock climber's note:** Although the Moqui-step exits are for rock climbers only, they are exciting to find, and their locations high on the walls of the river provide excellent vantage points. Both of the routes that exit to the south start with a moderate climb through an initial cliff band, then a traverse upcanyon to the highest cliff. Moqui steps will appear.
> The first set of Moqui steps is located at the tip of a long peninsula shown to the north of elevation 5304T (Class 5.4, 20'). This exit is used on the Overland Route to escape Escalante Canyon on the way to Scorpion Gulch.
> The second set of Moqui steps is located on a prow shown to the northeast of the same elevation and is visible from the river. This row of steps is exposed and intimidating (Class 5.3, 60').
> The Moqui steps that exit Escalante Canyon to the north go up a prow to the west of a drainage shown to the west of elevation 5081T. This exit is used as an entrance to Escalante Canyon on the Overland Route.

To the Moody canyons

Moody Creek comes in on the left (N). The Chinle Formation forms the floor of the canyon and Wingate walls tower high above.

There is good camping at its mouth, and medium springs a short distance upcanyon dispense clean water. (4.5–6.5 hours.)

Stay on the left side of the river. A poor path quickly turns into a horse trail that leads to the mouth of East Moody Canyon. There is good camping at its mouth, and medium springs are a quarter mile upcanyon. (1.0 hour.)

A short distance below East Moody Canyon is a large abandoned meander on the left (E) that is interesting to walk around. The walls of the canyon increase dramatically in height and the canyon narrows considerably. The mud-like Chinle becomes more prevalent the farther downcanyon you go. **(Map Twenty-two.)** Scorpion Gulch comes in on the right (SW). It contains large springs. At its mouth is a triangular, pinnacle-like tower. Campsites are available a short distance down the Escalante River or a mile up Scorpion Gulch. (5.0–8.0 hours.)

Up Scorpion Gulch

An established path through the Wingate-walled narrows near the mouth of the canyon eases the way through the thick vegetation and unavoidable stands of poison ivy. Pass a rockfall on the left (Class 4-). This signals the end of the running water for a mile. The Wingate walls peter out and the canyon widens as it enters the Kayenta. At a hard right turn a short stretch of large spring-fed pools line the floor of the canyon. (These pools are usually dry in the summer.) If you camp in the area, please stay in the sandy wash below the pools. Do not camp next to the pools. Before heading upcanyon, it is best to fill up with water. There is no reliable water along the route back to the trailhead.

A couple of minutes above the pools a short side canyon comes in on the right (N) (shown to the southwest of elevation 5048T).

> **Digression:** The short side canyon, though difficult to negotiate (Class 3+), leads to a fantastic view of the high Navajo dome country on the east side of Escalante Canyon, and provides egress from Scorpion Gulch. This is a highly recommended diversion. (1.0–2.0 hours round-trip.)

The canyon again divides. Go left (W) toward a huge overhang. A long string of large south-facing caves were used by Anasazi Indians.

> **Rock climber's note:** A couple of breaks in the Navajo that contain rows of Moqui steps can be used to exit the canyon.

A good trail leads through a stretch of deep ravines and thick underbrush. Water may be available but is often hard to get to. By

Spring-fed pools in Scorpion Gulch.

the time you cross a large sand dune that crosses the canyon from wall to wall the springs have ended. A sand dune on the right (NW), a short distance before the end of the canyon, is the exit. (2.5–3.5 hours.)

Back to the trailhead

From the top of the sand dune look west. A long, low ridge is visible a couple of miles away. In the middle of the ridge is an area of white slickrock. (The ridge contains elevations 5492T and 5387T on the **Egypt map**.) Hike west across small slickrock ridges and over the white slickrock to the top of the ridge. Go west-northwest across the ridge top. An arch should be visible a short distance down the hill. (The arch is one-quarter mile east of elevation 5283T.) If you cannot locate the arch, do not panic! Before you is a wide, shallow bowl. Behind it to the west is a ridge with a flattened dome on its right side. You may be able to see cars parked at the lower Early Weed Bench trailhead at the end of the road.

From the arch go northwest toward the right side of the flattened dome. Near the far side of the wide bowl intersect an old track that is now used by cattle and horses. It is the only track in the area. If you intersect deep draws or canyons that drop to the left (S), simply head them. You will eventually pick up the track. Follow it over the head of Brimstone Gulch and back to the trailhead. (3.5–4.5 hours.)

Spooky and Peek-A-Boo Gulches— The Long Loop—Hike #16

Season:	Any. Recent rains will make this a tough hike.
Time:	6.0 to 8.0 hours.
Water:	There may be no water along the route. Bring your own drinking water.
Elevation range:	4670' to 5480'.
Maps:	Egypt and Big Hollow Wash.
Skill level:	Moderate route finding. Class 5.0 climbing. The leader must be experienced with belay techniques and be capable of leading the climbing sections without protection. There may be some wading. This is a strenuous hike that is suitable only for those in excellent condition. Those on the stout side cannot make it through the incredibly tight narrows. **This slot is not suitable for claustrophobes, novice slot canyoneers, youngsters, or youth groups.**
Special equipment:	Wading boots and a forty-foot rope are required. Bring a small day pack; a large one will not fit through the narrows.
Land status:	This hike is in Grand Staircase-Escalante National Monument.

Often a landform with a bold, descriptive, mysterious name is enough to pique one's interest. Death Hollow, Harveys Fear Canyon, Hidden Passage Canyon, and Lost Eden Canyon are classic

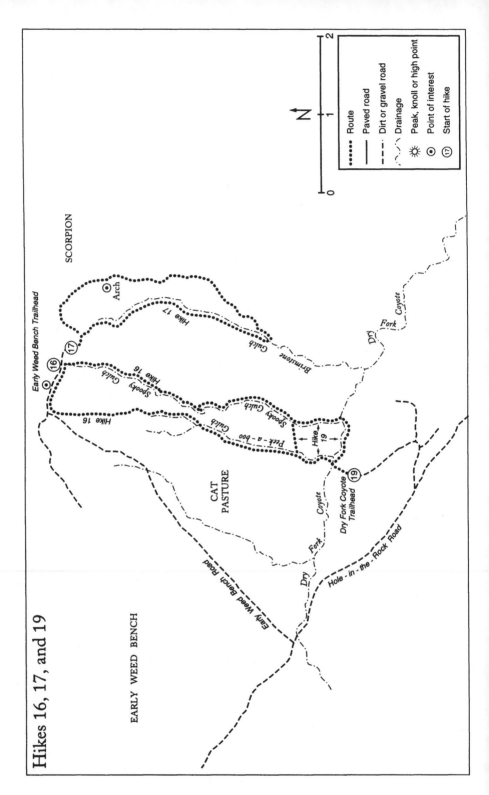

Hikes 16, 17, and 19

SCORPION

Arch

Early Weed Bench Trailhead

⊙ 16   ⑰ 17

Hike 17

Brimstone Gulch

Dry Fork Coyote

Spooky Gulch

Hike 16

Hike 16

Spooky Gulch

Peek-a-boo Gulch

Hike 19

CAT PASTURE

Dry Fork Coyote

Dry Fork Coyote Trailhead ⑲

Early Weed Bench Road

EARLY WEED BENCH

Dry Fork Coyote

Hole-in-the-Rock Road

N

0   1   2

- - - - - Route
―――― Paved road
― · ― · ― Dirt or gravel road
﹏﹏﹏ Drainage
☼ Peak, knoll or high point
⊙ Point of interest
⑰ Start of hike

Map Twenty-one

examples. It is harder, after all, to get excited about such colorless-sounding places as Cottonwood Wash, Cow Canyon, or Sheep Gulch.

The two elegant slots presented in this hike—Peek-a-boo and Spooky gulches—are of such high quality that they do live up to their enigmatic appellations. There has been some speculation about where their names came from. Shortly before his death in 1993, Escalante historian and schoolteacher Edson Alvey told me that they were suggested while he was exploring the two slot canyons with a group of schoolchildren on Halloween day in 1935.

The route starts on top of Early Weed Bench and descends the whole length of Spooky Gulch; it returns via most of Peek-a-boo Gulch.

Down Spooky Gulch

(**Egypt map, Map Twenty,** and **Map Twenty-one.**) Hike south into Spooky Gulch. (Spooky Gulch is not labeled on the map. It starts one-eighth mile east of elevation 5453T.) The canyon drops quickly and enters a long, tight slot. The crux of the route comes at a twenty-foot drop. Skirt along the right edge of the canyon for twenty-five yards to a point where the slot narrows considerably. Chimney down into the slot (Class 5.0, 12', belay as necessary). There may be some wading ahead. The canyon alternates between short slots and sandy stretches until it ends at Dry Fork Coyote. (**Big Hollow Wash map.**) (3.0–3.5 hours.)

Up Peek-a-boo Gulch

Hike up Dry Fork Coyote for fifteen minutes to the mouth of Peek-a-boo Gulch. (Peek-a-boo Gulch is not labeled on the map. It is located one-quarter mile east of elevation 4988.) A chiseled row of steps leads up a short wall into the canyon. The Peek-a-boo slot ends in a sandy wash. Follow the wash north until a canyon starts to develop, then divides (one-quarter mile east-southeast of elevation 5203T on the **Egypt map**). The main canyon goes left (NW). Hike into the canyon on the right (NE).

> **Digression:** Follow the main fork to the left. Though the canyon ends at a fall in a half mile, it is delightfully narrow. (1.0 hour round-trip.)

The canyon quickly ends. Scramble out of it and follow a ridge line north between Peek-a-boo Gulch on the left and Spooky Gulch on the right. A variety of multicolored domes, knobs, and heavily cross-bedded sandstone provides a fitting finish to a fine day. Hike the road back to the trailhead. (2.5–3.5 hours.)

Upper Brimstone Gulch—The Slot—Hike #17

Season:	Any. Recent rains will make this a tough hike.
Time:	5.0 to 7.0 hours.
Water:	There may be no water along this route. Bring your own drinking water.
Elevation range:	4800' to 5440'.
Maps:	Egypt and Big Hollow Wash.
Skill level:	Moderate route finding. Class 4 climbing. There may be some wading. This route is suitable for thin athletes only. The slot is so narrow that those of hefty build cannot make it through. **This slot is not appropriate for claustrophobes, novice slot canyoneers, youngsters, or youth groups.**
Special equipment:	Wading boots. Use the smallest daypack you can. A large pack will be difficult to maneuver through the narrowest sections. A forty-foot rope will prove useful.
Land status:	This hike is in Grand Staircase-Escalante National Monument.

Brimstone Gulch reminds me of one of my childhood heroes, David Innes, who, in Edgar Rice Burroughs's *At the Earth's Core*, made his way to Pellucidar, a land buried deep in the very bowels of the earth. Brimstone Gulch is often explored from its bottom end, but hikers there are stopped by its unrelenting narrows. Its upper section also contains long stretches of tight, sinuous narrows.

The route starts on top of Early Weed Bench and descends most of Brimstone Gulch. It returns to the trailhead along the rim of the canyon, providing an opportunity to view an exquisite and seldom seen arch.

Down Brimstone Gulch

(Egypt map, **Map Twenty** and **Map Twenty-one.**) From the parking area at the end of the road locate a Wilderness Study Area sign on a flexible post at the start of a no longer used track that goes downhill to the southeast. Follow the sandy track for five minutes until it crosses a short stretch of Navajo slickrock, dips into a shallow wash, then goes up a gentle rise—the first uphill section of the track. Do not go up the hill. Leave the track and hike southeast down the wash.

Easily skirt two small drops. Pass the third drop—a steep slot lined with large potholes—on the left by descending a broken wall

Arch above Brimstone Gulch.

to a bench that is above another slot. Follow the bench downcanyon until it intersects yet another slot. Find what seems to be an unlikely route south-southwest down a steep prow formed by the junction of the two slots into the main canyon. Ball-bearing rock covers the prow. Be careful!

The first narrows start shortly below the slab. If you cannot make it through them, it is time to call it a day. The slot only gets tighter and more difficult below. Now the canyon alternates between slots and sandy sections. Escapes from the canyon are manifold.

The ultra narrows are very long and incredibly tight. At the end of this section a small gully on the right provides egress from the canyon, if needed. Below, negotiate several large pools directly or, in every case, pass them on the right. The route ends at a high drop in the slot. You cannot continue past this point. (You are at about the "e" in Brimstone on the **Big Hollow Wash map**.) (3.0–4.0 hours.)

To the trailhead

Backtrack for several minutes to the first possible exit on the right (LUC)(E). Hike generally north through mesmerizing slick-rock domes, heading or crossing small canyons as needed. Eventually you will be forced to the rim of the canyon. Keep a sharp eye out for an arch near the rim. (It is located one-quarter mile west-northwest of elevation 5283T on the **Egypt map**.) Near the head of the canyon you will intersect the track you started on. Follow it back over the head of Brimstone Gulch to the trailhead. (2.0–3.0 hours.)

> **Digression:** The enthusiastic explorer can combine Brimstone, Spooky, and Peek-a-boo gulches into a slot canyon tour de force. Instead of exiting Brimstone Gulch on the left (LDC)(E), find a route out on the right (LDC)(W). Hike west over a rise into Spooky Gulch, the first canyon you encounter. It is a wide wash at this point. Now follow the directions in Hike #16. Peek-a-boo Gulch takes you back to the top of Early Weed Bench.

Scorpion Gulch and the Scorpion Horse Trail— Hike #18

Season:	Spring or fall. Due to a long, dry cross-country stretch, do not attempt this route in the summer or during periods of hot weather.
Time:	15.0 to 20.0 hours. This is a very long two-day hike. Three or four days are recommended.
Water:	Water availability is a problem on this route. The Escalante River has a perennial flow of water. Scorpion Gulch has large springs. The cross-country route back to the trailhead is dry. One dry camp is recommended.
Elevation range:	4200' to 5400'.
Maps:	Egypt and Scorpion Gulch. If you plan to do the rock climber's route, add the Stevens Canyon North map.

Along the Scorpion Horse Trail.

Skill level:	Moderately difficult route finding. There is one long cross-country stretch. Class 4- climbing without exposure. Some wading. This is a strenuous hike suitable for the experienced and fit backpacker. Low impact camping skills are essential.
Special equipment:	Wading shoes or boots. Have enough water capacity to deal with a dry camp. Two gallons for each person are recommended.
Note:	Lower Scorpion Gulch contains thick stands of poison ivy that are not avoidable.
Land status:	This hike is in Grand Staircase-Escalante National Monument and Glen Canyon National Recreation Area.

Sometimes redundancy is the better part of practicality. Although a route up Scorpion Gulch was described in Hike #15, Scorpion Gulch is such a popular hike that it only makes sense to describe the route going the other way—downcanyon. To add zest and to make the hike into a loop, the Scorpion Horse Trail, the finest ledge walk in the Escalante, is traversed on the return trip.

The route starts at the Early Weed Bench trailhead, crosses Scorpion, and goes down Scorpion Gulch. After a short trek down the Escalante River, the Scorpion Horse Trail is followed out of the canyon. A cross-country jaunt that heads Scorpion Gulch and crosses Scorpion leads back to the trailhead.

To Scorpion Gulch

(**Egypt map** and **Map Nineteen.**) From the end of the road,

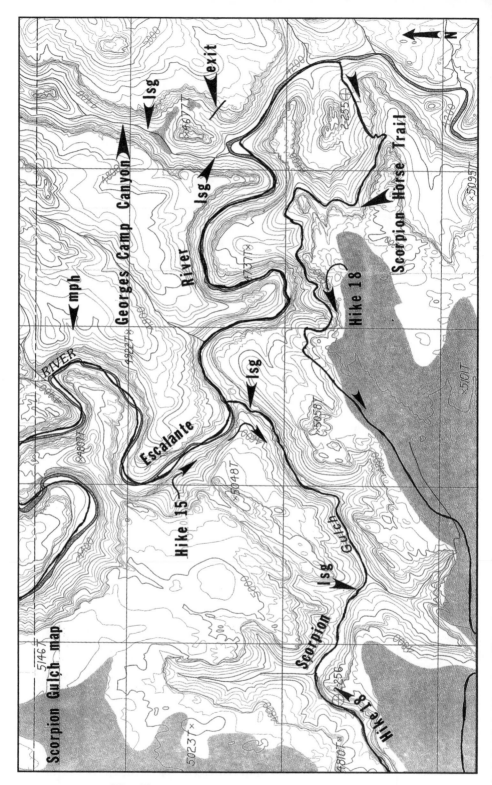

Map Twenty-two

look east. Below you is the gorge of Brimstone Gulch. Farther to the east is a long, low ridge (elevations 5492T and 5387T). In the background, with only its upper half visible, is Scorpion Point, a flat-topped slickrock mesa (elevation 5460 on the Scorpion Gulch map). On its right side is a small pointed dome; to its right is a small dark pinnacle (the tail of the scorpion).

From the parking area at the end of the road locate a Wilderness Study Area sign on a flexible post at the start of a no longer used track that goes downhill to the southeast. Follow the track as it turns northeast and goes over the head of Brimstone Gulch and past elevation 5378T before turning south for a short distance. When the track turns northeast again, watch for a small arch in the middle of the long, low ridge to the right (E). (The arch is one-quarter mile east of elevation 5283T.) Leave the track and hike to the arch. It is formed from a thin layer of limestone that composes the lowest member of the Carmel Formation.

Hike east to the top of the ridge. Scorpion Point will be visible to the east. (**Scorpion Gulch map.**) Note that a descending ridge (containing elevation 5253T) drops northeast from the highest point. Scorpion Gulch starts at the end of this ridge, which should be used as a landmark. A sand dune on the west side of Scorpion Gulch near its head leads into the canyon. (3.5–4.5 hours.)

Down Scorpion Gulch

An established trail leads down Scorpion Gulch. Water starts flowing just past a large sand dune, though it disappears underground from time to time. An area of large spring-fed pools at a sharp left bend in the canyon is a delight. These springs are dry in the summer. (**Map Twenty-two.**) If you camp in the area, please stay in the sandy wash below the pools. Do not camp next to the pools.

The canyon enters the Wingate and becomes more narrow. A large chockstone is passed on the right (Class 4-). Below the chockstone a riparian habitat develops and large springs are found. Poison ivy becomes a problem. There are a few small campsites near the Escalante River. (2.5–3.5 hours.)

> **Rock climber's note:** There are two difficult routes to the top of the Escalante escarpment on the opposite side of the river to the north. One consists of climbing a steep wall (Class 5.4, 25'); the other ascends a narrow rib dotted with Moqui steps that is a couple of hundred yards downcanyon from the mouth of Scorpion Gulch (Class 5.0, 60'). The route through the initial cliff band for both climbs starts 100 yards up the river.

To Georges Camp Canyon

Walk and wade down the Escalante River. Georges Camp Canyon is the first canyon on the left (N). Its mouth is marked by a large abandoned meander (elevation 4677T). The canyon to the left (W) of the abandoned meander contains a large freshwater spring and good campsites are nearby. (1.0–1.5 hours.)

Rock climber's note: A fine route suitable for rock climbers starts here. The hike takes 9.0–12.0 hours, requires several short climbing pitches, some wading, and perhaps a short swim or two.

Follow a rarely used horse trail up a steep hill to the right (E) side of the abandoned meander. The Wingate wall to the right (E), though it looks sheer from the ground, is broken in one place. (**Map Twenty-two.**) Find a route through a hole and up a chimney (Class 5.4, 60') to the top of the wall. You may see a worn row of Moqui steps on your way up. This route may take some scouting to find.

Follow the right (E) rim of the east fork of Georges Camp Canyon, staying on top of the Wingate or running along Kayenta benches for about three hours until it is possible to drop into the canyon. (There are many entrances once you are even with elevation 6318T on the Stevens Canyon North map).

Proceed downcanyon. The canyon narrows and short pour-offs into pools prove challenging (Class 5.5, 20'). You must deal with some directly; others you can find routes around. A wall on the left (LDC) in the middle of the narrows contains an amazing row of Moqui steps that go up an overhang. Pass a large fall on a thin ledge to the right (LDC); then climb down a short crack. The climbing difficulties are over, but there are still a couple of hours of boulder hopping and rough going ahead before you reach the Escalante River.

To the Scorpion Horse Trail

From Georges Camp Canyon continue down the Escalante River for twenty minutes to a large cliff dune on the right (W) (located at 2-255, an abandoned meander shown on the map). Before you leave the river, calculate your water needs. You will not find water along the route until back at the trailhead, 8.0 to 10.5 hours away. A jump start is advised. Hike up the dune. The Scorpion Horse Trail becomes apparent as you enter the Kayenta. A wide terrace on top of the Kayenta provides an excellent place to camp for the night. (1.0 hour.)

From the top of the Kayenta follow the horse trail upcanyon (NW) below towering Navajo walls. The trail heads several short canyons and in an hour it turns abruptly left (S) (one-quarter mile east of elevation 5058T), goes up a steep broken hill, through a brush fence, and disappears in the sand at the top of the escarpment. (1.5–2.5 hours.)

Alternate route: If water is a problem, you can enter Scorpion Gulch. Instead of following the Scorpion Horse Trail up the hill to the top of the escarpment, continue north on the Kayenta until you are above Scorpion Gulch. Now follow tiring Kayenta ledges up Scorpion Gulch until it is possible to descend to the canyon floor near the spring-fed pools.

To the trailhead

From the top of the escarpment, Scorpion Point is visible to the west-southwest. Using the point as a landmark, make your way along the rim of Scorpion Gulch to its head (2.0–2.5 hours.)

The sand dune you used initially to get into Scorpion Gulch will be visible a short distance downcanyon. Use directions from Hike #15 to get back to the trailhead. (3.5–4.5 hours.)

Dry Fork Coyote Road Section
Access to Hike #19.
Access is from the Hole-in-the-Rock road.
Map—Big Hollow Wash.

The Dry Fork Coyote road starts 25.9 miles down the Hole-in-the-Rock road at the "Dry Fork Trailhead 1.7 mi." sign (shown as a Jeep Trail at elevation 4884 on the **Big Hollow Wash map**). The track is suitable for high-clearance vehicles. There are several campsites along the track. (See **Map Fifteen**.)

0.0 — At the Hole-in-the-Rock road. Go east.

0.6 — "Y." Go left (W). The track you are now on is not shown on the USGS map.

1.6 — Start of Peek-a-boo and Spooky Gulches—The Standard Loop **Hike #19**. At a parking circle on the edge of a cliff. Limited camping. The trailhead is not shown on the USGS map. It is located one-quarter mile north of elevation 4932. You are in Navajo Sandstone.

Digression: Dry Fork Coyote provides alternative access to Hurricane Wash and Coyote Gulch. Although the wash in its upper reaches is sandy and tiring to hike, several short side canyons make it worthwhile. The text that follows notes water sources.

See Hike #19 for directions on entering Dry Fork Coyote. Once in the canyon, hike down it, passing the mouths of Peek-a-boo, Spooky, and Brimstone gulches. A short side canyon to the left (shown to the east of elevation 4803) contains a long string of medium potholes and a small natural bridge.

Boxelder Canyon (LKA), named for a small stand of those trees near its mouth, comes in on the left (N) (located to the east of elevation 4744). The canyon is sand-floored, pristine, and pretty. A medium pothole can be found near the end of the canyon on a bench below a hanging garden.

Grove Canyon (AN), twenty-five minutes down from Boxelder Canyon, and also on the left (N) (located to the east of elevation 4587), is difficult to locate because its mouth is obscured by a handsome grove of cottonwoods. A short distance up this side canyon, a slab on the right leads out of the canyon. Follow the rim upcanyon to a small drainage and a large pothole. At the end of the canyon, below a pour-off, is a medium pothole.

The hike down Dry Fork Coyote from Grove Canyon to Coyote Gulch is best described as a pretty chore. The vegetation which chokes the canyon and the seasonal ponds that form along its course can make for frustrating walking. See Hike #20 for details on continuing down Coyote Gulch. (King Mesa map.) (5.5 to 7.5 hours from the Dry Fork Coyote trailhead to Coyote Gulch.)

Peek-A-Boo and Spooky Gulches— The Standard Loop—Hike #19

Season:	Any. Recent rains can make this a tough hike.
Time:	2.5 to 4.5 hours.
Water:	There is no water along this route. Bring your own drinking water.
Elevation range:	4640' to 4960'.
Map:	Big Hollow Wash.
Skill level:	Easy route finding. Class 4+ climbing. The leader must be experienced with belay techniques and be capable of leading the climbing sections without protection. Exceptionally rotund hikers cannot squeeze through Spooky Gulch.
Special equipment:	A forty-foot rope will reassure beginners and youngsters. Large day packs will not fit through the slots.
Note:	On busy weekends these slots are packed with people. Try to do them during the week or in the off-season.
Land status:	This hike is in Grand Staircase-Escalante National Monument.

This is the premier and most popular short slot loop on the Colorado Plateau. Claustrophobically tight narrows, a host of natural bridges, and sensuous curves of cross-stratified sandstone combine to provide a magnificent experience.

The route starts by entering Dry Fork Coyote. It then goes up

Peek-a-boo Gulch, crosses a small ridge, and descends Spooky Gulch.

To Peek-a-boo Gulch

(**Big Hollow Wash map** and **Map Twenty-one.**) From the trailhead look north-northeast. Dry Fork Coyote is below you. On the far side of the canyon you will see one large vertical wall. To its right is a short narrow gap. This is Peek-a-boo Gulch. (Peek-a-boo Gulch is not labeled on the map. It is located to the east of elevation 4988.) A cairned trail takes you north down the initial cliff band and a small drainage that ends on the right side of a sand dune. Do not skirt along the top of the dune. Instead, descend straight down into a small canyon that leads to Dry Fork Coyote. Multiple trails are a problem in this area. Keep on the trail and off the sand dune.

The slots

Ascend a row of recently and needlessly carved steps into Peek-a-boo Gulch. Two sets of natural bridges, one large, the other small, are a major attraction for photographers. Small challenges lie ahead. One short section of slot is too tight to squeeze through. Exit the slot, walk the rim for a short distance, then drop back into the slot. It ends in a wash just about the time you are getting warmed up.

Cut due east across a low ridge for ten minutes (many options) to Spooky Gulch, which starts as the first wide sandy wash you intersect. (Spooky Gulch is not labeled on the map. It is located to the west of elevation 4970.) Proceed downcanyon. The wide wash quickly narrows and the fun begins. Tight slots, short drops, and a route through a chockstone jungle are a delight. The slot ends and a short walk down the wash leads back to Dry Fork Coyote.

> **Digression:** Brimstone Gulch is a short distance down Dry Fork Coyote and is worth exploring. Hike downcanyon along the wide, sandy wash. The canyon narrows and a large chockstone blocks the way. Pass it on the right (Class 5.0, 10'). The canyon again opens. A curtain of white guano marks a large bird nest on the right-hand wall. Brimstone Gulch enters from the left (N) shortly past the bird nest.
>
> Though wide and sandy at its mouth, Brimstone Gulch narrows into a spectacular slot. Squeeze your way up as far as you are comfortable. You cannot make it all the way through. When you return to Dry Fork Coyote, you can walk downcanyon for a couple of minutes to a slickrock slab on the right (SW). It leads to the rim of the canyon, which you can follow back to the trailhead.

To the trailhead

Hike up Dry Fork Coyote to the mouth of Peek-a-boo Gulch. You are in a broad sandy area. Look west. A narrow opening marks

Jack Dykinga in Spooky Gulch.

the mouth of upper Dry Fork Coyote. Ramble through its never-ending narrows. As the narrows die, pick one of many exits to the left (LUC) and follow a southeasterly course over low hills back to the trailhead.

. . .

Red Well Trailhead Road Section
Access to Coyote Gulch.
Access is from the Hole-in-the-Rock road.
Map—Big Hollow Wash.

The Red Well road starts 30.7 miles down the Hole-in-the-Rock road at the "Red Well 1.5 mi." sign (located one-quarter mile south of Liston Seep on the **Big Hollow Wash map**). The track is suitable for high-clearance vehicles. There are several campsites along the track. Do note that the Red Well trailhead is not located at Red Well, which is a mile to the southwest. (See **Map Fifteen**.)

0.0 — At the Hole-in-the-Rock road. Go northeast.

1.0 — Good camping in this area. The track becomes much rougher ahead.

1.3 — End of the track. Trailhead and trail register. Limited camping. The trailhead is located at the end of the track near elevation 4530. You are in Navajo Sandstone.

> **Digression:** The Red Well trailhead is located near the confluence of Big Hollow Wash and upper Coyote Gulch. It provides alternate access to Hurricane Wash and Coyote Gulch. Hike east down a track into Coyote Gulch. In thirty-five minutes Dry Fork Coyote comes in on the left (N). (King Mesa map.) Water may start to flow here. Pass a waterfall in a gorge on either side. The first side canyon below a hiker's maze, on the left (N), is Sleepy Hollow (LKA). (It is shown to the east of elevation 4500.)
>
> The canyon slowly deepens and narrows. Hurricane Wash comes in as a narrow defile on the right (W). (3.5–4.5 hours.) See Hike #20 for details on exploring Coyote Gulch from Hurricane Wash to the Escalante River.
>
> A popular continuation of this hike goes up the Escalante River from its confluence with Coyote Gulch to Fools Canyon. Make your way up Fools Canyon through a thick tangle of brush (some poison ivy), over and around beaver dams and ponds, down a cliff (Class 5.1, 30', belay and lower packs), until you are above a huge pool. (Immediately above the pool the thrashing ends and the canyon floor is slickrock.) Exit the canyon on the left (LUC)(SW) by way of a constructed cattle trail (described in Hike #21). Cross broken terrain to the west end of King Mesa (near elevation 5294). From there the Red Well trailhead may be visible. Descend into Coyote Gulch (many options) and return to the trailhead. (Four to five days for the complete loop.)
>
> **Historical note:** Red Well was developed by rancher Ursel "Red" Shirts. The Shirts family, consisting of Carl Shirts, his wife, and

nine children, was part of the first contingent of settlers to the Escalante area in 1875.

Hurricane Wash Trailhead Road Section
Access to Coyote Gulch.
Access is from the Hole-in-the-Rock road.
Map—Big Hollow Wash.

The signed Hurricane Wash trailhead is 33.8 miles down the Hole-in-the-Rock road and is located in a large pull-off on the right near several large tamarisk trees. (The trailhead is located one-eighth mile southeast of Willow Tank at a Jeep Trail on the **Big Hollow Wash map**.) There is camping at the trailhead. You are in the Carmel Formation. (See **Map Fifteen**.)

> **Digression:** Hurricane Wash provides easy and popular access to lower Coyote Gulch. From the parking area, cross the road and walk east on a track along the left side of Hurricane Wash to a trail register. Now either follow the track or the wash. The domes and goblins on the left are in Entrada Sandstone. The canyon walls build slowly and it is not until you reach a Glen Canyon National Recreation Area boundary sign that the wash changes to a canyon. (King Mesa map.) Water starts flowing a short distance above the confluence with Coyote Gulch. See Hike #20 for details on exploring the rest of Coyote Gulch. (2.5–3.5 hours from the trailhead to Coyote Gulch.)

Fortymile Ridge Road Section
Access to Hikes #20 through 23.
Access is from the Hole-in-the-Rock road.
Maps—Sooner Bench and King Mesa.

The Fortymile Ridge road starts 36.1 miles down the Hole-in-the-Rock road at the "40 Mile Bench" sign (located halfway between elevations 4766 and 4727 on the **Sooner Bench map**). The track is suitable for high-clearance vehicles for the first 4.0 miles. It is suitable for 4WD vehicles after that. There is limited camping along the track. (See **Map Fifteen**.)

0.0   —At the Hole-in-the-Rock road. Go northeast.

0.6   —Cattle guard.

4.0   —**(King Mesa map.)** Start of Coyote Gulch **Hike #20**. "Y." The track to the left (N) goes up a short steep hill to a large stock tank and the Coyote Gulch trailhead and trail register. There is good camping here. The trailhead is located at a bend in the track shown near elevation 4805. You are in the Carmel Formation.

The track ahead now gets rougher and is full of long sand traps. Only 4WD vehicle may be able to make it through them. Be careful.

5.3	—Cattle guard.
6.1	—Glen Canyon National Recreation Area boundary.
6.6	—Start of Stevens Canyon and the Waterpocket Fold **Hike #21**, Stevens and Fold Canyons **Hike #22**, and the Pollywog Bench Area **Hike #23**. At the Fortymile Ridge trailhead and trail register. There is good camping here. The trailhead is located just south of elevation 4678. You are in the Carmel Formation.

Coyote Gulch—Hike #20

Season:	Any.
Time:	Part 1—5.0 to 7.0 hours. Although the hike can be done in one day, there is so much to explore that it is best done as a two-day hike.
	Part 2—9.5 to 12.0 hours. This is best done as a two- or three-day hike.
Water:	Water availability is not a problem on this hike. Lower Hurricane Wash has large springs and Coyote Gulch has a perennial flow of water.
Elevation range:	Part 1—4060' to 4805'.
	Part 2—3720' to 4805'.
Maps:	Part 1—King Mesa.
	Part 2—Add Stevens Canyon South.
Skill level:	Part 1—Moderate route finding. Class 5.0 climbing with exposure. The leader must be experienced with belay techniques and be capable of leading the climbing section without protection. Lots of shallow wading. This is a moderate route. If done as an overnight hike, low-impact camping skills are necessary.
	Part 2—Moderate route finding. Class 3+ scrambling. Lots of shallow wading. This is a moderate route. Familiarity with low-impact camping techniques is essential.
Special equipment:	Part 1—Wading boots. A long, steep climb out of the canyon near Jacob Hamblin Arch dictates the use of a 165-foot climbing rope.
	Part 2—Wading boots. No ropes are needed.
Note:	Coyote Gulch is the most popular canyon in the Escalante region. Spring brings an overwhelming number of people into the canyon.

Lower Coyote Gulch.

Fall, with its cooler weather and the beauty of the leaves changing color, is the preferred season.

Remember, group size is limited to twelve. Dogs must be leashed. No fires are allowed. These rules are strictly enforced in Coyote Gulch.

Multiple and braided trails are a major problem in Coyote Gulch. Stay on the main trail. There are plenty of campsites; do not make your own. Be exceptionally careful with garbage. Carry out more than you brought in. **You must carry out your toilet paper and leftover food when in Coyote Gulch!**

Land status: This hike is in Grand Staircase-Escalante National Monument and Glen Canyon National Recreation Area.

Like James Joyce's difficult novel *Ulysses*, Coyote Gulch with its many superlative side canyons and slot-like tributaries, several arches, a massive natural bridge, waterfalls, and towering walls draped with variegated varnish takes many visits over a period of years to fully understand and appreciate. Once used by Anasazi and Fremont Indians during the growing season, Coyote Gulch has become the canyon to which all others in southern Utah are compared.

One problem with exploring Coyote Gulch in the past has been that the standard routes into it—Red Well, Dry Fork Coyote, Hurricane Wash, and Fortymile Ridge—force the explorer to hike the length of the canyon twice, which essentially doubles the human load in the canyon. This loop hike eliminates that problem.

> **Note:** Some may want to explore lower Coyote Gulch—from Jacob Hamblin Arch to the Escalante River—without hiking through the upper canyon. I recommend you do this in reverse order by going down Crack-in-the-Wall, hiking up Coyote Gulch, and exiting at Jacob Hamblin Arch. This keeps you from downclimbing the steep slab at the arch, which is very dangerous.

The route comes in two parts. Part 1 starts on the crest of Fortymile Ridge, enters Hurricane Wash just as it starts to narrow, and follows it down to Coyote Gulch. A climb out of Coyote Gulch near Jacob Hamblin Arch, which is halfway down the canyon, takes one back to the trailhead.

Part 2 continues downcanyon from Jacob Hamblin Arch to the Escalante River and returns to the trailhead via Crack-in-the-Wall.

Part 1: To Hurricane Wash

(**King Mesa map** and **Map Twenty-three.**) Before you start the hike look north-northeast and spot two squat domes. (The dome on the left is at elevation 4843.) For those doing Part 1, you will hike between these domes at the end of the hike.

From the trailhead you can see Chimney Rock, a lone pinnacle on a flat plain in the distance to the west-northwest. Hike across a blackbrush-covered plain and over a low rise toward Chimney Rock. Descend slickrock into a very wide bowl and follow any one of the small washes downhill. The washes, turning sharply and often, slowly funnel together. Pass a small arch perched atop a tower. The

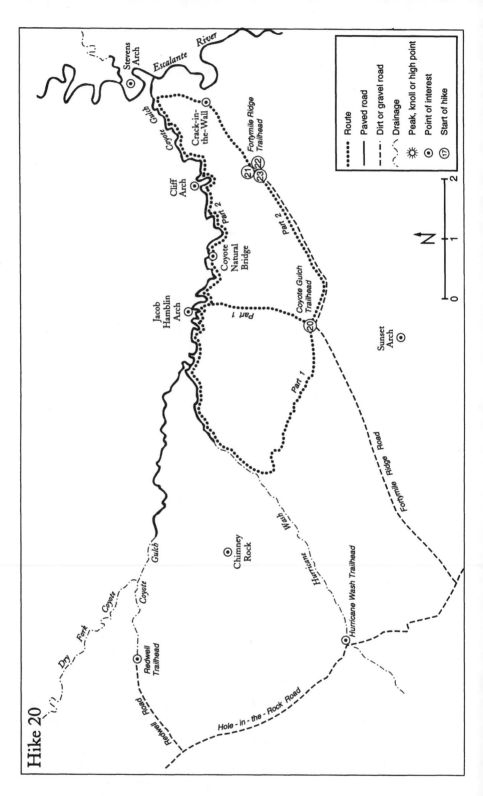

Hike 20

Stevens Arch

Escalante River

Coyote Gulch

Crack-in-the-Wall

Fortymile Ridge Trailhead

Cliff Arch

Part 2

Part 2

Coyote Natural Bridge

Jacob Hamblin Arch

Coyote Gulch Trailhead

Part 1

Part 1

Sunset Arch

Dry Fork Coyote

Coyote Gulch

Redwell Trailhead

Redwell Road

Chimney Rock

Wash

Hurricane

Hurricane Wash Trailhead

Fortymile Ridge Road

Hole-in-the-Rock Road

N

0   1   2

| Route |
| Paved road |
| Dirt or gravel road |
| Drainage |
| ☼ Peak, knoll or high point |
| ⊙ Point of interest |
| ⑰ Start of hike |

Map Twenty-three

gradient steepens and the wash enters a slot. This is the main drainage that flows into Hurricane Wash. (The drainage is shown to the north of elevation 4556.) Short sections of slot are interspersed with sandy washes. Rather than climbing through the slot, stay along its right (LDC) rim, skirting towers and scrambling over slickrock hills as necessary.

The slot turns into a deep gorge and intersects a wide sandy wash. A steep route down the slickrock at the confluence leads to the floor of the wash, as also do several easier slopes to the right. Follow the route downcanyon for a couple of minutes to Hurricane Wash. (1.5–2.0 hours.)

Down Hurricane Wash

You have intersected Hurricane Wash just as it gets interesting. The Navajo walls slowly build and narrow. Water starts flowing a half hour downcanyon and cottonwood-shaded benches make good campsites. Coyote Gulch, with its larger flow of water, comes up in a rush. There is good camping in the vicinity. (1.0–1.5 hours.)

Down Coyote Gulch

As you head down Coyote Gulch look for several rows of Moqui steps that lead out of the canyon on both sides. They are challenging to locate. The walking is serene along a trail that constantly crosses the creek. Arcadian stands of cottonwoods and enormous alcoves line the way. The canyon quickly constricts as it enters a stretch of "goosenecks," or tight meanders. Jacob Hamblin Arch has been cleaved by wind and water from a long fin of sandstone. Popular campsites proliferate in this area and a pit toilet is located a couple of hundred yards upcanyon from the arch on the left (LDC). (1.0–1.5 hours.)

Historical note: Jacob Hamblin Arch was originally named Lobo Arch by early ranchers out of respect for an old desert wolf that used to roam the area. The name Jacob Hamblin Arch was first suggested to local guide Burnett Hendricks by a man measuring silt on the Escalante River. Hendricks later mentioned the name to persons on a National Geographic expedition down Coyote Gulch in 1955. Robert Moore, a member of that expedition, described Jacob Hamblin Arch: "It looked to us as if a giant had thrust a fist through the rock wall to provide a peephole through which he might view the canyon beyond."

Jacob Hamblin, often called the "Mormon Leatherstocking," was sent to southern Utah in the 1850s by the head of the Mormon church, Brigham Young. Hamblin was the first Mormon missionary to visit the area and to befriend the local Indians. He was also a scout and an explorer who proved invaluable to John Wesley Powell during the latter's Colorado River adventures.

The dangerous climb near Jacob Hamblin Arch.

Exit Coyote Gulch

Hike past Jacob Hamblin Arch. Just as the arch disappears from view, ascend a steep trail to the right (LDC) to a sandy platform forty feet above the creek. Climb horizontally across a slickrock slab toward the arch (W) for fifty feet, then climb a steep slab (Class 5.0, 120', belay), using Moqui steps in places, to the top of the cliff.

> **Warning:** One evening my brother Ace, a couple of friends, and I sat on the rim of Coyote Gulch directly across from the Jacob Hamblin Arch exit slab. The spectacle we witnessed from our high perch still chills me. A group of adults and children were climbing the steepest part of the route—without a rope. We watched in horror as they slowly made their way upward by using shoulder stands, pulling small children up the cliff by their arms, and scratching for purchase on the polished rock.
>
> I remembered an incident many years ago when I had set my pack on a ledge while helping my group (on belay) up this same slab. One of the group grabbed my pack to use as a handhold (whoops). The pack was pulled off the ledge and I watched as it plummeted 150 feet to the floor of the canyon, bursting along the way.
>
> Now I envisioned a small body taking the same plunge, surely shattering as it bounced down the cliff. **This exit route, though used by many, is extremely dangerous. All due caution must be exercised. Belays MUST be used.**

Hike due south up the slickrock and pass through the two squat domes mentioned at the start of the hike. The trailhead is visible from the saddle. (1.5–2.0 hours.)

Part 2: Continuing on down Coyote Gulch

(**King Mesa map.**) From Jacob Hamblin Arch continue down-canyon. The character of the canyon changes. The narrow canyon widens and the way is lined with a lush and varied plant community. An hour down, Coyote Natural Bridge spans the canyon. Its sixty-eight-foot opening allows effortless passage and is a highlight of the trip. (1.0 hour.)

> **Historical note:** After walking through Coyote Natural Bridge, canyon explorer and environmental writer Edward Abbey wrote: "I walked under the bridge, feeling the sensuous pleasure of moving through a wall of stone, wading the stream that made the opening, standing in shadow and looking back at the upstream canyon bathed in morning light, the sparkling water, the varnished slick-rock walls, the fresh cool green of the cottonwoods, the pink and violet plumes of tamarisk."

The ensuing stretch of canyon contains several short side canyons that are worth a visit. The next major attraction is Cliff Arch, located high on a wall to the left. Early visitors called it Jug Handle Arch. (1.0 hour.)

Downcanyon the character of Coyote Gulch again changes. The creek has cut through Navajo Sandstone and into the Kayenta Formation. This formation, consisting of alternating layers of sandstones, siltstones, and mudstones, erodes into ledges that waterfalls now plummet over.

The canyon becomes harder to negotiate. Water, just an idle relic above Cliff Arch, becomes the focal point below. Springs gush from the walls and hanging gardens with maidenhair ferns, monkeyflowers, grasses, and columbines dangle from the cliffs. During the colder months icefalls drop from high alcoves to the floor of the canyon. Route finding around a panoply of waterfalls is a minor problem.

Near the Crack-in-the-Wall exit Stevens Arch becomes visible in the distance. (**Stevens Canyon South map.**) The lower section of a large sand dune is visible to the right (S). This marks the exit. (If you go too far downcanyon, you will intersect a log ladder, then the Escalante River. Backtrack for ten minutes.) (1.5–2.0 hours.)

> **Historical note:** Stevens Arch, the fifth-largest arch in canyon country, was named for Al Stevens, a rancher who used to run cattle in the area. Early cattlemen called it Stephen's Canyon Arch and river runner Harry Aleson noted it in his river logs as Sky Arch. Aleson wrote that it was "one spectacular bridge, with opening about 150 by 200 feet—the bridge hanging about 700 feet up in the canyon wall—blue sky filling the hondo-shaped opening. You will choke up with a feeling of beauty and awe when you first glimpse

it...." Stories are told of daredevil pilots illegally flying through the arch.

The exit

Hike south up the steep cliff dune on an established trail to Crack-in-the-Wall. Squeeze through the crack (Class 3 +) and walk to the top of the cliff. Look southwest. In the distance a vague sandy track runs up a hillside. Cross a large area of low slickrock hills to the track. **(King Mesa map.)** Hike up it to the Fortymile Ridge trailhead. (1.5–2.0 hours.)

It is now a 2.6-mile walk along the road back to the start of the hike. (1.0 hour.)

Stevens Canyon and the Waterpocket Fold— Hike #21

Season:	Spring until mid-May or fall after mid-September. Due to a lack of water along several sections of this hike, do not attempt it during periods of hot weather or an extended drought.
Time:	39.5 to 58.5 hours. Seven days minimum. Layover days and digressions can add more days to the length of the trip.
Water:	Water can be a major problem on this trip. Recent rains will ensure that potholes are full. Read the text about water sources and carefully assess current conditions before embarking on the trip.
Elevation range:	3700' to 6745'.
Maps:	King Mesa, Stevens Canyon South, Stevens Canyon North, and Scorpion Gulch.
Skill level:	Very difficult route finding. Class 5.2 rock climbing. The leader must be experienced with belay techniques and be capable of leading the climbing sections without protection. Some wading. This route is suitable only for exceptionally experienced canyoneers who are in excellent physical condition. Low-impact camping skills are essential.
Special equipment:	Wading shoes or boots. An eighty-foot rope is essential. Each person should have the capacity to carry at least two gallons of water.
Note:	There is one thick patch of poison ivy in Stevens Canyon near the Grotto that is impossible to avoid.
Land status:	This hike is in Glen Canyon National Recreation Area.

Edward Abbey, after a hike into Stevens Canyon, wrote, "I walked a mile or so up Stevens Canyon—rare, secret, lovely place it seemed." With its huge alcoves and overhangs, vast expanses of slick-rock, and a delightful stream choked with luminous green moss, it is indeed a special canyon. Starting at the crest of the Waterpocket Fold, Stevens Canyon drains a vast area on its twenty-mile march to the Escalante River. The length of the canyon, difficult route finding, and a lack of water in its upper reaches have kept the hordes at bay. Early ranchers and later uranium prospectors found routes into the canyon from the Waterpocket Fold, but little sign of their presence remains.

Two hikes into Stevens Canyon country are presented. Both are long, difficult, and fraught with danger. Water sources are difficult to find, and tricky climbing in a remote setting adds spice to these classic routes.

The first route starts at the Fortymile Ridge trailhead, drops into Coyote Gulch, and goes up Stevens Canyon. It then exits the right side of the canyon and goes to the top of the Waterpocket Fold. A complicated route leads back to the Escalante River, across Fools Canyon, and into Coyote Gulch. It is followed back to the trailhead. An expanded version of this hike, including an exit out the top of Stevens Canyon, was detailed in *Canyoneering 2: Technical Loop Hikes in Southern Utah*.

The second route into Stevens Canyon country is presented in Hike #22.

Down Crack-in-the-Wall

(**King Mesa map** and **Map Twenty-four.**) From the trailhead, follow a sandy track northeast down a hill and across a plain. When the track ends, follow a line of cairns northeast to the edge of an escarpment overlooking the Escalante River. (**Stevens Canyon South map** and **Map Twenty-five.**) The cairns are regularly knocked over. If the route is not apparent, simply continue northeast across Navajo slickrock to the edge of the escarpment.

> **Historical note:** The vague track you have been following was built by county officials in 1966 as part of a feasibility study for a proposed Trans-Escalante Federal Parkway road which would have tied Bullfrog Basin on Lake Powell to the town of Big Water in Arizona. For details on this road see the "Wilderness" chapter.

Locate a long fin of Navajo with a U-shaped gap extending northeast toward the river (shown one-half mile east of elevation 4484T). The Crack-in-the-Wall, a break in the Navajo, is 100 yards to the left (W) of the fin. After the first short drop it is most simple to lower packs down a twenty-five-foot wall rather than trying to squeeze them through the crack. Follow an established trail down a

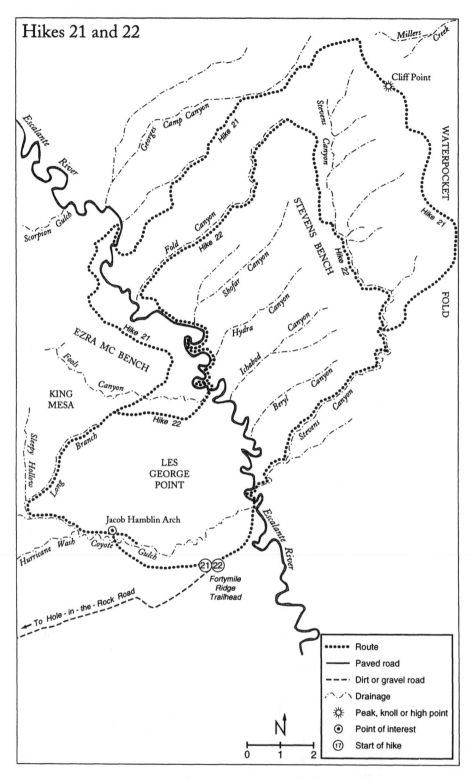

Hikes 21 and 22

Millers Creek

Cliff Point

Escalante River

Scorpion Gulch

George Camp Canyon

Hike 21

Stevens Canyon

WATERPOCKET

Fold Canyon

Hike 22

STEVENS BENCH

Hike 21

Hike 22

FOLD

Hike 21

EZRA MC BENCH

Fools Canyon

Shofar Canyon

Hydra Canyon

Ichabod Canyon

Canyon

KING MESA

Hike 22

Beryl Canyon

Sleepy Hollow

Long Branch

LES GEORGE POINT

Stevens Canyon

Jacob Hamblin Arch

Escalante River

Hurricane Wash

Coyote Gulch

21 22

Fortymile Ridge Trailhead

To Hole - in - the - Rock Road

	Route
	Paved road
	Dirt or gravel road
	Drainage
☼	Peak, knoll or high point
⊙	Point of interest
⑰	Start of hike

N

0   1   2

Map Twenty-four

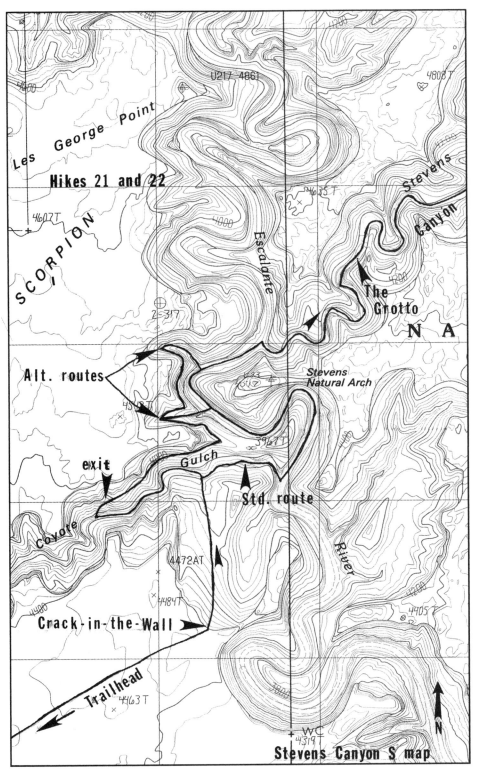

Map Twenty-five

Stevens Arch.

cliff dune to the left (W) side of a tower. **Multiple trails are a problem in this area. Stay on the trail!** Stevens Arch can be seen to the
northeast.

As you near Coyote Gulch, locate a trail that is thirty feet above
the bottom of the canyon. (Do not hike down the streambed.) Follow the trail downcanyon, cross a steep slickrock slab (Class 3 +),
and descend an eight-foot wall to the canyon floor. (1.5–2.5 hours.)

To Stevens Canyon

Wade down Coyote Gulch for ten minutes to its confluence with the Escalante River. Continue wading up the sand-bottomed Escalante River and under Stevens Arch to Stevens Canyon, the first canyon to the right (E). (1.0–1.5 hours.)

> **Alternate route:** This route must be used if the water level in Lake Powell is high. From the bottom of the sand dune trail, hike up Coyote Gulch for about fifteen minutes to the first area of camp-sites on the right (LUC)(N). They are ten feet above the canyon floor and are shaded by huge cottonwoods. A large spring flows from a wall 100 yards farther upstream on the right.
>
> From the downcanyon end of the campsite locate an estab-lished and cairned trail zigzagging up Kayenta ledges to the north. The trail turns northeast and traverses a talus slope to a saddle on a peninsula across from Stevens Arch (at elevation 3967T). The trail turns northwest. Follow it for ten minutes to the first side canyon dropping to the Escalante River (SE) (shown one-eighth mile east of elevation 4542T). You intersect the canyon before passing the fin containing Stevens Arch. Follow a cairned route down the canyon to the river.
>
> Should the lake be particularly full, continue traversing up-canyon to the next side canyon. This canyon is hard to descend (Class 4) and has an almost impenetrable barrier of vegetation at its mouth. Wade up the Escalante River to Stevens Canyon. (Add 1.0 hour.)

Up lower Stevens Canyon

Do not remove your wading shoes yet. The first mile of Stevens Canyon has a half-dozen or more crossings and is a bit of a thrash. Pass the first deep pool on the left (LUC) by climbing a stack of rocks and a row of Moqui-style steps (Class 5.0, 20', belay and hand up or haul packs). Go by the second pool on the right. Hikers have built a pyramid of rocks to ease the difficulty (Class 4+, 12'). The wading comes to an end after another quarter mile. (1.0–1.5 hours.)

In fifteen minutes a trail goes up a slippery, poison-ivy-choked rockslide. Before negotiating the hill, visit the Grotto, fifty yards to the left (LUC)(W). It is an exquisite alcove with a pool at its base topped by Hanging Arch, a unique natural bridge. Above the rock-slide, the canyon is intermittently dry.

The route continues up Stevens Canyon. It passes a nice side canyon (shown to the north of elevation 4819T) coming in from the right (E). There are occasional poison ivy patches, willow and tamarisk thickets, and other small obstacles to overcome. The bush-whacking ends in an area of wonderfully fluted slickrock and var-nished Wingate walls.

At the end of the slickrock the canyon is blocked by a pour-off

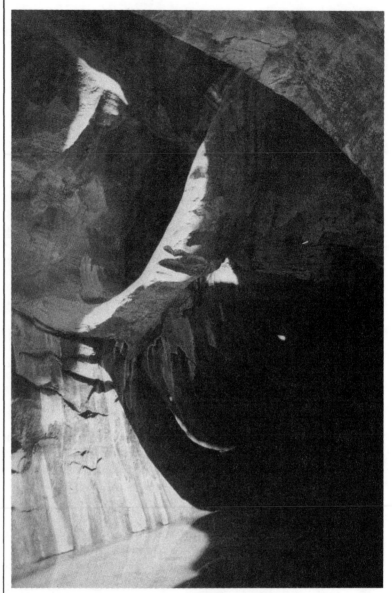

The Grotto and Hanging Arch in Stevens Canyon.

(north-northwest of elevation 4883T). Note the Moqui steps on the right-hand wall. They lead into a short dead-end slot (Class 5.8, 25'). Happily, there is no more poison ivy for the remainder of the trip. There are large potholes and good campsites in the area. (2.5–3.5 hours.)

. . .

Up middle Stevens Canyon

To continue up Stevens Canyon, backtrack from the pour-off for several hundred yards to the first rubble heap leading up the Wingate wall to the left (LDC)(E). Scramble up it, follow a wide ledge downcanyon for fifty yards, and ascend a steep slickrock ramp northeast to the top of the Wingate (Class 3 +). Hike upcanyon (NE) on the top of the Wingate and along Kayenta ledges. Stay near the rim of the canyon. At the first corner note the rockslide coming down from the Navajo wall to the right. This huge section of rock fell in the summer of 1991.

Continue hiking on top of the Wingate for almost two hours.

> **Digression:** The first steep slope dropping through the Wingate to the canyon bottom provides access to many medium potholes and short slots. There is excellent slickrock camping in the area. Do not continue up the floor of the canyon, since there is no easy exit out its top.

The trail descends the second steep slope back into the bottom of the canyon above a fall just as the Wingate wall to the right nearly disappears. Note the small natural bridge and large pothole at the top of the fall. (2.5–3.5 hours.)

In thirty minutes the canyon divides three ways (south-southwest of elevation 5087T). Watch carefully for this junction. It is somewhat hard to see. Turn left (W), staying in the main canyon. The canyon bottom is intermittently sand and slickrock floored. It has a seasonal flow of water and a string of inviting pools. In fifty minutes the canyon narrows for 100 yards. There are two large elongated potholes surrounded by slickrock—a perfect place for a break and a dip if the water is flowing. (**Map Twenty-six.**) It is important to recognize this area because the exit out of the canyon is a short way up and is hard to locate.

About nine minutes upcanyon from the elongated potholes the canyon turns right, from northwest to northeast. The Wingate wall to the right (E) is short and broken. At the far side of the corner a short section of constructed cattle trail is barely visible twenty-five feet above the ground. This is the Baker Trail and the exit route. (If you go too far upcanyon you will see a long straight stretch lined with grasses, willows, and cottonwoods that is marked as a spring one-quarter mile south-southwest of elevation 5170T on the map.) The spring has a large flow of water and there is camping in the area. (1.5–2.5 hours.)

> **Warning:** The next part of the hike, along the Baker Trail to the top of the Waterpocket Fold, takes a long day that includes a lot of elevation gain, route-finding problems, and no water. Make sure you

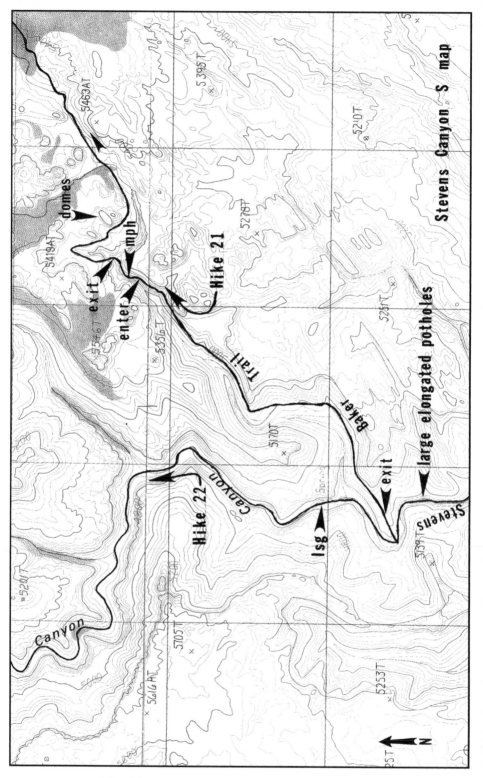

Stevens Canyon S map

domes

exit
mph
enter
Hike 21

Trail

Baker

exit

large elongated potholes

Stevens

Hike 22

Canyon

lsg

Canyon

N

5463AT

5395 T

5210 T

5278 T

5419AT

5546 T

5356 T

525 T

5170 T

5139 T

5207 T

5616 AT

5705 T

5253 T

Map Twenty-six

Wendy Chase and Solo in upper Stevens Canyon.

are prepared. A jump start the night before or a crack-of-dawn start is essential.

Exit Stevens Canyon

Exit the canyon via the Baker Trail to the northeast. The constructed part is very short and ends on Wingate slickrock. Follow the top of the Wingate northeast, staying near the rim of the canyon. Below you is the spring area with its numerous huge cottonwoods.

> **Historical note:** The Baker Trail was named for Eugene Baker, who moved his family from Escalante to a ranch at the mouth of Halls Creek in 1919. Baker and his sons built the trail to the top of the Waterpocket Fold and into Stevens Canyon to provide access for their cattle. The eastern section of the Baker Trail—from the crest of the Waterpocket Fold to Halls Creek—is often considered a part of the Black Trail. See Hike #23 for more details on the Baker and Black trails.

Within ten minutes intersect and follow the Wingate rim of a side canyon coming in from the east (shown to the east of elevation 5170T). Follow along the serpentine course of the side canyon on top of undulating waves of slickrock for a half hour until the Wingate tapers down and a trail drops to the bottom of the canyon. Hike up the canyon. There are medium potholes in the canyon and, if the potholes are full, this area could be used for camping.

(**Stevens Canyon North map.**) Minutes after you enter the canyon a very small side canyon comes in on the left (NW) at the end of the Wingate. One minute past the small side canyon there is

another small canyon to the left (N) with two cottonwoods and a
pinyon pine near its mouth (shown one-eighth mile south-southeast
of elevation 5419AT.) A large cairn is immediately downcanyon in
front of a large juniper tree. You will exit the canyon here. (If you go
too far, the canyon ends in a fall.)

Exit the side canyon
    Surmount a seven-foot wall (Class 4) behind the aforemen-
tioned pinyon pine and continue up the side canyon for a minute or
so until it is possible to exit it by scrambling up steep ledges to the
left (W) to the top of the Kayenta. There is a piece of the old cattle
trail near the top. Follow the rim of the side canyon north, head it,
and return to the rim of the main canyon. Continue upcanyon. In
several more minutes, after passing a series of Navajo domes that are
to the left (LUC), drop into the shallow upper part of the main
canyon. Do not head it; instead, go northeast up the sand-floored
canyon.
    The canyon divides almost immediately. Stay to the right
(NNE) (immediately north of the "5" in elevation 5463AT). In
about twelve minutes the canyon divides again, just before a split
pinnacle. Stay to the right (E). Several minutes later the canyon divides again. Stay to the right (NE) for several paces; then follow a
trail up a hill to the right (E).
    At the top of the hill you will find yourself in a shallow drainage
for 100 yards. The trail exits the drainage to the left (N) up a hillside
and quickly enters another shallow drainage going east-northeast.
The drainage goes generally northeast to the crest of the Waterpocket Fold. This section is confusing. If you miss the trail, do not
panic! Simply wend your way northeast up draws and around
domes until you are on the crest of the Waterpocket Fold. (You
should end up on the top of the Waterpocket Fold between elevations 5642T and 5658T.) (3.0–4.5 hours.)

> **Historical note:** As you walk along you will notice depressed areas
> containing innumerable flakes of chert, jasper, and chalcedony.
> These are called lithic scatters and are evidence of the Anasazi Indi-
> ans who roamed the Waterpocket Fold during the late Basketmaker
> II period (approximately A.D. 500). The scatters consist of the chips
> left over when the Indians flaked larger pieces of rock into cutting
> tools, spear points, and scrapers. The base rock used for chipping
> was not available on the top of the Waterpocket Fold; it was carried
> from outcrops found in the Halls Creek area. Please leave the chips
> in place and do not collect them.
>
> **Digression:** To locate the section of the Baker Trail that goes east
> down the cliffs to lower Halls Creek, first locate the small hill

shown at elevation 5658T. Pick up the trail a quarter mile northeast of the hill. It can be hard to follow in places, though cairns do help. The trail ends a quarter mile northeast of elevation 4032T on the Hall Mesa map. (2.0–3.0 hours.)

To Cliff

Follow the crest of the Waterpocket Fold generally north. This route looks straightforward, but there are several false summits and a couple of shallow canyons to cross. After recent rains there may be pothole water in scattered locations along the Navajo. "Cliff" (labeled on the map as Cliff at elevation 6745) is the highest point on this section of the Waterpocket Fold. There are several labeled bench marks on its Navajo summit. (5.0–7.0 hours.)

> **Water:** From Cliff look southwest into the bowl of upper Stevens Canyon. Note a large freestanding tower with a smaller tower on its right side down in the bowl (elevation 6361T). Walk directly toward the right side of the larger tower (SW). You are searching for a large shallow pothole with cattails in it that is 150 yards inland from the rim. A huge cattail-choked pothole can be found 200 yards to the east-southeast of the shallow pothole by going over a rise and dropping into a deep depression. (Both water sources are a quarter mile west-northwest of the spring shown on the map.) It may take some scouting to find the potholes. Remember that bighorn sheep and deer depend on these potholes. Camp at least 300 feet from them and do not visit them at night.

Finding the descent canyon

The descent canyon is hard to locate. Follow the directions and your map carefully. From Cliff look north into the square-topped head of Millers Creek Canyon. (**Map Twenty-seven.**) Make your way north along the top of the Fold until you are even with the northwest end of Millers Creek Canyon. Go northwest, following the crest of the Waterpocket Fold for another twenty minutes. You will pass the head of a white, shallow, Navajo slickrock-lined canyon. This is the descent canyon. (The canyon starts at elevation 6601AT and goes south-southwest. (1.5–2.5 hours.)

> **Essential Digression:** To make sure you descend the correct canyon, continue past the top of the canyon for about ten minutes until you can see the red Wingate walls of East Moody Canyon to the west-northwest. There are no other red-walled canyons in the vicinity. Backtrack to the descent canyon. **Do not try to find the descent canyon without first locating East Moody Canyon.** There are a couple of similar looking Navajo-lined canyons that feed into the descent canyon, but they contain impassable falls. (0.5 hours round-trip.)

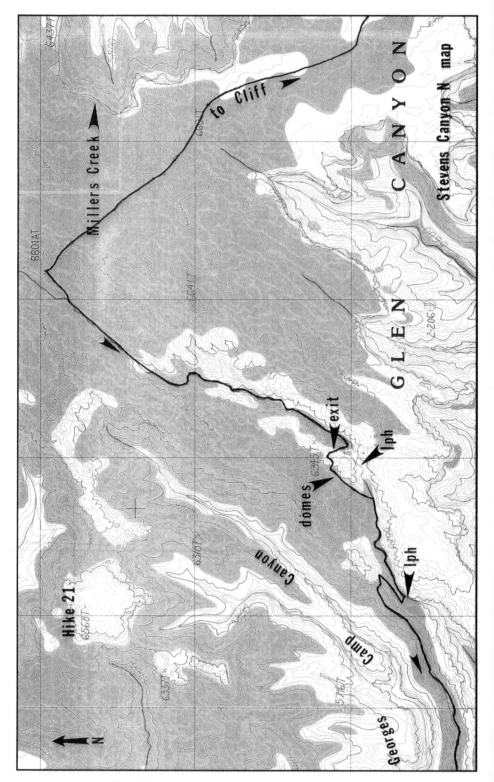

Map Twenty-seven

The descent canyon

Go southwest down the shallow sand-floored canyon for twenty-five minutes to a fall. Pass it on the right (LDC). There are a couple of small, easily negotiated falls before you reach a string of large potholes that are 200 yards above an impassable fall. There is camping in the area. (1.0–1.5 hours.)

To pass the fall, backtrack for a couple of hundred yards to the top pothole and ascend a slope to the left (LUC)(W) to the foot of a Navajo ridge (elevation 6345T). Follow the base of the ridge up-canyon until you are between the second and third domes. The first two domes have rounded tops; the third is more pointed. Scramble up between the domes and negotiate a short wall behind a juniper (Class 4) to a saddle.

From the saddle, look south at a ridge that drops into a shallow canyon to the north. Make your way to the ridge, using the branches of a pinyon pine to help ascend a short slab (Class 4). Descend very steep slickrock into the canyon (Class 4). A short distance down-canyon is another drop. Pass it via a less-than-vertical crack on the right (Class 4 +, 50', belay and lower packs). The Navajo walls and domes below are sublime.

At the next impassable fall there is a large reed-filled pothole. Exit the canyon up a short hillside to the right (NW) to a long thin saddle with fantastic views and excellent camping. The deep, impressive canyon to the north is Georges Camp Canyon (LKA). (1.5–3.0 hours.)

> **Historical note:** Georges Camp Canyon was named for rancher George Davis, who had a line camp behind an abandoned meander at the mouth of the canyon. Davis, an immigrant from Wales, moved to the Escalante area at the turn of the century and homesteaded north of town in lower Pine Creek. A man of many interests, Davis built a dance hall in town in 1901, belonged to the local band and dramatic troupe, had an interest in the People's Exchange dry goods store, was a director of the Pine Creek Irrigation Company, and delivered mail to some towns north of Escalante.

Canyon-hopping to the Escalante

The route gets complicated. Pay close attention to the text and to your maps. Proceed to the north end of the saddle until you come against a Navajo dome. Descend a chute to the west. Traverse southwest, following a bighorn sheep trail along Kayenta ledges. (Do not drop to the top of the Wingate.) **(Map Twenty-eight.)** Scramble up to the first notch in the Navajo ridge to the left (S). The notch has a dome in its middle. (The notch is one-half mile east-northeast of elevation 5816T.) (1.0–1.5 hours.)

From the notch, look south across the canyon to another notch

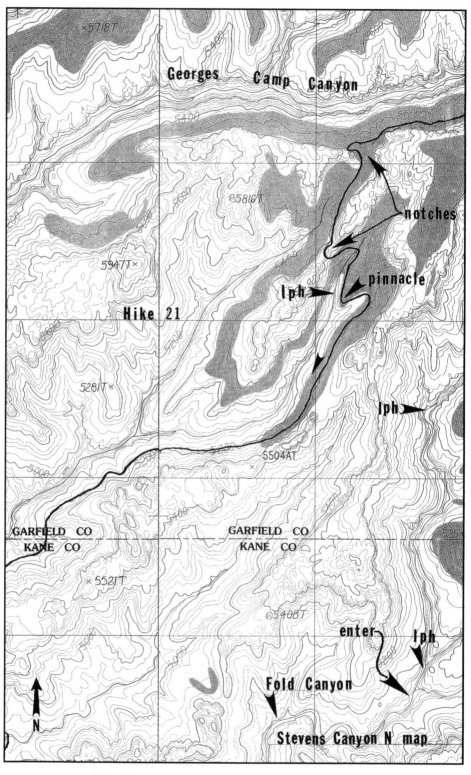

in the Navajo. Cross the canyon and hike into that notch. (The notch is one-eighth mile northeast of elevation 5673T.)

From the notch, look south into the next canyon. You will see two canyons coming together in a "Y," with a twenty-foot pinnacle at their junction (one-eighth mile east-southeast of elevation 5673T). Descend a steep Kayenta wall to the south. The route is tricky; it has loose rock and may take some scouting (Class 4, lower packs). Descend the canyon on its left (LDC) side until you are below the pinnacle at the "Y." Cross the short canyon that forms the left arm of the "Y." There are large potholes in both canyons. Hike southeast to the top of the Wingate. There is excellent slickrock camping in the area. (1.0–1.5 hours.)

Follow the top of the Wingate along the south edge of the canyon for an hour. (**Scorpion Gulch map.**) Locate a large, dominant, freestanding tower (elevation 5405T) on the opposite (W) side of the canyon. Several minutes past the tower you will be forced to the head of a short side canyon. From its top, look up to the east. The Navajo cliffs that have been to your left (S) end in a final tower that has two windows. Exit the canyon here by hiking to the top of the Kayenta ridge to the southeast (one-quarter mile east-northeast of elevation 5164T).

Descend Kayenta ledges south to the rim of another canyon (shown one-quarter mile south of elevation 5164T). Hike upcanyon along the rim of the canyon until you find a place to cross. The canyon does contain large potholes and there is good camping in the area. (1.0–1.5 hours.)

(**Map Twenty-nine.**) After crossing the canyon, follow its south rim west-southwest for a half hour to a notch to the south between the Navajo wall and a prominent dome, which is locally known as Yurt Dome (elevation 5441T, the one nearest the Escalante). Hike through the notch and descend Kayenta ledges south into a Wingate-lined drainage. Follow it west until you are on the rim of Escalante Canyon. Go southeast over a short ridge to the rim of a small canyon, head it, and return to the rim of Escalante Canyon.

Descend to the Escalante River

The route finding becomes even more tricky. Looking southwest, you will see a broken promontory of rock and a long talus slope extending northeast to southwest toward the Escalante River. (The promontory is shown one-quarter mile east of elevation 5095T and immediately south of a marked 4200-foot contour line.) Traverse southwest along the face of the escarpment, going up Kayenta ledges only as needed in order to make further progress. Look for a bighorn trail. After going about seventy-five feet above the Wingate,

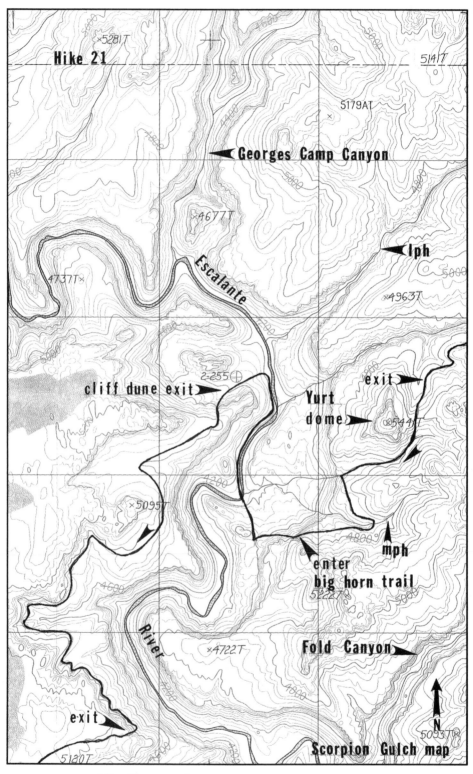

Map Twenty-nine

you will be forced onto a three- to five-foot-wide ledge. The ledge cuts horizontally across the face of the cliff for 200 yards and ends at the top of a slope leading out to the promontory. It is best to scout the route without a pack. Search carefully, as the ledge looks like it peters out in several places. (If you go too high, you will find yourself on a wide ledge below a Navajo cliff and you will walk above the desired ledge system.)

> **Warning:** The ledge is not technically difficult (Class 3+), but it is very scary. Belays can be utilized. In one place packs should be lowered to assure that hikers are not accidentally launched off the ledge.

Once on the promontory, descend a steep slope to the north and go down a shallow drainage to the Escalante River. There is good camping on a broad sandy beach across the river. The beach is in the Chinle Formation. (2.0–4.0 hours.)

Exit the Escalante

Hike north up the west side of the Escalante River (no wading) for twenty minutes to the base of a cliff dune that drops east through the Kayenta, Wingate, and Chinle formations. This is the only sand dune in the vicinity. (The cliff dune is south of an abandoned meander shown as 2-255.) Ascend the dune to the west. Near the top, find a cattle trail (LKA the Scorpion Horse Trail) going up the Kayenta to the south. Note the brush fence at the top. (1.0–1.5 hours.)

The Scorpion Horse Trail turns northwest at the brush fence. You will leave the trail here. Go generally south on a wide Kayenta bench, cross a couple of small canyons, and head others. After forty-five minutes the trail goes under the back of a larger canyon that has two distinct alcoves. Past this the trail crosses a wide plain in front of another side canyon. The Kayenta ledge narrows considerably and you will see a Navajo dome toward the end of a ridge on the right (LDC). This is the first break in the Navajo wall and it is the exit route. (If you go too far, the trail turns sharply south at a corner and goes toward the back of a long side canyon or bay.) (The ridge is shown one-quarter mile east-northeast of elevation 5120T and just northwest of a marked 4600-foot contour line.)

Climb up the Kayenta (Class 4, haul packs) and locate a pour-off between the Navajo wall and the Navajo dome. Ascend a crack on the right side of the pour-off (Class 5.2, 10' of climbing, 25' of exposure, belay and haul packs). Follow the drainage up for 100 yards until it divides. Go west up the prow between drainages and work southwest until you are between two squat, elongated, Carmel-topped domes. The dome to the left is flat-topped; the dome to the

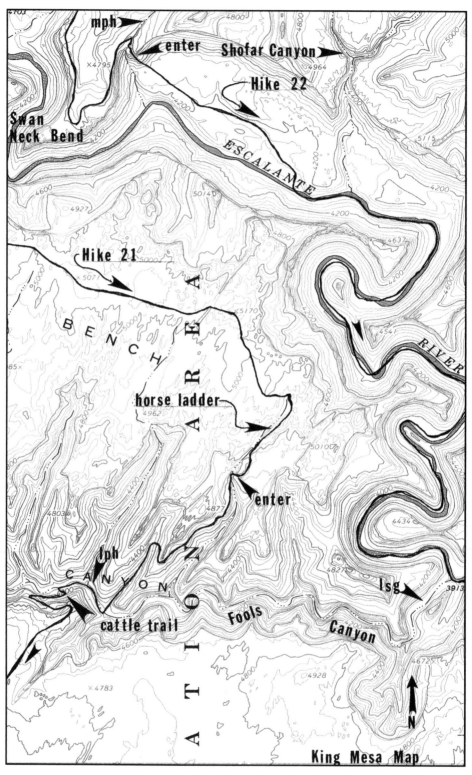

4703

mph ➤

4800 4800 5000

◀ enter

Shofar Canyon ➤

×4795 4964

Hike 22

5115

ESCALANTE 4200 4200 4200

Swan
Neck Bend

4200 4200

4600 4927 50140 4800

4200 4637 4200

4600

Hike 21

5075 5000

×507

B E N C H

5170 4200 4541 RIVER

4200

65×

A R E A

horse ladder

4962

5010

4600

enter

4877 50100 4000

4803 4400 4434

lph

C A N Y O N

4400 4827

cattle trail

Fools

lsg ➤ 3913

Canyon

4672×

A T I O

4783 4928 4800

N

King Mesa Map

Map Thirty

right is rounded. Without a pack, hike to the top of the dome to the left (E). (1.5–2.0 hours.)

Into Fools Canyon

(**King Mesa map.**) Walk to the southeast end of the dome and look east-southeast. Before you is the deep, wide side canyon or bay. The tallest, bare-topped, somewhat-pointed dome is marked elevation 5165 on the map. To the right of it, a couple of miles in the background, is a flat, Carmel-topped dome (elevation 5170). (**Map Thirty.**) This dome is your goal. It is easiest to pass the initial jumble of domes at the head of the long side canyon or bay by passing around its backside and dropping on steep slickrock into the canyon. (It is shown as a small drainage west of elevations 5110 and 5058.) There is a large pothole a quarter mile down this canyon in a section of narrows. Hike up the canyon back to the rim.

Once you are past the domes, stay within 200 to 300 yards of the rim of Escalante Canyon, hiking on pleasant slickrock and across sandy plains until you reach the top of the aforementioned destination dome (elevation 5170). (1.5–2.0 hours)

> **Historical note:** The area you are crossing, Ezra Mc Bench, was named for Ezra McInelly, a local rancher. The James McInelly family moved to Escalante in 1878 and built the first flour mill there. McInelly offspring, twelve in number, were active in the development of the area. Loral J. "Sixty" McInelly is credited with doing the initial bulldozer work on the Hell's Backbone road—a daring feat—in 1933. Arthur McInelly carried mail over the new road to Boulder in the late 1940s, and Arthur and Wells McInelly prospected for uranium in the Circle Cliffs Basin in the early 1950s.

From the top of the dome go south-southeast across a juniper-studded plain and down steepening slickrock to a bowl with a long, prominent, southwest-running rib on its west side. (The bowl is immediately west of elevation 5010.) You will see a long peninsula of red Navajo Sandstone jutting southwest far into Fools Canyon on the south side of the bowl (shown one-third mile west of elevation 4827 and immediately north of a 4400-foot contour line).

Make your way to the top of the rib and descend it, traveling southwest into the bowl. Note the steps hacked into the rock to facilitate getting horses up and down. Walk to the south end of the bowl. A wide side canyon drops into Fools Canyon, and the long peninsula will be on the left (LDC)(E). To the right of center is a rubble heap that goes down the Navajo and into the canyon.

Do not drop to the bottom of the canyon; instead, follow a game trail down the right side of the canyon on a Kayenta bench until the Navajo ridge on the right ends at a prow. From the end of the prow, descend to the bottom of a canyon to the right (NW) by first hiking upcanyon for 200 yards, then zigzagging down steep ledges to the floor of the canyon (Class 4-). Follow the canyon into Fools Canyon.

Thrash your way up Fools Canyon through thick vegetation for ten minutes until you are above a huge deep pool—the ultimate swim hole if water is flowing. (Immediately above the pool the thrashing ends and the canyon floor becomes slickrock.) There is camping in the area. (1.5–2.0 hours.)

Exit Fools Canyon
Hike upcanyon from the swimming hole for 100 yards to a trail coming in on the left (SW). (The trail starts to the north of a side canyon that is shown to the north of elevation 4783.) This is an old constructed cattle trail and is easy to follow as it makes its way up the Kayenta and Navajo.

The trail disappears near the top. Hike southwest to the rim of the canyon. (1.0 hour.)

To King Mesa
From the rim you will be able to see King Mesa, a long flat-topped Navajo ridge to the west-southwest. On its left (S) side is a rounded slickrock hill (elevation 5026). The mesa itself is split by a pass (shown at elevation 5020) near its south end. Make your way west-southwest over, around, and through a maze of domes and washes to the pass. (1.0–1.5 hours.)

> **Historical note:** Les George Point, the area between King Mesa and Fools Canyon, was named for Leslie George, a rancher, mail carrier, and bishop in the local Mormon church. King Mesa was named for John King, who emigrated from Scotland and arrived in Escalante in 1893.

Down the Long Branch of Sleepy Hollow
Descend along the left (LDC) rim of a slot canyon that starts at the pass and goes south. This slot is called the Long Branch of Sleepy Hollow (LKA).

> **Note:** Large potholes can be found in breaks in the slot and there is great camping along the slickrock. Remember, Coyote Gulch is being adversely impacted by campers. It is best to arrange your itinerary so you do not have to camp in Coyote Gulch.

The slot ends above lower Sleepy Hollow, a wide canyon with towering walls and a profusion of cottonwoods along its floor. Simply continue along the rim for another couple of minutes until you can descend moderate slickrock southwest into lower Sleepy Hollow. You may find a short piece of constructed cattle trail near the bottom.

> **Digression:** Lower Sleepy Hollow has a perennial flow of water. The upper reaches of the canyon are exceptional. A slot canyon that starts on King Mesa (between elevations 5112 and 5142) and ends at a fall in lower Sleepy Hollow has been named the Big Tony Fork of Sleepy Hollow. Tony Merten died on his farm in New Mexico in February 1996. His gargantuan size, unlimited physical strength, and unbridled persona perfectly match this slot canyon's character. With his wild red-blond hair and beard, Tony was instantly recognizable to all who encountered him in the canyons or along the windswept desert slickrock he loved so much and worked so hard to preserve. Perhaps all who pass will pay silent homage to Big Tony and to others who have cared about canyon country but can no longer be here to enjoy and be enthralled by it.

Hike down lower Sleepy Hollow to Coyote Gulch. (1.5–2.0 hours.)

Down Coyote Gulch

Now use the route description in Hike #20 for details on going down Coyote Gulch and exiting the canyon at Jacob Hamblin Arch. Once you are on top of the Navajo above the arch, cut east-southeast back to the Fortymile Ridge trailhead. (3.5–4.5 hours.)

Stevens and Fold Canyons—Hike #22

Season:	Spring until mid-May or fall after mid-September. Due to a lack of water along several sections of this hike, do not attempt it during periods of hot weather or an extended drought.
Time:	29.0 to 41.5 hours. Five to seven days.
Water:	Water can be a major problem on this trip. Recent rains will ensure that potholes are full. Read the text carefully about water sources and carefully assess current conditions before embarking on the trip.
Elevation range:	3700' to 5640'.
Maps:	King Mesa, Stevens Canyon South, Stevens Canyon North, and Scorpion Gulch.
Skill level:	Very difficult route finding. Class 5.0 rock climbing. The leader must be experienced with belay techniques and be capable of leading the climbing sections without protection. Some wading. This route is

suitable only for exceptionally experienced canyoneers who are in excellent physical condition. Knowledge of low-impact camping skills is essential.

Special equipment: Wading shoes or boots. An eighty-foot rope is essential. Have the capacity to carry at least two gallons of water per person.

Note: You will spend a couple of days walking along sloping slickrock with your ankles turned to the side. Many will find this uncomfortable; others may find it debilitating.

Land status: This hike is in Glen Canyon National Recreation Area.

This hike is a shorter and slightly easier variation of the Stevens Canyon and the Waterpocket Fold Hike #21. Instead of exiting the right side of Stevens Canyon and traversing the Waterpocket Fold, this route exits Stevens Canyon on the left. It then enters Fold Canyon, which is followed to the Escalante River. A circuitous route out of Escalante Canyon below Fools Canyon leads to Coyote Gulch and back to the trailhead.

Use the description in Hike #21 to get from the Fortymile Ridge trailhead to the Baker Trail exit in Stevens Canyon. It will take 10.0 to 15.0 hours—or two days—to reach this point. The route description picks up from the start of the Baker Trail.

To Fold Canyon
(**Stevens Canyon South map** and **Map Twenty-four.**) From the start of the Baker Trail continue up Stevens Canyon. (**Map Twenty-six.**) In seven minutes pass a side canyon coming in from the right (NE); huge cottonwoods partially obscure its mouth. Stay in the main canyon to the left (NNW) (west of elevation 5170T). The next section of canyon contains lots of vegetation and many large springs; the going can be tough.

In another thirty minutes a boulder-filled side canyon comes in from the right (NE) (shown to the west of elevation 5546T on the **Stevens Canyon North map**). Stay in the main canyon to the left (NW). In another ten minutes a side canyon comes in on the right (N) (shown to the east of elevation 5201T). There is a mining claim written on a boulder at its mouth. Follow the main canyon to the left (W). The vegetation and springs soon end.

In another fifty-five minutes two canyons enter from the right— the first from the northeast, the second from the north. (They are located to the south-southeast of elevation 5277T.) The Chinle Formation is visible at this junction. A mining claim painted on a boulder near the mouth of the canyon states, "Triple Kay Exp. June No. 1."

Playing in Fold Canyon.

From the mouth of the twin canyons continue up Stevens Canyon for fifteen minutes to the first break in the Wingate wall to the left (W). **(Map Thirty-one.)** (This is one-quarter mile east-southeast of elevation 5886T). Ascend broken rock to a wide ledge, follow it upcanyon for fifty yards, then friction up a steep slab for seventy feet to the top of the Wingate (Class 4).

Hike north along the top of the Wingate above Stevens Canyon for forty-five minutes. A pass in the Navajo to the left (LUC)(W) marks the head of Fold Canyon, which is your goal. (The pass is shown one-quarter mile northwest of elevation 5487AT.) You cannot see the pass from the Wingate. Instead, look for a long side canyon that comes into view on the right (E), across Stevens Canyon (shown to the north of elevation 5637T). When you are even with its mouth, start climbing west up the Kayenta (Class 4-). There are several route options. At the top of the Kayenta the pass will be apparent. (1.5–2.0 hours.)

Down Fold Canyon

From the pass, hike along Kayenta ledges on the left (LDC) side of the canyon to a steep slope that drops to the Wingate. Cross the canyon and follow its right rim across sheets of peerless slickrock. The gorge contains large potholes. The Navajo ridge on the right ends at a tower (elevation 5648T). Cross the gorge at the first suitable spot. There is excellent camping in the area. (1.0–1.5 hours.)

> **Digression:** An excellent dayhike starts here and takes you up both the Middle and North forks of Fold Canyon. On the way, you will

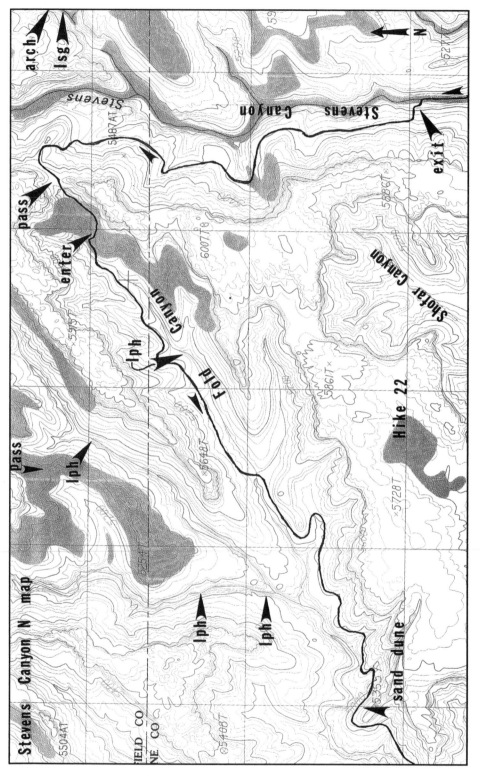

Map Thirty-one

cross three passes. Though there is some steep slab climbing, most of the route is along pleasant and spectacular Wingate and Kayenta benches. This route is highly recommended.

Instead of crossing Fold Canyon, continue down its right (N) rim for 200 yards to its confluence with the Middle Fork (shown to the north of elevation 5648T). Hike upcanyon along the Wingate rim for a short distance until you are forced up onto the Kayenta. Drop back to the Wingate when possible. A steep slickrock slab (Class 4) leads to the floor of the canyon and its many large potholes—the biggest in the area.

Hike upcanyon. At one point, a worn row of Moqui steps leads up a short wall and around a deep pool on its left (LUC) side. At the confluence with a small side canyon that comes in on the left (NW) (shown one-eighth mile south-southeast of elevation 5913T), climb a steep slab to the north to the top of the Wingate. Follow the left rim of the side canyon for a couple of minutes until a pass in the Navajo is visible to the west-northwest. Hike through the pass (shown one-quarter mile south-southwest of elevation 5913T). (1.0–1.5 hours.)

From the pass, follow a small drainage southwest down to the rim of the North Fork (shown to the north of elevation 5913T). Staying on the Wingate, follow the rim upcanyon for a couple of miles. Above a large fall the canyon becomes shallower. Drop into the canyon, which soon divides. Follow the right fork, then hike northeast up the Kayenta to the second pass (shown one-eighth mile northeast of elevation 6327T). This pass is locally known as Bob's Way. The bowl of upper Stevens Canyon is now before you to the east. (2.0–2.5 hours.)

Hike south along Kayenta ledges to the pass that marks the head of Fold Canyon. Follow your previous route down to your campsite. (2.5–3.5 hours.)

Continue hiking down Fold Canyon, but now on its left (S) rim. Stay on top of the Wingate. Medium potholes can be found in many of the short side drainages that you must head.

Digression: A short distance before crossing the only sand dune you will encounter you can enter Fold Canyon by way of a steep gully, which provides unlimited opportunities for exploration. There are large potholes and fine camping sites in the canyon.

To the Overland Route: At this point you have intersected the section of the Overland Route that goes between Scorpion Gulch and Fold Canyon.

You will intersect the escarpment that overlooks the Escalante River on a point. (**Map Thirty.**) The sharp bend in the river formed by the point was called the Swan Neck Bend by uranium miners. (You leave the **Stevens Canyon North map**, cross a corner of the

The Bobway.

Scorpion Gulch map, and end up on the **King Mesa map**. The Swan Neck Bend is a half mile southwest of elevation 4795.) (2.5–3.5 hours.)

The route to the river

From the Swan Neck Bend follow the rim of the escarpment downcanyon into a Wingate-lined side canyon (shown to the east of elevation 4795). Note the small twin arches on the far (E) rim of the canyon. Cross the canyon. It has medium potholes and there is good camping in the area. Hike to the arches. The descent route to the Escalante River is fifty yards southeast of the arches over a small rise. It consists of a short chimney dotted with Moqui steps (Class 5.0, 30'). A steep slope leads to the river. (1.5–2.5 hours.)

To Fools Canyon

Hike and wade down the Escalante River to Fools Canyon, the first side canyon that comes in on the right (SW). There are many good campsites along the river. Fools Canyon has a large spring and good camping near its mouth. (2.5–3.0 hours.)

> **Alternate route:** You can shorten the hike a little by leaving the standard route here. Go up Fools Canyon through a thick tangle of brush (some poison ivy), over and around beaver dams and ponds, down a cliff (Class 5.1, 30', belay and lower packs), until you are above a huge pool. (Immediately above the pool the thrashing ends and the canyon floor is slickrock.) Now join Hike #21 by exiting Fools Canyon at the constructed cattle trail.

To the exit route

Continue down the river to the first side canyon that comes in on the right (W) (shown to the east of elevation 4404T on the **Stevens Canyon South map**). Its narrow mouth can be a bit hard to see. (1.5–2.5 hours.)

This excellent narrow canyon contains the Bobway, an old constructed cattle trail. You will exit Escalante Canyon here. There may be no water along the route until you are in the Long Branch of Sleepy Hollow. Load up here. Hike up the Bobway. The inner gorge opens and the trail ends. Puff up a steep sand dune to the top of the canyon. (1.0 hour.)

To the Long Branch of Sleepy Hollow

Hike west across a slickrock plain to the foot of "Rock" (elevation 4961 on the **King Mesa map**), which is the dominant dome in the area.

> **Digression:** Rock, a huge rounded dome, is worth scrambling up. A spring to the southwest of Rock (shown on the map) is often dry, but if you follow the spring drainage upcanyon for a mile or more large potholes appear.

Continue hiking west along the north side of King Mesa until you see a pass through the mesa to the left. Hike to the pass (shown at elevation 5020). (If you try to hike along the south side of King Mesa to the pass you will encounter endless troubles.) (1.5–2.5 hours.)

You have now joined the Stevens Canyon and the Waterpocket Fold Hike #21. Follow the directions in that hike down the Long Branch of Sleepy Hollow into Coyote Gulch and back to the trailhead. (6.0–8.0 hours.)

> **Alternate route:** From Fools Canyon you can simply continue wading down the Escalante River to Coyote Gulch and back up Crack-in-the-Wall. (5.0–7.5 hours.)

The Pollywog Bench Area—Hike #23

Between Stevens Canyon, the Waterpocket Fold to the east, and the Pollywog Bench area at the confluence of the Colorado and Escalante rivers to the southeast are a series of marvelous and rarely explored canyons. These include Rose (AN), Cow, Fence, Bowns, and Long canyons.

The description of these canyons is brief. Just enough information is presented to give you a general feel for the area and to keep you out of serious trouble. Exercise caution before entering this remote country. A lack of water, difficult route finding, hazardous rock climbing, and long distances over rugged country make this area suitable only for hardcore canyoneers who are rock climbers. To explore the whole area takes fifteen to twenty days.

Water is a major concern in this area. Since most of the routes into the canyons cross vast areas of Navajo Sandstone which contain innumerable potholes, travel to these canyons should be limited to times following recent rains. Do not attempt to enter this area during periods of hot weather or drought. Early spring or late fall are the recommended seasons.

The maps you need to explore the entire area are King Mesa, Stevens Canyon South, Stevens Canyon North, The Rincon NE, and Davis Gulch.

There are two access routes to these canyons. One is via a difficult climb using a row of worn Moqui steps (Class 5.6, 90') located a quarter mile up the first side canyon in Stevens Canyon. (The side canyon is shown to the north of elevation 4819T on the **Stevens Canyon South map**.)

The second route is via the Baker Trail (described in Hike #21). It takes you out of middle Stevens Canyon to the crest of the Waterpocket Fold.

Rose Canyon

Rose Canyon, named for the profusion of cliff roses found in this delightful canyon, lies between Stevens and Cow canyons. (Rose Canyon is not named on the map. It starts just south of elevation 5017T on the **Stevens Canyon South map**.) Access to the canyon is easy throughout its length; breaks in its rounded Navajo walls are numerous. Huge potholes are scattered throughout the canyon.

Cow and Fence canyons

There is only one way to get into Cow and Fence canyons, and it is a bear. The route is for a team of three or more. One must be an accomplished rock climber; two are needed for a shoulder stand. The route enters the east fork of Cow Canyon between elevation 4626T and 2-315 on the **Stevens Canyon South map** and winds its way generally east down the Navajo. The crux of the route comes at the final drop, a series of worn Moqui steps descending, then crossing, a vertical fifteen-foot wall. Rappel anchors are nonexistent on the smooth slab above the drop. With a shoulder stand, the route into or out of the canyon is rated Class 5.9. Solo canyoneers cannot make this climb.

The east fork of Cow Canyon contains a fine stream. The west fork is less abundantly watered but does have small springs. Below the confluence of the forks are superb pools carved into the slickrock. It is an easy hike to the lake.

Access to Fence Canyon is from the mouth of Cow Canyon. Even in high water the traverse above the lake is no problem. Fence Canyon has plenty of water, good camping, and no exit routes.

Bowns Canyon

Bowns Canyon has several entrance points. The easiest is via the Bowns Trail, which is an extension of the Black Trail. (See Hike #29 for the history of the Black Trail.) The Bowns Trail exits the east fork of Bowns Canyon near its top (one-half mile north-northeast of elevation 4408AT on the **Stevens Canyon South map**).

> **Historical note:** William Bown established the Box Bar Ranch on Sandy Creek near the town of Notom to the northeast. According to his grandson Casey Bown, William Bown used both Long and Bowns canyons as winter range between 1909 and 1913. William called this once-fertile valley Meadow Canyon. He is credited with building the Bowns Trail out of the east fork of Bowns Canyon to its intersection with the Baker Trail at the top of the Waterpocket Fold. (See Map Thirty-seven and Hike #21 for information on the Baker Trail.)
>
> The Henry Mountain Oil Company used the Bowns Trail from 1920 to 1921 to bring supplies for its drilling activities from the Baker Ranch in Halls Creek to Oil Seep Bar near the mouth of Long Canyon. Horse packers still occasionally use the Baker and Bowns trails.

A horse ladder that descends an unbelievably spectacular sheet of steep slickrock provides entrance to the main fork of Bowns Canyon on its west side. (The ladder is located east-northeast of elevation 4465AT on the **Stevens Canyon South map**.) There is plenty of water in Bowns Canyon.

Long Canyon

From the mouth of Bowns Canyon above Lake Powell an old horse trail follows Kayenta ledges into Long Canyon.

> **Digression:** As you hike between the canyons you may find the remnants of an old constructed trail that goes down to Lake Powell.

An exit from Long Canyon to the west is via a very steep, exposed slab (Class 5.0, 90') (one-eighth mile south of elevation 4692T on **The Rincon NE map**). You can exit Long Canyon directly east of the western entrance by way of a steep slope and a hidden passage through the Navajo cliffs.

Harvey Halpern and Bud Evans on the horse ladder in Bowns Canyon.

Water availability in Long Canyon is somewhat of a problem. There are large potholes near the bottom end, medium potholes throughout the middle and upper sections, and large springs at the very upper end and in a side canyon shown just to the west of the "N" in National on **The Rincon NE map**.

> **Historical note:** Long Canyon contains Navajo Creek. According to Casey Bown, Navajo Indians used the canyon to graze their sheep in the late 1800s and early 1900s.

Pollywog Bench

Pollywog Bench is an outstanding area of Navajo slickrock domes that forms a "Vee" between the Escalante and Colorado rivers. From its lengthy rim one has superlative views of Wilson and Grey mesas, Navajo Mountain, the Straight Cliffs and Fiftymile Mountain, and the mouths of Willow Gulch, Fiftymile Creek, Davis Gulch, Clear Creek, and Indian Creek. Water is a definite problem on Pollywog Bench. Access to Lake Powell is via a horse ladder just north of elevation 3782T on the Davis Gulch map. This is just across the lake from the mouth of Clear Creek Canyon.

> **Historical note:** This horse ladder is part of the Black Trail, a route that went from the Hole-in-the-Rock road to the Escalante River north of Clear Creek Canyon, over Pollywog Bench, into Bowns Canyon, and eventually to the Baker Ranch at the mouth of Halls Creek. See Map Thirty-seven and the Historical note in Hike #29 for details on this trail.

Fortymile Creek and Willow Gulch—Hike #24

Season:	Spring, summer, or fall. Due to deep wading and a possible short swim, warm days are preferred.
Time:	7.5 to 9.5 hours. One long day or two pleasant days.
Water:	Water availability is not a problem on this hike. Both Fortymile Creek and Willow Gulch have perennial flows of water along their lower ends.
Elevation range:	3700' to 4260'.
Maps:	Sooner Bench and Davis Gulch.
Skill level:	Moderately easy route finding. Most of the hiking is Class 2, but there are several short Class 4 obstacles to overcome. There is a lot of wading and the potential for a short swim. This is a moderately strenuous hike. If you do this as an overnight hike, familiarity with low-impact camping techniques is essential.
Special equipment:	Wading shoes or boots. Dayhikers may be able to keep their gear dry, but overnight hikers need to bring an inner tube for floating packs. This route is moderately difficult.
Note:	There is one stretch of poison ivy in Fortymile Creek that is hard to avoid.
Land status:	This hike is in Glen Canyon National Recreation Area.

Fortymile Creek and Willow Gulch are like Bragi's story: they are always enchanting and never seem to end. Their opulent vales are intimate yet open; they contain hanging gardens, a waterfall, relics of prehistoric occupation, a huge arch, pools to play in, and side draws to explore. Although this route is a tad long on miles, it is worth the effort. Most do this hike in a day; the wise take two.

The route starts on the Hole-in-the-Rock road and goes down Sooner Wash, which quickly joins Fortymile Creek. It is followed to the mouth of Willow Gulch near Lake Powell. Willow Gulch and one of its slot-like tributaries lead back to the trailhead.

To Fortymile Creek

(**Sooner Bench map** and **Map Thirty-two.**) From the Sooner Wash sign, hike east down Sooner Wash. Just as you enter the light-colored Navajo Sandstone, there is a thirty-foot drop into a narrow gorge. Pass it by hiking along the left rim of the gorge to a slot that contains several large chockstones. Drop into the slot, clamber un-

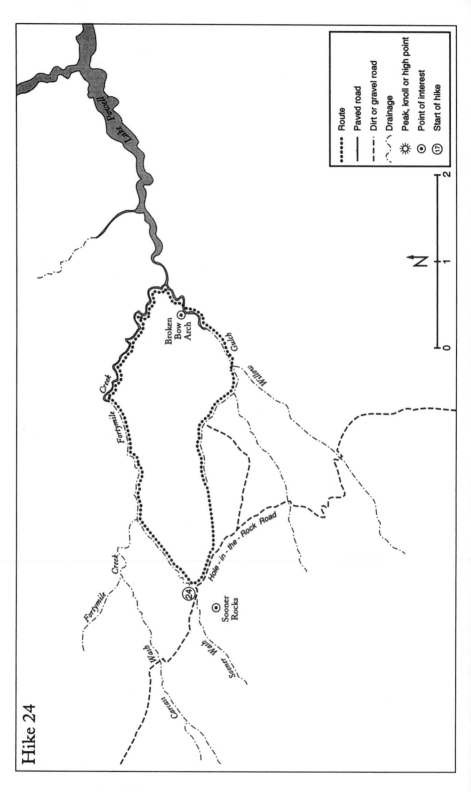

Hike 24

Lake Powell

Broken
Bow
Arch

Fortymile Creek

Willow Gulch

Hole-in-the-Rock Road

24

Sooner Rocks

Fortymile Creek

Wash

Sooner Wash

Carcass

Route
Paved road
Dirt or gravel road
Drainage
Peak, knoll or high point
Point of interest
Start of hike

N

0   1   2

Map Thirty-two

Harvey Halpern in Fortymile Creek Canyon.

der the chockstones, and descend into the canyon. There are several minor obstacles to deal with (Class 4, 8'). The first side canyon coming in on the left (NW) is Fortymile Creek. (0.5 hours.)

Down Fortymile Creek

The upper part of Fortymile Creek is wide and dry. By the time a canyon enters from the left (NW), water has started to flow from the creekbed and cottonwood trees line the canyon. Pass a waterfall at an abrupt left turn in the canyon on a steep trail to the right. It ducks under a grove of boxelder trees and through a healthy patch of poison ivy. From the base of the fall, look up and note a natural bridge. The canyon narrows and the walls are lined with small hanging gardens that contain maidenhair ferns, monkeyflowers, and columbines. (1.0–1.5 hours.)

The crux narrows
The wading starts shortly in a stretch of serpentine narrows. Depending on present conditions, there may be a couple of stretches of deep wading or even a stroke or two of swimming. Rock climbers can chimney over the deepest pools. Willow Gulch enters the canyon on the right (S) at a pronounced "Vee." (**Davis Gulch map.**) (1.5–2.5 hours.)

> **Digression:** The combined drainages of Fortymile Creek and Willow Gulch open downcanyon as you near Lake Powell. Adequate campsites and the lure of a swim make this a pleasant place to nest for a night.

Up Willow Gulch
Willow Gulch also contains a short stretch of narrows in its lower reaches that may require deep wading. A large chockstone blocked this gorge until 1955 when a local rancher "removed" the obstacle with twenty sticks of dynamite. The canyon soon opens and Broken Bow Arch appears. There is good camping in the area. (1.0 hour.)

> **Historical note:** Broken Bow Arch was named by Edson Alvey after he found a broken bow under the arch during a trip to the canyon in 1930. Alvey, born and raised in Escalante, taught school there for many years.

To the trailhead
A half hour above the arch the canyon divides in an area of cottonwoods and cattails. (**Sooner Bench map.**) The springs stop flowing in this vicinity. The sand- and rock-floored main canyon goes to the left (S). Go right (W) into a canyon partially blocked with vegetation. (0.5 hours.)

In ten minutes the canyon divides. A row of Moqui steps is visible from the confluence on a wall to the west-northwest. Go right (NW). The canyon (shown to the north of elevation 4202) immediately narrows, opens a tad, then really narrows. Tackle the slot, which is short and great fun, or pass it on the left (LUC).

Broken Bow Arch in Willow Gulch.

Digression: For those who left a car at the Willow Gulch trailhead, watch for a trail that climbs a sandy hillside to the left and goes by a formation that looks like a graduation cap, or mortarboard.

Continue up the ever-shallower canyon to the Hole-in-the-Rock road. Mosey a mile along the road back to the trailhead. (3.0–3.5 hours.)

EVERETT RUESS

Once more I am drunk with the lust of life and adventure and unbearable beauty. I have the devil's own conception of a perfect time; adventure seems to beset me on all quarters without my even searching for it...
Everett Ruess, 1934

In early November 1934 a young man riding a burro entered the small farm and ranch community of Escalante. After spending several weeks camping close to town on the Escalante River, socializing with locals, and exploring nearby canyons, the man headed east along the Hole-in-the-Rock road into the canyons of the lower desert. It was the last anyone would see of him. The mystery surrounding the disappearance of Everett Ruess is one of the enduring stories associated with the canyons of the Escalante.

Everett Ruess was born in California in 1914, the son of an artist and a minister. It was through them that he developed an interest in and a skill at writing, sketching, and wood-block carving. During a summer school break, the teenager set out on his first solo foray away from home, a three-month-long hitchhiking, backpacking, and camping loop. Starting in Los Angeles, Everett followed the California coast to Monterey, then headed east to Yosemite and the Sierra Nevada. The final leg of the journey led south to Mono Lake and back home.

Everett loved the freedom he had while traveling and delighted in the country he saw. The lure of wild places was intense and the joy he found there is reflected in his writings and artwork. After graduating from high school he again headed out, this time toward the canyons and mesas of the Four Corners region.

For eleven months Everett traveled, usually afoot, selling his art prints and picking up odd jobs as necessary. With a burro purchased in the Indian community of Kayenta, Everett made his way to the Grand Canyon, Monument Valley, southern Utah, and Zion National Park. He stopped to paint the famous ruins at Betatakin, Keet Seel, and Canyon de Chelly and stayed several days with John Wetherill, the man who discovered Mesa Verde.

Returning home, Everett enrolled at UCLA, but lasted only one semester before finding he needed to be on the road again. A friend received a letter from Everett expressing his dissatisfaction with college life: "How little you know me to think that I could still be in the University! How could a lofty, unconquerable soul like mine remain imprisoned in that academic backwater, wherein all but the most docile wallow in a hopeless slough?"

Trips to Yosemite and the Sierra, the redwoods of northern California, and the Pacific coast followed in quick succession. While in San Francisco, Everett hobnobbed with artist Maynard Dixon and photographers Dorothea Lange and Ansel Adams.

In April 1934 Everett's older brother Waldo dropped him off in Kayenta. For several months Everett wandered Arizona, spending much time with the Navajo Indians. July found him near Navajo Mountain, where he packed into Rainbow Bridge and then back to Arizona to participate in an archaeological dig.

That fall Everett visited Bryce Canyon, where he spent a couple of days before hiking over the Escalante Mountains to Escalante. He had heard of the beauty of the area from locals. Everett wrote a letter to Waldo from Escalante, telling him: "I stopped a few days in a little Mormon town [Escalante] and indulged myself in family life, church-going, and dances."

Apparently planning to spend the winter in the Escalante, Everett continued: "As to when I shall visit civilization, it will not be soon, I think. I have not tired of the wilderness; rather I enjoy its beauty and the vagrant life I lead, more keenly all the time. I prefer the saddle to the streetcar and star-sprinkled sky to a roof, the obscure and difficult trail, leading into the unknown, to any paved highway, and the deep peace of the wild to the discontent bred by cities." No more letters were sent by Everett.

On November 11, 1934, the twenty-year-old Everett left Escalante for the canyons of the lower desert. After not hearing from Everett for three months, his parents alerted the residents of Escalante. A search was launched in March 1935. Several canyons were checked before Everett's burros were located near the foot of the cattle trail leading out of Davis Gulch. Since his camp gear, food, and painting supplies were not with the burros, the searchers speculated that Everett left them and struck out on foot to explore the surrounding country. Bootprints matching Everett's were found throughout Davis Gulch, at the top of the Hole-in-the-Rock, and near the foot of the Kaiparowits Plateau. The search continued for several months before it was called off.

Three theories concerning Everett Ruess's disappearance have surfaced over the years. First, Everett may have fallen off a cliff, certainly a good possibility in the rugged Escalante country. Second, some residents of Escalante speculated that Everett crossed the Colorado River and disappeared in Navajo country. Everett had spent considerable time with the Navajos and felt a bond with them.

The theory that in retrospect seems the most plausible is that Everett was killed by cattle rustlers and his body and camp kit buried to hide the evidence. Rustlers were known to have been in the area and ranchers had had problems with them in the past.

Although the main search ended, various individuals kept looking for Everett for many years. Tantalizing bits of evidence surfaced from time to time, but none of the evidence was trustworthy. A human femur bone was discovered near Twilight Canyon by a boating party led by river runner Norm Nevills. He speculated that Everett's body may have washed down from the Kaiparowits Plateau.

Famed river runner Harry Aleson kept in touch with Stella and Christopher Ruess, Everett's parents. In 1950, in a cave near the mouth of Clear Creek Canyon, Aleson found an old Mackinaw jacket with potsherds in the pockets that he believed could have been Everett's.

In 1957, archaeologists found camping equipment in Reflection Canyon, which is a couple of miles south of the Escalante River; but the gear could not be positively identified as Everett's.

Reports from people claiming to have seen Everett came from Moab and Mexico; but all sightings led nowhere. It is unlikely that the final disposition of Everett Ruess will ever be determined. Shortly before his disappearance, Everett wrote a friend that, "When I go I leave no trace." These words, written at an encampment near Navajo Mountain, a rounded summit within sight of the rim of Davis Gulch, proved prophetic and puzzling. Perhaps Everett would have enjoyed the mystery surrounding his death or disappearance. More than his writing or artwork, Everett's departure has ensured his status in history, legend, and myth.

Fiftymile Creek—Hike #25

Season:	Any.
Time:	5.5 to 7.5 hours.
Water:	Water availability is not a problem on this hike. Lower Fiftymile Creek has a perennial flow of water.
Elevation range:	3700' to 4230'.
Maps:	Sooner Bench and Davis Gulch.
Skill level:	Easy route finding. Most of this hike is Class 2 walking. There are a couple of short Class 4 obstacles that few will have problems with. This is a moderate hike.
Special equipment:	If you are doing the rock climber's route, a 100-foot rope is essential. Those planning to swim in Lake Powell should bring wading shoes. There is a stretch of wet narrows before you reach the lake.
Land status:	This hike is in Glen Canyon National Recreation Area.

Young friends I hike with often baffle me with the descriptive words they use. I grew up with "cool," "boss," "radical," and "gnarly." They use "cashmere" for top quality; "dope" instead of cool or good; "chossy" for crumbly or lousy rock; and my favorite, "Baldwin," a term that derives from the handsome brothers of movie fame, which apparently means "the best." We used to "climb" a route; they'll say they "sent" it. I'd say Fiftymile Creek is an outstanding canyon; they'd say its "Shwang Betty" or a "Bo Derek" (a perfect 10). Whatever terms you do use to describe Fiftymile Creek, whether they are common and understandable or obtuse and idiomatic, you will find this route rewarding.

This partial loop starts at the Hole-in-the-Rock road and goes down an unnamed gorge to Fiftymile Creek. It is followed to Lake Powell. Another unnamed canyon and a cross-country jaunt lead back to the trailhead.

Down Fiftymile Creek

(**Sooner Bench map** and **Map Thirty-three.**) Look southwest toward the Straight Cliffs. The jut of land that projects east toward you is Cave Point. It will be an important landmark on the return trip.

Hike into a wash that goes east for 100 yards and then turns abruptly to the right (S). The wash quickly enters the Navajo and, after a short distance, drops into an inner gorge at a thirty-foot fall. Pass the fall on the left and enter the gorge.

In forty-five minutes a shallow canyon comes in on the right (S). (**Davis Gulch map.**) Continue down the main canyon. Note a cave on the left. Below it on a smooth wall is a row of Moqui steps to nowhere. At one time this may have led to a granary. A large canyon enters on the right (S). This is Fiftymile Creek. This spot will be called Fiftymile Junction in the text below. It will be the exit canyon at the end of the day. (The junction is one-quarter mile southeast of elevation 4207T.) (1.0–1.5 hours.)

> **Historical note:** Fiftymile Creek was called Soda Gulch by early ranchers, and it appears that way on old maps. Members of a National Geographic expedition into Escalante country in 1949 accomplished the first known descent of Soda Gulch. They found the upper part of the canyon wide and easy, but the lower part—now under Lake Powell—was a four-foot-wide constriction. Trip members described it as a "nightmare"; quicksand forced them to abandon their horses and they had to swim or chimney across long stretches of cold water.

Ten minutes downcanyon you reach the first cottonwood tree and the start of a riparian area. A minute below this first tree, on the

Hikes 25, 28, and 29

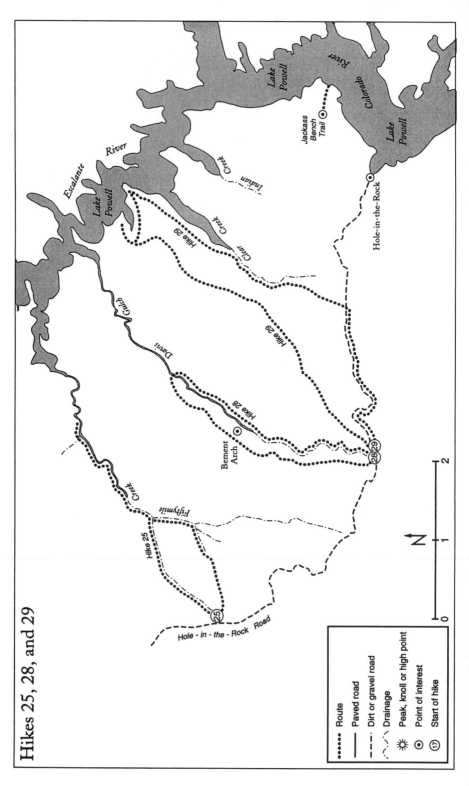

Map Thirty-three

Enjoying Fiftymile Creek Canyon.

wall to the right (E) and behind a large Fremont mahonia bush (it has holly-like leaves), is a vague row of Moqui steps. This is the return route for those doing the rock climber's route mentioned below. Intermittent springs appear from time to time on the canyon floor. The farther down one goes, the more water there is.

A large arch appears high on a wall to the left. This arch will help climbers orient themselves on their return trip. Downcanyon on the right, a cliff dune provides an alternate entrance to the canyon for those doing the rock climber's route. A side canyon enters from the left (SE) (shown to the west of elevation 4004T).

> **Historical note:** Below the mouth of the side canyon, on a wall to the left (LDC), is an inscription that reads:
> E Reus Hunters
> LCC 1935
> FB. RS. HC. AT. HS.
> June 6
> The inscription refers to a search party sent out to hunt for Everett Ruess after he was reported missing.

The canyon closes down. Short stretches of wading may be necessary if you are going to Lake Powell for a swim. (1.5–2.0 hours.)

Back to the trailhead
Return to Fiftymile Junction. (1.5–2.0 hours.)

> **Rock climber's note:** Instead of hiking back up the floor of the canyon, there is an enjoyable route that exits the canyon, runs its rim, and returns to the floor of the canyon near Fiftymile Junction. This route has Class 5.0 climbing and lots of exposure.
> From the Ruess hunters' inscription, go downcanyon for a couple of hundred yards and exit the canyon via a very steep slab on the right (LDC)(SW) (a couple of options). Hike to the rim of the canyon and follow it upcanyon. You can either reenter the canyon by going down the cliff dune or continue until you are past the arch and then climb down the aforementioned Moqui steps (Class 5.0, 40').

Go left (S) up Fiftymile Creek. In seventeen minutes the canyon divides (one-quarter mile west-southwest of elevation 4112AT). The main fork goes to the left (SE). Go right (SW). In two minutes the canyon divides again; the main canyon is to the left. Go right (WSW). The canyon above narrows and contains a couple of small obstacles (Class 4+, 7'). One may also pass this section on the right.
Above the slot the canyon becomes very shallow and Cave Point will be visible to the west-southwest. **(Sooner Bench map.)** Exit the wash and make your way across a blackbrush-covered plain back to the trailhead below Cave Point. (1.5–2.0 hours.)

Sixty Point and Twilight Canyon—Hike #26

Season: Spring until mid-May or fall after mid-September.

Time: 14.5 to 20.0 hours. Three to four days.

Elevation range:	3700' to 6000'.
Water:	Water availability is a major problem on this route. The text that follows notes water sources.
Maps:	Davis Gulch, Nasja Mesa, Navajo Point, and Sooner Bench.
Skill level:	Difficult route finding. Class 5.2 climbing with lots of exposure. The leader must be experienced with belay techniques and be capable of leading the climbing sections without protection. This is an exceptionally strenuous hike that is suitable for experienced canyoneers only. Low-impact camping skills are essential.
Special equipment:	An eighty-foot climbing rope is necessary.
Land status:	This hike is in Glen Canyon National Recreation Area.

Every great canyoneering route has four essential components: spectacular canyons, intimate narrows, big views, and physical challenges. This hike brings to the fore each of those elements: Twilight Canyon and its many slot-like tributaries, the daily views of Navajo Mountain and the surrounding country, and the demanding terrain you must cover to tie the individual pieces together. Off the beaten track and in obscure country, only those with extensive canyoneering experience should attempt this hike.

The route starts on the Hole-in-the-Rock road, goes up a steep slope to the top of Sixty Point, and then continues down Twilight Canyon to Lake Powell. A devious route out of the canyon and pleasant walking under the south end of Sixty Point leads to Hidden Passage and Reflection canyons and back to the trailhead.

To Sixty Point

(**Davis Gulch map** and **Map Thirty-four.**) From the trailhead look south-southeast. You will see a deep bay with huge walls. Two long green ridges run up the right side of the bay to the top of the cliffs. The ridge on the left ends below a cliff. The ridge on the right ends at the top of the cliff. Sharp eyes may be able to pick out a vague cattle trail. (The ridge is located one-eighth mile northwest of elevation 4730T.) Trudge 1,500 feet up the ridge on the right to its top. The cattle trail is apparent along thin sections of the ridge. You are now on Fiftymile Bench. Do not continue to the top of the Kaiparowits Plateau. (You cut a corner of the **Sooner Bench map** and will end up one-quarter mile east of elevation 5934 on the **Navajo Point map**.) (2.0–3.0 hours.)

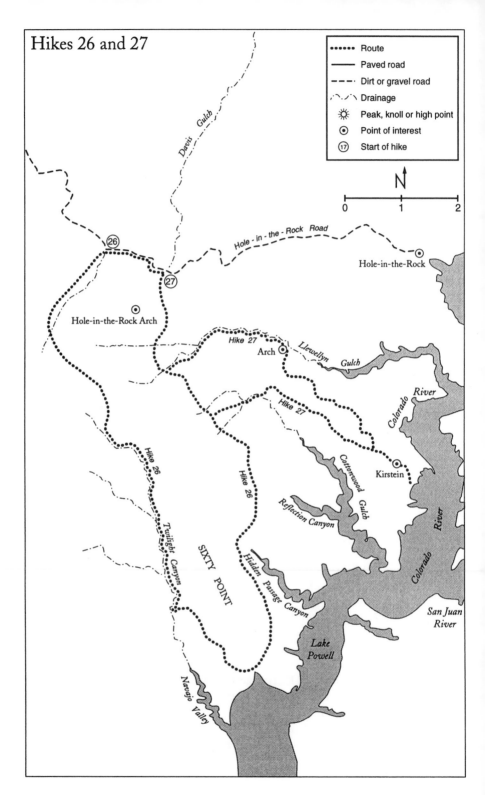

Hikes 26 and 27

Legend:
- •••••• Route
- —— Paved road
- – – – Dirt or gravel road
- ·–·–· Drainage
- ☼ Peak, knoll or high point
- ⊙ Point of interest
- ⑰ Start of hike

N

0   1   2

Davis Gulch

㉖

㉗

Hole - in - the - Rock Road

Hole-in-the-Rock

⊙ Hole-in-the-Rock Arch

Hike 27

Arch ⊙

Llewellyn Gulch

Hike 27

Colorado River

Hike 26

Kirstein ⊙

Hike 26

Cottonwood Gulch

Twilight Canyon

SIXTY POINT

Reflection Canyon

Colorado River

Hidden Passage Canyon

San Juan River

Lake Powell

Navajo Valley

Map Thirty-four

Historical note: Kaiparowits is a Piute word meaning "Big Mountain's Little Brother," referring to Navajo Mountain to the east. Although the name is now used to refer to the whole plateau, the Piutes used it to demarcate a small area of elevation near its north end. They called the whole plateau Miepakivav, or "mountain lying down." The Kaiparowits Plateau was inhabited by Kayenta and Virgin River Anasazi, with light use by the Fremont, during the Pueblo II and Pueblo III periods (A.D. 900 to 1275). In the 1800s and early 1900s, Navajo, Piute, and Ute Indians used the plateau for hunting and grazing. Early ranchers tell of a large lake, which is now just a shallow pond, on the plateau.

Hike generally southeast along Fiftymile Bench, over or across several ravines, and across the top of the bay onto the long, south-running Sixty Point. (It starts at elevation 6012T on the **Nasja Mesa map**.) Cattle trails make progress easy. Hole-in-the-Rock Arch on Fiftymile Point is visible to the northeast (near elevation 5944T). (1.0 hour.)

Digression: A short walk to the arch proves interesting. From the arch you can see Bement Arch deep in Davis Gulch, the old Hole-in-the-Rock airstrip, and the now abandoned Clear Creek Trail. (1.0 hour round-trip.)

Note: The long peninsula you are walking on has never had a formal name. Harry Aleson, in a letter to Otis "Dock" Marston in 1952, called it Sixty Point, a name I have used throughout this guide. It refers not to a specific spot but to the whole peninsula.

Hike south along the peninsula. Keep tabs of progress on your map. In about thirty minutes you will see a cone-shaped hill (elevation 5921T) in the middle of the peninsula. From the hill go right (SW) for a couple of minutes, then drop into a steep drainage that goes southeast. This drainage contains a spring with water that is hard enough to keep you hopping for a week. Avoid drinking it. The drainage ends at a high drop into Twilight Canyon. There is sublime, albeit dry, camping with wonderful views of Navajo Mountain and Lake Powell on a ledge to the left of the drop. (1.0–1.5 hours.)

Into Twilight Canyon

At the drop is an impossibly steep dirt slide that goes to the canyon floor. Do not go down the slide. (If you do go down it, there are overwhelming obstacles below.) Instead, head the canyon and follow its right rim, which presents itself as a steep, narrow crest of dirt. Hike south along the ridge, which is loose, difficult, and has an abundance of exposure. Take your time! A line of towers blocks the ridge

Along the ridge leading into Twilight Canyon.

at one point. Cut under the towers on the left, regain the ridge, and continue dropping. This is hairy! You are now between two canyons. (The canyon to the south is shown just north of elevation 5104T.) Near their confluence, drop off the ridge to the left into Twilight Canyon. There are several possibilities. (1.5–2.5 hours.)

> **Rock climber's note:** Once you are in the canyon, the narrows you bypassed while walking along the ridge are worth a look. There are several tough boulder-type problems to overcome.

> **Historical note:** The dual names of Twilight Canyon and Navajo Valley reflect the problem early explorers had in naming features in little-known country. Often they did not know of local names or names given by previous visitors. Sources as early as 1889 labeled this canyon Navajo Valley and noted that Navajo Indians used it as a route to the Kaiparowits Plateau. Escalante stockmen called it Boulder Canyon due to its boulder-strewn floor. River runner Norman Nevills, unfamiliar with its previous designations, named it Twilight Canyon because the walls were so overhung that the canyon, even at midday, was always dark.

Down Twilight Canyon

Hike downcanyon through a sinuous stretch of enchanting Entrada narrows. The canyon widens, then narrows as it enters the Navajo. (1.0 hour.)

There is one obstacle ahead—a drop. Although it at first looks intimidating, a closer view reveals that the drop comes in two ten-foot steps. Use a rope here.

Alternate route: You can bypass the obstacle by walking along the left (LDC) rim for ten minutes to a steep slope that drops back into the canyon.

You are now in a stretch of neverending narrows. As you wind downcanyon look for a fifteen-foot pinnacle with a sloping "hat" on its summit that is 100 feet above the canyon floor on the right. The exit route out of the canyon is a minute below the pinnacle and goes up a slab dotted with worn Moqui steps on the left (NE). (**Map Thirty-five.**) (The exit is immediately southwest of elevation 4147T.) (If you go too far downcanyon you will intersect a slot that enters the canyon at wash level on the right (W). It is shown to the north of elevation 4061T. Backtrack for ten minutes.) You will return to this exit route after a visit to the lake to obtain water.

Rock climber's note: This first slot is a joy to explore. There are many obstacles to work around. A white chockstone ten feet off the ground will stop most.

Continue downcanyon to the lake. Due to the flash-flood potential, you will have to exit the canyon at the Moqui steps before camping. (1.5–2.5 hours.)

The exit route
Backtrack to the Moqui-step exit route. (This is the first possible exit on the right (LUC) as you walk upcanyon.) Although the slab looks intimidating, the steps ease the difficulty (Class 5.2, 40'). At the top of the first slab, cut left (NW) under a cliff band for 100 yards, then exit the canyon on steep slickrock to the southeast (Class 4). A steep slickrock gully to the southeast of elevation 4147T contains medium potholes.

To Lake Powell
At the top of the slickrock look southeast. Your goal is to round the south end of Sixty Point. It is easiest to hike northeast to a cattle trail near the base of the escarpment. At the tip of the peninsula you will be between the cliff to the north and a wide V-shaped cut above the lake (at elevation 4241) to the south. (1.5–2.0 hours.)
Hike northeast parallel to Sixty Point for ten minutes. You may see a witness post/survey marker (elevation 4298T).

Digression: You can easily get to the lake from here. Simply go east down steep slickrock. There are large potholes and an excellent camping site near the lake (one-eighth mile north of elevation 3900T). (1.5 hours round-trip.)

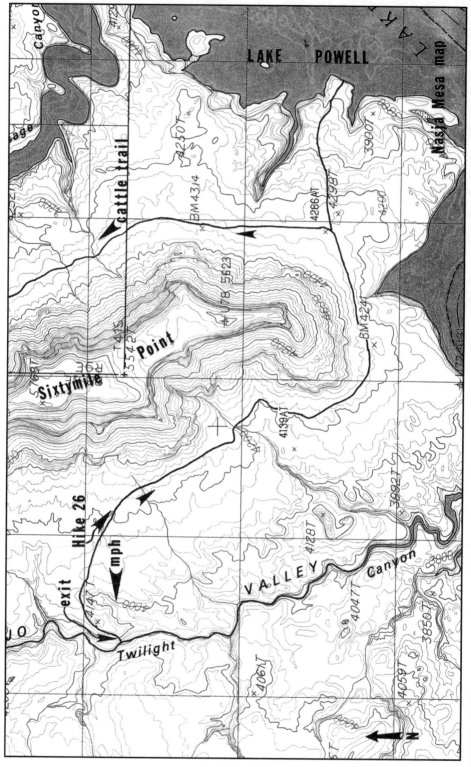

Map Thirty-five

The exit out of Twilight Canyon.

Historical note: The campsite is located above what was once Music Temple Bar before it was submerged with the flooding of Glen Canyon. The bar, a gravel terrace, was the site of a large placer-mining operation from the late 1880s through the 1890s.

To Hidden Passage Canyon

Proceed north to the top of Hidden Passage Canyon. There are no routes into the canyon; however, there are several medium to large potholes located on a slab between elevations 4352T and 4285T. They will take some searching to find. (1.5–2.0 hours.)

Historical note: It is unfortunate that there is no easy access into Hidden Passage Canyon from above. Before Glen Canyon was flooded, Hidden Passage Canyon attracted many visitors and received a surfeit of praise for its beauty. In September 1922 John Widtsoe, a member of a group looking for dam sites in Glen Canyon, described Hidden Passage Canyon: "It is a narrow, high winding gorge, with a small stream trickling down it. Near the entrance are dense groves of scrub oak, and large patches of poison oak. As we enter, the gorge narrows, a blue rift above is the sky. Where the gorge widens a vast overhanging canopy wholly shuts out the light. A little further on the gorge narrows and water fills the passageway....In this twilight-lighted, moist nook, vegetation is profuse climbing up the rocky slopes and fastening itself in really impossible places as it seems to us. Man-high is a shelf carrying a most perfect bed, perhaps 10 to 15 feet long, of beautiful maidenhair fern. We name the place Maidenhair Gorge."

River runners, not knowing of Widtsoe's designation, renamed the narrow gorge Hidden Passage Canyon. Cid Ricketts Sumner wrote of the canyon: "Hidden Passage—it was well-named. I could not make it stand forth to be seen....I looked ahead to where both walls drew in upon each other, curving away into what must be yet another mighty coil beyond my sight, and walked slowly on."

Explorer Weldon Heald noted, "what I will always remember about Hidden Passage is the upper waterfall at the head of the Canyon. There the corridor widens out into a vaulted hall at the head of which a slender thread of water falls into a clear pool. From the twilit room we looked up to the overhanging walls far above us, enclosing a narrow slit of sky between."

To Reflection Canyon

Walk along the cattle trail to the top of Reflection Canyon, the next canyon to the north. There is no easy access into Reflection Canyon. (1.0 hour.)

> **Rock climber's note:** There is very difficult and dangerous access into Reflection Canyon via a steep row of Moqui steps located to the south of elevation 3978AT (Class 5.6, 60', no protection possible).

Continue north, pass a jutting fin of Entrada Sandstone that comes down from Sixty Point (at elevation 4418), and follow a cattle trail along the base of the cliffs back to the trailhead. (2.5–3.5 hours.)

> **Digression:** This does not have to be the end of the trip. See Hike #27 for details on exploring Cottonwood and Llewellyn gulches, the next two canyons north of Reflection Canyon.

Llewellyn and Cottonwood Gulches—Hike #27

Season:	Spring or fall.
Time:	14.5 to 21.5 hours. Three to four days.
Water:	Water availability is a problem on this route. Lower Llewellyn and Cottonwood gulches have large springs.
Elevation range:	3700' to 4550'.
Maps:	Davis Gulch and Nasja Mesa.
Skill level:	Difficult route finding. Class 5.4 climbing. The leader must be experienced with belay techniques and be capable of leading the climbing sections without protection. There is some exposure on this route and long distances between water sources. This is a moderately

strenuous route that is for experienced canyoneers only. Familiarity with low-impact camping techniques is essential.

Special equipment: A fifty-foot rope is necessary.

Land status: This hike is in Glen Canyon National Recreation Area.

From the trailhead the terrain covered by this hike looks like Willa Cather country, a land "that keeps no secrets." What you cannot immediately see, though, are the splendid canyons that have cut deep into Navajo Sandstone as well as through the detritus that has fallen from the heights of Fiftymile Mountain. Just because these canyons do not end at the Escalante River does not mean they are second-rate. Like all classics, they deserve your utmost attention.

The route starts on the Hole-in-the-Rock road and follows the base of Sixty Point to the top of Llewellyn Gulch. It is followed down to Lake Powell. A cross-country hop leads to Lake Powell, then into Cottonwood Gulch. Follow the base of Sixty Point back to the trailhead.

To Llewellyn Gulch

(**Davis Gulch map** and **Map Thirty-four.**) From the parking area look southeast at Fiftymile Point (labeled on the **Nasja Mesa map**). On the top of the point is the small Hole-in-the-Rock Arch. To the south, beyond the arch and a prominent prow—and barely visible—is a bay that forms the head of the North Fork of Llewellyn Gulch. (The bay is shown to the east of elevation 5951T.) The second bay to the south (shown to the east of elevation 5952T) marks the top of the South Fork of Llewellyn Gulch, which is your immediate goal.

It is easiest to hike near the base of the cliffs below the reddish Entrada Sandstone. Once you find it, a cattle trail makes for casual hiking. Do not make the mistake of cutting straight toward the first bay from the trailhead or you will encounter insurmountable problems.

Cross the head of the North Fork.

> **Rock climber's note:** Instead of continuing to the South Fork, you can descend the North Fork. There are several rappels of up to thirty feet in length. Chockstones can be used to anchor a rope.

(**Map Thirty-six.**) Follow the cattle trail across several deep ravines into the second bay, which is marked by a couple of watering troughs. The South Fork starts as a wash at the troughs. (1.0–1.5 hours.)

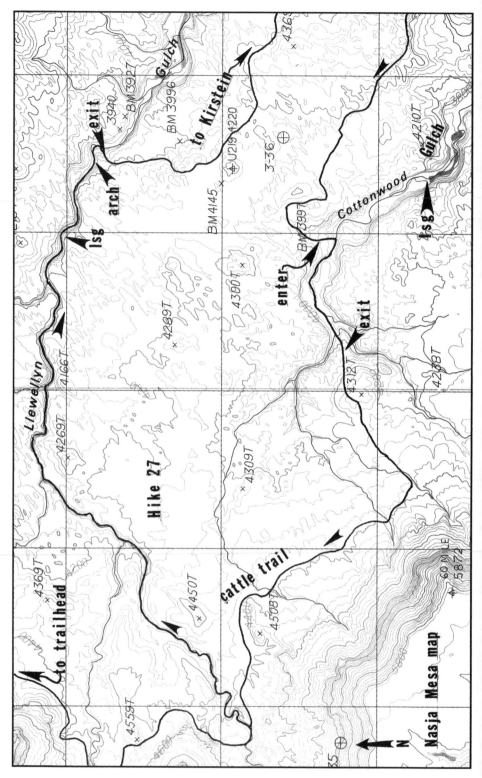

Map Thirty-six

Historical note: The canyon was named for Llewellyn Harris, for whom Harris Wash was also named. Harris ran cattle near the mouth of the Escalante River.

Before the Colorado River was dammed, river runners found an inscription in a cave that read: L. Harris April 24 1894. Arthur Chaffin, a river runner and Glen Canyon explorer, recounted a story about Llewellyn Harris to explorer Harry Aleson. Apparently a friend of his, gold miner Jack Butler, lent a burro to Harris, who used it on a trip into the Waterpocket Fold country. Caught in a snowstorm, Harris camped in a large cave for six weeks and ended up eating the burro. When asked about Llewellyn Harris years later, Butler told Chaffin: "That's the son-of-a-bitch that ate my burro!" The veracity of the story is not known.

Down Llewellyn Gulch

As you follow the wash down, it quickly turns into a narrow Navajo defile. There are several drops to negotiate (Class 5.4, 15'). All of them can be adequately belayed or hand lines can be used. These are some of the finest narrows in the Escalante area. The short side canyons you pass are worth exploring.

The canyon widens and water and large cottonwoods appear. Look for a thin arch on a wall to the right (LDC) (one-quarter mile west-northwest of elevation 3940). Go around the corner below the arch. A steep slope to the right (W) is the exit route. There is good camping in the area. (2.0–4.0 hours.)

> **Digression:** A stroll down to the lake is rewarding. Depending on the water level of the lake, there may be good camping near it. (2.0–3.0 hours round-trip.)

> **Rock climber's note:** Those wishing to exit the canyon on the left (LDC)(N) and return to the trailhead on a cross-country route over endless expanses of slickrock can do so. Twenty minutes down-canyon from the arch find two large overhangs divided by a steep prow. The prow is the only likely looking exit out of the canyon. Though the route is not technically difficult (Class 5.0, 100'), there is horrendous exposure.

To Lake Powell

Exit Llewellyn Gulch via the steep slope to the right (W) below the arch. Note the constructed section of an old cattle trail as you hike through the first band of Navajo Sandstone. Make your way southeast to the rim of the canyon. (0.5 hours.)

You are now in a harsh, barren wonderland of Navajo slickrock, domes, and small washes. The goal is to hike generally southeast to the highest point in the area (labeled as U76 or elevation 4535). As you work your way upward, the rounded bulk of Navajo Mountain becomes visible to the southeast. Walk toward the small peak that is on Navajo Mountain's left (N) side.

The high point is difficult to identify. There are several small knobs and domes that are all about the same elevation. The true high point has a small cairn on its summit and the name KIRSTEIN is inscribed on the rock below it. You may have to check several possible high points before you find the correct one. (2.5–3.5 hours.)

From KIRSTEIN, go east for a short distance and descend a steep slab into a steep south-running drainage. The drainage leads down to an expanse of slickrock below a cliff. There are several large potholes and excellent camping sites in the area. (0.5 hours.)

> **Digression**: To get to the lake, walk south and descend very steep slickrock (Class 4-). You may have to do some scouting to find the easiest route. There is fine camping at the lake.

To Cottonwood Gulch

Return to KIRSTEIN, then hike west-northwest to the rim of Cottonwood Gulch. Follow its rim upcanyon to the first obvious break in the canyon wall, a wide bowl (located one-eighth mile east of elevation 3997). A constructed cattle trail in the bowl takes you into Cottonwood Gulch, which was named by the USGS in 1951. (3.5–5.0 hours.)

Cottonwood Gulch

Immediately downcanyon are three large caves on the left. Rock climbers can have fun ascending Moqui steps into two of the caves. Water starts flowing a short distance downcanyon and there is good camping in the area. Lake Powell is a half-hour walk. There is much to see and explore in this canyon. (1.0 hour.)

Exit Cottonwood Gulch

Return to the foot of the cattle trail near the three large caves and proceed upcanyon for a couple of minutes. Rock climbers can duck into a scenic slot on the right and follow it up the canyon (Class 5.2, 10'). Others can hike up a brush-covered hillside to the left (LUC) of the slot and reenter the canyon in a quarter mile.

In fifteen minutes the canyon divides. Exit the canyon here by going southwest up a steep hill between the two forks of the canyon (over elevation 4312T) (Class 3+). (1.0–1.5 hours.)

> **Digression**: Both forks of the canyon contain impressive narrows.

Back to the trailhead

Hike to the foot of Sixty Point and follow the cattle trail back to the trailhead. (2.5–4.0 hours.)

Slot near Cottonwood Gulch.

Davis Gulch—Hike #28

Season:	Spring, summer, or fall. After recent rains there will be short stretches of wading and perhaps a stroke or two of swimming.
Time:	6.5 to 9.5 hours. It is very difficult to get packs through the narrows of Davis Gulch, making it unsuitable for an overnight trip.

Water:	Water availability is not a problem on this hike. A perennial stream starts flowing about halfway down Davis Gulch, below Bement Arch.
Elevation range:	3760' to 4315'.
Map:	Davis Gulch.
Skill level:	Easy route finding. There is one long cross-country stretch. Class 5.2 rock climbing. The leader must be experienced with belay techniques and be capable of leading the climbing sections without protection. There are short stretches of wading or swimming. This is a long strenuous dayhike that is suitable only for experienced canyoneers. **This route is not appropriate for novice canyoneers, youngsters, or youth groups.**
Special equipment:	A forty-foot rope and wading boots.
Land status:	This hike is in Glen Canyon National Recreation Area.

The Latin phrase *"multum in parvo"*—a great deal in a small space—accurately describes the Davis Gulch experience. This short canyon, once much longer before the flooding of its lower reaches by Lake Powell, packs a wallop. The upper part, a tight, difficult, and elegant slot, leads into a wide Navajo-walled canyon replete with rows of Moqui steps, beaver ponds, and a mammoth arch.

The route starts on the Hole-in-the-Rock road and goes through the narrows of Davis Gulch, past Bement Arch, and exits the canyon via an old cattle trail near Lake Powell. A rim walk takes you back to the trailhead.

> **Historical note:** Davis Gulch was named for the Davis brothers, George and Johnny, both early residents of Escalante. They ran sheep above the gulch.

The first narrows

(Davis Gulch map and **Map Thirty-three.)** Look west toward the Straight Cliffs. Hole-in-the-Rock Arch on Fiftymile Point is visible high on the skyline. It will be useful as a landmark at the end of the hike.

Walk north from the road into the shallow head of Davis Gulch. The canyon narrows quickly as it cuts deep into the Navajo Sandstone. Drops of up to ten feet over chockstones prove exciting. Belays may be necessary in places. The canyon opens. If the going seemed demanding during the initial section of the slot, this is the

Ginger Harmon in Davis Gulch.

time to bail out and return to the trailhead. The going gets even tougher and more technical ahead. (0.5 hours.)

The second narrows

The canyon again narrows and the walls rise as you negotiate a plethora of moderate problems. A slide into an often deep pool is the crux. The first person down should be belayed while checking water depth.

Warning: At this point, the route may not be reversible. Once over the slide, you are committed to finishing the route through the narrows, which eases somewhat beyond the pool. Remember, too, that the hike from the mouth of the narrows to the cattle trail exit and back to the trailhead is a long one.

Historical note: Toward the end of the slot, high on a wall to the right, is the difficult-to-locate Everett Ruess memorial plaque. It reads:

EVERETT RUESS
"I HAVE BEEN THINKING MORE AND MORE THAT I
SHALL ALWAYS BE A LONE
WANDERER IN THE WILDERNESS"

"Oh but the desert is glorious now
With marching clouds in the blue sky,
And cool winds blowing.
The smell of the sage is sweet
in my nostrils,
And the luring trail leads onwards."

The quotes are from Everett's writings. The plaque was installed in 1984.

The slot continues for another couple of hundred yards, then opens into a sand-floored canyon. The large tree below the slot is a netleaf hackberry. Sacred datura plants with their large green leaves and huge white flowers can often be seen in profusion. (1.0–2.0 hours.)

To Bement Arch

The canyon below contains three sets of Moqui steps. The first is several minutes from the mouth of the slot and is on the left. It goes up a curve of rock. These steps, though undoubtedly of Anasazi origin, were probably enlarged by Navajo or Piute sheepherders in the late 1800s.

The second row of Moqui steps is also on the left. It is difficult to locate. Near the top of its run it makes a spectacular traverse across a near-vertical wall. The third row is on the right, a short distance above Bement Arch. A steep trail leads through the arch, affording fine views of the canyon. (1.0–1.5 hours.)

Historical note: Davis Gulch was the last known campsite used by Everett Ruess. He inscribed "NEMO 1934" on a wall near Bement Arch. The name Nemo was used several times by Everett in his writings. Speculation has it that Nemo was either from the Greek word meaning "no one" or from Captain Nemo, who shunned humankind by disappearing under the sea in Jules Verne's *Twenty Thousand Leagues Under the Sea*.

Bement Arch was locally called Nemo Arch or Gothic Arch. Harry Aleson suggested the name Everett Ruess Natural Window in 1950. Members of a National Geographic expedition in 1955 renamed it for Harlon W. Bement, the director of the Utah State Aeronautics Commission. Bement was an avid explorer of canyon country on both foot and from the air and is credited with discovering several arches. The USGS Board on Geographic Names was faced with the problem of officially naming the arch after Bement since he was still alive and landform names generally honor the dead.

To the cattle trail exit

Below Bement Arch a riparian habitat develops. A perennial flow of water and a string of beaver ponds hinders progress. There may be some wading, though indistinct trails do lead around most of the ponds.

A constructed cattle trail is used to exit the canyon. It is on the left and ascends the first easy break in the wall. (The trail goes between the "l" and the "c" in Gulch.) Scattered near the foot of the trail are pieces of a log fence. If you miss the trail, the walls again steepen and you will end up at Lake Powell. (1.5–2.0 hours.)

> **Historical note:** The lower three miles of Davis Gulch, now under water, were strewn with Anasazi cliff dwellings and Fremont Culture pictographs. The flooding of Lake Powell destroyed these sites. Harry Aleson, in a letter to Stella Ruess, Everett Ruess's mother, described a trip into the canyon in May 1949 while looking for signs of the long-missing Everett. While there, Aleson stumbled onto a major cliff dwelling. Aleson reported that he "Climbed into the first large cave on Right (So. Exp.). This was an old Moki Cave for 20 or so families. Many shards, charcoal, metates, side by side in boulders, old maize cobs, 3 rock lookouts, remains of Moki House, 4 ft walls in place—White pigment paintings farthest to Eastward. To West, outside of main cave, & on lower level is a fine Moki Granary, stick, stone and mud. Door below it. No white man ever here?"

The cattle trail exit

The first portion of the cattle trail consists of a series of steps cut into the rock. After the initial rise, the trail follows the rim upcanyon for a couple of hundred yards; it then turns west and zigzags up a shallow slickrock drainage.

> **Historical note:** This trail proved problematic to cattlemen. Rancher McKay Bailey is quoted as saying, "This spot is tricky. We had a horse do a two-and-a-half gainer off the cliff here, and once a pack mule landed in the cottonwood trees below."

The trail fizzles at the top of the cliff. You can either follow the rim of the canyon back to the trailhead or take a faster route that cuts southwest to higher and less convoluted ground. Use Hole-in-the-Rock Arch on Fiftymile Point as a guide as you route-find back to the trailhead. (2.5–3.5 hours.)

Clear Creek and the Cathedral in the Desert— Hike #29

Season:	Any.
Time:	9.0 to 12.5 hours. A very long dayhike or a pleasant overnight hike.
Water:	Water availability is a minor problem on this route. Upper Clear Creek has large potholes. Water is available at Lake Powell. The cross-country route back to the trailhead is dry.
Elevation range:	3700' to 4480'.
Map:	Davis Gulch.
Skill level:	Moderate route finding. There is one long cross-country stretch. Class 3 scrambling. This is a moderate hike. If done as an overnight hike, familiarity with low-impact camping skills is essential.
Special equipment:	None.
Land status:	This hike is in Glen Canyon National Recreation Area.

I was one of the lucky ones. In 1968 a group of friends and I visited the Cathedral in the Desert by boat. Lake Powell was still filling then and, although the lower canyon was awash, we were able to climb a thin row of Moqui steps up a vertical wall into the upper cathedral. And what a wonderful place it was! The tan Navajo walls, streaked with a thick patina of brown-and-black desert varnish, curved skyward in Gothic arcs that nearly met at the top, leaving just a thin slit of sunlight to illuminate the small stream that ran down from the chancel, through the nave, and disappeared under a wall beyond the narthex.

With the filling of Lake Powell, the cathedral was inundated and we lost a very special place. An early visitor, Mrs. Howd Veater from Escalante, thought the canyon looked like a cathedral with pennons hanging along the walls and suggested the name.

The route starts on the Hole-in-the-Rock road and goes down Clear Creek to a fall. It then follows the canyon rim to a pleasant campsite on Lake Powell. A cross-country jaunt leads back to the trailhead.

Along the Hole-in-the-Rock road

(**Davis Gulch map** and **Map Thirty-three.**) From the trailhead follow the Hole-in-the-Rock road east. In twenty-five minutes Hole-in-the-Rock well, with its green pump and stock reservoir, appears on the right. Beyond it, a plaque erected in 1957 by the Utah Pioneer Trails and Landmarks Association is on a wall to the right. It reads:

The naming of this arch honors
the historic trek of the MORMON PIONEERS
called by
BRIGHAM YOUNG
To Colonize San Juan County
in 1879 – 1880

The arch—Hole-in-the-Rock Arch—can be seen on the skyline to the southwest.

To Clear Creek

In another thirty-five minutes, after ascending a long hill, you will intersect the first side track to the left (NNE). An orange "No Vehicles" sign on a flexible post marks the track. (The track is not shown on the map. It starts one-quarter mile east-northeast of elevation 4422.) (1.0 hour.)

Down Clear Creek

Walk north up the track for three minutes, then leave it, cutting northeast down a hill into the shallow upper part of the Clear Creek drainage. Proceed down the sandy wash. As the drainage narrows and deepens into an inner gorge, small drops in the Navajo Sandstone impede progress. Exit the canyon and walk along its left (W) rim. The gorge below contains many large potholes and ends at a dramatic pour-off into Clear Creek Canyon. (1.5–2.0 hours.)

> **Historical note:** Stockmen and early explorers to the lower Escalante Canyon, tired of drinking the often dirty river water, relished the "champagne-clear" water flowing from springs in Clear Creek Canyon.

To Lake Powell

Your goal is to hike north-northeast along the left (W) rim of Clear Creek Canyon until you reach Lake Powell. It is easiest to stay

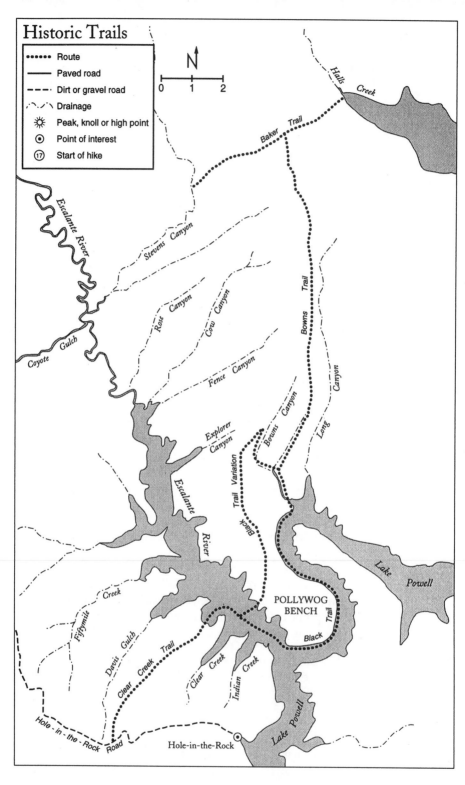

Map Thirty-seven

high above the canyon to avoid a couple of deep side drainages. A jutting point of slickrock (at elevation 3814T) provides access to the lake by means of a steep slickrock descent (Class 3). It may take some scouting to find the route. There is good but limited camping near the lake. (2.0–3.0 hours.)

> **Digression:** From the water's edge look east across the lake. A steep slab behind an island leads north up to Pollywog Bench. This slab contains a variation of the Clear Creek Trail, an old constructed cattle trail. See the Historical note below for details.

To the Clear Creek Trail

Look at your map. One-half mile to the west is a short west-tending inlet. Your goal is to go around the west end of the inlet, then follow its north rim east to another jutting point of slickrock. Near the end of the point pick up a cairned and constructed cattle trail that leads to a narrow defile. It will take you to the lake (southwest of the second "A" in AREA). There is good but limited camping near the lake. (1.0–1.5 hours.)

> **Historical note:** The route the cattle trail follows was first used by Anasazi Indians. Several caves near the trail were surveyed by archaeologists in 1957. They found rock shelters, storage cists, and assorted artifacts which have now been inundated by Lake Powell.
>
> The cattle trail, which runs from the Hole-in-the-Rock road to Halls Creek, was built in sections by three local cattlemen in the early 1900s. (**Map Thirty-seven.**) The first section was constructed by John Black, an Escalante and Boulder cattleman. The Black Trail started at the Hole-in-the-Rock road and entered Escalante Canyon at this point. This section of the Black Trail is now called the Clear Creek Trail.
>
> Robert Moore, after ascending this portion of the trail in 1955, wrote: "First we had to follow a zigzag path up a sand slope, a trail so steep that the pack horses refused time and again to start up it. Above this, the path mounts a narrow, sharply tilted ledge of slickrock in which cowboys have blasted and chipped a few crude footholds. Even when we had negotiated that precipitous incline, there were sand slopes and slickrock so steep that we had to climb afoot, leading our horses."
>
> The Black Trail then followed the canyon floor downriver for a couple of miles and went partway out of the canyon on the left to a Kayenta bench, which is now under water. The trail followed the bench out to the Colorado River and upcanyon to the mouths of Bowns and Long canyons.
>
> The second part of the trail—from the east fork of Bowns Canyon to the top of the Waterpocket Fold—was constructed by William Bown. The Bowns Trail is described in Hike #23.
>
> The third part of the trail—from the crest of the Waterpocket

Fold into Halls Creek—was built by Eugene Baker. The Baker Trail is described in Hike #21.

An important variation of the Black Trail exited Escalante Canyon via the cattle trail that is almost directly across from the mouth of Clear Creek Canyon. It then crossed Pollywog Bench and entered Bowns Canyon by way of a spectacular horse ladder. (See Hike #23.)

Return to the trailhead

The route back to the trailhead is dry. Load up with water before leaving Lake Powell. You will follow the course of the old Clear Creek Trail, which used to be passable by car; however, it is unlikely that you will see signs of the road.

Historical note: The Clear Creek Trail road was "built" by the U.S. Geological Survey to reach a gaging station it had erected on the Escalante River at the foot of the trail. Burnett Hendryx, a horse packer from Panguitch, noted that "the Government built the cheapest highway in history. Seven miles with a gallon of paint!" White streaks of paint left on the slickrock marked the "road."

In April 1956 explorer J. Allan Crocket and a group of friends drove this "road." Crocket wrote: "That trip is absolutely unbelievable over the steep, slick-rock, ups and downs that I wouldn't have believed even a jeep could take." The remains of a camp for those monitoring the river is near the top of the trail.

Simply set a compass course south-southwest and hike through a maze of small domes and washes. The prospect of having few landmarks to help guide the way should not intimidate the novice canyoneer. The Straight Cliffs provide a general direction. If you go too far west Davis Gulch will appear. Intersect the Hole-in-the-Rock road and return to the trailhead. (3.5–5.0 hours.)

IV
The Burr Trail—The Eastern Escalante

The eastern Escalante is bounded by Highway 12 to the west, the Circle Cliffs to the north, the Waterpocket Fold to the east, and the Escalante River to the south. The Circle Cliffs, an immense circle-shaped escarpment of Wingate Sandstone that surrounds a huge basin, defines the area. Unlike the western Escalante, which is dominated by Navajo Sandstone, the east side of the river contains a panoply of geologic formations that give the Circle Cliffs Basin and the canyons that flow through it a distinctive character.

Almon Thompson of the second Powell expedition was the first white man known to have entered the Circle Cliffs Basin, which he named. Geologist Grove Karl Gilbert, unaware of Thompson's designation, called the cliffs both the Howell Fold and the Escalante Fold during an expedition in 1875.

The first wagon road into Circle Cliffs Basin was scouted and built by Charles Hall in the early 1880s as a replacement for the difficult Hole-in-the-Rock route. The Hall route went from the town of Escalante down Harris Wash, up Silver Falls Creek, across the Circle Cliffs Basin to Muley Twist Canyon, and down Halls Creek to the Colorado River.

The Burr Trail, which cuts through the heart of the Circle Cliffs Basin, was built in the late 1880s by John Atlantic Burr. Burr's unusual middle name was in honor of his birth while his parents were crossing the Atlantic Ocean in the early 1870s. He built the Burr Trail to move cattle from the Aquarius Plateau to Bullfrog Basin on the Colorado River. Burr died alone on the desert while trying to remedy a urinary tract blockage with a piece of wire.

In 1920 the Ohio Drilling Company built the first automobile road into the Circle Cliffs Basin. This road went down Harris Wash and up Silver Falls Creek to the Wagon Box Mesa area.

Local ranchers built a rough road through the upper gulch to the northern Circle Cliffs Basin in 1936 to install watering troughs at Brinkerhoff Seeps.

Turning the Burr Trail into a road started in earnest in 1947. By 1950 a good road had been built through Long Canyon, and in 1951 the switchbacks down the face of the Waterpocket Fold had been completed. Uranium miners, arriving in large numbers in the

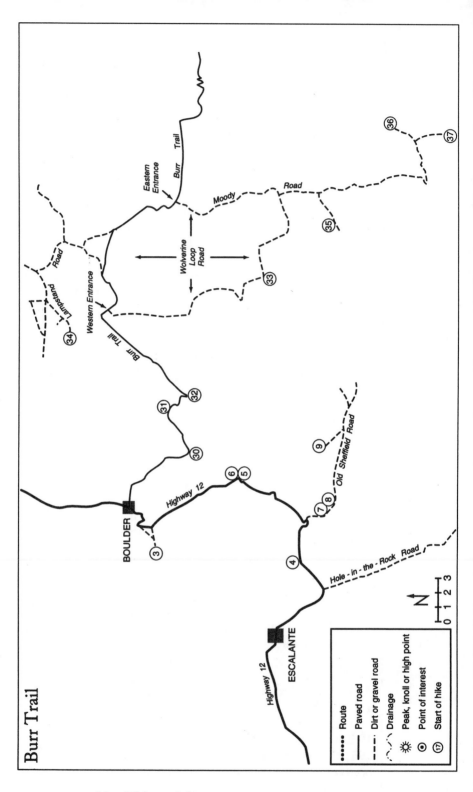

Map Thirty-eight

mid-1950s, pushed roads into nearly every corner of the Circle Cliffs Basin.

Burr Trail Road Section
Access to Hikes #30 through 37.
Access is from Highway 12.
Provides access to the Lamp Stand road, Wolverine Loop road—the Western Entrance, and Wolverine Loop road—the Eastern Entrance (the Moody road).
Maps—Boulder Town, Calf Creek, King Bench, Steep Creek Bench, Lamp Stand, Bitter Creek Divide, and Wagon Box Mesa.

The Burr Trail starts at milepost 87.1 on Highway 12 (located one-eighth mile north-northeast of elevation 6794 on the **Boulder Town map**). The road is suitable for light-duty vehicles to the Capitol Reef National Park boundary at mile 30.5, which marks the end of the pavement. Beyond that point, light-duty vehicles may not be able to continue. High-clearance vehicles are recommended. The dirt portion of the road may be impassable after rains. This is a long road. Make sure to carry plenty of gas and water. There is camping near the road. (See **Map Thirty-eight**.)

0.0 —On Highway 12 at the Burr Trail junction. A sign reads "Boulder–Bull Frog Scenic Road." Go east.

2.5 —(**Calf Creek map**.) Cattle guard. The occasional large evergreens are ponderosa pines. The white checkerboard wall to the right is Navajo Sandstone topped with brownish Carmel Formation limestone.

6.2 —(**King Bench map**.) Start of Deer Creek **Hike #30**. Signed Deer Creek crossing. Just before the creek is a parking area and trail register on the right. Past the creek on the left is a small BLM campground. It has outhouses, picnic tables, and trash barrels, but there is no drinking water. You are at the crossing shown between "Deer" and "Creek" on the map. You are in Navajo Sandstone.

7.1 —Top of a hill.

7.5 —Yellow fifteen-miles-per-hour sign on the right.

7.9 —Start of Steep Creek and Hot Canyon **Hike #31**. "Tee." A short track to the left (NE) starts just before a Navajo dome that is right next to the road. There is parking past the dome. The dome is located one-quarter mile north-northwest of elevation 6177.

10.1 —Start of The Gulch and Horse Canyon **Hike #32**. Short road signed "Trailhead Parking" to the right (W). There is a trail register and limited camping. You are at a sharp bend in the road between a labeled cliff dwelling and a corral. You are in the Kayenta Formation.

10.3 | —The Gulch is to the right. You are now in Long Canyon.

10.6 | —Bridge crossing The Gulch. You are in Wingate Sandstone. As you drive up Long Canyon you will enter the colorful hills of the Chinle Formation.

15.8 | —(**Steep Creek Bench map.**) The canyon to the left (N) is Upper Long Canyon. (It starts just as you go off the Steep Creek Bench map.)

> **Digression:** A delightful route goes up colorful Upper Long Canyon. The first section is easy, as it goes along the canyon floor. (Lamp Stand map.) The middle section gets tougher, with boulder hopping and minor bush bashing. The upper section, after you enter the Wingate, narrows into a slot. One move up a short chimney (Class 5.2, 10') is the crux. Above, the canyon stays narrow and near the top it divides. Go right, to the edge of an escarpment, which provides inspiring views of the Circle Cliffs, Henry Mountains, Navajo Mountain, and the Kaiparowits Plateau. (4.0–6.0 hours round-trip.)

16.7 | —(**Lamp Stand map.**) You are on the top of a hill at the Long Canyon Overlook sign. The long escarpment of red Wingate Sandstone in the distance (NE) is the Circle Cliffs. The Henry Mountains are in the far background.

18.4 | —"Tee." A sign for the road to the right (SSW) starts with "Capitol Reef 11 mi."; listed below are Horse Canyon, Wolverine Canyon, and Little Death Hollow. This road provides access to **Hike #33**. See the Wolverine Loop road—the Western Entrance for details.

19.5 | —The small wash you cross is Horse Canyon. You are in the Moenkopi Formation.

21.8 | —"Tee." The first signed road to the Lamp Stand is to the left (NE). This road provides access to **Hike #34**. See the Lamp Stand Road Section for details.

22.5 | —Cattle guard.

24.2 | —"Tee." The second signed road to the Lamp Stand is to the left (NNW). You are on White Canyon Flat.

27.6 | —(**Bitter Creek Divide map.**) Through the Studhorse Peaks. The name comes from stud horses that stood high on the slopes of the peak while guarding their mares.

27.8 | —Cattle guard.

28.0 | —Stock pond on left.

28.8 | —(**Wagon Box Mesa map.**) "Tee." A sign for the road to the right (S) starts with "Wolverine Loop Road." Listed below are Silver Falls Creek, Little Death Hollow, Wolverine Canyon, etc. This road provides access to **Hikes #35 through 37**. See the Wolverine Loop road—the Eastern Entrance for details. This road is also called the Moody road.

29.8 | —Cattle guard.

30.5 | —Enter Capitol Reef National Park. This marks the end of the pavement and the end of the road section. It is now 5.1 miles to a "Tee" at the foot of the Waterpocket Fold. From there it is thirty-three miles north to Highway 24 and thirty miles south to Highway 276.

Deer Creek—Hike #30

Season: Late spring after spring runoff, summer, or fall. This route cannot be done during periods of high water or cold temperatures.

Time: 14.5 to 19.5 hours. Two long days or three moderate days.

Water: Water availability is a minor problem on this hike. Deer Creek has a perennial flow of water. Large potholes can be found along the return route.

Elevation range: 5080' to 5850'.

Map: King Bench.

Skill level: Moderate route finding. Class 5.0 climbing with moderate exposure. The leader must be experienced with belay techniques and be capable of leading the climbing sections without protection. Lots of wading. This is a moderately strenuous hike. Familiarity with low-impact camping skills is essential.

Special equipment: Wading boots. One inner tube per group for floating packs will help if you are unable to climb around the pools. An eighty-foot climbing rope is essential.

Note: Poison ivy is found along Deer Creek. It is avoidable.

Land status: This hike is in Grand Staircase-Escalante National Monument.

In the days of yore came the man O'roöndates, who loved the woman Stati'ra, the widow of Alexander the Great. Although a woman of perfect beauty, Stati'ra was treacherous and deceptive. She

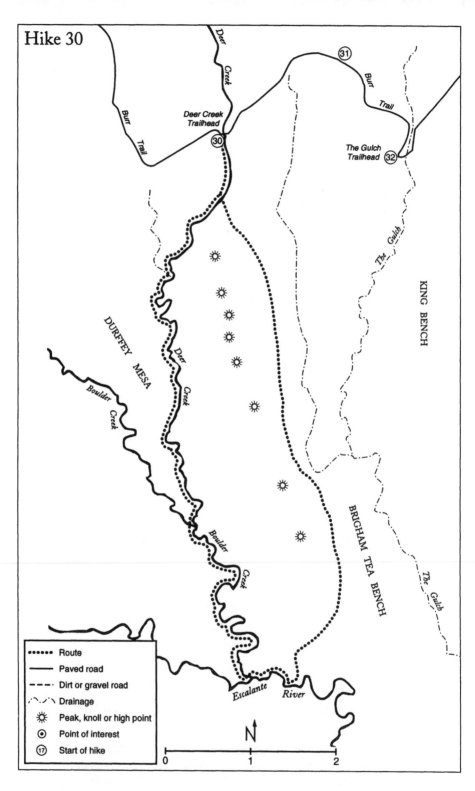

Hike 30

Deer Creek

Burr Trail

31

Burr Trail

Deer Creek
Trailhead

30

The Gulch
Trailhead

32

Burr Trail

The Gulch

KING BENCH

DURFFEY MESA

Deer Creek

Boulder Creek

BRIGHAM TEA BENCH

The Gulch

Boulder Creek

Escalante River

•••••• Route
——— Paved road
– – – Dirt or gravel road
⌇·⌇·⌇ Drainage
☼ Peak, knoll or high point
⊙ Point of interest
17 Start of hike

N

0   1   2

Map Thirty-nine

forced O'roöndates to tackle a series of dangers and difficulties before allowing him to take her hand. For many a year O'roöndates toiled on, with thoughts of Stati'ra's charms propelling him, until at last the hardships ended and she had to accept him as her husband. Like O'roöndates, you will have to overcome a series of difficulties in the flowing waters of Deer Creek in order to possess the beauty you are seeking.

The route starts on the Burr Trail and goes down Deer Creek to the Escalante River. It is followed downcanyon for a short distance. A cattle trail exit leads to a day-long stretch of walking superb slickrock under a remarkable dome-topped escarpment, which you follow back to the trailhead.

Along Deer Creek

(**King Bench map** and **Map Thirty-nine.**) From the trailhead locate a path that goes along the right (W) side of Deer Creek. It is easy to follow for the first two miles. The route then cuts up onto slickrock and crosses a couple of small side canyons before returning to the rim of Deer Creek. Cairns mark the route through this section. Follow the trail until Durffey Mesa, a Navajo escarpment on the right (W), forces you down to the creekbed (one-eighth mile east-northeast of the "a" in Durffey Mesa). Do not make the mistake of dropping into the canyon too soon or you will have to contend with thick vegetation. (1.5–2.0 hours.)

Down Deer Creek

The crux of the route lies ahead and consists of many miles of wading and thrashing through long stretches of willows. The dominant trees are boxelders, with leaves that have irregularly notched teeth arranged in clumps of three, and dogwoods with their purplish bark. Small groups will find plenty of campsites in this section, but large groups will have problems. Watch for a couple of rows of Moqui steps and two constructed cattle trails that exit the canyon on the left (LDC). They provide access to the rim and good camping.

A couple of hundred yards before you reach Boulder Creek, which enters on the right (W), is a large patch of poison ivy. Boulder Creek is the first side canyon to enter Deer Creek. You will not miss it. There is excellent camping in the area. (3.5–5.5 hours.)

Down Boulder Creek

Below the confluence of Deer and Boulder creeks the united canyons are called Boulder Creek. The route downcanyon now consists of long stretches of slickrock walking interspersed with areas of willow bashing and wading. In an hour, after passing an old USGS water-gaging station that is on the right side of the creek, you reach

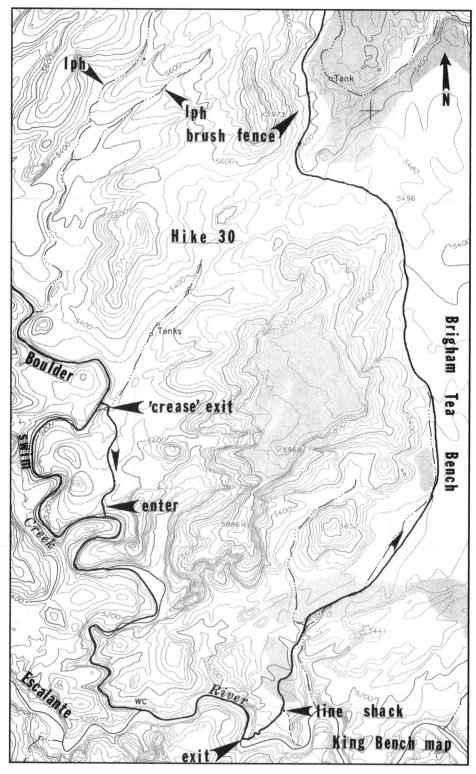

Map Forty

a stretch of splendid narrows and idyllic swim holes. You can probably spot both brown and rainbow trout in the pools. The narrows are a trial to negotiate and are presented below as a digression. Most will want to hike around the narrows. (1.0 hour.)

Around the narrows

From the start of the narrows, backtrack for 100 yards. Locate a steep crease in the cross-stratified Navajo sandstone wall on the right (LUC)(E). **(Map Forty.)** This is the only break in the wall in this vicinity. The crease (Class 4+, 60') provides egress from the canyon. Good camping is available on the slickrock above the canyon. (The crease is located just upcanyon from where a "Tanks" drainage shown on the map enters Boulder Creek.)

> **To the Overland Route:** This crease marks the point where the section of the Overland Route that goes between Highway 12 and Silver Falls Creek exits Boulder Creek.

> **Digression:** The trip through the narrows is short, exciting, and entails moderate stretches of swimming. Once through, return to the top of the narrows by exiting the canyon to the left (LDC), walking the rim upcanyon, and descending via the aforementioned crease. (1.5–2.5 hours round-trip.)

Follow the rim of the canyon down for ten minutes or until you can see the end of the narrows. A trail down a draw leads back to Deer Creek. Below, the canyon narrows for short stretches in a couple of places, forming deep pools. Most can climb around them (Class 5.0, 25'), but some may need to float packs across on inner tubes. There is poor camping at the junction with the Escalante River, but good campsites appear a short distance downcanyon. (3.0–4.0 hours.)

Down the Escalante River

Follow a good trail along the Escalante River for fifteen minutes to a barb-wire fence. Two minutes past the fence, the trail crosses the river. One hundred yards downcanyon and partway around a corner locate a constructed cattle trail on the left (N). You will leave the river here. Water sources are now far apart and are located a distance from the route. Load up with water. (0.5 hours.)

Follow the trail through a barb-wire gate to an old line shack on the top of the hill.

> **To the Overland Route:** You can join the section of the Overland Route that goes between Highway 12 and Silver Falls Creek at the line shack. The location of the line shack is shown as a small black square and is correctly placed on the USGS map. The trail from the

Narrows of Boulder Creek.

shack to the river is not accurately drawn, however; instead of going down a point to the southeast of the shack, the trail goes down
the point to the southwest.

To the trailhead

There is a narrow canyon to the east of the line shack (shown to
the west of elevation 5441). Follow its left (LUC)(W) rim north un-

til the narrows end, then follow a sandy wash northeast. It skirts around the east side of a very long north-running Navajo escarpment and dies in the slickrock. Your goal is to follow the east side of the escarpment north for many miles. Stay within a couple of hundred yards of the cliff; you will encounter serious obstacles if you do not. This long, lovely escarpment is broken in places by domes, towers, and turrets and is easy to follow.

A couple of landmarks along the route below the escarpment will help you keep track of your progress. First, you will pass over a brush fence that is located one-eighth mile east of elevation 5973. Immediately to the east is a canyon (with a labeled "Tank" on the map). A constructed cattle trail leads into the canyon, which contains medium pools near both of its heads. (2.0–2.5 hours.)

> **Digression:** If water is a problem, follow the "Tank" canyon down for a half hour to The Gulch, which has a perennial flow.

The second landmark is a labeled "Spring" an hour north of the "Tank." It rarely contains water, but a gap in the escarpment to the left (SW) (shown one-eighth mile north of elevation 6209) leads to a wide, wonderful slickrock-floored canyon lined with ponderosa pines and a string of large potholes. There is excellent camping in the area. (1.0–1.5 hours.)

> **Digression:** If the large potholes are not full and you are desperate for water, continue hiking down the slickrock-floored canyon until you are on a cliff above Deer Creek. Hike upcanyon along the rim for a quarter mile and cross a drainage that drops from the northeast. Descend a Class 3 slab to the creek.

The escarpment you have been following ends (north of elevation 6043). The valley containing Deer Creek is visible to the west and northwest, although you cannot see the creek itself. You should also recognize Durffey Mesa, which you hiked under on the first day. Simply continue north and find a way through low cliffs to Deer Creek. Cross the creek and follow the trail on the west side back to the trailhead. (2.0–2.5 hours.)

Steep Creek and Hot Canyon—Hike #31

Season: Spring or fall.

Time: 9.0 to 12.0 hours. Two days.

Water: Water availability is a problem on this hike. Steep Creek has large springs in several sections. Hot Canyon is dry.

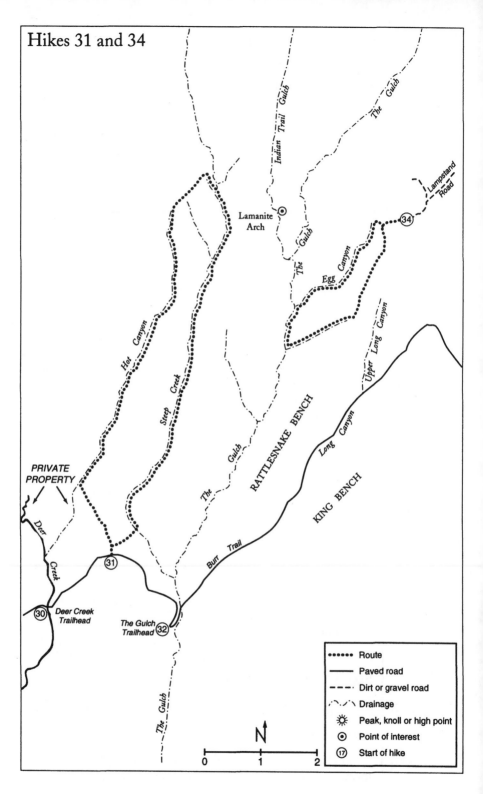

Hikes 31 and 34

Indian Trail Gulch

The Gulch

Lampstand Road

34

Lamanite Arch

The Gulch

Egg Canyon

Hot Canyon

Upper Long Canyon

Steep Creek

The Gulch

RATTLESNAKE BENCH

Long Canyon

KING BENCH

PRIVATE PROPERTY

Deer Creek

31

Burr Trail

30 Deer Creek Trailhead

The Gulch Trailhead 32

The Gulch

N

0   1   2

••••••	Route
——	Paved road
– – –	Dirt or gravel road
⌐⌐⌐	Drainage
☼	Peak, knoll or high point
⊙	Point of interest
⑰	Start of hike

Map Forty-one

Elevation range:	5720' to 7000'.
Maps:	King Bench and Steep Creek Bench.
Skill level:	Difficult route finding. Class 3 scrambling. This is a moderately strenuous hike. Some wading. Familiarity with low-impact camping skills is essential.
Special equipment:	Wading shoes.
Land status:	This hike is in Grand Staircase-Escalante National Monument.

Steep and hot. Not exactly two adjectives one would want to see used to describe canyons on a proposed hike. Although there is some correlation between the canyons on this route and their names, the connection is not absolute. Steep Creek really isn't, for the most part, and Hot Canyon isn't, if the weather is cooperating.

There are some who put this hike down due to the cattle damage in lower Steep Creek. The initial cow-pie-lined trudge, though, leads to one of the finest and least-visited sections of canyon in the Escalante.

The route starts on the Burr Trail and follows a constructed cattle trail into Steep Creek. It then goes up Steep Creek, crosses a high ridge, and descends Hot Canyon. A short cross-country jaunt leads back to the trailhead.

Into Steep Creek
(**King Bench map** and **Map Forty-one.**) Hike northwest along the track. In two minutes it divides. The main track goes to the left (S). Go right (N). In 100 yards the track dies in the sand. You are now in a gap between two domes. (The dome to the north has a "WC" [witness corner] labeled on its south side on the map.)

An established and still used cattle trail begins at the gap and goes northeast along the left (NW) side of a shallow northeast-running drainage. As you near Steep Creek, pass through a wire gate and descend a constructed portion of cattle trail to the canyon floor. You are in the Kayenta Formation and there are large springs in this section of the canyon. (0.5 hours.)

Note: This cattle trail, and a line shack in Steep Creek, are incorrectly placed on the King Bench map.

Up Steep Creek
(**Steep Creek Bench map.**) Cattle trails ease your passage through thick vegetation as you proceed upcanyon. An old tin line

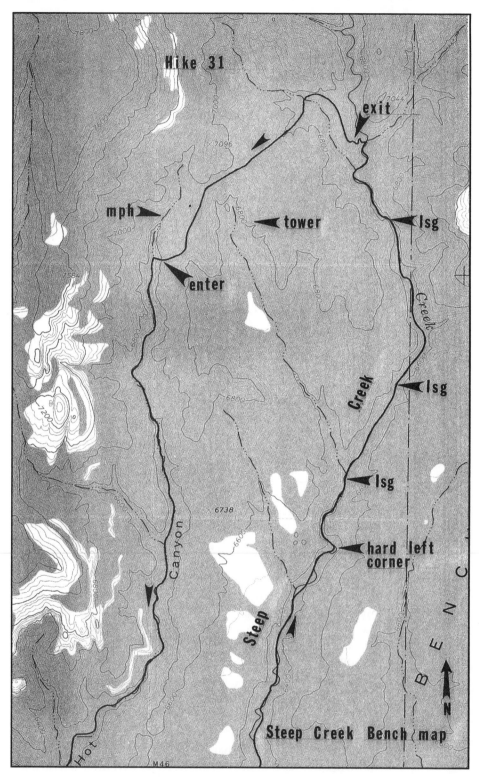

Map Forty-two

shack soon becomes visible on the right bank. The canyon is remarkably uniform in structure, making it hard to tell exactly where you are on the map. In 1.5 hours you will reach a barb-wire fence. This marks the start of Wingate Sandstone, which is characterized by vertical cliffs pocked with holes. Water stops running here and will not return for an hour or more. (You are near "Steep" on the map.) (1.5–2.0 hours.)

The next landmark is a hard left corner an hour upcanyon from the barb-wire fence (shown one-half mile to the east-southeast of elevation 6738). (**Map Forty-two.**) The ambience of the canyon changes. Flowing water soon reappears and the bush bashing ends. Large lava rocks are strewn along the stream and the channel is lined with ponderosa pines. Signs of cattle decrease. This area is idyllic. The canyon narrows considerably and there may be some minor wading until you reach a small fall and a deep pool in a narrow gap. You can either tackle this directly (deep wading) or backtrack for 150 yards, clamber up a very steep boulder-choked gully to the right (LUC)(NE), and pass the fall.

Also pass the second pool on the right (LUC). The third pool must be tackled head on (knee- to waist-deep wading). The Wingate canyon narrows even more and there is some minor climbing and wading. This section is unbelievably beautiful, with red Wingate walls framed by a variety of greenery. As the canyon enters the Kayenta, the wading ends. After passing a couple of small waterfalls you will find an excellent camp spot along the only wide section of the canyon.

Above the camping area note where the stream has cut under a long, but not high, overhang on the left. This is the only overhang of its type in the area and it is obvious. A minute past this the canyon divides. The main canyon is on the left (NW). The canyon on the right (NE) has a small arch on its left side and a stepped slickrock drop at its mouth. (You are one-eighth mile south-southwest of elevation 7044.) There may not be water along the route. Load up here. (1.5–2.5 hours.)

To Hot Canyon
Exit Steep Creek by scrambling west up a steep hillside and through short cliffs to the top of a sharp ridge covered with lava boulders. This is tough. Look west. Below you is a deep drainage. Behind it is a long ridge with a tree-covered top (elevation 7900). On its left (S) side is a lower bump with trees on its top and white Navajo Sandstone visible on its left side (elevation 7584). Your goal is to get to the rim of Hot Canyon, which is immediately below the middle of the hill that is at elevation 7584.

You will cross the heads of two drainages on the way. The first drainage is below you. The second drainage—a wide tree-covered valley—has a forty-foot tower just below its left (E) rim near its top.

If you try to enter Hot Canyon too far upcanyon you will find yourself in a steep slot that you cannot get through. This slot does contain medium potholes that you can reach. Descend steep slopes that are due east of the middle of the hill that is at elevation 7584 into Kayenta-walled Hot Canyon. There are many options. (1.5–2.0 hours.)

Down Hot Canyon

Hot Canyon, like Steep Creek, is quite uniform throughout its length, making it difficult to keep track of where you are on the map. The following landmarks will help you keep track of your progress. After about two hours the wall on the left, which was not too tall before, rises, becomes vertical, and changes color to dirty white for a short distance. This wall is obvious. Shortly below it the canyon widens and you will encounter the first cottonwood trees. Small springs may also appear.

Twenty minutes downcanyon from the dirty white wall, look for a large white Navajo escarpment in the distance to the right (LDC). It is the first plainly visible escarpment you will see from the canyon floor. (This is elevation 6969.) A couple of minutes later a side canyon enters on the right (N) (shown at the "C" in Canyon). If you are not sure if this is the correct canyon, walk up it for a few paces and locate a double-fist-sized hole in the wall ten feet off the deck on the right. (2.5–3.0 hours.)

The main canyon now becomes crowded with vegetation. In thirty minutes another drainage enters on the right (WNW). This one is really hard to see, as the low cliffs become even lower, at least along the right side of the canyon. A very thick stand of tamarisks, the first such stand encountered, starts here. If you are still unsure you are in the right place, hike up a hillside to the right (NW) and look at the cliff across the canyon to the south-southeast. Locate a small triangular-shaped cave high on the cliff. (0.5 hours.)

Exit Hot Canyon

Hike downcanyon for five minutes and exit the canyon to the left (SE). There are a couple of options. (Exit to the southeast of the "H" in Hot.)

> **Note:** Do not continue downcanyon to Deer Creek. Although this appears tempting on the map, there is private property ahead. Please respect the privacy and private property rights of others.

From the top of a sandy ridge look southeast. Before you is a small drainage. Behind it is a lopsided triangular-shaped dome (elevation 6232). Hike to the south shoulder of the dome. Look south-southeast and locate a sandy high point on a ridge. Make your way to it. From its crest look east. You will see a long flat-topped dome (elevation 6294). To its right (S) are two small rounded domes. (**King Bench map.**) The trailhead is to the right of the right-hand dome. (1.0–1.5 hours.)

The Gulch and Horse Canyon—Hike #32

Season:	Spring or fall.
Time:	19.0 to 25.5 hours. Three to four days.
Water:	Water availability is a moderate problem on this route. The Gulch, the Escalante River, and lower Horse Canyon have perennial flows of water. The cross-country route back to the trailhead is dry.
Elevation range:	4840' to 5640'.
Maps:	King Bench and Red Breaks.
Skill level:	Moderately difficult route finding. There is one long cross-country stretch. Class 5.0 climbing. The leader must be experienced with belay techniques and be capable of leading the climbing section without protection. Lots of wading. This is a moderate hike. Familiarity with low-impact camping skills is essential.
Special equipment:	Wading boots. A fifty-foot rope is essential.
Land status:	This hike is in Grand Staircase-Escalante National Monument.

The word "canyon" is derived from the Greek *kanna* and the Latin *canna*. Both refer to hollow reeds. The Spanish borrowed from the Latin and Greek to form the word *caña*, or "tube." Caña then became the root of the Spanish word *cañon*, which means a narrow chasm.

The word cañon made its way first to central Mexico with the conquistadors, then north into what is now the western United States. There it became Anglicized, with spelling variations that included cannion, cannon, cannyon, kanyun, and kenyon. It was not until Zebulon Montgomery Pike, the famous explorer of the West, wrote about his adventures in the early 1800s that the modern American spelling of "canyon" was introduced. The modern spelling was not used universally until the 1900s. Diarists on the Powell expeditions in the 1870s generally used cañon, and it is spelled that way in an 1879 edition of *McGuffey's Eclectic Spelling-Book*.

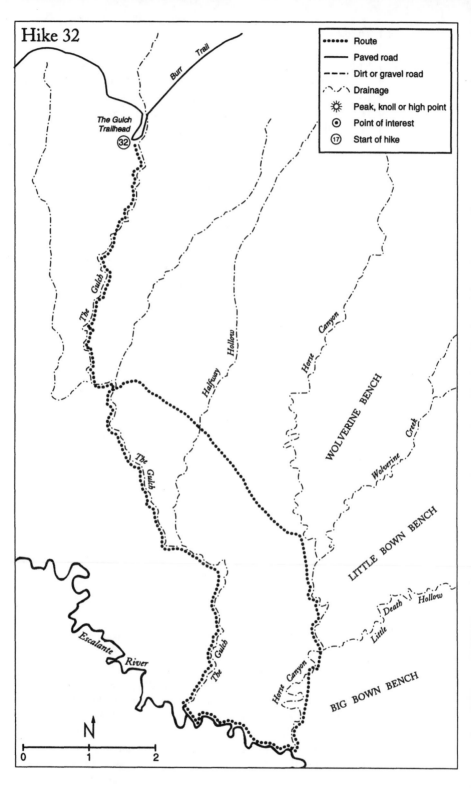

Route
Paved road
Dirt or gravel road
Drainage
Peak, knoll or high point
Point of interest
Start of hike

Burr Trail

The Gulch Trailhead

(32)

The Gulch

Halfway Hollow

Horse Canyon

WOLVERINE BENCH

Wolverine Creek

The Gulch

LITTLE BOWN BENCH

Death Hollow

Little

Escalante River

The Gulch

Horse Canyon

BIG BOWN BENCH

N

0   1   2

Map Forty-three

However spelled, the two canyons covered on this route are classics. The Gulch is similar in ambience to Harris Wash: a small stream wends its way through park-like glens shaded by huge cottonwoods, evidence of Fremont and Anasazi occupation abounds, and opportunities for side exploration seem endless.

The downside to hiking in The Gulch is that its upper reaches have been trashed by cattle. Horse Canyon, wide and highwalled throughout, is akin to a major highway interchange — constructed cattle trails and canyons branch off every which way.

The hike starts on the Burr Trail and goes down The Gulch to the Escalante River. After following the river for a short distance, the route turns into Horse Canyon and goes partway up it. A cross-country stretch across King Bench leads back into The Gulch, which is followed to the trailhead.

Down The Gulch

(**King Bench map** and **Map Forty-three.**) Ramble down the wide, flat-floored bottom of The Gulch. A cattle trail following the general course of an old road that used to go down the canyon makes for easy hiking. During periods of high water there may be some shallow wading as the trail crisscrosses the stream.

> **Digression:** Note a constructed cattle trail going up the cliff wall on the left (E) just a few minutes downcanyon from the trailhead. Some may want to use this trail on the return hike.

The first landmark is a line shack on the right (shown on the map). (1.5–2.0 hours.)

The next landmark is another line shack, this one on the left (located one-quarter mile south-southeast of the "e" in The.) (2.0–2.5 hours.)

Below the second line shack the canyon narrows. During periods of high water there may be some deep wading. At an abrupt left turn, the stream drops over a short fall into a narrow gorge (south-southeast of elevation 5412). It is wisest to explore these narrows from the bottom. To get around the narrows, first look downcanyon (E). Note a beautiful wall streaked with black-and-brown desert varnish framed by the narrows. Remember this wall.

Backtrack upcanyon for about four minutes to an indent in the wall to the left (LUC)(W). There is a log against the cliff. Ascend a slab on downsloping holds to the right of the log (Class 5.0, 20', belay). This is the first possible exit out of the canyon. Continue up steep slabs to the top. Follow the rim downcanyon until you are even with the black-and-brown-varnish-streaked wall. Look southeast. Below you is a vegetation-covered bench. A hiker-developed

The Gulch.

path will be visible. Go down a steep slab to the bench and follow the path into the canyon (Class 4). (2.0–3.0 hours.)

> **To the Overland Route:** To intersect the section of the Overland Route that runs between Highway 12 and Silver Falls Creek, hike down The Gulch for an hour from the base of the narrows you just skirted, then start looking for three potential exit canyons. These three narrow canyons are on the left (LDC)(E); they parallel each other and are only a minute or so apart. (The three canyons are located to the east of the "The" on the Red Breaks map.) You will join the Overland Route here.

The canyon fluctuates between being moderately narrow and a tad wide. **(Red Breaks map.)** Beaver ponds can be a trial in the lower part of the canyon. There is poor camping at the mouth of The Gulch. Better camping is found a short distance down the Escalante River. (2.0–2.5 hours.)

Down the Escalante River

It takes two hours of pleasant hiking and wading down the river to reach the wide mouth of Horse Canyon. There is good camping in the area and Horse Canyon has a clear flow of water. (2.0–3.0 hours.)

Up Horse Canyon

Horse Canyon is wide and sandy throughout its length. It takes an hour to reach the mouth of Little Death Hollow, which comes in on the right (LUC)(E). (Little Death Hollow is labeled as Death Hollow on the map.) (1.0 hour.)

Ten minutes above the mouth of Little Death Hollow is a line shack on the left. The springs that feed Horse Canyon start here. (The line shack and the spring are shown on the map.) This is the last reliable water until you reach The Gulch, 3.5–5.0 hours away. Load up here.

Exit Horse Canyon

Ten minutes upcanyon from the spring, a constructed cattle trail exits the canyon to the left (NW). (The first part of the trail is shown to the north, east, and southeast of elevation 5678 on the **King Bench map**.) The trail is tricky to find. It goes up the first low spot in the Kayenta, and you pass it while cutting corners on a track. Look for a large cairn ten feet above the canyon floor. The trail is easy to follow as it winds its way around domes and up cliffs. It fades in an area of drift sand near the top of the hill. (1.5–2.0 hours.)

To The Gulch

You now have a choice. If water is a concern, follow the standard route into The Gulch. If speed is your goal, see the alternate route below.

Continue following the cattle trail as it leads initially northwest across King Bench. In places it is six feet or more wide, revealing that it is still used.

> **Historical note:** King Bench was named for John King, a rancher who moved to the Salt Gulch area near the town of Boulder in the early 1890s.

Before reaching Halfway Hollow the trail turns west, then drops into The Gulch (west of elevation 5322). (This is not the same cattle trail shown to the northwest of elevation 5685.) If you do lose the cattle trail, do not panic! Simply continue west across King Bench. Halfway Hollow is reasonable to cross at almost any point and it is not difficult to find a route through the low Navajo walls that line The Gulch. (3.5–5.0 hours.)

> **Alternate route:** This route follows a direct line from Horse Canyon to the top of The Gulch near the Burr Trail. It avoids the long walk back up The Gulch. There is no water and it is easy to get confused as to exactly where you are on the top of King Bench. Only experienced canyoneers should attempt this route.
>
> From the top of the cattle trail above Horse Canyon set a course northwest. Once past Halfway Hollow, go north-northwest. Your aim is to intersect The Gulch near the Burr Trail. You can use the constructed cattle trail mentioned at the start of the hike to en-

ter The Gulch. (It is located one-quarter mile south of elevation 6224.) There are several other routes into the canyon in the vicinity.

To the trailhead
Simply retrace your steps up The Gulch to the trailhead. (3.5–4.5 hours.)

Wolverine Loop Road—The Western entrance Road Section
Access to Hike #33.
Access is from the Burr Trail.
Maps—Lamp Stand, Pioneer Mesa, and Wagon Box Mesa.
The Wolverine Loop road—the Western Entrance starts 18.4 miles down the Burr Trail at a sign that begins, "Capitol Reef 11 mi." (located at elevation 5915T on the **Lamp Stand map**). This graded road is suitable for high-clearance vehicles except after recent rains; then even 4WDs will have problems. There is good camping along the road. (See **Map Thirty-eight.**)

0.0   —On the Burr Trail. Go south-southwest.

2.8   —**(Pioneer Mesa map.)** The shallow head of upper Horse Canyon is starting to develop on the left. You are in the Moenkopi Formation.

4.2   —The road enters the wash of Horse Canyon and crosses it several times in the next mile.

5.4   —Stand of large cottonwoods.

5.5   —"Tee." Stay on the main road to the left (SE). Signed Horse Canyon track is to the right (SW). You are near elevation 5682T. The Horse Canyon track is not shown on the map.

Side track down Horse Canyon

0.0   —On the main road. Go right (SW). This track goes down Horse Canyon and ends near the mouth of Wolverine Creek. It is suitable for high-clearance vehicles except after recent rains. Then even 4WDs will have problems. There is good camping along the track. A battle between Garfield County officials and environmental groups is brewing over this track. It may be closed in the future. Early explorers located a petrified wood area they called the Black Forest in upper Horse Canyon.

0.4   —Corral on the right. The start of a spring area that may make the next mile tough.

1.2   —You are in the Chinle Formation.

5.0   —(King Bench map.) Enter another bothersome spring area.

6.4	—The canyon narrows as it enters Wingate Sandstone.
9.0	—Wire gate. This is often closed.
10.2	—A line shack is barely visible to the left. Although the track continues for another mile, it is best to leave your vehicle here. Hikers doing the Little Death Hollow-Wolverine Creek loop and other hikes in the area will appreciate not seeing or hearing vehicles along their route. Please be courteous. It takes less than a half hour of walking to reach the mouth of Wolverine Creek.

End of side track

5.6	—The white vertical cliffs on both sides of the road are in the Shinarump Member of the Chinle Formation.
6.1	—Cattle guard.
9.3	—The road starts crossing the shallow upper end of Wolverine Creek. Water in the wash may be a seasonal problem.
10.7	—"Tee." Stay with the main road to the left (E). Short signed Wolverine trailhead road to the right (SW). There is a trail register. This road provides access to the main fork of Wolverine Creek.
10.4	—The white slickrock area to the left that looks like a freshly baked pan of biscuits is in the Shinarump Member of the Chinle Formation.
11.8	—"Tee." Stay with the main road to the left (SE). The short road to the right (SSW) goes to the signed Wolverine Petrified Wood Natural Area and provides access to the south fork of Wolverine Creek.
12.6	—Start of Little Death Hollow and Wolverine Creek **Hike #33**. "Tee." Short signed Little Death Hollow trailhead track to the right (S). There is adequate parking and camping near a corral. You are a quarter mile southeast of elevation 5712T and are in the Chinle Formation.
13.1	—"Tee." Stay with the main road to the right (E). The track to the left (N) goes to the Studhorse Peak area.
14.4	—Cattle guard. Pioneer Mesa is to the left (NE).
16.9	—The North Fork of Silver Falls Creek is on the right (S).
19.4	—(**Wagon Box Mesa map.**) "Tee." Signed Wolverine Loop road— the Eastern Entrance (the Moody road). The Burr Trail is to the left (N). To visit Silver Falls Creek and the Moody canyons, go right (S). You are at mile 8.0 on the Wolverine Loop road—the Eastern Entrance Road Section.

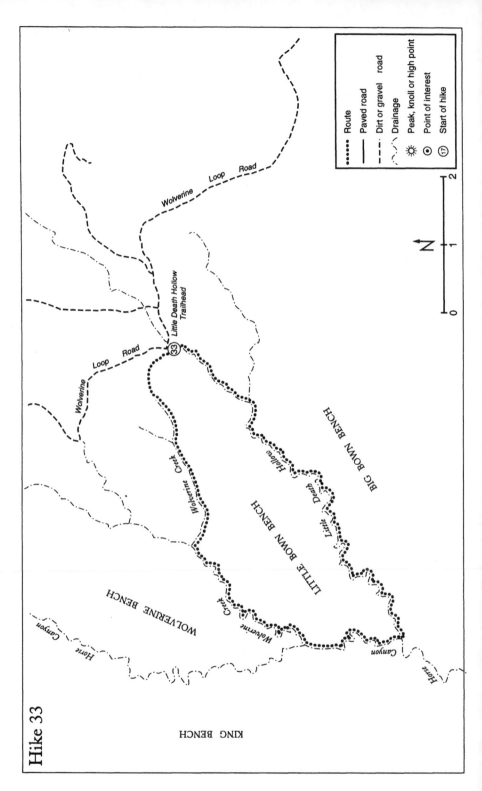

Hike 33

Map Forty-four

Little Death Hollow and Wolverine Creek—
Hike #33

Season:	Spring or fall. Recent rains can make Little Death Hollow a chore to descend.
Time:	8.0 to 11.5 hours. This can be done as a very long dayhike or a moderate two-day hike.
Water:	Water availability is a moderate problem on this hike. Water is procurable at the confluence of Horse Canyon and Little Death Hollow. Medium potholes may be found in middle and lower Little Death Hollow and in lower Wolverine Creek.
Elevation range:	4950' to 5600'.
Maps:	Pioneer Mesa, Silver Falls Bench, Red Breaks, and King Bench.
Skill level:	Moderate route finding. Class 5.0 climbing with exposure. The leader must be experienced with belay techniques and be capable of leading the climbing sections without protection. Some wading. This is a moderate hike. If you do this as an overnight hike, familiarity with low-impact camping techniques is essential.
Special equipment:	Wading shoes or boots. A forty-foot rope is necessary. Each member of the party should have the capacity to carry at least six quarts of water.
Land status:	This hike is in Grand Staircase-Escalante National Monument.

When I was young, my father and I would go on long cross-country backpacking trips. Often, when the choice of a route was between a lower easier path or a higher, more difficult, and perhaps slightly technical and exposed passage, I would lobby for the latter. Dad would then call out his favorite saying: "Terra firma—the more the firma, the less the terra," and we would follow the easier track. Little Death Hollow, a superb and marginally technical slot canyon, can be taken at several levels. Any way you do it is engaging and enjoyable. Wolverine Creek Canyon is rarely talked about, which is unfortunate. It is a fine Wingate-walled defile.

The route starts on the Wolverine Loop road and goes down Little Death Hollow to Horse Canyon. Wolverine Creek is followed back to the trailhead.

Down Little Death Hollow
(**Pioneer Mesa map** and **Map Forty-four.**) From the corral follow a track southwest. The upper part of Little Death Hollow is

Little Death Hollow.

wide, choked with Russian thistle, and not inspiring. Cattle trails do make the hiking easy, however. The canyon walls slowly constrict as you enter the Wingate. Watch for an arch high on the left wall. (It is one-eighth mile northeast of elevation 5464T.)

After passing the arch and going through a short stretch of narrows, a narrow canyon comes in on the right (NW). Five minutes below it a slot canyon comes in on the right (NE) (shown to the east of elevation 5828T). Trees partially block its mouth. A large pothole is located 100 yards up this sand-floored canyon. There is no camping near the pothole due to the potential for flash floods. Slickrock benches a couple of minutes downcanyon can be used for camping. (2.0–2.5 hours.)

The canyon constricts into breathtaking narrows. There are small obstacles to overcome (Class 5.0, 10'), minor route-finding challenges, and perhaps a short section or two of wading before reaching the crux narrows. (**Silver Falls Bench map.**)

The crux narrows

The crux narrows start at an eight-foot drop over a boulder into a pool. If the pool is shallow, it is easiest to wade across. Tall, strong climbers (basketball centers and the like) can chimney over the pool with a pack. To bypass the crux, hike back upcanyon for 100 yards and exit via a steep crack/slot (Class 3) to the left (LUC)(WSW). Scramble to the top of the Wingate—not to the top of the Kayenta—and follow it downcanyon for several minutes until you are forced up the Kayenta to the top of a peninsula that runs west to east. Proceed to the east end of the peninsula and descend a steep chute (Class 3) into the canyon. The bottom of the chute is choked with wood.

To Horse Canyon

The remainder of Little Death Hollow holds no surprises. (**Red Breaks map.**) Short narrows can be easily skirted on ledges. There is good camping and medium potholes. After the canyon cuts through the Wingate and into the Kayenta, it intersects Horse Canyon, which has a large flow of water. (2.0–4.0 hours.)

To Wolverine Creek

Hike ten minutes up Horse Canyon to a line shack. The springs that feed the canyon start here. (The line shack and spring are shown on the map.) The canyon above is usually dry. This is the last reliable water until back at the trailhead. There is fair camping in the area. Continue up Horse Canyon for twenty minutes to the mouth of Wolverine Creek, which comes in on the right (ENE). (**King Bench map.**)

Up Wolverine Creek

The first section of Wolverine Creek is wide, but the canyon quickly narrows as it enters the Wingate. There may be short stretches of shallow wading after recent rains.

> **Historical note:** Prospectors heading to the Circle Cliffs Basin mining area from the town of Escalante sometimes went up

Hugh Kearns in Wolverine Creek Canyon.

Wolverine Creek. The narrows were so tight that their pack animals could not fit through when fully loaded. The miners would unload their animals, carry their gear for 100 or so yards, then reload.

After seventy-five minutes the canyon starts to widen, then divides. **(Pioneer Mesa map.)** The main canyon goes left (N). Go right (E) into the south fork of Wolverine Creek (shown to the south of elevation 5883T). You are now walking in the Chinle Formation and may see segments of an old mining road. Several small side canyons branch off to the left. Always stay with the main canyon to the right.

The canyon widens and ends as you pass through the Circle Cliffs. Huge petrified logs litter the area, which was called the "Fallen Giant Forest" in the past. Simply stay parallel to the Wingate wall to the right as you circle around and start heading south into Little Death Hollow and back to the trailhead. You will pass across a corner of the Wolverine Petrified Wood Natural Area. You are not allowed to collect petrified wood here. (If you go too far out the top of the canyon, you will intersect the Wolverine Loop road. Follow it southeast back to the corral.) (4.0–5.0 hours.)

Lamp Stand Road Section
Access to Hike #34.
Access is from the Burr Trail.
Map—Lamp Stand.

The Lamp Stand road starts 21.8 miles down the Burr Trail at a Lamp Stand sign (located at elevation 6294T on the **Lamp Stand map**). This graded road is suitable for high-clearance vehicles except after recent rains. Then even 4WDs will have problems. There is camping along the road. (See **Map Thirty-eight**.)

0.0	— On the Burr Trail. Go northeast.
0.4	— Cattle guard.
1.9	— "Y." Stay on the main road to the left (N).
2.5	— Cattle guard.
3.2	— "Tee." Stay on the main road to the left (NNW).
4.1	— Stock pond on the left.
4.7	— The Lamp Stand is on the right (N). It is not a significant feature. It has a brown Moenkopi base topped with the white Shinarump Member of the Chinle Formation. A scramble-up route is available on the back side.
4.9	— Stock tank on the left.
5.1	— "Tee." Stay with the main road to the left (W).
6.0	— "Tee." Stay with the main road to the left (W).

> **Digression:** The track to the right (N) ends in 0.4 miles. Walk north up the wash for a short distance and locate a large pothole on the left (LUC) that has Moqui steps leading into it.

7.6	— "Y." At a cattle guard. There is a corral to the left. Go left (SW). The road to the right (NW) goes to The Gulch in 2.6 miles.
9.5	— Start of Egg Canyon and Lamanite Arch **Hike #34**. End of the road at several old miners cabins. There is parking and camping in the area. You are at a junction shown one-quarter mile southwest of elevation 6220T and are in the Moenkopi Formation.

Egg Canyon and Lamanite Arch — Hike #34

Season:	Spring or fall.
Time:	3.5 to 5.0 hours. Add 3.0 to 4.0 hours if you plan to visit Lamanite Arch.
Water:	Water availability is not a problem on this hike. The Gulch has a perennial flow.

Elevation range:	6300' to 6520'.
Maps:	Lamp Stand and Steep Creek Bench.
Skill level:	Moderately easy route finding. Class 2+ walking. This is a moderate hike.
Special equipment:	None.
Land status:	This hike is in Grand Staircase-Escalante National Monument.

Egghead, eggbeater, eggnog, egg roll, egg plant, eggshell, egg white, egg crate, egg coal, egg money, egg jockey (bomber pilot), egg orchard (a chicken farm), eggs Benedict, egg on, rotten egg, a bad egg, a good egg, go lay an egg, egg in one's face, egg in your beer, kill the goose that laid the golden egg, put all one's eggs in one basket, have an egg in the nest. After all that, can there be anything else to associate with eggs? How about an Egg Canyon?

Yes, there is one, and it is located in the Escalante. And like the eggs above, this egg is full of surprises and variety. This easy hike leads to a landscape of a type not seen elsewhere in the area. Do not expect huge vertical walls in Egg Canyon, but do expect huge color-ful hills and a narrow defile carved in Chinle Formation mudstones and siltstones. Also, you will hike through what is arguably the finest petrified forest in the area.

The route starts in the Lamp Stand area near the northern end of the Circle Cliffs Basin and goes down Egg Canyon to The Gulch. An unnamed canyon and an old mining track take you back to the trailhead. A digression leads up a side canyon to Lamanite Arch.

Down Egg Canyon

(**Lamp Stand map** and **Map Forty-one.**) From the parking area follow a mining track south-southeast. After four minutes the track divides just before it crosses a wash. Go left (SW). The track goes up a steep hill, dividing twice along the way. Stay to the right at both junctions. You are in the Chinle Formation.

After topping the hill, continue along the track for 100 yards. Look south. Locate a small arch high on a Wingate escarpment. The canyon to its right marks the return route. To the right of the canyon is another Wingate escarpment and to its right is a wide U-shaped pass formed from the pink sands of the Chinle Formation. This "Pink Pass" marks the head of Egg Canyon.

Follow a mining track until you are below the Pink Pass. (There are a couple of mining tracks in the area. Take your pick.) Leave the track, scramble over the pass, and descend through a superb petrified forest into Egg Canyon. Pioneers initially called it Egg Box Canyon. The derivation is not known. Work your way down a deep ravine cut into the Chinle Formation to The Gulch. **(Steep Creek Bench map.)** (1.5–2.0 hours.)

> **Digression:** To visit Lamanite Arch, hike up The Gulch for a half hour to the first side canyon that enters on the left (NW) (shown to the west of elevation 6912). This canyon is Indian Trail Gulch (LKA). It contains medium springs and is a thrash to get up, though cattle trails do help. Lamanite Arch takes forty-five minutes to reach and is located on a Wingate cliff to the right (LUC)(E). Mormons believe that "Lamanites" were the ancestors of the American Indians. Return the way you came to the mouth of Egg Canyon. (2.5–3.5 hours.)

The return canyon

Hike down The Gulch for twenty minutes to the first canyon that enters on the left (ENE). Follow this easy canyon to a pass at its upper end. **(Lamp Stand map.)** Near the top you will find a constructed trail. From the pass look north-northeast. A quarter mile away you will see the head of a canyon marked by a short vertical white cliff (Shinarump Member of the Chinle Formation). Descend the wash below you toward the canyon. Before reaching it, intersect a track that cuts over the head of the canyon. Follow the track to the left (N). It dithers about for ten minutes, then divides. You have now rejoined the original route. The Pink Pass will be visible to the left (WSW). Follow the track to the right (NE) back to the start. (2.0–3.0 hours.)

Wolverine Loop Road—The Eastern Entrance Road Section
This is also called the Moody road.
Access to Hikes #35 through 37.
Access is from the Burr Trail.
Maps—Wagon Box Mesa, Horse Pasture Mesa, and Deer Point.

The Wolverine Loop road—the Eastern Entrance starts 28.8 miles down the Burr Trail at the Wolverine Loop road sign (located at elevation 6767T on the **Wagon Box Mesa map**). This graded road is suitable for high-clearance vehicles except after recent rains. Then even 4WDs will have problems. There is camping along the road. (See **Map Thirty-eight**.)

0.0	—On the Burr Trail. Go south.
2.4	—Huge sand pile on the right.

2.9	—Wire corral on the right. Wagon Box Mesa, named for a wagon abandoned by early settlers, is straight ahead (E).
5.8	—Stock pond on the left. The road descends into the North Fork of Silver Falls Creek.
6.4	—Road exits the wash. You are in the Shinarump Member of the Chinle Formation.
7.6	—Top of a rise. Fine views of Navajo Mountain and the Circle Cliffs to the south.
8.0	—"Tee." Stay to the left (SSE). The signed road to the right (SW) is part of the Wolverine Loop road and goes to Wolverine Canyon, Horse Canyon, Little Death Hollow, and back to the Burr Trail. This road is described in the Wolverine Loop road—the Western Entrance Road Section. (You are one-eighth mile north of elevation 6278T.)
10.7	—(**Horse Pasture Mesa map.**) "Tee." Stay to the left (SE). The road to the right (W) goes to Silver Falls Creek and Hike #35. (You are at elevation 5708T.)

Side road to Silver Falls Creek and Choprock Canyon Hike #35

0.0	—Follow the road to the right (W).
0.9	—Mine tunnels at the head of a draw to the left (SE).
1.0	—The road enters the wash. After recent rains this may be as far as you can drive.
2.1	—Vague track to the left (ESE). This is where Hike #35 ends.
2.2	—Start of Silver Falls Creek and Choprock Canyon **Hike #35**. Stock corral on the right. This is the end of the graded road. The track beyond quickly deteriorates. There is parking and camping in the area. You are near elevation 5420T and are in the Shinarump Member of the Chinle Formation.

End of side road

11.5	—Cross the wash of upper Moody Creek.
11.7	—Wire gate. Enter the wash of upper Moody Creek.
11.8	—Wire gate. Line shack on the right. Colt Mesa is to the east. You are in the Moenkopi Formation.
11.9	—Road leaves the wash on the right.
13.3	—Moenkopi-walled upper Moody Creek is to the left.

13.9 | —Large stock pond on the right (shown at elevation 5349T).

Digression: There is direct access to the head of Choprock Canyon from the stock pond. Hike up a draw to the west-northwest and over a rise to the head of Choprock Canyon.

14.1 | —A U-shaped gap in the Wingate and Chinle cliff to the right (SSW) (between elevations 6281T and 6114T) provides difficult access to one of the southern forks of Choprock Canyon. On the far side of the gap is the finest Chinle tower "garden" in the area. These gardens form when a hard caprock protects the underlying rock from weathering, leaving behind stands of thin pinnacles. In 1875 explorer Grove Karl Gilbert noticed towers like these during his geologic and geographic explorations of the Escalante area. He called them "witch pinnacles."

16.7 | —Enter Moody Creek and Glen Canyon National Recreation Area. The road gets rougher.

18.8 | —Start of a spring area. Tamarisks line the wash and the canyon narrows. After recent rains this area may not be passable. There is a corral on the right.

19.0 | —The track leaves the wash to the left. This is a trailhead for those wanting to hike down the main fork of Moody Creek to the Escalante River.

Digression: A break in the Wingate wall to the northwest (one-quarter mile south-southeast of elevation 5881T) provides Class 3 access to Baker Bench. The route is tucked into a corner and cannot be seen fully from here.

19.1 | —Large parking and camping area on the right, halfway up a hill.

22.3 | —"Y." Follow the road to the right (ESE). (This road is not shown on the map.) The track to the left (NE) provides access to **Hike #36.**

Side track to Deer Point—An Ascent Hike #36

0.0 | —Follow the track to the left (NE). This track is for high-clearance vehicles only.

1.4 | —"Tee." Stay on the main track to the left (E).

3.1 | —Start of Deer Point—An Ascent **Hike #36.** You are on a level plain below colorful Chinle hills. This is one of the best and most isolated car-camping spots in the Escalante area. You are at the end of a 4WD track shown one mile northwest of elevation 6010AT on the Deer Point map.

End of side track

22.5 —Short, steep hill. This may stop some vehicles.

24.3 —Start of Moody Creek Canyons **Hike #37**. At the end of the track and a "No Vehicles" sign. There is adequate parking and camping. You are near elevation 5198T on the north rim of Middle Moody Canyon. The white slickrock sheet and the canyon to the south are in the Shinarump Member of the Chinle Formation.

Silver Falls Creek and Choprock Canyon—Hike #35

Season:	Spring or fall.
Time:	13.5 to 19.5 hours. Two to three days. There is a lot to explore along this route. Adding an extra day is advised.
Elevation range:	4600' to 5840'.
Water:	Water availability is a problem on this hike. Lower Silver Falls Creek and lower Choprock Canyon have large springs. Water is always available on the Escalante River.
Maps:	Horse Pasture Mesa and Silver Falls Bench.
Skill level:	Easy route finding. Class 2 walking. Lots of wading. This easy route is suitable for most. Familiarity with low-impact camping skills is essential.
Special equipment:	Wading boots.
Land status:	This hike is in Grand Staircase-Escalante National Monument and Glen Canyon National Recreation Area.

Sesquipedalian substitutes are long expressions used in place of short, easily understood words or terms. Two classic examples are Winston Churchill's use of "terminological inexactitude" for the word "lie" and George Orwell's "involuntary conversion" of an airplane for a plane "crash." Using sesquipedalian substitutes, one could describe Silver Falls Creek as a brobdingnagian defile that curves like Hogarth's Line of Beauty through brentian sandstones as though cut by Thor's mighty mj`lnier and descends to an Alphian river deep in the amaurot. Understandable imagery? Perhaps only to a prud'homme, like Mark Tapley, who would relish this skimble-skamble amphigouri as an interesting challenge—if he wasn't in a zist.

Enough said. In short: great canyons, diverse terrain, and good, uncomplicated hiking. A must for all enthusiastic admirers of the Escalante.

The route starts at the Moody road and goes down Silver Falls Creek to the Escalante River. After a short stroll down the river, Choprock Canyon is followed up to the Circle Cliffs. An old mining road that ducks under the east end of Silver Falls Bench is used to regain Silver Falls Creek.

Down Silver Falls Creek

(**Horse Pasture Mesa map** and **Map Forty-five.**) From the trailhead, hike downcanyon on a track that crisscrosses the usually dry creekbed. This old road is part of the historic Halls route from Escalante to Halls Crossing. You are in the Chinle Formation, with vertical red walls of Wingate Sandstone high above. (**Silver Falls Bench map.**) By the time you reach the North Fork of Silver Falls Creek, which comes in on the right (NW), you have entered Glen Canyon National Recreation Area.

The canyon quickly narrows below the North Fork. Emigrant Spring, which has a medium flow, is located next to a monolithic abandoned meander on the left. Past the abandoned meander watch for the George Hobbs inscription and explanatory plaque under an overhang on the right. It reads:

> GEORGE BRIGHAM HOBBS
> CHOPPED HIS NAME HERE ON HIS 24th BIRTHDAY FEB. 22nd
> 1883.
> HE WAS TAKING FOOD TO THE SAINTS AT MONTEZUMA, WAS ALONE
> AND HAD ONE HORSE AND MULE LOADED WITH SUPPLIES.
> CAUGHT IN A STORM HE DID NOT THINK HE WOULD SURVIVE BUT
> AFTER FIVE DAYS IN SNOW HE WAS ABLE TO RESUME HIS JOURNEY.
>
> ERECTED BY FAMILY JULY 5th 1957.

Below the Hobbs inscription there is often a small flow of water in the creekbed. As you approach the Escalante River the canyon narrows even more. The Chinle Formation and the old Halls road disappear. Wingate walls topped with Kayenta slopes now dominate. The Wingate disappears near the river, leaving Kayenta slopes capped by sheer walls of Navajo Sandstone. There is good camping and medium seeps in the canyon floor near the confluence. (3.5–5.5 hours.)

To the Overland Route: You can intersect the section of the Overland Route that runs between Silver Falls Creek and Choprock Canyon here. See the Overland Route description for details.

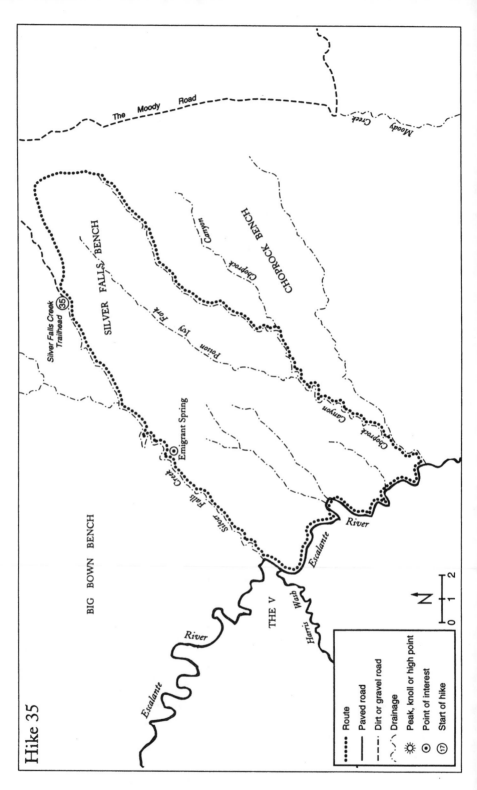

Hike 35

Map Forty-five

Down the Escalante River to Choprock Canyon

Hike and wade down the Escalante River. Harris Wash comes in on the right (LDC)(W) in fifteen minutes. The first canyon on the left (NE) is a true box with no escape routes out its top. The second and third canyons on the left (shown to the east and west of elevation 5252T) are a joy to explore if you are a rock climber.

The fourth side canyon that comes in on the left (NE) (shown to the west of elevation 5293T) has a constructed cattle trail that starts near its mouth on its downcanyon side. This trail provides easy access to Silver Falls Bench. Choprock Canyon comes in on the left (ENE) in another half hour. (Choprock Canyon is not named on the map. It is the long drainage to the west of elevation 5103T.) There is good camping and a string of large springs a short stroll up-canyon. (3.5–5.0 hours.)

Up Choprock Canyon

A couple of minutes upcanyon a cattle trail on the right (LUC)(E) goes up a Wingate wall.

> **To the Overland Route:** You can intersect the section of the Overland Route that runs between Choprock Canyon and Twentyfive Mile Wash here. See the Overland Route description for details.

The East Fork of Choprock Canyon enters on the right (NE) in twenty minutes (shown to the east of elevation 5264T). This may be the last reliable water along the route during the dry season.

> **Digression:** The East Fork is lush, narrow, and ends at a large pool below an impressive pour-off. (1.0 hour round-trip.)

The canyon quickly narrows and the Wingate walls rise. There may be some shallow wading or moderate stemming across potholes. Medium seeps in the canyon floor appear from time to time. There are plenty of good campsites. The West Fork of Choprock Canyon comes in on the left (N) (shown to the east of elevation 5290AT) and marks the end of the narrows. There are medium seeps in the vicinity. (2.0–3.0 hours.)

> **Rock climber's note:** An absolutely fabulous but very long, difficult, and technical dayhike goes up the West Fork of Choprock Canyon, through two natural bridges, and returns along its rim. This route is only for very experienced canyoneers who are rock climbers. My friends and I call the West Fork the Poison Ivy Fork because it is filled with the plants.
>
> Before starting this loop, you must first locate the descent route you will use to get back into Choprock Canyon at the end of the day. This downclimb is nearly impossible to find from above.

Jim Finch in the Poison Ivy Fork of Choprock Canyon.

From the confluence of the main and West forks of Choprock
Canyon, hike down the main canyon for eighteen minutes. Look
for a long row of Moqui steps on a southwest-facing wall on the
right (LDC). You must look upcanyon to see them. Climb the steps
(Class 5.4, 50') and then work your way to the top of the Wingate.
Locate a route through the Kayenta. Memorize the route. Return
to the mouth of the West Fork.

Hike north up the West Fork of Choprock Canyon. There is much bush bashing, boulder scrambling, and other assorted obstacles. Medium springs and potholes appear from time to time. As you near the top of the canyon, it narrows and steepens. Climb directly up a pour-off (Class 5.6, 25'). The second challenge is a difficult face (Class 5.7, 10') that starts in a pool below a large natural bridge. The canyon above contains a second large natural bridge and a pothole arch. If the pour-offs below the bridges are too difficult, pass them on the right (LUC).

To exit the canyon, climb over the second bridge and up to a ledge system on the right (LUC)(E) side of the canyon. Follow ledges downcanyon past several large caves for ten minutes to the first possible exit to the left (E), a row of Moqui steps that goes over the left edge of a cave (Class 5.5, 60').

Hike northeast to the top of the Navajo and to elevation 6042T. Follow the rim of the West Fork north until it is possible to cross it. Hike south along its west rim—along the Kayenta—to the Moqui steps you explored earlier. (7.5–11.0 hours.)

The likelihood of finding water diminishes rapidly the farther up Choprock Canyon you hike. By the time the canyon divides—in fifty minutes—you are in the Chinle and the canyon will be dry. Stay in the main canyon to the left (NW) (shown to the east of elevation 5665T).

Pieces of an old mining track now appear. Follow the track as closely as possible. At the head of the canyon (near elevation 5626AT on the **Horse Pasture Mesa map**) the track becomes more pronounced. Passing through the Circle Cliffs, the track turns first northeast, then north, and passes under the eastern prow of Silver Falls Bench (elevation 6618T). The track goes near the edge of a cliff. The dry, sinuous bed of Moody Creek will be visible from time to time to the east.

As you pass Colt Mesa the remnants of a uranium mining encampment will be visible on its west side. (This is at mile 11.8 on the Moody road.) The track turns southwest into Silver Falls Creek and after a mile drops to the floor of the canyon. Depending on where you left your car, go up or down the canyon back to the trailhead. (4.5–6.0 hours.)

Deer Point—An Ascent—Hike #36

Season:	Any.
Time:	5.0 to 7.0 hours.
Elevation range:	6080' to 7265'.

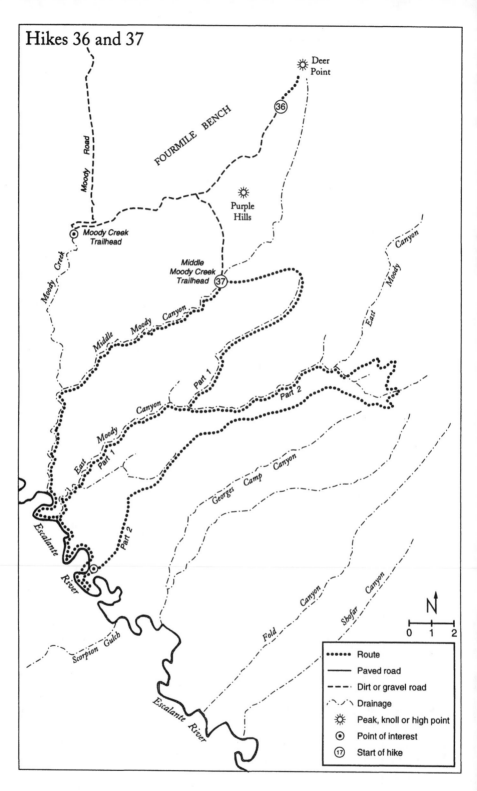

Hikes 36 and 37

☀ Deer
Point

㊱

FOURMILE BENCH

Moody Road

☀
Purple
Hills

East Moody Canyon

⊙ Moody Creek
Trailhead

Middle
Moody Creek
Trailhead ㊲

Moody Creek

Middle Moody Canyon

Part 1

Canyon

Part 2

East Moody
Part 1

Georges Camp Canyon

Escalante River

Part 2

⊙

Fold Canyon

Shofar Canyon

N

0   1   2

Scorpion Gulch

Escalante River

	Route
•••••	Route
——	Paved road
- - -	Dirt or gravel road
·–·–·	Drainage
☀	Peak, knoll or high point
⊙	Point of interest
㊲	Start of hike

Map Forty-six

Water:	There is no water along the route. Bring your own drinking water.
Map:	Deer Point.
Skill level:	Easy route finding. Class 3+ scrambling. There is a great deal of elevation gain, making this hike suitable only for the fit.
Special equipment:	None.
Land status:	This hike is in Grand Staircase-Escalante National Monument.

Sometimes lovers of the "inverted mountains" miss much by staying between canyon walls. It is difficult to assess an area's character by seeing only a small part of the whole. Deer Point, a small mesa that straddles the Waterpocket Fold between the Circle Cliffs and the Halls Creek section of Capitol Reef National Park, gives one the opportunity to see how many of the little pieces of the canyon puzzle fit together. The hike to the top of Deer Point does not form a loop, but it does offer an unsurpassed vantage point for viewing the surrounding country.

To Deer Point
(**Deer Point map** and **Map Forty-six.**) From the parking area one can clearly see the two arms of Deer Point to the north and northeast. A steep slope at the back of the "Vee" formed by the arms provides access to the top of Deer Point. Hike east for a few minutes over low Chinle hills to an old mining track. Follow it along the rim of Middle Moody Canyon until it crosses the valley that leads north-northeast up to the "Vee." Leave the track and scramble and boulder hop up the valley.

At the Wingate, the valley turns into a shallow canyon. Follow it to the top of the mesa. A bench mark from 1934 denotes Pockets, a dome to the left (W). The highest elevation on Deer Point is to the right (E) (elevation 7265T). From the high point the view of the surrounding desert is amazing:

East-northeast: The two summits of the Little Rockies. The peak to the left is Mt. Holmes (7,998'), the one to the right is Mt. Ellsworth (8,253').
Northeast: The LaSal Mountains are in the far distance.
North-northeast: The three summits of the Henry Mountains. From left to right the peaks are Mt. Ellen (11,506'), Mt. Pennell (11,132'), and Mt. Hillers (10,737'). Below you are the Navajo escarpment of the Waterpocket Fold and the Halls Creek gorge. Early explorers variously called Halls Creek Hoxie Creek, Grand Gulch, Waterpocket Canyon, or Canopy Canyon.
North-northwest: The white Navajo domes of Capitol Reef. The southern reef of the San Rafael Swell is barely visible in the far

background to the right of Capitol Reef. To the left of Capitol Reef is Thousand Lake Mountain.

Northwest: The Aquarius Plateau and Boulder Mountain. The white cliffs are Death Hollow and Sand Creek. The red cliffs are the Circle Cliffs.

Southwest: The Kaiparowits Plateau is in the distance, with the Circle Cliffs in the foreground.

South-southeast: The rounded summit of Navajo Mountain (10,346').

Southeast: Lake Powell, with the towers of Monument Valley in Arizona in the background.

Though there is no water on top, Deer Point is a great place to camp. Return the way you came.

Moody Creek Canyons—Hike #37

Season:	Part 1—Spring, fall, or winter. Part 2—Spring or fall.
Time:	Part 1—11.0 to 16.0 hours. Two to three days. Part 2—21.0 to 32.0 hours. Three to five days.
Elevation range:	Part 1—4360' to 5720'. Part 2—4320' to 6260'.
Water:	Part 1—Water availability is a minor problem on this route. Both lower Moody canyons have medium springs and the Escalante River has a perennial flow. Part 2—Water availability is a big problem on this route. On the return route you rely on pothole water. The text that follows notes water sources.
Maps:	Parts 1 and 2—Horse Pasture Mesa, Scorpion Gulch, Stevens Canyon North, and Deer Point.
Skill level:	Part 1—Easy route finding. Class 3 scrambling. This is a moderate hike suitable for anyone in good shape. You must be familiar with low-impact camping skills. Part 2—Difficult route finding. Class 5.1 climbing with lots of exposure. The leader must be experienced with belay techniques and be capable of leading the climbing sections without protection. Some wading. This is a strenuous, technical route suitable only for experienced canyoneers who are also rock climbers. Familiarity with low-impact camping skills is essential.
Special equipment:	Part 1—Have the capacity to carry a full day's supply of water. Part 2—As above; you will also need wading boots and a 120-foot climbing rope.

Land status: These hikes are in Glen Canyon National Recreation Area.

Fantasia, a word most commonly used to describe a musical creation, has two meanings: it is a composition of freeform structure that follows the whims of the composer, and it is a medley of familiar themes broken by variations and interludes. The Moody canyons are fantasias: the stalwart walls of Wingate Sandstone are the beat of the music; the potpourri of abandoned meanders strewn along its path and its ceaseless walls draped with iridescent-purple desert varnish are the flights of fancy.

The route comes in two parts. Part 1 starts on the Moody road and goes down Middle Moody Canyon and Moody Creek to the Escalante River. A short walk on a horse trail leads downriver to East Moody Canyon, which is followed up to the West Fork of East Moody Canyon. An old mining road leads out of this canyon back to the trailhead.

Part 2 leaves the standard route at the mouth of East Moody Canyon and goes down the Escalante River for several miles to a devious route out of the canyon to the benchlands above. A complex and energetic route leads over broken country to the head of East Moody Canyon, which is followed to its confluence with the West Fork of East Moody Canyon where it joins the standard route.

Part 1: Down Middle Moody Canyon

(**Horse Pasture Mesa map** and **Map Forty-six.**) From the "No Vehicles" sign walk a few yards southeast into a shallow canyon. Follow it down, working over and around several large boulders (Class 3) to the floor of the inner gorge of Middle Moody Canyon. Across the canyon, to the southeast, is a long, low horizontal cave. On its right side is a ledge system that leads up to a small drainage. This will be the return route at the end of the trip.

Hike downcanyon by thick stands of rabbitbrush and Apache plume. (**Scorpion Gulch map.**) After a short walk, cottonwoods and tamarisks denote an area of medium springs. The walls of these narrows are the Shinarump Member of the Chinle Formation and contain a fascinating array of sculpted patterns. When the inner gorge ends, exit the canyon on the right and follow an old mining track downcanyon.

Historical note: The Moody canyons were named not for their temperament but for John Moody, one of the first settlers in the town of Escalante. His second daughter, Etta, is credited with being the first child born in Escalante, in 1876.

The track ends soon. Follow the wash downcanyon through colorful Chinle hills. Before you reach the main fork of Moody

Creek there is a short stretch of medium springs along the canyon floor. The main fork comes in on the right (N). (2.0–3.0 hours.)

Down Moody Creek

The canyon narrows. A couple of abandoned meanders on the right prove interesting. Getting behind the first abandoned meander requires a stiff scramble. Its outer wall contains a small but exquisite arch. The second abandoned meander is for rock climbers only. Access is through a tight slot (Class 5.2, 25').

Medium springs appear from time to time before you reach the Escalante River. There is good camping near the confluence. (1.5–2.5 hours.)

To East Moody Canyon

Stay on the left (LDC) side of the Escalante River as you head downcanyon. After a short stretch of troublesome walking along a vague path, the path widens into an oft-used horse-packer's trail that leads to the mouth of East Moody Canyon. There is good camping at the confluence. (1.0 hour.)

Up East Moody Canyon

The hike up East Moody Canyon back to the trailhead takes one long day and, unless there have been recent rains, the canyon may be dry. Slower groups will want to jump start the day. Load up with water at the river.

The canyon itself starts as a narrow Wingate-walled cleft lined with medium springs and large cottonwoods. Photographer Philip Hyde made the heavily varnished walls of East Moody Canyon famous through his images. The canyon slowly widens as it enters the colorful gray, green, and purple slopes of the Chinle Formation.

The West Fork of East Moody Canyon comes in on the left (N) and is the one you want to follow. (This fork is not named on the map. It contains elevation 5037AT.) There are medium springs a short distance up both forks. Watch carefully for this fork. If you miss it and go up the main fork to the right, you will be in deep dodo. (2.5–3.5 hours.)

Up the West Fork of East Moody Canyon

The West Fork is narrow and boulder-choked, and it has a short section of an old mining track along its right side. The mining track disappears quickly in the rubble-filled streambed. When the track does reappear, follow it through rolling Chinle hills. The track re-enters the wash, then turns left (N), and goes through a pass in the Wingate. (You have gone off the Scorpion Gulch map, onto the **Stevens Canyon North map** for a short distance, and are now one-half mile west of elevation 6270AT on the **Deer Point map**.) From the pass, Deer Point is visible to the north. (2.0–3.0 hours.)

To the trailhead

The mining track winds north down a Chinle hill past several mine shacks into a wash. It exits the wash on the left (W) (hard to see) and continues above the inner gorge of Middle Moody Canyon. You will see the trailhead on the opposite side of the gorge. Drop into the aforementioned drainage that is directly across from the trailhead and near the horizontal cave. There is one place along the ledge system that may require lowering packs a couple of feet. (2.0–3.0 hours.)

Part 2: Down the Escalante River

(**Scorpion Gulch map** and **Map Forty-seven.**) From the mouth of East Moody Canyon hike and wade down the Escalante River. In fifteen minutes a large abandoned meander on the left proves interesting to walk around (shown at elevation 4745T). Forty-five minutes past it, after making first a left bend, then a right bend, look for a white Navajo tower with an archlet or window on its left side high above the river to your left. It will disappear from view as you go under it. You will walk to this tower later. (The white Navajo tower is located halfway between elevations 5022T and 4807T, at the neck of a "dog bone" bend in the river.)

The river makes another right bend, then a quick left turn (shown one-quarter mile south of elevation 4795T.) It then straightens out and goes southeast for a quarter mile. Watch for a triangular-shaped cliff dune on the right (SW) side of the river that ends at the edge of a cliff forty feet above the water. It is the only cliff dune in the vicinity. Across the river (E) from the cliff dune is a wide ledge that goes upcanyon (NW) above a cliff band. (2.0–2.5 hours.)

The exit route

Walk upcanyon along the ledge past a cave, then ascend a slot (Class 4+, 20'). Proceed upcanyon on the next ledge until stopped by a precipice overlooking the river. A 100-foot slab above the drop contains a row of Moqui steps. They may not be apparent until you start climbing (Class 5.1, 100'). Belays should be used and packs can be hauled.

Hike northeast out of the canyon and along a Kayenta ridge to the white Navajo archlet tower mentioned earlier. There are expansive views of the river in two directions. The white-and-red domes and walls to the northwest and northeast are in the Navajo. (0.5–1.5 hours.)

Follow the Kayenta ridge north-northeast (over elevation

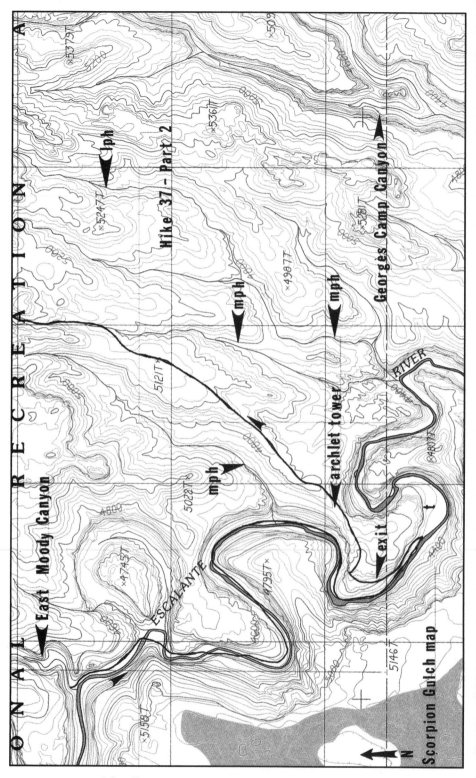

Map Forty-seven

5121T). Drainages are on either side of you. At a low Navajo prow, stay to the right (E) and walk near the Kayenta/Navajo interface. Drop into the upper part of the now shallow drainage that is to the right (E). There are medium potholes here.

Follow the drainage up. It divides at a small red slickrock sheet. Go right (NE). The drainage fizzles out. Hike northeast over a rise. A ridge of Navajo domes that goes north to south is on the right (SE) and a Kayenta-walled canyon is to the left (NE). (You will pass the left (W) side of elevation 5449T.) The terrain forces you east between the ridge and the canyon. (The canyon is shown to the south of elevation 5401T). Drop to a Kayenta ledge that goes along the right side of the canyon. The ledge will drop you to the floor of the canyon near its head. There are medium potholes and good camping in the area. (1.5–2.5 hours.)

Across the benchlands

Exit the canyon on its left (LUC) side. Hike north-northeast. At the top of a rise you will see a Siamese-twin dome of white Navajo Sandstone (elevation 5822T) to the north. The dome on the left is the larger of the two and there is a small tree in the saddle between them. To the right of the Siamese dome is a beehive-shaped Navajo dome (elevation 5885T). Pass the beehive-shaped dome on its right (E) side and gain the rim of East Moody Canyon. Follow Navajo ledges northeast between the canyon on the left and Navajo domes on the right. Do not descend to the Kayenta.

(**Map Forty-eight.**) Eventually you will be forced onto the top of a ridge that divides East Moody Canyon on the left from the north fork of Georges Camp Canyon on the right. (Georges Camp Canyon is not labeled on the map. It is shown to the south of elevation 6027AT on the **Stevens Canyon North map.**) This canyon will be readily recognized for its vast area of smooth Wingate slickrock that creases into an impenetrable inner gorge.

Follow the ridge as it parallels East Moody Canyon and takes you over the head of a couple of small canyons that drop south into Georges Camp Canyon. One of these has a squat, white, twenty-foot-tall Navajo pinnacle on a prow. You can clearly see Wingate sandstone a short distance down from the rim. This canyon contains medium and large potholes. The largest and deepest of these may require the use of a pot on a rope to obtain water. (This drainage is one-quarter mile east of elevation 6027AT.) (1.5–2.0 hours.)

Continue along the rim of East Moody Canyon (passing over or near elevations 6163T and 6321T). As you near its head, a large expanse of slickrock and a 100-foot pinnacle in one of its several arms becomes visible (located one-eighth mile north of elevation 6431T). Your goal is to make your way to the base of the pinnacle.

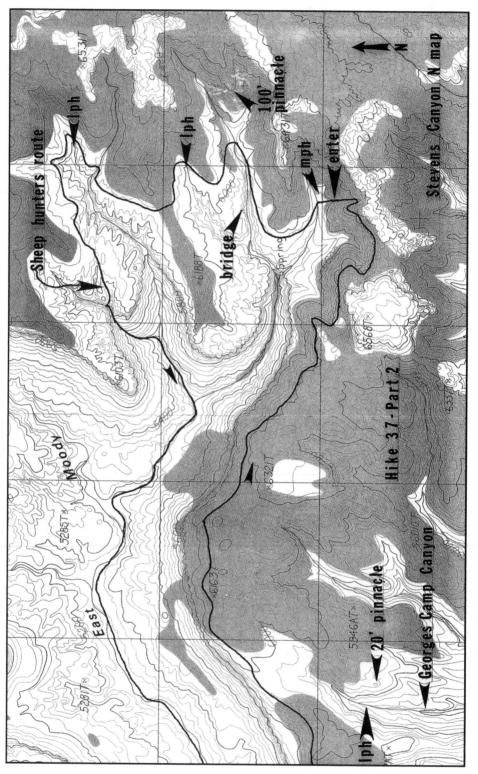

Map Forty-eight

Continue traversing the rim of the canyon until you are forced onto an intermediate Navajo ledge. Follow the ledge until it is possible to descend a steep chute to the Wingate.

The canyon with the pinnacle contains a large natural bridge on its left (LUC) side. Large potholes and excellent camping can be found in the upper arms of this canyon. (2.0–3.0 hours.)

Staying on the Wingate, head the next small side canyon. It also contains large potholes. The next side canyon is a long one (shown to the west of elevation 6531T). It also has large potholes in its upper reaches and good camping in the vicinity. (1.5–2.5 hours.)

The descent route into East Moody Canyon

Follow the north rim of the canyon west. You will be forced away from the rim by a couple of short side canyons. Return to the rim. Start to head the next short side canyon (shown one-quarter mile east of elevation 6103T). The descent route is located in a steep west-running chute that descends the south side of the short side canyon. It is choked with trees and bushes. This route is locally known as the Sheep Hunters route, since bighorn hunters often use it. When in doubt, stay to the left. A short row of Moqui steps above a large pothole and spring area helps ease the difficulty (Class 4, 10'). Descend steep boulder-strewn Chinle slopes into the main fork. This route will take some scouting to find. (1.5–2.5 hours.)

Down East Moody Canyon

The hardpacked surface of East Moody Creek makes for fast hiking. Near its junction with the West Fork are medium springs and good camping. (The West Fork is not labeled on the map. It contains elevation 5037AT on the **Scorpion Gulch map**.) (2.0–3.0 hours.)

From the junction of the East Fork and the West Fork, join the standard route back to the trailhead. (4.0–6.0 hours.)

The Overland Route—General Description

The Overland Route describes a cross-country hike that runs parallel to the Escalante River and, with a few exceptions, stays on the high ground above the river. Skipping over benchlands and zooming in and out of canyons, this route is designed to be used in conjunction with other hikes in the guide. It starts on Highway 12 and ends at the Fortymile Ridge trailhead near Coyote Gulch. No effort has been made to make this a direct route; rather, I have chosen to make it interesting throughout its length.

The route incorporates sections that have already been described in the hikes and also includes new material. It is not intended to be done in one push, though that would be an incredible accomplishment. It is meant for those looking for remote and seldom-explored country and to provide options for those doing other hikes in the guide.

Most sections of the Overland Route are appropriate only for hardcore canyoneers who are also experienced rock climbers. Difficult climbing on steep walls, demanding route-finding problems, long distances between known water sources, and other assorted perils await the bold explorer.

Often the route descriptions are brief. You must be well versed in map reading and not be intimidated by long stretches of complex and convoluted terrain. You will not find the Overland Route marked on the maps in the guide. The dedicated and adventurous will be forced to assemble the puzzle on their own.

> **Warning:** Do not take any of the Overland Route lightly. It is intricate, at times trying, and, without a doubt, dangerous.

The Overland Route—Highway 12 to Silver Falls Creek

Highway 12 to Boulder Creek
(**Calf Creek map.**) The route starts on the Haymaker Bench portion of Highway 12. You are in Grand Staircase-Escalante National Monument. Use the route description detailed in Hike #5 to get into Boulder Creek and to its confluence with Deer Creek. Use the route description in Hike #30 to go down Boulder Creek to the narrows an hour below the confluence of Boulder and Deer creeks. (**King Bench map.**) Exit the canyon by way of the "crease" to the rim of the canyon. You are now at the mouth of the "Tanks" drainage just above Boulder Creek.

To The Gulch
From the mouth of the "Tanks" drainage, look southeast. On the right is a large brown-gray dome; to the left is a red-and-white Navajo-walled escarpment. Hike through the gap between the dome and the escarpment and follow a canyon (shown a quarter mile west of elevation 5886) south until you are on a short cliff above Boulder Creek. Go down the creek for 150 yards and exit the canyon via a steep slot to the left (ENE). The slot (Class 4) becomes narrower and the rock looser near the top. Exit the top of the slot and work southeast, then south, to a handsome old line shack on a flat plain.

> **Note:** The location of the line shack is shown as a small black square and is correctly placed on the USGS map. A trail from the

shack to the river is not accurately drawn—instead of going down a point to the southeast of the shack, the trail goes down the point to the southwest.

There is a narrow canyon to the east of the line shack (shown one-quarter mile west of elevation 5441). Follow its left (LUC)(W) rim north until the narrows end; then cut southeast across Brigham Tea Bench on rolling terrain and enter The Gulch via an old cattle trail that enters the canyon in a small draw shown at the "h" in The on the **Red Breaks map.** (2.5–3.5 hours.)

Out of The Gulch

Directly across The Gulch from where you entered it are three narrow east-tending canyons. You will exit the canyon via one of the three. The middle canyon, its mouth partially blocked by a V-trunked cottonwood, is the easiest of the three if a pothole 100 yards up-canyon at the base of a short fall is not full. Scramble up the fall (Class 4, 30') and immediately exit the canyon to the right (SE) by scrambling to the top up short walls and steep slabs. There is superb camping on the undulating slickrock overlooking The Gulch. (0.5 hours.)

To Horse Canyon

Walk east up the slickrock. A prominent Navajo ridge with a U-shaped notch becomes visible to the east (elevation 5562). Continue east across King Bench and pass over the southern shoulder of the prominent Navajo ridge. From the shoulder, you can see the walls of Horse Canyon. The dark red ledge-forming layer below the Navajo is the Kayenta Formation. To the northeast is the Kayenta-walled mouth of Little Death Hollow.

Continue east, over the head of a small drainage that runs south, to the edge of Horse Canyon. One bend downcanyon from the mouth of Little Death Hollow is a shallow east-facing indent in the otherwise vertical Navajo wall. The indent contains a steep slide and an old constructed cattle trail. Follow it to the canyon floor. There is a perennial flow of water and fair camping along this stretch of Horse Canyon. (1.0–1.5 hours.)

The exit route out of Horse Canyon

From the bottom of the cattle trail, go up Horse Canyon for several minutes to a fence. To the right (E) is a constructed cattle trail going up a break in the Kayenta. Fill up with water before going up the trail. The next reliable water source is in Silver Falls Creek, 4.0–6.0 hours away. Follow the cattle trail as it traverses east along Kayenta ledges and above the mouth of Little Death Hollow. A pumphouse and metal pipe are visible at the confluence. The pipe joins the trail at the interface between the Kayenta and Navajo. Follow the trail and pipe to a stock tank. You are now on Big Bown Bench. (0.5 hours.)

> **Historical note:** Big Bown Bench was named for William Bown, a rancher who ran cattle and sheep in the area.

Across Big Bown Bench

You will notice a black rubber pipe going east from the stock tank. Follow it to the top of a hill, across a wide shallow valley, to the crest of another hill, and into a shallow canyon (shown one-quarter mile east of elevation 5626T on the **Silver Falls Bench map**). Drop into the canyon and follow it south. There are a couple of medium potholes in the canyon. A small side canyon comes in from the left (NE) just before a fall (shown to the west of elevation 5594T). There is a medium pothole above the fall. (1.0–1.5 hours.)

Go southeast across a flat plain. The goal is to cross the top of the next side canyon that comes up from the Escalante River (shown to the west of elevation 5321T). This canyon has no water. You have now entered Glen Canyon National Recreation Area.

> **Rock climber's note:** A route into this canyon can be followed to the Escalante River. Follow the left (LDC)(E) rim of the canyon south for a couple of hundred yards past a large, level slickrock slab to the only likely looking descent route. Downclimb a couple of short walls (Class 5.0, 15'), then zigzag down ledges into the canyon. Note the line of Moqui steps near the top of the cliff. Follow the canyon down to the Escalante River.
>
> To return, go up a Kayenta prow to the north (toward elevation 5217T) on a constructed cattle trail. This will take you to the top. Follow the rim of the canyon back to the start. (2.0–3.0 hours.)

Proceed south into an area of Navajo domes and intersect a wash going southwest (shown to the west of elevation 5356T). Follow it down a long stretch of shallow narrows until you are near the rim of a canyon. The farther down you go, the more likely you are to find small potholes (0.5–1.0 hour.)

Exit the canyon to the left (LDC)(E) (the exact point you exit is not important) and go southeast across broken ground to the rim of Silver Falls Creek. It is difficult to find the descent route, which starts at Cliff Spring (shown on the map). (0.5 hours.)

Into Silver Falls Creek

Assuming you have intersected the rim of Silver Falls Creek south of the spring, follow the rim upcanyon. Stay near its edge. You are on Navajo slickrock and the spring is at the interface between the

Navajo and Kayenta. You cannot see the actual spring from the rim. First, find a Navajo prow with a vertical crack running up its middle on the far (E) side of Silver Falls Creek. The prow is directly across the canyon from the spring. (It is located one-half mile west-north-west of elevation 5234AT.) This will get you in the general area. Look for the bright white and green deposits that typically mark seeps on a wall and for a round, silver water tank with a white-tipped fence that runs to it on a Kayenta bench. You may see a cattle trail on the bench.

Make your way down the Navajo on the upcanyon (N) side of the spring. Follow the cattle trail to the spring, which has a medium flow of water. A cattle trail now runs generally southwest along the Kayenta bench below the Navajo cliffs into Silver Falls Creek. Silver Falls Creek has a medium flow of water where you join it. If the creekbed is dry, simply walk downcanyon to the Escalante River. (1.0–1.5 hours.)

The Overland Route—Silver Falls Creek to Choprock Canyon

Out of Silver Falls Creek
(Silver Falls Bench map.) From the Escalante River, hike up Silver Falls Creek for about twenty-three minutes. Locate a prow of Navajo high on the wall to the right. It has a prominent vertical crack running up its west face. This is the same prow used to find Cliff Spring. A hundred yards upcanyon from the prow is a cattle trail to the right (E) that goes up a short slope to a bench. (If you go too far upcanyon, a wall of Wingate rises out of the streambed and there is no possible exit. Backtrack for a couple of hundred yards.) This trail can be difficult to find.

Follow the trail upcanyon along a bench for fifty yards. It then turns right (SE) and goes up a heavily gullied Kayenta slope. Once you are on the trail, it is easy to follow as it winds its way along ledges to the top of the cliff. You are now on Silver Falls Bench. (0.5 hours.)

> **Historical note:** You will pass a cowboy glyph from Peter Deuel— June 15, 1915, Marion Woolsley—April 10, 1924, and Carter Or- mond. The Deuel and Woolsley families were some of the first to move to Escalante, in 1876. The Ormonds arrived in the 1890s.

Across Silver Falls Bench
The trail disappears on the top of the cliff. Hike east for twenty minutes over an escarpment to the rim of a wide canyon that con- tains two drainages. A large tower (elevation 5511T) will be visible to the southeast. (The two drainages are shown to the east and west of elevation 5511T.)

Your goal is to make your way east across the two canyons—and several smaller washes—and end up on the Navajo rim of Choprock Canyon. (Choprock Canyon is not named on the map. It is shown between elevations 5293T and 5103T.) None of the canyons is difficult to cross. A medium spring and a cattle trough are one-quarter mile south of elevation 5681T. (1.5–2.5 hours.)

Into Choprock Canyon

Follow the west rim of Choprock Canyon south. Stay on top of the Kayenta. An old cattle trail helps in places. Near a Navajo dome (elevation 5293T) the Kayenta ledge narrows and drops through several short cliff bands. From a distance the drops do not look promising, but with perseverance you will find a way through them. Hike along the top of the Wingate. Two hundred yards before reaching the Escalante River locate a row of Moqui steps that descend a crease in the cliff to the canyon floor (Class 5.1, 50'). The steps are hard to see unless you are right at the edge of the canyon. Good camping and large springs are in the area. (2.0–3.0 hours.)

The Overland Route—Choprock Canyon to Twentyfive Mile Wash

To Neon Canyon

(**Silver Falls Bench map.**) From the Escalante River hike up Choprock Canyon for a couple of hundred yards. A constructed cattle trail cuts up the Wingate wall on the right (LUC)(E). A short barb-wire fence will help you locate the trail. Go up the trail, which leads southwest until you are above the Escalante River. Hike south along Kayenta and Wingate benches. (**Egypt map.**)

You will be following a trail. Follow the trail only for as long as it stays near the Wingate. Once the trail starts cutting uphill, leave it. Stay near the top of the Wingate or you could find yourself in the wrong place.

> **Digression:** A couple of steep slabs can be used to descend to the river before you reach Fence Canyon. It is visible across the river to the west.

Turn the corner into Neon Canyon. (Neon Canyon is not named on the map. It is shown to the west of elevation 5270T.) Descend a cattle trail that goes down the first bowl into the canyon. There is good camping near the river. Do not camp up Neon Canyon. (1.5–2.0 hours.)

To Ringtail Canyon

Hike down Neon Canyon to the Escalante River. Wade down-river for a couple of hundred yards and exit the canyon at the first opportunity by using an old constructed cattle trail (NE). It will take you to the top of the Wingate and to the rim of a Kayenta-walled side canyon. Leave the trail here and continue the along-the-rim traverse.

> **Alternate route:** The purist may not want to hike down the Escalante River even for a short distance. To avoid wading, do not drop into Neon Canyon on the cattle trail. Instead, follow ledges northeast along the top of the inner gorge of Neon Canyon for a mile to the first place you can enter the inner gorge (east of elevation 5133T). A handline down a twenty-foot wall is recommended. Good camping and large potholes are in the area. Exit the east side of the gorge by using a row of Moqui steps (Class 5.1, 30'). Now make your way south-southeast past the east side of a prominent dome (elevation 5270T) and follow a shallow drainage until you are above the Escalante River. You may find an old constructed cattle trail. Catch the standard route here.

Ringtail Canyon (AN) is the next canyon encountered. (Ringtail Canyon is not named on the map. It is shown between elevations 5235T and 4988T.) Cross the canyon at the first opportunity. Large potholes can be found up- and downcanyon. (1.5–2.0 hours.)

> **Rock climber's note:** Ringtail Canyon is an excellent short technical slot. It usually requires wading, and after recent rains, extensive swimming. There are a couple of moderate (Class 5.6, 20') drops. A fifty-foot rope is essential. Moqui steps festoon one of the drops. Near the bottom of the slot it gets very dark. To return to the top of Ringtail Canyon, hike down the Escalante River for a quarter mile and locate a constructed cattle trail that goes east to the rim of the canyon. Follow the rim north to Ringtail Canyon. (2.5–4.0 hours.)

To Baker Canyon

Return to the rim of the Escalante escarpment and head south. After you head several small side canyons a major canyon comes in from the northeast. This is Baker Canyon. (Baker Canyon is not named on the map. It is shown one-half mile east of elevation 4990T.) (1.5–2.0 hours.)

Baker Canyon is very long, ending near the Circle Cliffs, and can only be crossed near its many-branched head. Most of these branches contain large potholes that may take some scouting to find. (**Scorpion Gulch map.**)

After heading the canyon, return to the rim of the Escalante escarpment. A unique arch in a huge pothole on the rim of the canyon is worth searching for. (**Egypt map.**)

Historical note: The arch is named Downcanyon from Charlie Arch (AN). Charlie Olojas was an inveterate canyon explorer who was one of the first to come to Escalante country with the express goal of backpacking. Charlie died in 1995 at the age of eighty-five.

To Twentyfive Mile Wash

Again, head south along the rim. After a couple of hundred yards, locate a fifteen-foot Kayenta pinnacle/archlet. The main drainage to the south—which is in a maze of small drainages— contains a large pothole. There is great camping in the area. (3.0–4.5 hours.)

Twentyfive Mile Wash soon becomes visible across the canyon to the west.

> **Rock climber's note:** There are two routes to the river in this vicinity. Both contain Moqui steps and will take some exploring to find. One is located directly across from the mouth of Twentyfive Mile Wash and starts on a steep ramp that goes down an initial cliff band to a broad terrace (Class 4+). Hike southwest until you are near the south end of the terrace to the edge of the final cliff. A steep slab lined with Moqui steps (Class 5.2, 60', lots of exposure), a near-vertical gully, and a final drop down a short vertical wall (Class 5.5, 10') take you to the river. A cottonwood tree can help for the last ten feet.
>
> The second route descends a long row of worn Moqui steps on a steep cliff that is a couple of hundred yards northeast of elevation 4538T (Class 5.1, 50').

The Overland Route—Twentyfive Mile Wash to Scorpion Gulch

To the Escalante River

(**Egypt map.**) From the rim of the Escalante escarpment opposite the mouth of Twentyfive Mile Wash go downcanyon along the rim. Head two short side canyons (shown to the east and west of elevation 5206T on the **Scorpion Gulch map**). Both canyons contain medium potholes. Cross the neck of a long south-running peninsula (elevation 4801T), head a short Wingate side canyon, and walk to the rim of a larger side canyon (shown to the west of elevation 5081T).

You need to locate a route to the Escalante River. Follow the west rim of the larger side canyon south until you are above the river. A cliff band above a black cryptobiotic-soil-covered plain is descended via a short, steep gully. A couple of Moqui steps help ease the difficulty (Class 5.0, 50'). Hike downcanyon to a break in the final cliff and descend to the river. (3.0–5.0 hours.)

Digression: There is a direct route from Twentyfive Mile Wash into Moody Creek. On your map, pinpoint an abandoned meander shown at elevation 4836T that is about a mile up Moody Creek from the Escalante River. Your goal is to make your way over the heads of several canyons and gain the rim of Moody Creek. Locate the abandoned meander and hike to its north side. Descend a maze of steep slickrock slabs, washes, and ridges and locate a low cliff. A fifteen-foot rappel with a large boulder for an anchor leads to the top of a slab. Steep rock (Class 5.0, 80') leads to the ground behind a tower in the middle of the abandoned meander. Circle it to the south, then east. A tight vertical slot (Class 5.2, 25') takes you into Moody Creek, which is followed downcanyon to the river. This route will take much scouting to find. (4.0–7.0 hours.)

Out of Escalante Canyon
Cross the river and hike upcanyon for a couple of hundred yards. A break in the wall to the left (LUC)(W) leads to a bench above the river. Follow the bench upcanyon until you are near the end of a point. Find a log and a row of Moqui steps in a crack that leads to the canyon rim (Class 5.4, 20'). (The steps are one-quarter mile northeast of elevation 4801T.) (1.0–1.5 hours.)

To Scorpion Gulch
Your goal is to head generally southeast far above the Escalante River across broken terrain to Scorpion Gulch. On your map find elevation 5048T, which is near the mouth of Scorpion Gulch. A short, steep canyon leads southwest from the west side of this elevation. Follow the canyon down into Scorpion Gulch. Large springs and good camping are in the area. If you do stay here, camp in the wash below the springs. (The springs are dry in the summer. Large springs appear a mile downcanyon.) (4.0–6.0 hours.)

The Overland Route—Scorpion Gulch to Fold Canyon

Out of Scorpion Gulch
(Scorpion Gulch map.) Hike down Scorpion Gulch for a couple of minutes and gain the Kayenta on the right (LDC)(S). Run Kayenta ledges generally east-northeast along the south side of Scorpion Gulch. Turn a corner (past elevation 5058T). Follow the Kayenta generally east high above the Escalante River. The Kayenta ledges narrow. You will pick up the Scorpion Horse Trail as you walk along. (The horse trail is described in Hike #18.) Follow the horse trail along the Kayenta for about a half hour until you are above a huge sand dune (located to the southwest of 2-255, an abandoned

meander shown on the map). Descend the dune to the Escalante River. There is good camping in the area. (2.5–3.5 hours.)

The exit route

Hike downcanyon along the right side of the river for a half hour. Locate the first break in the Wingate wall on the left (LDC)(SSE) side of the river at the top of a huge Chinle hill. Trudge up the hill and find a thin ledge that cuts left across the Wingate. (This bighorn trail is the descent route used in Hike #21. It is located a quarter mile east of elevation 5095T.) Make your way to the top of the Wingate and turn south.

Follow the rim of Escalante Canyon downcanyon to the first major side canyon you intersect (located one-half mile southeast of elevation 5222T). This is Fold Canyon (LKA). (2.0–3.0 hours.)

Across Fold Canyon

Follow the north rim of Fold Canyon northeast for several miles along pleasant Wingate slickrock until you intersect a long side canyon that comes in from the north (shown a quarter mile west of elevation 5254T on the **Stevens Canyon North map**). A couple of hundred yards before the mouth of the long side canyon locate a hole or slot that leads down the Wingate cliff into Fold Canyon (Class 5.0, 30'). This will take some scouting. Good camping and large potholes are in the canyon. (2.5–3.5 hours.)

To the Escalante escarpment

Walk downcanyon for about twenty minutes and exit the canyon to the south at the first break in the canyon wall (northeast of elevation 5355T). Cross a sand slide and follow the south rim of Fold Canyon southwest. You will end up on a point high above the Escalante River. The sharp bend in the river formed by the point was named the Swan Neck Bend by uranium miners. (The bend is mentioned in Hike #22.) (You leave the **Stevens Canyon North map**, cross a corner of the **Scorpion Gulch map**, and end up on the **King Mesa map**. The Swan Neck Bend is one-half mile southwest of elevation 4795.) (2.5–3.5 hours.)

The Overland Route—Fold Canyon to the Fortymile Ridge Trailhead

Sandwiched between Fold Canyon to the west and Stevens Canyon to the east are four indescribably beautiful and remote canyons. The route into these canyons from the confluence of Fold Canyon and the escarpment that overlooks the Escalante River is to simply follow Wingate and Kayenta benches high above the river into each canyon. The canyoneer then goes up each canyon as far as necessary to head it or cross it and return to the rim of Escalante Canyon.

There are exits from each canyon up to Stevens Bench (AN). (Stevens Bench is not named on the maps. It is located between the heads of the four canyons described below and Stevens Canyon. Some locals call this Stevens Plateau.) With careful study, one can put together a variety of routes that take you from one canyon, over Stevens Bench, and into another canyon. If you do go up on Stevens Bench, water availability is a problem. There are medium potholes near the rim of Ichabod Canyon. Other than those, water may not be available on Stevens Bench.

There are three routes to the Escalante River from the four canyons. Choose the route that best fits your needs.

To Shofar Canyon
   (**King Mesa map.**) From the Swan Neck Bend follow the rim of the escarpment downcanyon into a Wingate-lined side canyon (shown to the east of elevation 4795). Note the small twin arches on the far (E) rim of the canyon. Cross the canyon. It has medium potholes and there is good camping in the area.

> **Digression:** The first exit to the Escalante River is located here. Hike to the arches. The descent route to the Escalante River is fifty yards southeast of the arches over a small rise. It consists of a short chimney dotted with Moqui steps (Class 5.0, 30'). A steep slope leads to the river.

Again, follow the rim of the Escalante escarpment. There is one place along the cliffs that, from a distance, looks mighty narrow. Once at it, though, you will find that looks can be deceiving. The first major canyon encountered is Shofar Canyon (AN). Shofar is Hebrew for horn, which accurately describes many of the canyon's pinnacles, especially one in particular that looks like a horn. (Shofar Canyon is not named on the map. It is shown to the east of elevation 4964 and contains two major forks. Some locals call this Sheep Canyon.)

> **Digression:** Great Old Broads for Wilderness Arch (AN) in Shofar Canyon is located in a small drainage a quarter mile northeast of elevation 4995T on the Stevens Canyon North map.
>   The exit out of Shofar Canyon to Stevens Bench is via a steep slope to the left (N) of a large tower (shown one-quarter mile southwest of elevation 5375T on the Stevens Canyon North map).

Cross the west fork of Shofar Canyon a quarter mile south of el-

Shofar Canyon.

evation 5014T (on the **Scorpion Gulch map**). Large potholes and good camping are found in the canyon. The east fork of Shofar Canyon is crossed a short distance up it. After exiting the canyon, return to the rim of the Escalante escarpment. (You will cross a corner of the **Stevens Canyon North map**, then a small section of the **Scorpion Gulch map**, and will intersect the Escalante escarpment near elevation 5115 on the **King Mesa map**.) (3.5–5.5 hours.)

> **Digression:** The second route down to the Escalante River is near this point. Hug the rim of the Escalante escarpment for a couple of hundred yards as you work downcanyon. Look for a slump block (or tower) and a steep slope below the rim. Find a tricky, exposed route (Class 5.0, 15') that takes you to a gap between the tower and the main wall—which is covered by unique and beautiful gypsum varnish—and descend a steep, loose slope to the river.

> **Note:** If you have chosen one of the first two routes to the Escalante River, your best option for rejoining the Overland Route is to hike and wade downriver to Fools Canyon. See Hike #21 for details on the route from Fools Canyon to the Fortymile Bench trailhead.

To Hydra Canyon

The first canyon to the east of Shofar Canyon is Hydra Canyon (AN). (Hydra Canyon is not named on the map. It is shown to the south of elevation 5099T on the **Stevens Canyon South map**.) The canyon was named after the many-headed serpent from Greek

Great Old Broads for Wilderness Arch.

mythology that grew two heads every time one was cut off. The name accurately reflects this canyon's many side drainages.

Instead of hiking the rim of the Escalante escarpment between Shofar and Hydra canyons—which is difficult—it is easiest to climb to the top of the cliffs to the northeast, cross elevation 5100AT on Stevens Bench, and enter Hydra Canyon by way of a steep slope that drops southeast immediately south of elevation 5135T.

Once at the rim of the inner gorge of Hydra Canyon, hike up-canyon for a couple of minutes to a short north-tending side canyon (shown one-eighth mile east of elevation 5135T). Follow the short side canyon's east rim south and find a steep (Class 4+) route to the floor of the canyon. Easier entrances are available farther upcanyon. Large potholes and good camping are found in the canyon. (3.5–5.5 hours.)

To the Escalante escarpment
The exit out of Hydra Canyon is across from the place you dropped into the canyon. Follow the east rim of Hydra Canyon south down to the Escalante escarpment. (You will end up one-eighth mile south-southwest of elevation 4797T.) (1.5–2.0 hours.)

To Ichabod Canyon
Follow the rim of the Escalante escarpment for a short distance, then turn north and head a short multiheaded canyon (shown one-quarter mile east-northeast of elevation 4797T). Its eastern arm contains large potholes. Clamber east through a pass (located one-

quarter mile northeast of elevation 4769T) and drop to the rim of
Ichabod Canyon (AN). It was named for Washington Irving's Icha-
bod Crane, who was chased by the headless horseman in the "Leg-
end of Sleepy Hollow." (Ichabod Canyon is not named on the map.
It is shown to the east of elevation 4769T. Some locals also call this
Sheep Canyon.) (2.0–3.0 hours.)

> **Digression:** The exit from Ichabod Canyon to Stevens Bench is a
> steep slab (Class 5.0, 50') near the Navajo rim of the canyon that is
> one-quarter mile east-southeast of elevation 5163T. This is the
> hardest and least recommended of the exit routes. It will take much
> scouting to locate.

Across Ichabod Canyon

The third route to the Escalante River is by way of the floor of
Ichabod Canyon. The route used to enter the canyon is tricky. It is
located a quarter mile upcanyon from the confluence of the two
forks of the canyon (Class 5.8, 40'). A rappel from a tree can be
used. Large potholes and good camping are found in the canyon.

> **Alternate route:** If this entrance is too difficult, head Ichabod
> Canyon and hike down to its east fork (shown one-half mile south
> of elevation 5876T). Most of the side drainages have large pot-
> holes. Enter the inner gorge of the upper part of the east fork of
> Ichabod Canyon. Hike downcanyon and locate a route on the
> canyon's north side that descends a steep sloping ramp above a ten-
> foot drop (Class 5.0, 25'). Look for Moqui steps. (Add 4.0 hours.)

> **Digression:** Although Beryl Canyon (AN), the canyon to the east
> of Ichabod Canyon, does not provide a way to the Escalante River,
> it is worth visiting. (Beryl Canyon is not named on the map. It is
> shown to the south of elevation 5173T.) The derivation of the
> name Beryl is twofold. First, Beryl is a mineral, one of whose vari-
> eties is aquamarine. Second, the lady Beryl of myth was a laughing,
> loving beauty full of innocence and sunshine. Both accurately de-
> scribe this lavishly watered canyon lined with large colorful pools.
> This canyon is the shortest of the quartet.
>   Use the route detailed in the Alternate route above to exit Icha-
> bod Canyon. Hike to the rim of the Escalante escarpment and fol-
> low it downcanyon to Beryl Canyon.
>   The exit out of Beryl Canyon to Stevens Bench is located a
> quarter mile south of elevation 4957T.

To the Escalante River

Simply hike down Ichabod Canyon to the Escalante River. The
lower end of the canyon is choked with poison ivy that is hard to
avoid. (1.0 hour.)

Sarah Michael and Ginger Harmon at Great Old Broads for Wilderness Arch.

To the Bobway

From the mouth of Ichabod Canyon hike down the Escalante River for forty-five minutes to the first side canyon that comes in on the right (W) (shown to the east of elevation 4404T). Hike #22 details the Bobway and the route to the head of the Long Branch of

Sleepy Hollow. Hike #21 has directions on following the Long Branch of Sleepy Hollow to Coyote Gulch and to the Fortymile Ridge trailhead.

> *We had left a part of us back there in the twisting canyons among the red-and-white rocks, a part we would not find again until we came back the next time.*
>
> Philip Hyde, 1987

Bibliography

Abbey, Edward, and Philip Hyde. *Slickrock: The Canyon Country of Southeast Utah*. San Francisco: Sierra Club Books, 1971.

Allen, Steve. *Canyoneering: The San Rafael Swell*. Salt Lake City: University of Utah Press, 1992.

——. *Canyoneering 2: Technical Loop Hikes in Southern Utah*. Salt Lake City: University of Utah Press, 1995.

Atkins, Victoria M., ed. *Anasazi Basketmaker*. Salt Lake City: United States Department of the Interior, Bureau of Land Management, 1993.

Baars, Donald L. *Canyonlands Country: Geology of Canyonlands and Arches National Parks*. Revised Edition. Salt Lake City: University of Utah Press, 1993.

——. *Red Rock Country: The Geologic History of the Colorado Plateau*. Garden City, NY: Doubleday, 1972.

Backer, Howard, M.D. "Field Water Disinfection." *Journal of the American Medical Association* 259 (1988): 3185.

Breed, Jack. "First Motor Sortie into Escalante Land." *National Geographic* 96 (September 1949): 369–404.

——. "Roaming the West's Fantastic Four Corners." *National Geographic* 101 (June 1952): 705–42.

Brown, Lenard E. *The Baker Ranch—A History*. Washington, D.C.: Office of Archaeology and Historic Preservation, U.S. Department of the Interior, National Park Service, 1970.

Bureau of Land Management. *Utah Statewide Wilderness Study Report. Volume IIA—Summary Analysis of Study Area Recommendations*. Salt Lake City: Bureau of Land Management, 1991.

Castleton, Kenneth B. *Petroglyphs and Pictographs of Utah. Volume Two: The South, Central, West and Northwest*. Salt Lake City: Utah Museum of Natural History, 1990.

Chidester, Ida, and Eleanor Bruhn, eds. *Golden Nuggets of Pioneer Days: A History of Garfield County*. Panguitch, UT: Daughters of Utah Pioneers, 1949.

Committee on Interior and Insular Affairs. "Canyonlands National Park and Glen Canyon National Recreational Area. Hearing before the Subcommittee on Parks and Recreation of the Committee on Interior and Insular Affairs. United States Senate.

Ninety-first Congress...May 5, 1970." Washington, D.C.: U.S. Government Printing Office, 1970.

Controtto, Eugene L. "By Power Scooter Through the Wild Red Yonder." *Desert Magazine* (August 1961).

Crampton, Gregory C. *Ghosts of Glen Canyon*. St. George, UT: Publishers Place, Inc., 1986.

———. *Historical Sites in Glen Canyon—Mouth of San Juan River to Lee's Ferry*. University of Utah Anthropological Paper #46 (Glen Canyon Series #19). Salt Lake City: University of Utah Press, 1960.

———. *Standing Up Country: The Canyon Lands of Utah and Arizona*. New York: Alfred A. Knopf, 1964.

Davidson, E.S. *Geology of the Circle Cliffs Area, Garfield and Kane Counties, Utah*. U.S. Geological Survey Bulletin 1229. Washington, D.C.: U.S. Government Printing Office, 1967.

Dietrich, Richard V., and Brian J. Skinner. *Rocks and Rock Minerals*. New York: John Wiley and Sons, 1979.

Doolittle, Jerome. *Canyons and Mesas*. New York: Time-Life Books, 1974.

Dutton, Clarence E. *Report on the Geology of The High Plateaus of Utah*. Washington, D.C.: U.S. Government Printing Office, 1880.

Fowler, Don D. *1961 Excavations, Harris Wash, Utah*. University of Utah Anthropological Paper #64 (Glen Canyon Series #19). Salt Lake City: University of Utah Press, 1963.

Fowler, Don D., and C. Melvin Aikens. *1961 Excavations, Kaiparowits Plateau, Utah*. University of Utah Anthropological Paper #66 (Glen Canyon Series #20). Salt Lake City: University of Utah Press, 1963.

Fowler, Don D., et al. *The Glen Canyon Archaeological Survey*. University of Utah Anthropological Paper #39 (Glen Canyon Series #6). Salt Lake City: University of Utah Press, 1959.

Geary, Edward A. *The Proper Edge of the Sky*. Salt Lake City: University of Utah Press, 1992.

Gregory, Herbert E., and Raymond C. Moore. *The Kaiparowits Region: A Geographic and Geologic Reconnaissance of Parts of Utah and Arizona*. U.S. Geological Survey Professional Paper 164. Washington, D.C.: U.S. Government Printing Office, 1931.

Gunnerson, James H. *1957 Excavations, Glen Canyon Area*. University of Utah Anthropological Paper #43 (Glen Canyon Series #10). Salt Lake City: University of Utah Press, 1959.

Hauck, F.R. *Cultural Resource Evaluation in South Central Utah*. Salt Lake City: Bureau of Land Management, 1977.

Henderson, Randall. "Glen Canyon Voyage." *Desert Magazine* (October 1952).

———. "Petrified Forests in Utah's Circle Cliffs." *Desert Magazine* (June 1956).

———. "We Camped on Kaiparowits." *Desert Magazine* (September 1951).

———. "When the Boats Wouldn't Float—We Pulled 'em." *Desert Magazine* (September 1950).

Historic American Engineering Board. *Escalante River Bridge*. Denver: National Park Service, n.d.

Houk, Rose. *Dwellers of the Rainbow*. Torrey, UT: Capitol Reef Natural History Association, 1988.

Hunt, Charles B. *Cenozoic Geology of the Colorado Plateau*. Geological Survey Professional Paper 279. Washington, D.C.: U.S. Government Printing Office, 1931.

Hunt, Charles B., ed. *Geology of the Henry Mountains, Utah, as recorded in the notebooks of G.K. Gilbert (1875–76)*. Boulder, CO: Geological Society of America, 1988.

Huntoon, Peer W. "Phanerozoic Structural Geology of the Grand Canyon." In *Grand Canyon Geology*. New York: Oxford University Press, 1990.

Jennings, Jesse D. *Glen Canyon: A Summary*. University of Utah Anthropological Paper #81 (Glen Canyon Series #31). Salt Lake City: University of Utah Press, 1966.

Jones, Raymond Smith. "Last Wagon Through the Hole-in-the-Rock." *Desert Magazine* (June 1954): 22–25.

Lavender, David. *River Runners of the Grand Canyon*. Tucson: University of Arizona Press, 1985.

LeFevre, Lenora Hall. *The Boulder Country and Its People*. Springville, UT: Art City Publishing, 1973.

Leigh, Rufus Wood. *Five Hundred Utah Place Names*. Salt Lake City: Deseret News Press, 1961.

Lipe, William D. "Anasazi/Pueblo Culture Periods in the Northern Southwest (Pecos Classification)." Typescript.

Lister, Florence C. *Kaiparowits Plateau and Glen Canyon Prehistory: An Interpretation Based on Ceramics*. University of Utah Anthropological Paper #71 (Glen Canyon Series #23). Salt Lake City: University of Utah Press, 1964.

Lister, Robert H. *The Glen Canyon Survey in 1957*. University of Utah Anthropological Paper #30 (Glen Canyon Series #1). Salt Lake City: University of Utah Press, 1958.

Lister, Robert H., and Florence C. Lister. *The Coombs Site. Part III, Summary and Conclusions*. University of Utah Anthropological Paper #41 (Glen Canyon Series #8). Salt Lake City: University of Utah Press, 1961.

Lowry, Nelson. *A Social Survey of Escalante, Utah*. Provo: Brigham Young University, 1925.

Madsen, David B. *Exploring the Fremont.* Salt Lake City: Utah Museum of Natural History, 1989.

Mortensen, A.R., ed. "A Journal of John A. Widtsoe." *Utah Historical Quarterly* 23 (July 1955): 195–231.

Miller, David E. *Hole-in-the-Rock.* Salt Lake City: University of Utah Press, 1959.

Moore, W. Robert. "Escalante: Utah's River of Arches." *National Geographic* 108 (September 1955): 399–425.

Murphy, Alexandra. "Happy Ending to Utah Grazing Conflict." *High Country News* (August 24, 1992): 5.

Nabhan, Gary Paul, and Caroline Wilson. *Canyons of Color: Utah's Slickrock Wildlands.* New York: HarperCollins Publishers, 1995.

National Outdoor Leadership School. *Leave No Trace—Desert and Canyon Country.* Lander, WY: National Outdoor Leadership School, 1994.

Pattison, Natalie B., and Loren D. Potter. *Prehistoric and Historic Steps and Trails of Glen Canyon-Lake Powell.* Albuquerque, NM: National Science Foundation, University of New Mexico, 1977.

Peterson, Fred, and G.N. Pipiringos. *Stratigraphic Relations of the Navajo Sandstone to Middle Jurassic Formations, Southern Utah and Northern Arizona.* Washington, D.C.: United States Government Printing Office, 1979.

Peterson, Fred, and Christine Turner-Peterson. *Geology of the Colorado Plateau.* Washington, D.C.: American Geophysical Union, 1989.

Porter, Eliot. *The Place No One Knew: Glen Canyon on the Colorado.* New York: Ballantine Books, 1963.

Reay, Lee. *Incredible Passage.* Salt Lake City: Publishers Press, 1980.

Reilly, P.T. "The Lost World of Glen Canyon." *Utah Historical Quarterly* 63 (Spring 1995): 122–34.

Ruess, Everett. *On Desert Trails with Everett Ruess.* El Centro, CA: Desert Magazine Press, 1940.

Rusho, W.L. *Everett Ruess, Vagabond for Beauty.* Salt Lake City: Peregrine Smith, 1983.

Schneeberger, Jon. "Escalante Canyon—Wilderness at the Crossroads." *National Geographic* 142 (August 1972): 270–84.

Schroedl, Alan R. "Paleo-Indian Occupation in the Eastern Great Basin and Northern Colorado Plateau." *Utah Archaeology* (1991).

Spencer, Deloy. "A History of Escalante." Utah Historical Society Library, Salt Lake City, Utah, 1960. Typescript.

Stanton, Robert B. *The Hoskaninni Papers. Mining in Glen Canyon, 1897-1902.* University of Utah Anthropological Paper #54 (Glen Canyon Series #15). Salt Lake City: University of Utah Press, 1961.

Utah State Planning Board. "The Proposed Escalante National Monument: A preliminary report." Utah Historical Society Library, Salt Lake City, Utah, 1936. Typescript.

United States Department of the Interior. *A Survey of the Recreational Resources of the Colorado River Basin*. Washington, D.C.: United States Government Printing Office, 1950.

Utah Wilderness Coalition. *Wilderness at the Edge*. Salt Lake City: Utah Wilderness Coalition, 1990.

Van Cott, John W. *Utah Place Names*. Salt Lake City: University of Utah Press, 1990.

Wilderson, James A. *Medicine for Mountaineering*. Third Edition. Seattle: The Mountaineers, 1990.

Woolsey, Nethella Griffin. *The Escalante Story*. Springville, UT: Art City Publishing Co., 1964.

Woodsbury, Angus M. *Notes on the Human Ecology of Glen Canyon*. University of Utah Anthropological Paper #74 (Glen Canyon Series #26). Salt Lake City: University of Utah Press, 1965.

Acknowledgments

Many friends and canyoneers helped in researching and writing this book. Often they took time out from business and family to hike with my route descriptions in hand and give advice. Their efforts have added immeasurably to the quality of this guide.

Jeff Grathwohl and Rodger Reynolds at the University of Utah Press were wonderful to work with and provided indispensable support.

Bill Feeny took my hand-drawn maps and somehow turned them into computerized masterpieces. A belated thanks for tackling the same chore for *Canyoneering 1* and *2*.

A hundred or more backpackers spent time with me in the backcountry while I was preparing this guide. Their comments and criticism were welcome and invaluable. Special thanks go to Ace Allen, Bob Bordasch, Mike Brennan, Tom Browne, Glen Buelteman, Ronnie Egan, Jim Finch, Joan Hoffman, Marge Hoffman, Eric Husby, Jack Dykinga, Della Lewis, Barbara Moore, Don Murch, Marcey Olajos, Rob Roseen, Randy Rudderman, David Sanders, Tony and Carol Somkin, Laverne Waddington, Chip Ward, Florence Williams, and Hansjorg Wyss.

Ginger Harmon hiked many of the routes with me; others she tackled using my descriptions. Content editing and excellent advice are Ginger's forte. Many thanks for taking the time and sharing your love of the desert with me.

Wendy Chase spent a lot of time in the backcountry with me and even more time editing the manuscript and designing the geology cross-section chart. Endless thanks.

Harvey Halpern and Bud Evans spent many months in the Escalante with me, usually on two- or three-week-long expeditions. Their attention to detail, pointed and accurate advice, and route-finding abilities were essential.

Joe Breddan always added a new dimension to the hikes we did. His red pen made mincemeat out of the original draft of the manuscript. Thanks, Joe.

Tom Messenger is a fine companion in the backcountry and his encyclopedic knowledge of the canyons and their geology proved indispensable. Tom and I co-wrote the "The Geology of the Escalante

Region" and "The Strata" chapters. Tom and I both thank geologists Russell Dubiel and Fred Peterson for their observations and comments. Any errors in those chapters are mine.

Charles Bagley sent excellent comments and notes on Stevens Canyon and the lower Escalante.

Del Smith educated me in the newest low-impact camping techniques. Her input is indispensable in helping keep the wildlands pristine.

Bert Fingerhut took time out from the score of environmental battles he leads to hike the backcountry with me and to write the Foreword.

The owners of Escalante Outfitters, Barry and Celeste Bernards, provided me with a home away from home. Their ongoing encouragement during the five-year-long course of this project and their knowledge of the land and its history were crucial. Barry and Celeste are exceptional people; everyone passing through Escalante should stop in and meet them.

Personnel at the Interagency Office in Escalante read the manuscript and offered constructive advice. Especially helpful were Jim Bowman, Craig Sorenson, Bill Wolverton, and Jeannie Linn.

Several people were not able to join me on the hikes but were, nonetheless, essential. Thanks to Dr. Jim Anderson, Augie and Melanie Bernardo, Joe Bauman, Brant Calkin, Susan Harris, Mac LeFevre, Ann Perius-Parker, Rick and Beverly Upham, and Tom Weinreich.